W9-CKH-810

Microprocessor Applications Handbook

OTHER MCGRAW-HILL HANDBOOKS OF INTEREST

American Institute of Physics • American Institute of Physics Handbook
Baumeister • Marks' Standard Handbook for Mechanical Engineers
Beeman • Industrial Power Systems Handbook
Brady and Clauser • Materials Handbook
Burington and May • Handbook of Probability and Statistics with Tables
Condon and Odishaw • Handbook of Physics
Considine • Energy Technology Handbook
Coombs • Basic Electronic Instrument Handbook
Coombs • Printed Circuits Handbook
Croft, Carr, and Watt • American Electricians' Handbook
Dean • Lange's Handbook of Chemistry
Fink • Electronics Engineers' Handbook
Fink and Beaty • Standard Handbook for Electrical Engineers
Giacoletto • Electronics Designers' Handbook
Harper • Handbook of Components for Electronics
Harper • Handbook of Electronic Packaging
Harper • Handbook of Electronic System Design
Harper • Handbook of Materials and Processes for Electronics
Harper • Handbook of Thick Film Hybrid Microelectronics
Harper • Handbook of Wiring, Cabling, and Interconnecting for Electronics
Hicks • Standard Handbook of Engineering Calculations
Hunter • Handbook of Semiconductor Electronics
Huskey and Korn • Computer Handbook
Ireson • Reliability Handbook
Jasik • Antenna Engineering Handbook
Juran • Quality Control Handbook
Kaufman and Seidman • Handbook of Electronics Calculations
Kaufman and Seidman • Handbook for Electronics Engineering Technicians
Korn and Korn • Mathematical Handbook for Scientists and Engineers
Kurtz and Shoemaker • The Lineman's and Cableman's Handbook
Machol • System Engineering Handbook
Maissel and Glang • Handbook of Thin Film Technology
Markus • Electronics Dictionary
McPartland • McGraw-Hill's National Electrical Code Handbook
Perry • Engineering Manual
Skolnik • Radar Handbook
Smeaton • Motor Application and Maintenance Handbook
Stout and Kaufman • Handbook of Microcircuit Design and Application
Stout and Kaufman • Handbook of Operational Amplifier Circuit Design
Truxal • Control Engineers' Handbook
Tuma • Engineering Mathematics Handbook
Tuma • Handbook of Physical Calculations
Tuma • Technology Mathematics Handbook
Williams • Electronic Filter Design Handbook
Woodson • Human Factors Design Handbook

Microprocessor Applications Handbook

David F. Stout *Editor-in-Chief*

Vice President of Engineering
Dataface, Inc.
Santa Clara, California

McGraw-Hill Book Company

New York St. Louis San Francisco Auckland
Bogotá Hamburg Johannesburg London Madrid Mexico
Montreal New Delhi Panama Paris São Paulo
Singapore Sydney Tokyo Toronto

Library of Congress Cataloging in Publication Data

Main entry under title:
  Microprocessor applications handbook.

  Includes index.
  1. Microprocessors. I. Stout, D. F.
TK7895.M5M463   621.3819'58   81-11787
                                      AACR2

1234567890   KPKP   8987654321

ISBN 0-07-061798-8

The editors for this book were Harold B. Crawford and Ruth L. Weine,
the designer was Naomi Auerbach (with binding design by Mark E. Safran),
and the production supervisor was Teresa F. Leaden.
It was set in Melior by University Graphics.
Printed and bound by The Kingsport Press

Contents

Contributors

ABRAMS, C. W. *International Business Machines Corp.* (CHAPTER 15)

CANNON, L. E. *Washington State University* (CHAPTER 6)

CARTER, C. W. *Corning Glass Works* (CHAPTER 17)

CASTRO, C. *Casheab* (CHAPTER 10)

GRAPPEL, R. D. *Hemenway Associates* (CHAPTER 11)

HEABERLIN, A. *Casheab* (CHAPTER 10)

KARSTAD, K. *RCA Corporation* (CHAPTER 4)

KOPERDA, F. *International Business Machines Corp.* (CHAPTER 14)

KREAGER, P. S. *Washington State University* (CHAPTER 6)

LANDAU, J. V. *Teradyne, Inc.* (CHAPTER 16)

LE VASSEUR, D. *NASA Ames Research Center* (CHAPTER 2)

LI, K. *Signetics Corporation* (CHAPTER 7)

MELVIN, D. K. *Intel Corporation* (CHAPTER 9)

NEGRO, V. C. *U.S. Department of Energy* (CHAPTER 5)

STOUT, D. F. *Dataface, Inc.* (CHAPTERS 1, 8, 12, AND 13)

WALL, E. L. *ITT Telecommunications* (CHAPTER 3)

Preface

We are in the midst of an era in electronics that requires intelligent
instruments, machines, and systems in all technological and scientific
fields. These systems obtain their intelligence from microprocessors,
microcomputers, and other large-scale integrated circuits operating
under control of programs stored in memory. Intelligent systems are
designed by a specialized class of individuals who must be talented
in both hardware and software. This book is primarily addressed to
such a group of people, and to those who are aspiring to become
members of the group. These individuals must be familiar with many
aspects of both digital and analog electronics; they must be able to
design software programs that fully exploit the capabilities of the
hardware and understand the many tradeoffs required to achieve the
proper balance between hardware and software in each particular
system.

During the initial design phase of an intelligent system, designers
need to draw upon proven ideas from many reference sources
because they cannot afford to "re-invent the wheel" for each new
task. The design process often can be expedited or simplified if the
designer has access to finished plans of similar applications. Some
people may argue the ethics of using other people's designs, but this
is the only way the human race makes progress. We must build upon
previous designs to expand the state of the art. Typically, the
designer may be able to borrow 10 to 20 percent of the design from
each of several references. The remaining 60 to 80 percent must be
original work. However, even in the remaining "original" design the
designer can shorten work time by using ideas from proven concepts.

This handbook clearly presents a wide variety of microprocessor
applications, based upon contributions from specialists in many diver-

sified fields. Most chapters contain an ample treatment of both hardware and software aspects of microprocessor system design and discuss specific design information gathered during the development of actual microprocessor applications.

There are literally millions of potential applications for microprocessors, microcomputers, and LSI/VLSI devices. A single volume dedicated to applications of these programmable instruments must, of necessity, be limited to a finite set of devices, technologies, and hardware. This handbook discusses applications using the following types of microprocessors: 1802, 2650, 6800, and the 8080; the types of microcomputer chips included are the 2920, 3870, 3872, 6801, 6802, and 8088. The handbook also covers the following LSI devices operating from a microprocessor data and address bus: parallel ports 6820, 6821, 68488, and 8255; serial ports 6850, 6852, and 8251; LSI instruments discussed in various chapters include analog-to-digital and digital-to-analog converters, communications devices, timers, clocks, and video interface chips.

In years past, real-time processing tasks were difficult to handle using microprocessors because of the machines' slow speed and small data-word size. Recently, many breakthroughs have been achieved using faster microprocessors, better instruction sets, wider buses, and improved algorithms. Several of these real-time tasks are included here. For example, Chapter 3 discusses real-time error correction, which is becoming more important as more compact memory systems are developed. Chapter 6 discusses a smart lumber-grading machine that analyzes each board as it momentarily pauses on a conveyor belt. Chapter 9 covers many concepts in telephony, which requires fast microcomputers and well-designed software to speed up telephone traffic and reduce cost. Chapter 10 presents design guidelines for a digitally programmable waveform synthesizer used in music synthesis. Although the high-speed portions of this circuit use MSI, the functions requiring decisions and input-output in real time are performed with a 6800 microprocessor. Chapter 11 has design guidelines for real-time digital filters and describes low-, high-, and bandpass filters implemented with an A/D converter, a microprocessor board, and a D/A converter. Chapter 14 describes techniques for real-time voice recognition using multiple microprocessors to increase processing speed.

Applications using several standard interfacing circuits are described in Chapters 2, 5, 8, 12, and 13. These include the IEEE-488 bus standard in Chapter 2; the bus is used to interface a programmable calculator to a microprocessor-controlled airborne distance-measuring device. Serial and parallel interfaces using a single-chip microcomputer are thoroughly examined in Chapter 5. A number of A/D converter interfaces to microprocessor systems are explained in Chapter 7. Parallel and serial interfaces are further described in Chapter 12, using both synchronous and asynchronous data transfer. Human interfaces through keyboards and thumbwheel switches are presented in Chapter 13.

Video systems have innumerable application possibilities for microprocessor control. Chapter 4 describes in detail several features of a color TV receiver that may be placed under microprocessor control. Design techniques for various types of video games using a microprocessor to control a specialized game chip are described in Chapter 7. Chapter 15 describes how this technology is used for radio facsimile transmission and in scientific and technical fields because it processes video information at rates compatible with standard microprocessors.

Designing an intelligent system is a form of art. It is difficult to state generally those things that should first be put down on paper. Some designers start with a familiar microprocessor circuit and design the software around it; others work on flowcharts and algorithms long before the logic devices are chosen. There are many advocates for either approach. Chapter 16 is a well-presented example of the "algorithm first" approach, wherein an industrial sewing machine controller is designed using state variable description techniques. Many complex systems can be reduced to more manageable algorithms using the ideas presented in this chapter.

Because of wide usage, microprocessors and microcomputers are no more expensive than most of the other MSI/LSI components on a circuit board, which is why many designers use two or more microprocessors/microcomputers to implement the desired function. In all cases, however, one device must be programmed as the master and the others must be slaves. The master contains the EXECUTIVE or MAIN program, and the other devices process INPUT/OUTPUT routines and other dedicated tasks. Chapter 17 clearly describes one approach to the multiple-microcomputer design philosophy.

It has been a mentally stimulating task to work with the contributors of this handbook for the past two years. Although I have been working with microprocessors for many years, these contributors gave me many new insights concerning the design process. I wish to express my appreciation to these contributors, who spent numerous hours working with me to help produce a useful and widely diversified handbook.

I also wish to express my appreciation to my wife Mildred, and to my two sons Michael and Matthew, who did much of the manuscript typing and proofreading. Many of my colleagues at Ford Aerospace and Communications Corp. and Dataface, Inc., also deserve thanks for their helpful suggestions and moral support.

DAVID F. STOUT
Cupertino, California

Microprocessor
Applications
Handbook

CHAPTER ONE

Survey of Microprocessor Technology

David F. Stout

Dataface Incorporated,
Santa Clara, California

THE EVOLUTION OF THE MICROPROCESSOR

Few areas of electronics have experienced the rapid progress now occurring in the field of microprocessors, microcomputers, and associated integrated circuits. The complexity of integrated circuit (IC) devices has doubled approximately every year since the first device was developed in the early 1960s. Projections indicate that, if the present trend continues, devices containing hundreds of millions of transistors per chip will be available in the 1990s. Figure 1 shows the maximum number of components (transistors, diodes, capacitors, and resistors) on state-of-the-art IC chips for the past 20 years. The dashed line indicates the expected chip density for the next 10 years, assuming certain present technical barriers are surmounted.[1] Many difficult barriers have been overcome to bring ICs up to their present, mature state of technology, and humankind will continue to make substantial progress in this area to achieve the dashed line shown in the figure because new processes are being developed continually as each process reaches the end of its capabilities.

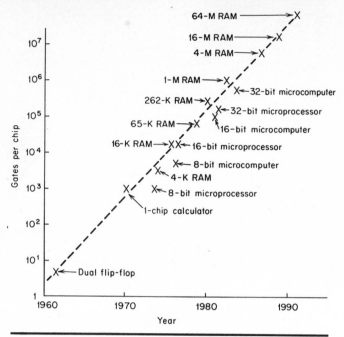

FIG. 1 *With IC chip density doubling every year we may expect to see chips containing hundreds of millions of devices in the 1990s. (From Ref. 1 with permission)*

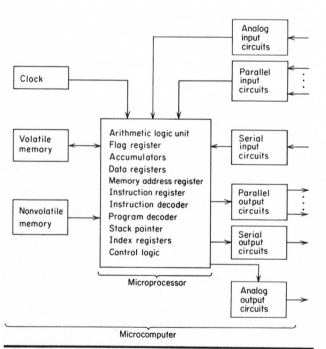

FIG. 2 *Simplified block diagram showing the microprocessor as the major component in a microcomputer.*

In the early 1960s, the first gate was fabricated by using a chip of silicon. As more gates were added to ICs over the years, the functions performed by these devices grew more complex. In just a few years after the first chip was developed, nearly all the logic and arithmetic functions performed by today's microcomputer devices were available to a user on a large assortment of IC devices. The arithmetic logic unit (ALU) chip developed in the 1960s could add, subtract, rotate, and shift, just as a microprocessor or microcomputer device can today. However, not until the early 1970s was the ALU combined (on a single chip) with a sequential circuit (flip-flops, shift registers, and so on) to make a rudimentary microprocessor. This had not been feasible until the IC developers were able to place at least 1000 transistors on a single chip. It took only several more years until input-output (I/O) circuits, read-only memory (ROM), random access memory (RAM), and clock circuits were also placed on the chip; the device was then called a microcomputer.

The line of demarcation between microprocessors and microcomputers is not well-defined. Generally, a microprocessor sequentially executes instructions, whereas a microcomputer executes instructions and provides (1) I/O circuitry for a user in serial and/or parallel modes, (2) ROM or programmable ROM (PROM) on which users may permanently store their program, (3) large quantities of RAM for a user to store temporary data and programs, and (4) a clock circuit requiring only an external crystal or RC network.

A microcomputer chip is sometimes referred to as a "computer on a chip." This term is really a misnomer because no matter how much logic is put on the chip, large devices such as a keyboard, display, and power supply are required. Many microcomputer systems still require several dozen other chips to interface the system with some outside process. And the limited number of pins available on a microcomputer package is a major drawback. Although chips containing millions of gates are predicted for the 1980s, the real problem with using these devices will be interfacing them to the outside world.

Figure 2 illustrates that a microprocessor is the central device in a microcomputer. Some microcomputer chips contain less than all the blocks shown; some contain more. Many special-purpose microcomputers contain on-chip I/O interfaces applicable to only a small class of applications. These interfaces may be keyboard scanners, video monitor circuitry, alphanumeric driver circuits, relay or lamp drivers, and so forth. The potential list of specialized microcomputers is endless.

1.1 Elements of a Microprocessor

The Arithmetic Logic Unit (ALU)   As mentioned, the microprocessor was an outgrowth of the ALU. For example, the 74181 is a 4-bit ALU with 75-gate complexity. It performs 16 separate operations on two 4-bit input words, with results appearing on a 4-bit output word plus four miscellaneous outputs. The function SELECT is made on four other input lines. Figure 3 shows the logic representation of the 74181. This device is cascadable up to any I/O word size. The 16 functions performed by the 74181 are listed in Table 1. If control

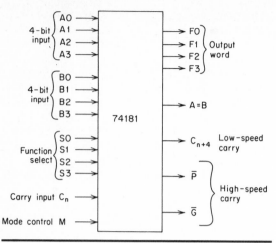

FIG. 3   *Logic representation of the 74181 ALU. (From Ref. 1 with permission)*

TABLE 1   **Arithmetic operations of the 74181 ALU***

Function SELECT				Arithmetic output function	Logic output function
S3	S2	S1	S0	$M = C_n = 0$	$M = 1$
0	0	0	0	$F = A$	$F = \overline{A}$
0	0	0	1	$F = A + B$	$F = \overline{A + B}$
0	0	1	0	$F = A + \overline{B}$	$F = \overline{A} \cdot B$
0	0	1	1	$F = -1$ (2s complement)	$F = 0000$
0	1	0	0	$F = A$ plus $A \cdot \overline{B}$	$F = \overline{A \cdot B}$
0	1	0	1	$F = (A + B)$ plus $A \cdot \overline{B}$	$F = \overline{B}$
0	1	1	0	$F = A - B - 1$	$F = A \oplus B$
0	1	1	1	$F = A \cdot \overline{B} - 1$	$F = A \cdot \overline{B}$
1	0	0	0	$F = A$ plus $A \cdot B$	$F = \overline{A} + B$
1	0	0	1	$F = A$ plus B	$F = \overline{A \oplus B}$
1	0	1	0	$F = (A + \overline{B})$ plus $A \cdot B$	$F = B$
1	0	1	1	$F = A \cdot B - 1$	$F = A \cdot B$
1	1	0	0	$F = A$ plus $A = 2A$	$F = 1111$
1	1	0	1	$F = (A + B)$ plus A	$F = A + \overline{B}$
1	1	1	0	$F = (A + \overline{B})$ plus A	$F = A + B$
1	1	1	1	$F = A - 1$	$F = A$

*+ = logical OR, · = logical AND, ⊕ = logical XOR.
SOURCE: See Ref. 1.

input $M = 0$, then arithmetic and logic operations are implemented. With $M = 1$, the output word F represents only logical combinations of words A and B. When utilizing a device that performs both "plus" and OR, we must be careful not to use the + symbol for both. In the following discussion we use + for OR and "plus" for addition. The basic operations of a general-purpose ALU are summarized in Table 2.

TABLE 2   *Basic operations of a general-purpose* ALU*

Function	Description (in any operation A and B can be interchanged)
$F = A$ plus $\mathbf{1}$	Increment A (or B)
$F = A - \mathbf{1}$	Decrement A (or B)
$F = A$ plus B	Add A and B
$F = A - B$	Subtract B from A
$F = A \cdot B$	Compute logical AND of inputs
$F = A + B$	Compute logical OR of inputs
$F = A \oplus B$	Compute logical XOR of inputs
$F = 2A$	Shift A left
$F = A/2$	Shift A right
$F = $ ⟳	Rotate A left
$F = $ ⟳	Rotate A right
$F = \overline{A}$	Complement A
$F = 0 \cdot A$	Clear A

*Assume two input buses A and B and an output bus F.
SOURCE: See Ref. 2.

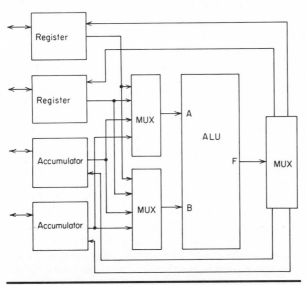

FIG. 4   *By adding registers, accumulators, and multiplexers to the ALU a simple microprocessor begins to formulate. Each line shown represents a data bus of 4, 8, or 16 lines. (From Ref. 1 with permission)*

Registers   The ALU in a microprocessor is capable of little more than those operations listed in Table 2. A microprocessor gains its additional power by attaching several storage *registers* to the ALU, as shown in Fig. 4. The ALU can operate on data from only one or two of the registers at a time. Some of these registers are more versatile than the rest and are therefore labeled "accumulators."

Devices called *multiplexers* transfer selected register contents into either ALU input port. Another multiplexer moves the ALU output to a destination register, where it is held until needed by some outside circuit. All these operations are controlled by a sequential circuit that is attached to all registers and multiplexers. For example, for an 8-bit microprocessor, the registers, accumulators, and multiplexers are all 8-bit-wide parallel-in/parallel-out devices.

The next step in the development of a full-scale microprocessor is to add a program counter, condition code register, instruction register, instruction decoder, and memory. Because these devices are all interrelated, they must be added as a group. Figure 5 shows the interrelationship of these circuits. For a microprocessor the memory is typically external to the chip. However, microcomputer devices contain much of the memory on the chip.

Program Counter A typical 8-bit microprocessor has a 16-bit *program counter*. This counter keeps track of the sequence of operations for all microprocessor circuits; that is, the number in the program counter is the line number being executed in the program. This is the memory address which is active at that time. A 16-bit program counter allows programs to be written to a maximum length of 65,535 steps. Most programs are only a few hundred or a few thousand steps long, so the 65,535 limit is seldom reached.

Memory and Instruction Register As indicated by Fig. 5, the program counter does not directly sequence the ALU through various operations. As the program counter sequences through the numbers associated with a program stored in memory, the data word at each corresponding memory location is sequentially presented to the instruction register. Here the data word is temporarily stored while the instruction decoder determines which operation the ALU and/or the program counter must perform. If the instruction decoder discerns a Branch or Jump instruction, the program counter is changed to a new value and the memory is read at that location. The ALU is not accessed in this case. However, if the instruction decoder finds an instruction like one in Table 1 or 2, the ALU and its associated registers are placed into operation. Data moves in and out of the ALU on a data bus having 4, 8, 16, or more parallel lines. This is the same data bus used by memory. Information can flow in either direction on this bus as controlled by sequential logic. In most systems this bus is tristate. All receivers and transmitters connected to the bus are normally deactivated. When a particular instruction is being executed, the instruction decoder decides which transmitter and receiver are activated. During that instruction execution, the bus carries information only between those two devices.

Condition Code Register (CCR) While the ALU is performing its task, the special-purpose register called the *condition code register* (CCR) becomes activated. Each bit in this register represents a terse summary of various types of results possible during ALU operations. For example, if an ALU register goes to an all-zero state, then a CCR bit called the zero bit (O or Z bit) is set to the HIGH state. If a carry was generated, then $C = 1$. If no carry (NC) was gen-

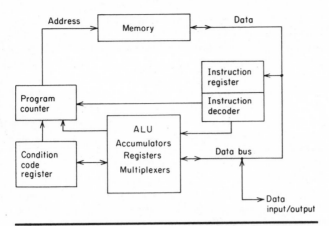

FIG. 5 Development of the microprocessor showing how the program counter, condition code register, instruction register, instruction decoder, and memory support the ALU and its registers. (From Ref. 1 with permission)

TABLE 3 CCR flags

Flag-bit name	Description
Z	Results = 0
NZ	Results ≠ 0
C	Results produce a carry
HC	Results produce a half carry (BCD operations)
NC	Results produce no carry
B	Results produce a borrow
NB	Results produce no borrow
E	Two input words equal
P	Results positive
N	Results negative
PA	Parity is odd
OV	Operation overflows register
I	Interrupt mask bit
GT	One input > another input
GE	One input ≥ another input
LT	One input < another input
LE	One input ≤ another input

SOURCE: Adapted from Ref. 1.

erated, we obtain NC = 1. This register is also called the "status" or "flag register" by various manufacturers.

A number of other types of flags are possible; Table 3 summarizes some of the more commonly used ones. Because most 8-bit microprocessors use an 8-bit flag register, the list in Table 3 is usually scaled down somewhat. Some microprocessors use as few as six flags.

Most of the branch instructions are dependent upon the results stored in the CCR. For example, if a Branch If Not Equal (BNE) instruction is being processed, the instruction decoder must allow the ALU to complete its operation before instructions are sent over to the program counter. If the ALU results are not equal to zero, the instruction decoder provides a new starting address (number) for the program counter. If the results of the ALU are equal to zero, the program counter is told to advance its count by one. The section of logic that decodes the CCR and sends control signals to appropriate sections of the microprocessor is called *conditional branch logic*. This logic is one of the more complex parts of the chip.

The Control Section   Microprocessors contain some supervisory logic called the *control section*. This section usually consists of the program counter, instruction register, and instruction decoder. The control section links all diverse registers in the microprocessor to perform the requirements of a particular instruction. Each instruction of a user's program might require up to 10 internal steps to implement. These internal steps are called microcycles; each step typically uses 1 cycle of the system clock.[2]

A microinstruction is required to direct each microcycle. Some microcycles hold intermediate results in registers not shown in Fig. 5. For example, there is sometimes a block between the program counter and memory called the memory address register (MAR). Between the memory and instruction register, another register, called the memory data register (MDR), is sometimes used. A set of instructions is stored in the microprocessor that remembers all the particular microinstructions required to complete each external instruction. These microcycle instructions are stored in a ROM called the control ROM or micro ROM. Most microprocessors have this ROM on the chip, but some multiple-package microprocessors have a separate ROM chip, which enables designers to change some of the microinstructions to fill their particular requirements. Microprocessors of this type are referred to as "microprogrammable." Because sequential addressing of the micro ROM is required, a small program counter called the micro PC is utilized. This counter needs to be only 3 to 4 bits wide.

Index Register   As an aid to efficient programming, one or more *index registers* are included in most newer microprocessors. In 8-bit microprocessors the index register is typically 16 bits wide. The usefulness of the index register, which is fully realized only through good programming, allows a programmer to automatically scan through one section of memory (for example, picking up entries from a table of data) while the program counter is executing instructions in the main program. In effect, two program counters are operating simultaneously while the index register is being utilized. The 16-bit index register can address the full 65,535-word memory.

Stack Pointer (SP)   The *stack pointer* (SP) is another register whose potential can be fully realized only by good programming. The SP is 16 bits wide in most 8-bit microprocessors and can therefore address (point to) any section of memory space. The "stack" pointed to by the SP is any prescribed group of memory locations in RAM. This section of RAM may be internal or external to a microcomputer chip. The assignment of a specific area of RAM for the stack is arbitrary and left to the programmer. However, the stack location must be identified in the initialization portion of the computer program.

The stack provides an easily programmable means of storing and retrieving successive data words. It is convenient for storing blocks of data (several data words) when the microprocessor receives an interrupt command from an external device. The interrupt line may be hard-wired to some peripheral device. When this device needs the services of the microprocessor, it pulses the interrupt line, causing the microprocessor to stop its present task. The microprocessor then stores the program counter on the stack so it can remember where to restart the program after the peripheral device has been serviced. In response to an interrupt, the microprocessor also stores the contents of the flag register, all accumulators, all index registers, and so on. When the peripheral routine is complete, all these registers are reinstated and the program resumes.

The stack is also used to remember the old program counter address when the program jumps to a subroutine. At the end of the subroutine a Return-From-Subroutine instruction directs the microprocessor to restart the program counter at one instruction past the number stored in the stack.

Input-Output Microprocessors have an internal data bus that transfers information between various registers. Bidirectional buffers are required to transfer this low-level bus to or from the higher-power-level outside circuits. Most of the internal registers also contain a set of bidirectional buffers for moving data to or from the device over the internal data bus. A typical bidirectional buffer is shown schematically in Fig. 6. This type of buffer is also used outside

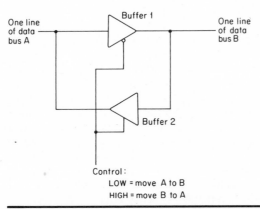

FIG. 6 *An individual bidirectional gate of the type used inside a microprocessor, for interfacing the internal data bus to the outside, and for transferring the internal data to various devices outside the microprocessor. (From Ref. 1 with permission)*

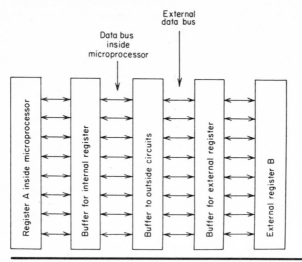

FIG. 7 *A microprocessor and its external system require many bidirectional buffers to move data back and forth between various types of registers. Some applications require data to flow in only one direction. (From Ref. 1 with permission)*

the microprocessor to move data between the microprocessor and other devices. A transfer of data from a register inside the microprocessor to a device outside the microprocessor might therefore require the use of three bidirectional buffer arrays, as shown in Fig. 7. The direction of information flow on the internal and external data buses is controlled automatically via software. For example, in Fig. 7 suppose the instruction Store A in B is encountered: All three bidirectional gates simultaneously transfer information to the right, and in less than several microseconds we have A = B.

External Memory A microprocessor stores nearly all its permanent and temporary data and instructions in devices outside its package. A microcomputer chip might store all or most of the temporary data and instructions inside the chip, and many microcomputer devices also contain ROMs (either permanently programmed or user-alterable) for holding nonvolatile data and instructions. In either case, programming of the microprocessor or microcomputer proceeds along identical lines. However, it is much more dificult to design the external memory hardware than to have it already available on the microcomputer chip.

Many factors must be considered when interfacing external memory to a microprocessor. Designers must first decide which area in memory space is to be utilized by the block of external memory. They must then design addressing circuitry that will properly time the address bus with the data bus, read-write line, and several other signals.

1.2 *Microprocessor and Microcomputer Software*

Every type of microprocessor and microcomputer understands a slightly different language. All these languages are merely extensions of the basic computer instructions listed in Table 2. From a programmer's point of view, microprocessor instructions[3] can be conveniently sorted into three classes:

1. *Data movement:* I/O, Load, Store, Exchange, Move
2. *Data manipulation:* Add, Subtract, Multiply, Divide, Complement, Clear, Shift, Rotate, Increment, Decrement, AND, OR, XOR
3. *Program manipulation:* Jump, Skip, Branch, Call, Return, Halt

We now discuss each class in detail.

Data Movement Data can be moved about in a variety of ways—inside or outside the microprocessor. Figure 8 briefly illustrates a few important types of data movement, that is, data transfer. Certain types of data transfer require more than one instruction, but in most microprocessors the majority of data transfers can be performed with one instruction. Data to be moved reside in

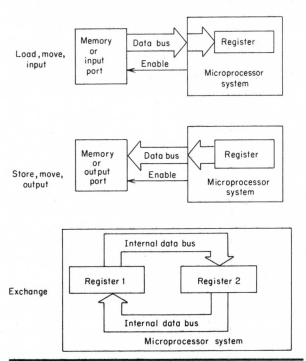

FIG. 8 *Simple illustrations summarizing a few of the more important types of data movement. (From Ref. 1 with permission)*

internal registers, internal memory, or external memory. Specialized external devices such as I/O ports, timers, number crunchers, and so forth all appear as external memory to the microprocessor. Data movement can therefore be classified as one of four types:

1. Register to register
2. Register to memory (including output ports)
3. Memory to register (including input ports)
4. Memory to memory

All microprocessors handle these first three data transfers with one instruction. Two instructions, such as number 3 followed by number 2, were required to achieve instruction number 4 in the first- and second-generation microprocessors. Third- and fourth-generation microprocessors and microcomputers can perform the fourth type of data transfer by using a single instruction.

Many variations of the four basic data-movement instructions are available with various microprocessors. The Z80 microprocessor,[4] a third-generation device, has seven of the type 1 data-movement instructions, nine of type 2, seventeen of type 3, and five of type 4. It also has ten exchange instructions, each of which is a type 1 instruction done in both directions simultaneously. But this is not all. Some of the instructions, such as LDr,r', have 64 possible combinations of any r with any r'. This instruction loads any of the 8r registers with the content of any of the 8r' registers. When all the possible combinations within each instruction are considered, a grand total of 188 data-movement instructions are possible with the Z80. The fourth-generation microprocessors such as the 16-bit 68000 device offer an even more flexible instruction set.

Addressing Modes   Before discussing the other two classes of instructions, we need to explore the concept of addressing modes. Most 8-bit microprocessors and microcomputers use a 16-bit address word capable of addressing $2^{16} =$ 65,536 memory locations. If an instruction refers to a memory address using the *extended addressing mode,* all 16 bits of the memory address are attached to the 8-bit instruction. This is called a 3-byte instruction, the least efficient method for finding an address. When the address immediately follows the instruction, the mode is called *immediate addressing.* If the required address is in the first 256 words of memory, then the *direct addressing mode* may be used. This mode requires one 8-bit word following the instruction. An 8-bit word can select 256 memory locations in the first page of memory (that is, the first 256 words of memory space).

The technique of indexed addressing also allows a 16-bit address to be generated without providing all 16 bits following the instruction. The 16-bit index register is used to keep track of the memory address. This register can be loaded, incremented, decremented, or tested for zero using other instructions. For example, suppose we want the A accumulator to be successively loaded with numbers from a section of memory starting at 4100 and ending at 43FF. For each value loaded into A, a subroutine is entered where the data is processed. If the 6800 microprocessor is used, the program might be set up as follows (note that # means immediate date and $ means hexadecimal data):

	LDX	#$4100	LOAD INDEX REGISTER WITH 4100
LOOP	LDAA	O,X	LOAD A WITH DATA AT ADDRESS EQUAL TO VALUE OF X
	JSR	NAME	JUMP TO SUBROUTINE WHERE A IS USED
	INX		INCREMENT INDEX REGISTER
	CPX	#$43FF	COMPARE X WITH 43FF
	BNE	LOOP	GO TO LOOP IF X ≠ 43FF

Although the 8080 microprocessor does not have an index register, its *register indirect addressing mode* allows a programmer to perform indexed addressing. For example, the previous program could be executed as follows using the 8080:

	LXIB	#$4100	LOAD REGISTER PAIR BC WITH 4100
LOOP	LDAX	B	LOAD A INDIRECT USING ADDRESS IN BC
	CALL	NAME	JUMP TO SUBROUTINE WHERE A IS USED
	INXB		INCREMENT REGISTER PAIR BC
	LXIH	#$−43FF	LOAD REGISTER PAIR HL WITH −43FF
	DADB		HL = HL + BC
	JNC	LOOP	GO TO LOOP IF BC ≠ −HL

In this example we used the register pair BC as a 16-bit index register. The 8080 does not have a 16-bit Compare or Subtract instruction, but it does have a 16-bit Add called DAD rp. This instruction adds register pair rp (here we used rp = BC) to the contents of the HL register pair. In this case we started with HL = −43FF. If BC = 43FF, then a carry is generated and the Jump instruction is disregarded.

Data Manipulation   The real power of a microprocessor instruction set is established if it has a large and versatile set of data-manipulation instructions. Many software/hardware designers choose a microprocessor for its ability to perform mathematical and logic calculations with minimum instructions. Referring to Table 2, note that all basic ALU instructions fit into the category of data-manipulation instructions. Each new generation of microprocessors or microcomputers has new types of data-manipulation instructions; early devices had only the basic ALU instructions listed in Table 2. An expanded listing of these instructions available in second- and third-generation microprocessors is in Tables 4 and 5. Some of the instructions, such as Multiply and Divide, require a large number of microinstructions within the basic instruction.

TABLE 4 *Arithmetic data-manipulation instructions available in second- and third-generation microprocessors*

Name	Description of instruction options
Add	Carry bit not added
	Add carry bit
	Add register to accumulator
	Add one accumulator to another
	Add immediate data to accumulator
	Add memory data to accumulator by
	Direct addressing
	Extended addressing
	Relative addressing
	Indexed addressing
	Indirect addressing
	Multiple-precision capability (carry bit)
	BCD-add capability (decimal adjust)
Subtract	Carry (borrow) bit not included
	Subtract using carry (borrow) bit
	Subtract register from accumulator
	Subtract one accumulator from another
	Subtract immediate data from accumulator
	Subtract memory data from accumulator by
	Direct addressing
	Extended addressing
	Relative addressing
	Indexed addressing
	Indirect addressing
	Multiple-precision capability (carry bit)
Clear	Clear accumulator
	Clear register
	Clear memory location by
	Direct addressing
	Extended addressing
	Indexed addressing
Multiply	Multiply register by another register
Divide	Divide register pair by another register
Increment	Increment accumulator
(decrement)	Increment register
	Increment memory location by
	Extended addressing
	Indexed addressing
	Increment stack pointer
	Increment register pair
	Increment index register
	Increment and skip if **0**
Negate	Complement accumulator and add **1**

SOURCE: See Ref. 1.

TABLE 5 Logic data-manipulation instructions available in second- and third-generation microprocessors

Logic instruction name	Description of instruction options
Complement	Exchange 1s and 0s in accumulator
Rotate	Rotate right, including carry
	Rotate left, including carry
	Rotate accumulator
	Rotate register
	Rotate memory location by
	Extended addressing
	Indexed addressing
	4-bit rotate
	Rotate register pair
Shift	Arithmetic shift left, 0s into LSB
	Arithmetic shift right, keep MSB unchanged
	Arithmetic shift, any accumulator
	Any register
	Any memory location
	Extended addressing
	Indexed addressing
	Logical shift right, 0s into MSB
AND	Accumulator AND register
	Accumulator AND immediate data
	Accumulator AND memory location by
	Direct addressing
	Extended addressing
	Indexed addressing
OR	Accumulator OR register
	Accumulator OR immediate data
	Accumulator OR memory location by
	Direct addressing
	Extended addressing
	Indexed addressing
XOR	Accumulator XOR register
	Accumulator XOR immediate data
	Accumulator XOR memory location by
	Direct addressing
	Extended addressing
	Indexed addressing
Compare	Compare accumulator with register
	Compare accumulator with immediate data
	Compare accumulator with memory data by
	Direct addressing
	Extended addressing
	Indexed addressing
	Compare accumulator with register, decrement another register

SOURCE: See Ref. 1.

Although not explicitly shown in the tables, third-generation microprocessors also have many instructions that repeat an indexed process until a given counter goes to zero. For example, in the Z80 microprocessor, the block Transfer and block Search group of instructions belong to this class. These types of instructions reduce the program size but still require many steps to complete. The main improvement in each generation of microprocessors is in the option list for each data-manipulation instruction. Addressing modes are being added or improved continually so that routines can be written more compactly. Two or more index registers in some microprocessors allow several operations to be carried on simultaneously.

Program Manipulation   Data-manipulation and data-movement instructions are concerned primarily with the data contained in registers, accumulators, and memory locations. These two classes of instructions affect the status of the program counter only indirectly. Program-manipulation instructions, however, directly control the actions of the program counter. These instructions change the order in which the program instructions are carried out. Program-manipulation instructions are either unconditional or conditional. *Unconditional program-manipulation instructions* cause the program counter to assume a value specified in the second, or second and third, word(s) of the instruction whenever the instruction is encountered in the program. *Conditional program-manipulation instructions* cause the program counter to assume a value specified in the second, or second and third, word(s) of the instruction only if given conditions are met. These conditions are specified by particular bits in the CCR or by the content of a given general-purpose register.

The Jump instruction changes the program counter content to the value specified in the second and third words of the instruction. From our earlier discussion of addressing modes, recall that this is the extended addressing mode. If this instruction is conditional, it is ignored (that is, skipped) until the conditions are met. An Indexed Jump instruction loads the program counter with a number found in one of the index registers. This addressing mode allows the Jump destination to be dynamically modified as the program proceeds.

The Jump Relative or Branch instructions are two different names for an instruction that requires only one additional word to specify the new value for the program counter. In 8-bit microprocessors this additional word specifies an address within ±127 words of the present program counter number. This second word, often referred to as the "relative offset," uses signed twos complement notation; that is, the most significant bit is 1 for negative offsets.

The Call and JSR instructions are extended addressing commands that cause the program counter to jump to the beginning of a subroutine. The RET or RTS instructions at the end of the subroutine are also extended addressing commands that return the program counter to one instruction past the Call or JSR instruction leading into the subroutine. Some microprocessors also offer conditional Call and RET instructions.

1.3   *Fundamentals of Microprocessor System Design*

Applications involving microprocessors and microcomputers will invade nearly every facet of human endeavor in the years to come. This handbook provides in-depth examples of several useful applications for these devices; no book could possibly discuss the design of every application. Our applications cover a wide range of topics, so most microprocessors users will be able to find some areas of common interest. There is a balance of hardware and software throughout the book.

This section presents steps useful to consider while designing a microprocessor-operated system. These steps can be a checklist for the design of many classes of systems. Some applications may involve only a few of these steps, whereas others may use nearly all of them.

STEP 1. Before beginning any work on a project, write a *statement of requirements and objectives.* Both large and small projects benefit from written system-performance requirements available before design begins. This not only assists the designer but gives management and others an opportunity to review, critique, and suggest improvements. Each hour spent on this phase of the project may prevent the designer from wasting hundreds of hours working on incorrect concepts.

STEP 2. Draw a *simplified hardware block diagram* using the statement of requirements as the only input data. This procedure begins to test the completeness of the statement of requirements and helps determine whether it should be modified or expanded. This step also gives the designer a first impression of the cost of the project. At this point some of the larger or long-lead items required for the project could be ordered.

STEP 3. Next, make a *simplified flowchart* that shows the relationship of the executive or supervisory program to the major subroutines. Assign specific subroutines that are to handle inputs and outputs. A minimum of these specific control functions and detailed calculations should be handled by the supervisory program. The main program should serve only as a link between the various subroutines; all the work should be performed within the subroutines.

STEP 4. Make *preliminary processing-speed calculations.* Using various I/O constraints now available, estimate an upper limit on the speed of each subroutine. From this, make an approximate upper limit on the total loop time around the supervisory program. If some or all of the subroutines are accessed using interrupts, then processing limits can be estimated for each INTERRUPT SERVICE routine. If speed is of no concern, most of this step can be deleted.

STEP 5. Make specific assignments as to the nature and speed of all I/O devices. This information is required for most of the following steps. Is the I/O port parallel or serial, synchronous or asynchronous, with or without a clock, latched or gated, and so forth?

STEP 6. Choose *data- and address-word sizes.* Should the microprocessor data word be 4, 8, 16, or 32 bits wide? This decision is often dictated by the type of I/O devices used, accuracy and speed of calculations required, or availability of a development system for a particular microprocessor. The address-word width depends upon the size of memory required.

STEP 7. Perform *tradeoffs* on cost, availability, software support, speed, support chips, addressing capability, on-chip RAM and ROM, I/O capability, power, interrupt capabilities, and instruction-set capabilities of several candidate microprocessors or microcomputers. Often a designer's facility has only one type of microprocessor development system (MDS), but the designer can still perform this tradeoff because one MDS will usually support software development for several microprocessors in a given class.

STEP 8. Choose the *large-scale integration (LSI) support chips* once the candidate microprocessor has been selected. Make certain these parts are proven and well-documented by the manufacturer.

STEP 9. Design the central processing unit (CPU), clock, bus drivers, and main address decoding circuits. These are the heart of the system and must have drive capability sufficient to handle the entire system, with margin for growth.

STEP 10. Design the *memory system* using RAM, ROM, PROM, electrically alterable ROM (EAROM), and so on. Choose a microcomputer chip with as much RAM and ROM on board as possible. If high-volume production is anticipated, choose a chip with both PROM available for development and mask programmable ROM available for production.

STEP 11. Design the *I/O circuits* using LSI devices having a good history and adequate documentation. Keep the main microprocessor data and address buses within a few inches of the microprocessor itself. Whenever interfacing with other boards or I/O devices, use secondary data buses and decoded address lines. Many development problems are prevented by keeping all low-level and primary buses on one board within a tightly controlled area.

STEP 12. Design the *control panel* and other *human interfaces*. Make certain as many debugging features are designed into the system as are economically feasible. By making the front panel of the system totally software-operated (both inputs and displays), one can incorporate into hardware and software some highly useful tools that will save hundreds of hours of debugging. These features are invaluable during development of the system and for fault isolation in the field.

STEP 13. Design the *power distribution system*. Most system designers purchase rather than design power supplies. Be sure the current capability of all supply voltages has sufficient margin for growth. Choose established manufacturers who will provide a guarantee and quick turnaround for failed units. Design all printed circuits, cables, and connectors to handle the currents from each supply. Provide adequate numbers of bypass capacitors on each board to keep power supply ripple in the millivolt levels.

STEP 14. Now that more is known of the system, draw a more *detailed flowchart* of the supervisory program. List tradeoffs on locations, sizes, types, and quantities of the various subroutines. Use true modular programming. Keep subroutines as independent as possible. The optimum subroutine is only 20 to

30 statements long, which makes software debugging and corrections easier for the original programmer or for anyone else called upon to isolate problems.

STEP 15. Construct a useful and informative *memory map*. Keep this map in the front of the program listing, where it can be continually edited along with the program.

STEP 16. Write the *supervisory program* and all subroutines. Assemble, debug, reassemble, and prepare the program for test. If possible, simulate the hardware using the MDS system and attempt to run the program.

STEP 17. Load the *assembled program* into RAM, PROM, or a ROM simulator and test on the designed system. Debug, redesign, and rewrite the program as required to get the system operating. This is always the most time-consuming part of system design. Projects usually survive or die in this phase of development.

STEP 18. In the front of the program listing, *list* all design parameters, temporary registers, scratchpad registers, I/O ports, and so on. Describe each item fully.

REFERENCES

1. Stout, D. F., and M. Kaufman: *Handbook of Microcircuit Design and Application,* McGraw-Hill, New York, 1980, pp. 18–20.
2. Nemec, J., and S. Y. Lau: "Bipolar Microprocessors: An Introduction to Architecture and Applications," *EDN,* September 20, 1977, p. 63.
3. Weiss, C. D.: "Software for MOS/LSI Microprocessors," *Electronic Design,* vol. 7, April 1, 1974, p. 50.
4. Ungermann, R., and B. Peuto, "Get Powerful Microprocessor Performance by Using the Z80," *Electronic Design,* vol. 14, July 5, 1977, p. 54.

CHAPTER TWO

A Microprocessor-Based Interface for the IEEE-488 Bus

Dan LeVasseur

*Sperry Flight Systems, NASA Ames Research
Center, Moffett Field, California*

INTRODUCTION

Microprocessors have made engineers and technicians acutely aware
of the need for standardized busing in modular systems. Indeed,
were it not for the need to connect systems or devices in a
standardized manner, busing would not be necessary because each
component would have its own specialized connection to the rest of
the world, as was the case with many instruments and systems
before the advent of the microprocessor. The microprocessor has
promoted and hastened the development of standard buses. One bus
that has enjoyed increasingly widespread popularity is described in
the IEEE-488 specification.[1,2]

2.1 The IEEE-488 Standard

The 488 bus was derived from an asynchronous data-transfer
protocol originated by Hewlett-Packard Co.; it was called the HPIB
(Hewlett-Packard Interface Bus). The IEEE-488-1975 specification[3] is
the document that formalizes this standardization.

Many large-scale integration (LSI) devices have been developed to help the designer implement systems that interface with the 488 bus. Here we discuss the Motorola MC68488 interface chip, but should be aware that other devices could be used just as well. However, because the 6802 microprocessor is used as the main controlling device in the application described in this chapter, it is best to design the rest of the system using 6802-compatible devices.

Bus Description The IEEE-488 bus accommodates a variety of devices that operate in one of three basic modes.[4] A *listener only* mode accepts data from the bus, a *talker* sends data over the bus, and a *controller* assumes supervisory control by addressing other devices or granting permission for talkers to use the bus. Connected devices can embody any combination of the three functions, but only one bus controller or talker can be active at a time.

Connected devices are assigned unique addresses. The controller addresses as many listeners as required, although at any one time information is typically transferred between only two devices: one functioning as a talker and the other as a listener.

When designing circuitry for use with the bus, keep track of cable lengths. Devices typically terminate signal lines with 3-kΩ pull-down resistors, maintaining uniform line impedance and improved noise immunity. Drivers must sink 48 mA (receivers use Schmitt-type inputs). Limit the maximum number of devices connected to 14, and restrict cable lengths so that the total length is less than 2 m times the total number of devices. (In any case, limit cable lengths to a maximum of 20 m; longer lengths might cause timing violations that will result in unreliable operation.)

The Signal Lines of the 488 Interface The 488 bus[5] employs a byte-serial, bit-parallel, "low-true" logic scheme with three functional groups of transistor-transistor logic (TTL)-level signals (see Fig. 1):

1. The eight bidirectional data lines (DIO_{1-8}) carry a byte of address or data information or a command.
2. The byte-transfer-control lines function as follows:
   a. When the data valid (DAV) line is forced LOW by the talker, the information on the bus is valid and can be read by all listeners.
   b. When a listener is ready to accept a byte of information, it releases the wire-OR'd not ready for data (NRFD) line, letting that line float HIGH.
   c. Participating listeners release the wire-OR'd not data accept (NDAC) line after accepting the information presented on the data bus. When this line goes HIGH, the talker removes the message. Data transfers therefore proceed at the rate of the slowest listening device.
3. The interface-management lines consist of the following signals:
   a. ATN (attention)—The controller pulls this line LOW, indicating that the information currently on the data lines is an interface address or command.
   b. IFC (interface clear) resets all interfaces to a particular known condition. One can use it as a hard-wired RESET line.

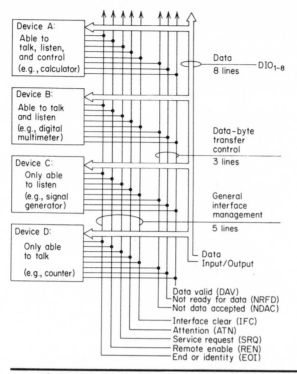

FIG. 1   The IEEE-488 bus signal lines interconnect different devices over a common data path of TTL-level signals.

    c. SRQ (service request)—A device requiring service captures the controller's attention by asserting this wire-OR'd line LOW.

    d. REN (remote enable) allows remote control of a device—from front-panel controls if the device is an instrument.

    e. EOI (end or identify) is asserted by a talker (denoting the end of a message-transfer sequence) or as a command from the controller (asking a device to identify itself in response to an SRQ). The device responds to the identify command by placing its assigned address on the bus during the polling sequence.

The "Handshake" Data-Control Interface   Every byte transfer is accompanied by an asynchronous 3-wire "handshake" on the byte-transfer-control lines; the timing diagram (Fig. 2) shows how this procedure works. After making sure the listeners are ready, the talker pulls DAV LOW, thereby announcing that the DIO lines carry valid information. Acknowledging DAV LOW, the fastest listener pulls NRFD LOW, signifying that it is busy with the current byte. When the slowest participating listener releases NDAC (held LOW since

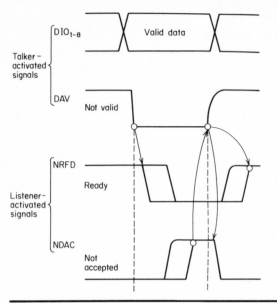

FIG. 2   A bus timing diagram shows how every byte transfer is accomplished by an asynchronous 3-wire handshake on the byte-transfer control lines.

the previous transfer), all listeners have accepted the byte. Sensing NDAC HIGH forces the talker to remove the message and pull DAV HIGH.

Upon sensing that signal, all listeners prepare for the next transfer. They pull NDAC LOW, signifying that they are ready and able to accept another byte. During this time, the talker prepares the next byte for transfer and subsequently asserts DAV as soon as NDAC is LOW and NRFD is HIGH.

2.2   Implementing a Microprocessor-Based 488 Interface

The microprocessor-based interface described herein is an implementation of the 488 bus. It adapts a generalized parallel- or serial-input device to the bus. The interface itself is essentially a self-contained microcomputer; it is programmable, dynamically reconfigurable, and has computational capability. Moreover, it consumes little power and requires only 10 integrated circuits (ICs). The circuit could be placed in a single very large-scale integration (VLSI) with two bidirectional ports: one to the 488 bus, the other to the user device. The IC would only require that the user define the functions of the device interface via ultraviolet PROM (UVPROM) code.

Interface Hardware   As shown in Fig. 3, the 6802 microprocessor forms the heart of this universal interface (UI).[6] An MC68488 general-purpose interface adapter (GPIA) interfaces the microprocessor to the IEEE-488 bus. The addition of memory, two peripheral interface adapters (PIAs), and an asynchronous-communications interface adapter (ACIA) completes the system. Note that literally any microprocessor could be used in the circuit to perform the control function. Also, other 488 chips are available, such as Texas Instruments' TMS9914, the Intel chip set 8291 and 8292, and the Philips' HEF4738.

Figure 4 shows a detailed schematic of the UI. The capabilities of the interface board include:

1. Complete listener and talker functions.
2. Single or dual primary and secondary address recognition (it can recognize multiple 488 bus addresses).
3. Serial or parallel interface capability.
4. Synchronous or asynchronous 488 bus transfers.
5. Multilevel programmable interrupts.
6. Direct memory access (DMA) data acceptance with the addition of a DMA controller.
7. Adaptability to many microprocessors.

The GPIA does not embody the entire IEEE-488 specification; it primarily encompasses listener and talker functions. Controller functions can be implemented with this chip by incorporating some supporting logic. In any event, the GPIA considerably simplifies interfacing to the IEEE-488 bus because one need not fully understand 488 protocol to use it.

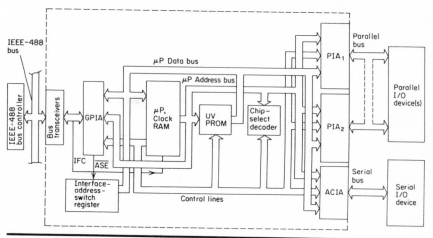

FIG. 3   *This universal interface can connect a variety of devices to the IEEE-488 bus. It accommodates serial or parallel I/O devices, is programmable and dynamically reconfigurable, and possesses computational capability.*

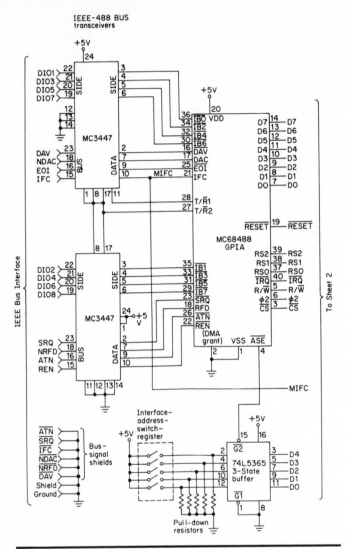

FIG. 4   *Detailed schematic of the bus interface. Sheet 1.*

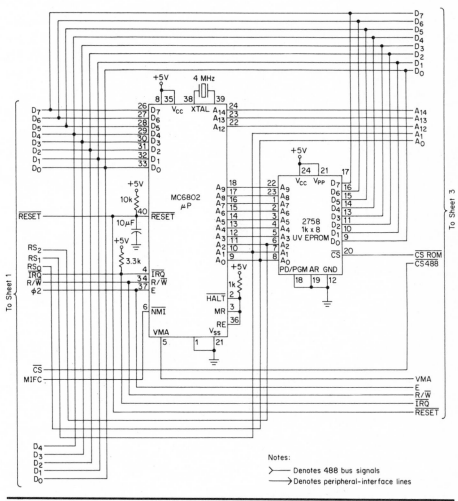

FIG. 4 (Cont.) Sheet 2

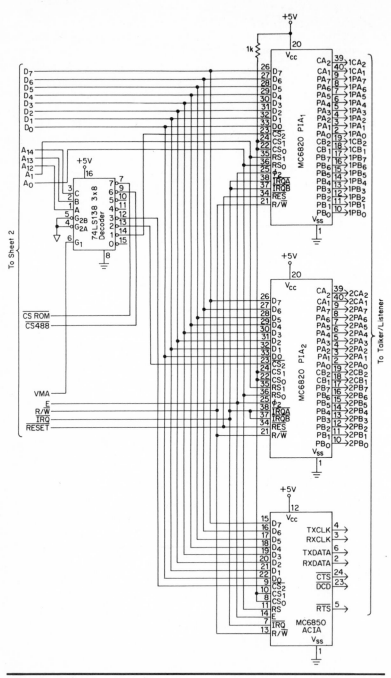

FIG. 4   (Cont.) Sheet 3

The GPIA chip is an LSI NMOS device with fifteen 8-bit registers addressable by the microprocessor: Seven of these registers are write-only, and the remaining eight are read-only. These 15 registers are addressed by the microprocessor using the read-write (R/$\overline{W}$) line and the 3 least significant bits (LSBs) of the address bus. The chip-select ($\overline{CS}$) line to the 488 chip must be LOW to allow addressing. Some of the 8 read-only registers contain bits that indicate the GPIA's dynamic state before, during, or after a bus transaction. Some of these bits might be present for only several clock periods; others indicate particular GPIA device states and can be used to interrupt the microprocessor.

During multibyte transfers, the microprocessor must control data handshakes because it cannot read the received data and process that data at the high speed of the system controller and GPIA. If the microprocessor did not perform this function, the data might be inadvertently overwritten. In some applications, DMA of an external device to the RAM in the system being designed could be used for dedicated listener interfaces. This approach would allow data acceptance at maximum speed and not tie up the bus.

The MC3447 transceivers provide appropriate electrical interfacing directly to the 488 bus. These chips incorporate the bus terminations and receiver hysteresis required by the 488-1975 specification.

The 6802 microprocessor incorporates a clock and 128 bytes of random access memory (RAM) in addition to exhibiting the features of its predecessor, the 6800. Because all other ICs in the interface are MOS or low-power Schottky, the microprocessor can drive the address bus and control lines shown in Fig. 4 without buffering. However, if the system is expanded much beyond that shown in Fig. 4, bidirectional transceivers on the microprocessor data bus or unidirectional buffers on the address bus and control lines may be required.

The interface also includes a 2758 erasable PROM (EPROM), which stores 1024 words with only single-supply operation. As an alternative, one could use the 2716 (2048 words), the 2732 (4096 words), or the 2764 (8192 words).

The 6820 PIAs allow control of multiple devices through programmable interrupt lines and individually programmable data lines running to the appropriate peripheral device. Sixteen data-in lines on PIA_1 and 16 data-out lines on PIA_2 provede communication with such a peripheral.

The 6850 ACIA interfaces asynchronous serial-data-oriented peripherals. With minor modifications, the circuit could be designed around the 6852 synchronous serial-data adapter. Both the PIA and ACIA outputs can drive one TTL load on each line. If necessary, one could add a second circuit card for buffers or drivers, current-loop converters, RS-232C drivers, and so on.

2.3 IEEE-488 Application—Distance-Measuring Equipment (DME)

This UI is designed to handle a multitude of applications in different environments. The following application describes an aircraft distance-measuring equipment (DME) system[7] and an HP 9825A calculator that use the IEEE-488 interface. (See sec. 2.4, *DME Principles of Operation.*) The calculator is used as the controller for this IEEE-488 interface.

A DME transceiver determines the distance between an airplane and a radionavigation station on the ground. The DME is tuned to a particular station frequency, and by transmitting and receiving coded pulses to and from that station, it determines slant distance. The calculator triangulates DME data from several stations, thus pinpointing the plane's exact location. In this application, the HP 9825A controls the DME through the UI. The UI software flowchart is shown in Fig. 5; Fig. 6 lists the corresponding firmware. The HP 9825A calculator program is listed in Fig. 7.

Software allows the UI to communicate with the calculator via a macrocode. In this example, the UI accepts 2 sequential data bytes representing a DME station frequency followed by an SRQ permit macrocommand. The latter synchronizes interrupts between the calculator and UI. Before the UI can

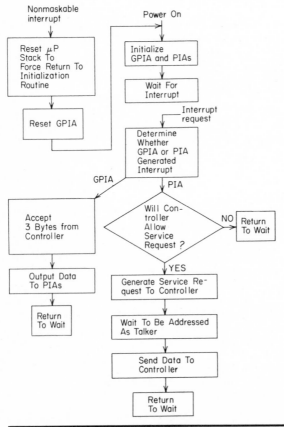

FIG. 5 *The universal interface software waits for an interrupt from the bus (through the GPIA) or from a peripheral (through the PIAs).*

```
◆◆◆◆◆◆◆◆◆◆◆◆◆◆◆◆◆◆◆◆◆◆◆◆◆◆◆◆◆◆◆◆◆◆◆◆◆◆◆◆◆◆◆◆◆◆◆◆◆◆◆◆◆◆◆◆
◆  488 BUS/DME PROGRAM ◆◆◆◆◆◆◆◆◆◆◆◆◆◆◆◆◆◆◆◆◆◆◆◆◆◆◆◆◆◆◆◆◆◆◆
◆◆◆◆◆◆◆◆◆◆◆◆◆◆◆◆◆◆◆◆◆◆◆◆◆◆◆◆◆◆◆◆◆◆◆◆◆◆◆◆◆◆◆◆◆◆◆◆◆◆◆◆◆◆◆◆
◆  RECEIVE 2 BYTE DME FREQUENCY PLUS SRQ INTERRRUPT
◆  ENABLE BYTE; SEND 2 BYTE SLANT RANGE DISTANCE FROM
◆  DME TO CALCULATOR
◆
◆  MEMORY MAP:  0XXX=RAM
◆               1XXX=PIA1
◆               2XXX=PIA2
◆               6XXX=GPIA
◆               7XXX=ROM
◆
◆◆◆◆◆◆◆◆◆◆◆◆◆◆◆◆◆◆◆◆◆◆◆◆◆◆◆◆◆◆◆◆◆◆◆◆◆◆◆◆◆◆◆◆◆◆◆◆◆◆◆◆◆◆◆◆
                       OPT    S,O,NOP,M
7000                   ORG    $7000
7000 8E 007F BEGIN     LDS    #$007F   ;STACK POINTER
7003 86 FF             LDA A  #$FF     ;PIA1-16 BITS IN
7005 B7 2000           STA A  $2000    PIA2-16 BITS OUT
7008 B7 2002           STA A  $2002
700B 86 34             LDA A  #$34     ;PIA1-CA1 INACTIVE
700D B7 1001           STA A  $1001    CA2-LOAD OUTPUT
7010 86 0C             LDA A  #$0C     ;PIA1-CB1 INACTIVE
7012 B7 1003           STA A  $1003    CB2-INT INPUT
7015 86 04             LDA A  #$04     ;PIA2-INTERRUPTS DISABLED
7017 B7 2001           STA A  $2001
701A B7 2003           STA A  $2003
701D 4F                CLR A           ;ZERO OUT PERIPHERAL LINES
701E 97 00             STA A  $0000    AND INTERRUPT FLAG FROM
7020 97 01             STA A  $0001    CALCULATOR
7022 97 02             STA A  $0002
7024 8D 26             BSR    STROB
7026 B6 6004 ZERO      LDA A  $6004    ;INITIALIZE INTERFACE ADDRESS
7029 84 1F             AND A  #$1F
702B B7 6004           STA A  $6004
702E 4F                CLR A           ;CLEAR RESET BIT IN GPIA
702F B7 6003           STA A  $6003
7032 86 04             LDA A  #$04     ;RFD DATA HOLD-OFF OPTION
7034 B7 6002           STA A  $6002
7037 86 80             LDA A  #$80     ;PARALLEL POLL ADDRESS=128
7039 B7 6006           STA A  $6006    DECIMAL
703C CE 0000           LDX    #$0000   ;DATA BUFFER POINTER
703F 86 81             LDA A  #$81     ;ENABLE MP INTERRUPTS ON BI
7041 B7 6000           STA A  $6000
7044 0E                CLI             ;CLEAR MASK
7045 BD 70F2 WAIT      JSR    CODE     ;CODE IS EXECUTIVE
7048 01                NOP
7049 01                NOP
704A 20 F9             BRA    WAIT
```

FIG. 6 *Sequential steps of universal interface firmware from address $7000.*

```
704C CE 0000 STROB  LDX    #$0000   ;DATA BUFFER POINTER
704F A6 00          LDA A  00,X     ;SEND OUT FIRST DATA BYTE
7051 B7 2000        STA A  $2000
7054 A6 01          LDA A  01,X     ;SEND OUT LAST DATA BYTE
7056 B7 2002        STA A  $2002
7059 86 3C          LDA A  #$3C     ;STROBE LOAD LINE
705B B7 1001        STA A  $1001
705E 86 34          LDA A  #$34
7060 B7 1001        STA A  $1001
7063 CE 0000        LDX    #$0000   ;RESET DATA POINTER
7066 39             RTS
7067 B6 6000 IRQ    LDA A  $6000    ;CHECK GPIA FIRST
706A 06             TAP
706B 24 24          BCC    PERI
706D B6 6002 CALC   LDA A  $6002    ;ADDRESSED AS A LISTENER?
7070 C6 86          LDA B  #$86
7072 10             SBA
7073 26 F8          BNE    CALC
7075 5F             CLR B           ;INITIALIZE COUNTER
7076 B6 6007 NEXT   LDA A  $6007    ;READ DATA BYTE
7079 A7 00          STA A  0,X      ;STORE DATA IN BUFFER
707B 86 40          LDA A  #$40     ;RELEASE HANDSHAKE
707D B7 6003        STA A  $6003
7080 08             INX             ;INCREMENT BUFFER POINTER
7081 5C             INC B           ;INCREMENT COUNTER
7082 C1 03          CMP B  #$03     ;BOTH DATA BYTES AND
7084 27 08          BEQ    END      INTERRUPT FLAG RECEIVED?
7086 B6 6000 LOOP   LDA A  $6000    ;WAIT FOR BI
7089 06             TAP
708A 24 FA          BCC    LOOP
708C 20 E8          BRA    NEXT     ;GET SECOND DATA BYTE
708E 8D BC  END     BSR    STROB    ;OUTPUT DATA TO PIA
7090 3B             RTI
7091 B6 1003 PERI   LDA A  $1003    ;CHECK PIA FOR INTERRUPT
7094 85 40          BIT A  #$40
7096 26 01          BNE    OK
7098 3B             RTI             ;ACIA VECTOR GOES HERE
7099 96 02  OK      LDA A  $0002    ;WILL CALCULATOR PERMIT AN
709B 44             LSR A           INTERRUPT?
709C 25 05          BCS    SRQ
709E B6 1002        LDA A  $1002    ;SRQ NOT PERMITTED;
70A1 20 2D          BRA    EXIT     CLEAR PIA INTERRUPT
70A3 97 02  SRQ     STA A  $0002    ;CLEAR PERMISSION FLAG
70A5 86 C0          LDA A  #$C0     ;SEND SRQ AND SERIAL
70A7 B7 6005        STA A  $6005    POLL ADDRESS=192 DECIMAL
70AA B6 6002 SEND   LDA A  $6002    ;ADDRESSED AS A TALKER YET?
70AD C6 89          LDA B  #$89
70AF 10             SBA
70B0 26 F8          BNE    SEND
70B2 5F             CLR B           ;INITIALIZE COUNTER
70B3 CE 1000        LDX    #$1000   ;LOAD POINTER
```

FIG. 6   *(Cont.)*

```
70B6 B6 6000 TALK    LDA A  $6000    ;BO SET YET?
70B9 85 40           BIT·A  #$40
70BB 27 F9           BEQ    TALK
70BD A6 00           LDA A  0,X       ;GET DATA BYTE
70BF B7 6007         STA A  $6007     ;SEND IT TO CALCULATOR
70C2 08              INX              ;CHECK IT TO SEE IF
70C3 08              INX              BOTH DATA BYTES WERE SENT
70C4 5C              INC B
70C5 C1 02           CMP B  #$02
70C7 26 ED           BNE    TALK
70C9 CE 0000         LDX    #$0000    ;RESET DATA BUFFER POINTER
70CC 4F              CLR A            ;CLEAR SRQ!
70CD B7 6005         STA A  $6005
70D0 3B      EXIT    RTI
70D1 4F      NMI     CLR A            ;CLEAR COUNTER
70D2 31      SADJ    INS              ;ADJUST SP=SP-7
70D3 4C              INC A
70D4 81 07           CMP A  #$07
70D6 26 FA           BNE    SADJ
70D8 86 00           LDA A  #00       ;RETURN TO BEGIN
70DA 36              PSH A
70DB 86 70           LDA A  #$70
70DD 36              PSH A
70DE 4F              CLR A            ;PUT 00'S ON STACK
70DF 5F              CLR B
70E0 36      PUSH    PSH A
70E1 5C              INC B
70E2 C1 04           CMP B  #$04
70E4 26 FA·          BNE    PUSH
70E6 86 10           LDA A  #$10      ;SET INTERRUPT MASK
70E8 36              PSH A
70E9 86 80           LDA A  #$80      ;RESET GPIA
70EB B7 6003         STA A  $6003
70EE B6 1002         LDA A  $1002     ;CLEAR POSSIBLE PIA INTERRUPT
70F1 3B              RTI
70F2 86 40   CODE    LDA A  #$40      ;RELEASE RFD HANDSHAKE
70F4 B7 6003         STA A  $6003
70F7 01              NOP              ;PROGRAM
70F8 01              NOP              GOES
70F9 01              NOP              HERE!
70FA 39              RTS
73F8                 ORG    $73F8
73F8 7067   VEC1     FDB    IRQ
73FA 0002   VEC2     RMB    2
73FC 70D1   VEC3     FDB    NMI
73FE 7000   VEC4     FDB    BEGIN
                     END
```

FIG. 6   (Cont.)

```
0:  "DME Routine"
:oni 7,"POLL";
.eir 7;255→r3
1:  ent "STATION
#?",X;shf(X,
8)→r1;band(X,
r3)→r2;wtb 724,
r1,r2,1
2:  "WAIT":dsp
"SRQ enabled...
wait for DME
data"
3:  gto "WAIT"
4:  "POLL":dsp ;
prt rds(724)→A;
spc
5:  rdb(724)→B
6:  rdb(724)→C
7:  cmd 7,"T";B*
2↑8→B;(B+C)/
10→D
8:  prt "DME STAT
ION","DISTANCE(
nm) = ",D;wtb
724,r1,r2,1
9:  eir 7
10: iret
*5792
```

```
                          |Serial Poll Address
           192.00  ←──────|
                          |And SRQ

DME STATION
DISTANCE(nm) =
           5.60
```

FIG. 7 *A programmable calculator can serve as the interface's bus controller with the aid of a simple program like this one for the application given in the text.*

interrupt the calculator with distance information, it must look at the SRQ permit macrocode stored from the previous 3-byte transfer. If that code is **0**, the UI cannot interrupt the calculator via SRQ, in which case it ignores the DME distance data. If the code is **1**, the calculator permits a service request. Employing the macrocode avoids potential lockup problems, which can occur when a PIA-generated interrupt masks the GPIA's interrupt line while the calculator tries to address the interface.

After each transfer back to the calculator, the microprocessor disables its own interrupt capability by clearing the macrocode SRQ permit stored in RAM. The microprocessor stays disabled until the calculator reenables it during the next 3-byte transfer.

Routine **BEGIN** The firmware shown in Fig. 6 steps sequentially from address $7000 ($ denotes hexadecimal) after power-up. (Note that RAM addresses reside between $0000 and $0FFF, PIA addresses between $1000 and \$2FFF, GPIAs from \$6000 to \$6FFF, and ROM code in \$7000 through \$7FFF.) Starting at \$7000, the system initializes PIA$_1$ to accept a 16-bit word from the DME through the 1PA$_{0-7}$ and 1PB$_{0-7}$ signal pins. PIA$_2$ provides a 16-bit parallel-output word that tunes the DME. Strobe 1CA$_2$ goes HIGH, forcing the DME to accept the station frequency on the output lines. Interrupt 1CB$_2$ goes LOW when the DME has acquired distance data for the calculator.

Routine ZERO   This section of read-only memory (ROM) reads the device primary interface address on the interface-address switch register and stores it in the GPIA. The switches determine the DME address on the 488 bus. When ATN is active, the GPIA looks for this primary interface address on the DIO$_{1-8}$ lines. Next, the reset bit in the GPIA must be cleared in location \$6003. Storing \$04 in GPIA address \$6002 chooses the NRFD hold-off option. This option is used because more than 1 data byte is being accepted. If the data are accepted without the microprocessor's intervention via NRFD, it may overrun. At address \$7039 a parallel-poll address is sent to the GPIA. The GPIA interrupts the microprocessor when the first data byte after a listener-addressed- and listener-active–state transition sequence ends. The GPIA enables the microprocessor interrupts on BI (byte in) at program address \$7041.

Routine STROB   After each initialization routine (BEGIN), routine STROB transfers the station frequency to the DME and toggles the load line 1CA$_2$. The frequency (previously received from the calculator) is stored in RAM at \$0000 and \$0001.

Routine IRQ   The program branches to routine IRQ when the microprocessor is interrupted via the $\overline{\text{IRQ}}$ line. This routine places the highest interrupt priority on the calculator by first checking the GPIA. If the GPIA interrupts the microprocessor, it is checked for listener-addressed status.

Routine CALC   This routine is accessed only if the interrupt came from a listener. If interrupt-driven operation is not required, the microprocessor loops on CALC while waiting for information from the calculator to determine when the calculator is addressing the UI as a listener. Such noninterrupt operation avoids having to save the stack after the interrupt and also saves the subsequent polling routine execution time. This feature results in faster data acceptance. However, in this case the PIA data ready line (1CB$_2$) must also be monitored.

Routine NEXT   If the calculator addresses the UI, the program executes NEXT. A data byte is read, and a 3-wire handshake (NRFD, NDAC, and DAV) is ended via a bit (in location \$6003) that toggles NRFD. The system clears BI (bit 0) of location \$6000 in the GPIA whenever the microprocessor reads data from address \$6007 in the GPIA (the data-in register). BI is set when the next byte arrives. After receiving the 3 expected data bytes, the UI relays the station frequency to the DME via PIA_2.

Routine PERI   If the PIA initiates an interrupt to the microprocessor, routine PERI replaces CALC. The UI checks location $0003 (which holds the SRQ permit macrocode) before generating a service request to the calculator. If such a service request is not permitted, the UI clears the data ready line and exits the INTERRUPT routine. If the request is allowed, both SRQ and a serial-poll address are sent out via the GPIA. The calculator responds to this service request by reading the serial-poll address of the interrupting device on the 488 bus. The GPIA handles all bus protocol for the interface.

Routine TALK   Once addressed as a talker in SEND, the UI enters TALK. A bit termed BO (byte out) in GPIA location $6000 indicates that all designated listeners (those instructed to handshake on data) are ready to accept a byte from the UI. The microprocessor reads a byte from the PIA and sends it to the bus listeners via the data-out register (address $6007 in the GPIA). Note that address $6007 doubles as the data-in and data-out register. This sequence repeats, after which a bit at GPIA address $6005 must be cleared to make SRQ passive.

Routine NMI   This routine initializes the system. Activating MIFC (via IFC on the bus) by pushing the RESET button on the calculator executes this routine. NMI reloads the stack and forces the microprocessor to return execution to the beginning of the program after resetting the GPIA.

Routine CODE   Although no user program is shown, it can be placed starting at $70F7 in ROM. Routine CODE is a subroutine of the ZERO routine. However, before CODE can be accessed, the NRFD bit must be toggled in the GPIA after a return from the TALK routine. If this procedure does not occur, the next time the calculator tells the UI to listen, the UI will not accept the first data byte because the handshake was not sequenced in the GPIA. However, the listener address will be accepted. Because a Wait for Interrupt (WAI) instruction does not allow for this sequencing, it will not work in the UI firmware.

The Calculator Controls the Bus   As noted, the HP 9825A controls the bus. Its program (Fig. 7) first initializes the UI with a station frequency and SRQ permit macrocode and then waits for an interrupt. When the UI indicates a service request, the calculator reads and prints the serial-poll address of the interrupting device, along with 2 data bytes. These bytes, representing the DME station frequency, then go back to the UI, followed by another SRQ permit macrocode, which allows a service request interrupt. (Sending the macrocommand as the third contiguous byte saves bus overhead because the UI does not have to readdress listeners and talkers for another byte transfer.) The calculator then returns to lines 2 and 3 and waits for a new service request.

2.4 DME *Principles of Operation*

The DME is a distance/ground speed/time-to-station measuring unit, used primarily in aircraft up to 45,000 ft (13 km). It electronically converts elapsed time to distance by measuring the length of time between the transmission of a radio signal to a preselected very-low-frequency omnidirectional radio *tactical* station (vortac) ground facility to the reception of the reply signal. This distance, which is then available to an indicator, is normally measured on a slant angle from air to ground, commonly referred to as slant distance (which is different from actual ground distance). Note that the error between ground and slant distance is smallest at low altitude and long range; conversely, the error is greatest in close proximity to a vortac facility. However, if the range is three times the altitude or greater, this error is negligible.

The effective range of DME depends upon factors such as aircraft altitude, location and altitude of the ground transmitter, transmitter power output, and the integrity of both the aircraft and ground facility. The operating channel frequencies lie between 108 and 117.95 MHz in the VHF band.

The range information is available in $\frac{1}{10}$-nautical mile (185-m) increments [the LSB value of the digital range]. Closure rate in knots and time to station in minutes are also available from the DME. Warning information is available when a station is lost or the unit is rechanneling (acquiring a new station).

In utilizing the DME output, the information presented indicates zero when the aircraft ground track is perpendicular to the bearing from the vortac. For this reason, a computer-controlled interface (described in Sec. 2.3) that can automatically triangulate between several stations is desirable.

Basic DME *Principles* The airborne DME (see Figs. 8 and 9) interrogates the DME ground station by transmitting pulse pairs on the receive frequency of the ground station. These pulse pairs are received by the ground station, delayed 50 μs, and then retransmitted to the airborne DME on the receive frequency of the airborne DME, which is 63 MHz away from the ground-station frequency. After the airborne DME transmits a pulse-pair interrogation, it waits 50 μs before beginning to "count out" the time interval prior to receiving the return pulse pair from the DME ground station. The time between the end of the 50-μs period and the return pulse pair is used by the airborne DME to compute the slant distance to the ground station.

For example, the time required for a radio frequency (RF) signal to go 1 mi (1.6 km) round-trip is 12.36 μs. If the round-trip time after subtracting the 50-μs delay of the pulse pair is 37.08 μs, the ground station would be 3 mi (4.8 km) away.

DME *Ground Station* The DME ground station transmits up to a pulse-pair rate of 2700 per second, consisting of replies to interrogations by airborne DMEs and random pulses. When the ground station receives more than 2700 pulse-pair interrogations per second from airborne DMEs, it lowers its receiver sensitivity, thus dropping out the weaker interrogations. Figure 8 shows the relationship between the airborne DME and the ground station.

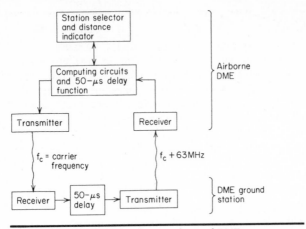

FIG. 8   *Block diagram of the airborne and ground DME.*

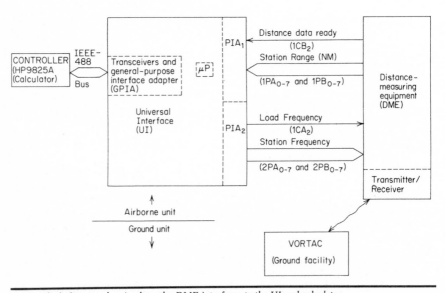

FIG. 9   *Block diagram showing how the DME interfaces to the UI and calculator.*

2.5   Application Summary

Figure 9 represents the interconnection between the three components of the system, specifically, the (1) 488 bus controller (a calculator), (2) UI (universal interface), and (3) airborne DME and ground facility. Using a standardized bus with a generalized interface, we are able to interface a specialized piece of avionics equipment to a general-purpose calculator to perform a navigation function for an aircraft. Two station "fixes" (radio-determined position) pinpoint two possible positions of the aircraft, and a third station fix isolates the aircraft location by triangulation.

The microprocessor-controlled 488 bus interface described in Sec. 2.3 can be used to adapt a generalized parallel- or serial-input device to a computer via the IEEE bus. The interface is actually a self-contained microcomputer that is programmable and can be reconfigured in a real-time environment by accepting "macrocodes" (Sec. 2.3) that can be used to determine various operating characteristics of the interface. For example, when interrupts are not desirable while the bus controller is executing critical sections of code, it may selectively "mask out" interrupts from devices with intelligent interfaces with an SRQ permit macrocode. A danger in bused systems is to devote too much overhead processing time to I/O interrupt servicing. Intelligent interfaces can alleviate this situation if implemented properly. Additionally, a programmable interface can relieve the bus controller or main processor of a part of its workload by sharing some of its processing tasks.

The IEEE-488 bus is one of many parallel buses,[8] such as the STD bus, the S-100 bus, and Intel's Multibus. With available LSI devices such as the 68488 GPIA, which can readily adapt most instruments to the 488 bus, this standard will continue to gain widespread acceptance. Many minicomputer and desktop calculators now have a 488 port as standard equipment. In fact, connecting two computers can be a trivial task if both are equipped with a 488 data link.

REFERENCES

1. Baunach, S.: "An Example of an MC6800-Based GPIB Interface," *EDN*, Sept. 20, 1977, p. 125.
2. "IEEE Standard Digital Interface for Programmable Instrumentation," IEEE Instrumentation and Measurements Group, New York, 1975.
3. "Getting Aboard the 488-1975 Bus," App. Note, Motorola Semiconductor Products Inc., Austin, Tex., 1977.
4. Ricci, D., and G. Nelson: "Standard Instrument Interface Simplifies System Design," *Electronics*, November 1974, p. 95.
5. Triffani, J.: "Bus Standard Brings New Power to Benchtop Instrumentation," *Electronic Products*, July 1976, p. 31.
6. LeVasseur, D.: "Multifunction Interface Simplifies IEEE-488 Use," *EDN*, Mar. 5, 1979, p. 105.
7. "KDM705 Distance Measuring Equipment Installation Manual 006-0082-00," King Radio Corporation, Olathe, Kan., 1973.
8. Conway, J.: "What You Should Know About the 488 and 583 Interface Standards," *EDN*, August 5, 1976, p. 49.

CHAPTER THREE

Hamming Code Error Correction for Microcomputers

Ernst L. Wall

ITT Telecommunications, Shelton, Connecticut

INTRODUCTION

With the recent introduction of large, dynamic random access memories (RAMs) such as the 64K and 256K devices, massive, inexpensive computer memories have become possible for a wide range of applications. However, it has been discovered that alpha particles produced by trace amounts of naturally occurring radioactive elements in the packaging material of the RAMs occasionally create momentary ion paths in the silicon, discharging one of the dynamic storage elements.[1,2] Furthermore it is even possible that cosmic radiation can produce similar ion paths, especially at high altitudes or in space.[3] Although the probability of causing an error in a single, given RAM cell may be quite small, the probability of an error in a large array of cells or chips may become significant. These effects in large arrays, along with the growing demand for large numbers of small, inexpensive, but highly reliable microprocessors in systems such as unattended rural telephone exchanges and biomedical monitoring equipment, have created a need for methods of detecting and automatically correcting memory errors.

Although several algorithms are available,[4,5] Hamming code is the most widely used method because it requires a minimum overhead in memory. For simple correction, a given word requires just enough bits to form a binary number equal in value to the number of bits in the word plus 1. The Hamming code was invented by Richard W. Hamming of Bell Laboratories and was the earliest error-correcting code.[6]

Many books have been written about error correction, but as a rule they emphasize mathematical theory rather than useful application. To avoid a mathematical approach, here we offer an approach that provides typical hardware engineers with an understanding of simple error correction and several circuits which can be adapted to their needs with minimum modification.

We cover a simple, real-time circuit for an 8-bit microprocessor; a real-time approach for a 16-bit machine; and a method of using hardware to detect an error, with firmware providing a correction algorithm.

3.1 Error Detection by Means of Parity

Before discussing Hamming code, we must first discuss error detection via simple parity.[7] The parity of a binary word is determined by counting the number of 1s in it. If there is an odd number of 1s, the parity is odd, or **1**. If there is an even number of 1s, the parity is even, or **0**. Suppose we have the binary word **011011**, in which there is an even number of 1s. The parity of this word is therefore **0**. An equation for the parity of this word may be written:

$$0 \oplus 1 \oplus 1 \oplus 0 \oplus 1 \oplus 1 = 0$$

where the symbol $\oplus$ means EXCLUSIVE OR (this is also referred to as addition modulo 2). Similarly, the parity equation of a binary word **0110111** (that is, an odd number of 1s) is written as

$$0 \oplus 1 \oplus 1 \oplus 0 \oplus 0 \oplus 1 \oplus 1 \oplus 1 = 1$$

Suppose we wish to use these ideas to detect errors in stored or transmitted data. We simply measure the parity of the word and store or transmit the parity of the word along with the word itself. If, upon later reading the stored word or receiving the transmitted word the parity has changed, we know that an odd number of bits has changed. If an even number of bits has changed, then the parity will be unchanged, so the error will not be detected. Therefore, this method is usable only when the probability of a single bit changing is extremely small, making the probability of a double error in the word completely negligible. In any case, this method does not correct errors; it only notifies the system that there has been an error. During a computer data processing operation it would be necessary to notify the computer operator that the error had occurred so that the data could be reprocessed. In the case of data transmission, retransmission would be necessary.

Devices Used for Parity Measurement The simplest implementation of parity measurement is for a 2-bit word by means of an EXCLUSIVE OR gate, such as the 7486 device, which is shown in Fig. 1, along with its parity equation. A 4-bit parity checker made up from an array of EXCLUSIVE OR gates along with its parity equation is portrayed in Fig. 1*b*.

A more useful approach to parity testing uses the 74280 device shown in Fig. 1*c*. This chip can measure the parity of nine inputs. By grounding the ninth input when an 8-bit word is being written into memory, the parity of the word can be obtained and the parity output then stored in memory, along with the word itself. When the word is read back from memory, the parity of the word plus the stored parity bit is obtained. If there is no error, the resultant parity is **0** because a word with an odd parity combined with the additional odd parity bit **(1)** has even parity. Conversely, a word with an even parity combines with the even parity bit **(0)** to produce an even parity. In either case, if an error occurred between the time the word was written and read, the overall parity on readback is odd, notifying the system that there has been an error.

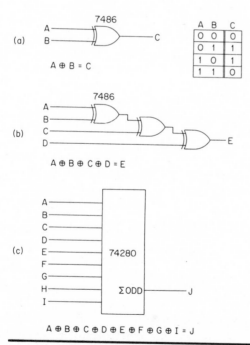

FIG. 1   Three examples of parity measurement: (a) shows a 2-input EXCLUSIVE OR gate, the standard TTL 7486, together with its truth table. If either input alone is **1** the output will be **1**. This is an indication of odd parity. If both inputs are either **1** or **0** simultaneously, the output becomes **0** indicating even parity. Example (b) is an array of 7486s arranged to measure the parity of a 4-bit word, and (c) is a standard TTL device, the 74280, which measures the parity of a 9-bit word.

3.2 Hamming Code Theory

To understand how Hamming code works, refer to Table 1. The top row, Bit Content, shows the structure of a 16-bit data word. The 5 H_i bits are parity, or Hamming bits, and the 16 D_i bits are data. The Bit Position row is the numerical position of each bit. Beneath each position number is a column containing a 5-bit binary number numerically equal to the position number itself (the upper bit is the least significant bit; the bottom bit is the most significant). A single-bit error will produce this associated 5-bit pattern as a pointer that can be used by hardware or software to correct the error. If there is no error, then the pointer should remain at **0**.

The 5-bit pointer can be constructed by generating parities over the related bits as follows: Note that to the left of each row of binary numbers is a parity indicator P_j. Each parity indicator can be represented as an equation that is the parity of those bits in the word, with a **1** beneath it in the row for P_j. These equations are shown for each P_j, with the appropriate bit brought down from the Bit Content row directly above. Note further that an error in a Hamming or a data bit will be found by using this technique.

The Hamming bits are generated as the parity over the data bits in each equation and written into memory along with the data. The result is that the parity sum of the data and the Hamming bits, when combined, is **0** for each P_j. During a subsequent read from memory, the parity of the data and Hamming bit is summed by the parity circuitry for each equation. If none of the bits has changed value since being written, then the five equations will all be **0**. But if 1 bit has changed value, the parity of each equation containing that bit will be **1**. By concatenating the parities P_0 to P_4, we form the previously mentioned 5-bit error pointer in such a manner that it can be utilized by hardware or software to make the correction.

In Table 1, suppose that an error has occurred in D_2 since it was written. This is bit position 6. When the word is read, the parity-measuring circuitry shows that D_2 in the equations for P_1 and P_2 changed from 0 to 1 (see the circled characters in the table). Hence, these pointers show that bit 6 is in error and must be inverted.

Note that each H_i is in a location in the word where only 1 pointer bit is equal to **1**. This makes each Hamming bit independent of the others in that they each occur in only one of the equations. Also note that for an 8-bit word, only the first four equations are needed along with the 4 Hamming bits. Furthermore, each equation is reduced to those characters set off by parentheses.

Protection from Multiple Errors per Word Unfortunately, the approach just described works for only a single-bit error per word. For two or more errors, the pointer indicates an error in the wrong bit. If the probability of accumulating more than one error in a single word prior to reading that word and correcting it is infinitesimally small, then the scheme is adequate as it stands.

As protection from a double error, a simple parity check over all bits, Hamming and data, can be added to the procedure. Because an odd number of bit errors generates an even parity, we can use this mechanism to distinguish

TABLE 1 Structure of a 16-bit word with 5 Hamming bits. (The binary number in each column is numerically equal to the decimal-position number above it. The parity equation of each pointer is the parity sum of those bits having a 1 beneath them in the row of the respective pointer. The location of the Hamming bits is such that each occurs in only one of the equations, making them independent of each other. The circled characters are those that will be affected if D_2 is in error. The values for the equations shown in the box on the right of the equations are those for the no-error case and the case of an error in D_2.)

Bit content	H_0	H_1	D_0	H_2	D_1	D_2	D_3	H_3	D_4	D_5	D_6	D_7	D_8	D_9	D_{10}	H_4	D_{11}	D_{12}	D_{13}	D_{14}	D_{15}
Bit position	1	2	3	4	5	6	7	8	9	10	11	12	13	14	15	16	17	18	19	20	21
P_0	1	0	1	0	1	0	1	0	1	0	1	0	1	0	1	0	1	0	1	0	1
P_1	0	1	1	0	0	1	1	0	0	1	1	0	0	1	1	0	0	1	1	0	0
P_2	0	0	0	1	1	1	1	0	0	0	0	1	1	1	1	0	0	0	0	1	1
P_3	0	0	0	0	0	0	0	1	1	1	1	1	1	1	1	0	0	0	0	0	0
P_4	0	0	0	0	0	0	0	0	0	0	0	0	0	0	0	1	1	1	1	1	1

(Rows P_0–P_4 form the Pointer word.)

Equations (with box values: No-error case → and Error in D_2 →):

$$P_0 = (D_{15} \oplus D_{13} \oplus D_{11} \oplus D_{10} \oplus D_8 \oplus D_6 \oplus D_4 \oplus D_3 \oplus D_1 \oplus D_0 \oplus H_0) = 0 = 0$$

$$P_1 = (D_{13} \oplus D_{12} \oplus D_{10} \oplus D_9 \oplus D_6 \oplus D_5 \oplus D_3 \oplus \boxed{D_2} \oplus D_0 \oplus H_1) = 0 = 1$$

$$P_2 = (D_{15} \oplus D_{14} \oplus D_{10} \oplus D_9 \oplus D_8 \oplus D_7 \oplus D_3 \oplus \boxed{D_2} \oplus D_1 \oplus H_2) = 0 = 1$$

$$P_3 = (D_{10} \oplus D_9 \oplus D_8 \oplus D_7 \oplus D_6 \oplus D_5 \oplus D_4 \oplus H_3) = 0 = 0$$

$$P_4 = (D_{15} \oplus D_{14} \oplus D_{13} \oplus D_{12} \oplus D_{11} \oplus H_4) = 0 = 0$$

No-error case → $0\ 0\ 0\ 0\ 0$

Error in D_2 → $0\ 1\ 1\ 0\ 0$

between a single- and a double-bit error. If we assume the probability of one error is both small and random, then the probability of two errors is much smaller than that of one error, and the probability of three errors is much smaller than that of two errors. Hence the probability of having more than two errors must be negligible within the framework of the scheme. We conclude that we can correct a single-bit error in a word and detect two.

An 8-Bit Example   As an example of how the code is used, suppose we have an 8-bit word that we wish to write into memory as shown:

$$D_7\ D_6\ D_5\ D_4\ D_3\ D_2\ D_1\ D_0$$

1 0 1 0 1 1 1 0

With the values for H_0 to H_3 set equal to 0, the parity equations for P_0 to P_3 are written:

$$P_0 = \mathbf{0 \oplus 0 \oplus 1 \oplus 1 \oplus 0 \oplus 0} = \mathbf{0}$$
$$P_1 = \mathbf{0 \oplus 1 \oplus 1 \oplus 1 \oplus 0 \oplus 0} = \mathbf{1}$$
$$P_2 = \mathbf{1 \oplus 1 \oplus 1 \oplus 1 \oplus 0} = \mathbf{0}$$
$$P_3 = \mathbf{1 \oplus 0 \oplus 1 \oplus 0 \oplus 0} = \mathbf{0}$$

Writing these values for P_0 to P_3 into memory at the same address as the data word itself and renaming them H_0 to H_3, we have for the 4 Hamming bits stored in memory:

$$H_3\ H_2\ H_1\ H_0$$

0   0   1   0

When the word is read from memory, the 4 Hamming bits are combined with the data bits in the equations, giving a value of **0** for each equation if there is no error. If there is a single error, then one or more of the equations will become **1**, causing correction to take place.

Now suppose that in the time between the writing of the word into memory and the reading of the word, bit D_2 has become **0**. The result is that upon reading the word, the equations (using the previous values for H_0 to H_3) for P_1 and P_2 become **1**, giving for the binary pointer word

$$P_3\ P_2\ P_1\ P_0$$

0   1   1   0

which is numerically equal to the decimal value 6, the position number of bit D_2 in Table 1. Hence we have a number that identifies the erroneous bit. The procedure will also identify Hamming bits that have changed.

It is also interesting to observe that this method works just as well with serial-data transmission as it does with parallel-data storage. The order of the bits is unimportant; it is necessary only that their identity be maintained so that during transmission the Hamming bits may be appended to the end of the data or intermixed as desired.

3.3 A Hamming Equation Calculator/Corrector

Figure 2 is a circuit that solves the equation for P_0. It uses a standard 9-bit transistor-transistor logic (TTL) parity chip, the 74280. Because there is a total of 11 terms in the equation, the parity of two of the lines may be combined with the output of the parity chip by means of EXCLUSIVE OR gates, such as the 7486.

Only the parity of the data from the central processing unit (CPU) is measured during a write into memory because the Hamming input is grounded. If the parity is odd, the combined output of the parity chip and the EXCLUSIVE OR gates, designated P_0, is stored in the Hamming memory as a **1** (or a **0** if the parity is even).

During a read from memory, this stored parity bit is combined with the parity of the data bits via this parity array. If a single error (or odd number of

$$P_0 = H_0 \oplus D_0 \oplus D_1 \oplus D_3 \oplus D_4 \oplus D_6 \oplus D_8 \oplus D_{10} \oplus D_{11} \oplus D_{13} \oplus D_{15}$$

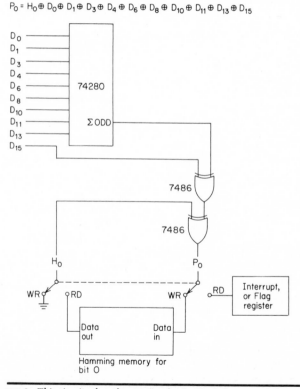

FIG. 2 This circuit solves the equation for P_0. Since there are more inputs than the 74280 can accommodate, it must be combined with two 7486s. During a write into memory, H_0 is grounded so that the parity of the CPU data alone is measured and written back into memory. During a read from memory, H_0 is combined with the CPU data for parity measurement. The output is used as an interrupt or to strobe a flag register. The equations for P_1 to P_4 are solved by similar circuits.

errors) has occurred since the write cycle, the net parity of H_0 and the data bits is **1**, causing corrective action to be taken. If there are no errors, there is no action. Similar circuits solve the equations for P_1 to P_4.

Having obtained a value for the pointer word, we now need to be able to use it to correct an erroneous bit. As shown in Fig. 3, the pointer word is sent to a 4:16 line decoder. P_0 to P_3 go to the A, B, C, and D inputs of the decoder, selecting 1 of the 16 outputs of the chip. If there are no errors, location 0 is selected and its output goes LOW. If there is an error, another output goes LOW and output **0** stays HIGH. Output **0** can therefore serve as a strobe for a flag register or a counter.

The decoder outputs must be inverted before they can be used in the EXCLU-SIVE OR array. If one input of an EXCLUSIVE OR gate is HIGH, the other input is reversed as it goes through the gate. If one input of an EXCLUSIVE OR gate is held LOW, the other input is not changed as it passes through.

As an example, suppose D_2 is in error, as in the previous case. The input pointer word P_0 to P_3 will be binary number 6. Position 6 will be selected, corresponding to bit D_2. Correction line C_2 will go HIGH, inverting bit D_2 at the EXCLUSIVE OR gate.

There is no reason to invert the Hamming bits if they are discovered to be

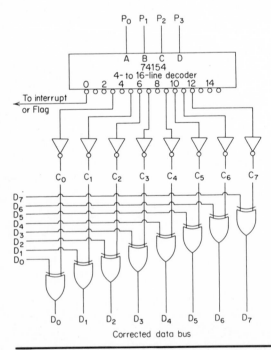

FIG. 3   *The pointer word P_0–P_3 is fed into the 4-to-16 line decoder, selecting the appropriate bit to invert. For example, if D_2 is in error, output 6 is selected, causing C_2 to go HIGH. This causes the* EXCLUSIVE OR *gate to invert D_2, thereby correcting it.*

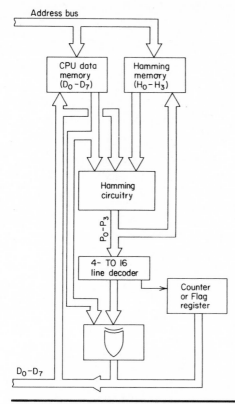

FIG. 4   *Block diagram of an 8-bit real-time error-correction circuit. The address bus selects the appropriate word in both the CPU and memory. During a write into memory, the CPU writes directly to memory while the Hamming data is generated by the Hamming circuitry. During a read from memory, the CPU memory data is combined with the Hamming memory data at the EXCLUSIVE OR array. Any errors strobe the counter or flag register.*

incorrect because they are not used by the CPU. This could be done, but the hardware needed to accomplish the task would be cumbersome. If the same data must be stored in RAM for months or years, then it would probably be worthwhile to occasionally correct any incorrect Hamming bits. Otherwise, if a data error occurred in the same word as the Hamming bit error, the data error could not be corrected.

3.4   Real-Time Error Correction (8 Bits)

For a practical application of the foregoing, we now look closely at an 8-bit real-time error-correction circuit. Refer to the block diagram in Fig. 4. The address bus selects an 8-bit CPU data location and a corresponding 4-bit

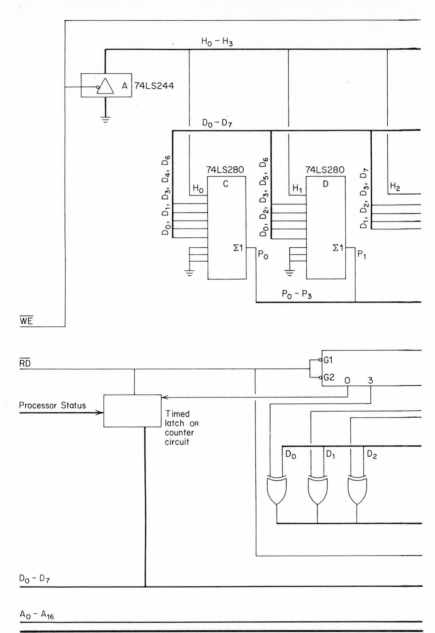

FIG. 5 *A detailed schematic of an 8-bit real-time Hamming code circuit. During a write into memory, chip A grounds the Hamming inputs to the parity chips C through F so that the parity of the CPU data alone is measured and written into memory. During this time, the CPU data is transferred to the parity chips by chip G. During a read from memory, Hamming and CPU data are combined by the parity chips. If there is no error, there is no correction. If there is an error, the 4-to-16 line decoder selects the appropriate output line and inverts the erroneous bit via the EXCLUSIVE OR array J.*

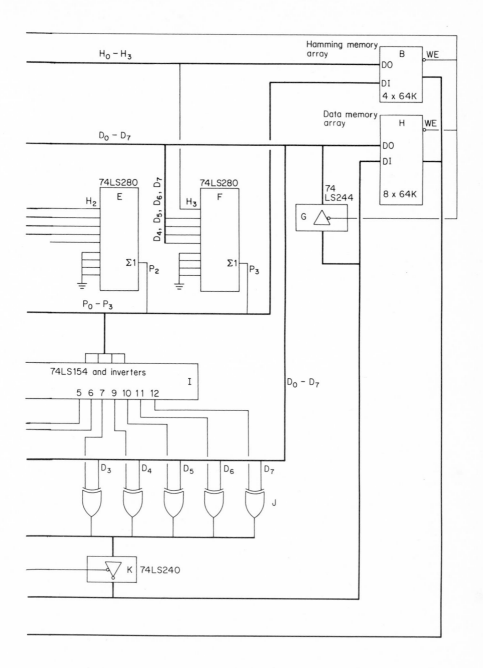

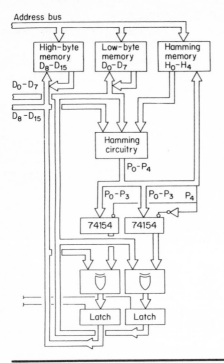

FIG. 6   *This figure outlines the operation of the 16-bit real-time Hamming circuit. It is similar in nature to the 8-bit version, but since the HIGH byte and the LOW byte can be accessed separately, it is necessary that the byte not being accessed by the CPU during a write into memory be supplied by the memory via one of the latches. This is required so that parities can be calculated over all 16 bits of data. Note that P_0 to P_3 go into both 4-to-16 line decoders, but the appropriate decoder is selected by P_4.*

Hamming data location. During a write into memory, the Hamming circuitry generates a 4 bit word, P_0 to P_3, and stores it in the Hamming memory as H_0 to H_3.

During a read from the same address, the Hamming circuitry compares the data from the CPU and Hamming memories via the parity circuits. If there is an error, one or more of the lines P_0 to P_3 go HIGH, causing the counter (or flag register) to trip for later reference. At the same time, the 4:16 line decoder outputs are combined with the CPU memory data via the EXCLUSIVE OR gates, thus correcting the erroneous bit. Periodically, the latch or counter is scanned to determine if an error has been detected. If there has been an error, at some convenient time each word in memory is read (thus correcting it) and then rewritten back into memory. If there is no error, the data is left unchanged.

Figure 5 shows the memory array with separate data in (DI) and data out (DO), as in the case with typical 16K or 64K RAMs. As mentioned, assume that each word will either be accessed at least once or periodically scanned in a much shorter interval than the mean time between failure. If an error is encountered during a memory read, it is corrected before it reaches the processor while a latch or counter is tripped. The latch or counter can be periodically checked for errors. If an error has occurred, it is necessary to read each word in memory (thus correcting it) and rewriting it into memory. Because of this frequent access, it is assumed that the probability of double errors, although finite, is negligibly small, so no overall parity is taken to check for double errors.

During a memory write, the Hamming lines H_0 to H_3 are grounded by buffer chip A, and the data being written into memory is admitted to the parity chips C through F by the tristate buffer G. As with the previously described Hamming calculator, this permits the parities of the CPU data alone (that is, with H_0 to H_3 being **0**) to be summed and stored in the Hamming memory via lines P_0 to P_3.

During a memory read, each parity chip sums the parities of data and Hamming bits. This parity data is routed to the 4:16 line decoder via lines P_0 to P_3. If there is an error, this pointer is converted to a specific data output line 1 through 12, so that it effectively points at the incorrect bit and corrects it. Each output line is combined with its respective data bit D_0 to D_7 as per the error position of Table 1. This combination is accomplished by the EXCLUSIVE OR array J. Note that because the output of the decoder is active LOW, it is necessary to invert the result by using an inverting buffer so that the 74LS86 will operate correctly.

If any errors occur, the decoder's **0** output line goes HIGH. This result may be used to trip a latch or counter. However, time must be allowed for the data to be accessed and propagated through the circuitry; otherwise, propagation skew will cause false error indications. The propagation time is about 150 ns when LS TTL logic is used.

3.5   Real-Time Error Correction (16 Bits)

In general, the 16-bit processor is treated similarly to the 8-bit machine, but all five equations must be solved. In addition, the operation itself is slightly more complicated. This is illustrated in the block diagram in Fig. 6, where we see that for a given memory location there is a LOW byte (D_0 to D_7), a HIGH byte (D_8 to D_{15}), and a 5-bit Hamming word. During a write into memory, the CPU may write to both banks simultaneously, with the Hamming circuitry functioning similarly to the 8-bit version. Or, the CPU may write into the HIGH or LOW byte individually, with the other corrected byte being first generated by the Hamming circuitry from all the old data stored at the memory location. This corrected byte is stored in a latch and combined with the other byte from the CPU. The new Hamming data is derived from this combined data, and all three data groups are written at their respective addresses.

During a read from memory, the Hamming data and the data from the CPU memory are combined by the Hamming circuitry, where any errors cause one or more of the lines P_0 to P_4 to go HIGH. The output from one of the 4:16 line

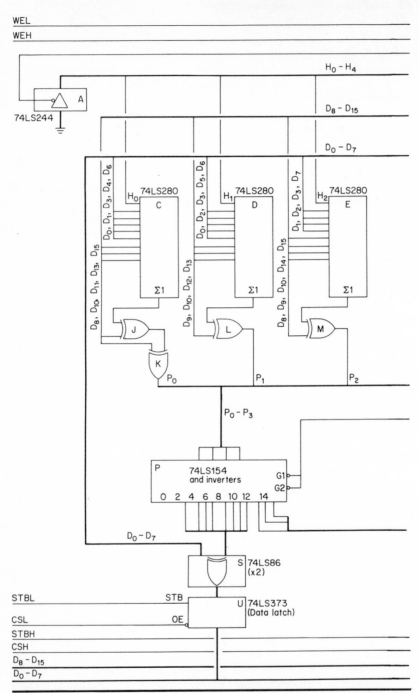

FIG. 7   *A detailed schematic of the 16-bit Hamming circuit. The operation is quite similar to the 8-bit circuit, but here all five complete equations are solved. Note that P_4 enables the lower decoder chip P for errors in data bits less than D_{11}, and enables the upper decoder chip Q for errors in data bits D_{11} and above. Key: WE = write enable, STB = strobe, CS = chip select, OE = output enable, L = low, H = high, DO = data out, DI = data in.*

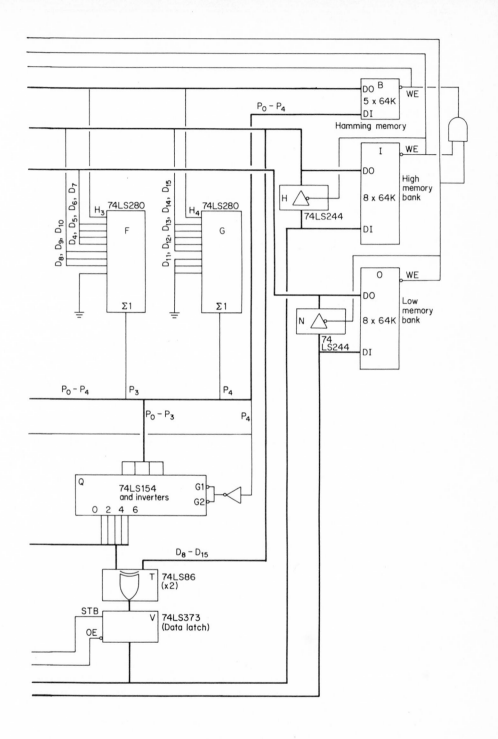

decoders then combine with the data in the EXCLUSIVE OR array or correct any single incorrect bit.

Figure 7 shows the 16-bit real-time error-correction circuit in more detail. As in the block diagram (Fig. 6), the 16-bit memory array is divided into an 8-bit bank (D_8 to D_{15}), an 8-bit LOW bank (D_0 to D_7), and the 5-bit Hamming bank. This permits writing to each bank separately. For example, suppose we wish to write into the HIGH but not the LOW bank. First the memory is accessed, but the write enable (WE) signal is disabled by an arbitrator circuit. This causes the corrected data to be read into the latches U and V. The output of latch U is enabled, causing the corrected LOW byte to be read from memory onto data lines D_0 to D_7. The output of latch V is not enabled. We then enable the write signal so that the HIGH byte from the microprocessor is written into the HIGH bank while the LOW byte from the latch is written into the LOW bank. At the same time, the lines H_0 to H_4 are grounded by tristate buffer A, and both the HIGH and LOW byte data are admitted to the parity chips C through G via buffers H and N. The parity outputs P_0 to P_4 are then written into the Hamming bank.

Because the 74154 will only point to 16 bits, we must use 2 of them for this circuit. When P_4 is **0**, the LOW bank pointer chip P is selected. When P_4 is **1**, the HIGH bank pointer chip Q is selected. P_0 to P_3 then select the appropriate output line on the enabled chip.

As in the case of the timed interrupt circuits, no circuit is shown for arbitrating the HIGH byte-LOW byte sequence described here because it is dependent upon the timing required for a specific processor and memory.

3.6 A Hardware/Firmware Approach to Hamming Code Correction

In addition to using the pointer-corrector circuit of Fig. 3, we can use firmware to provide the actual correction once an error has been detected by the parity circuits of Fig. 2. All that are needed are accessible latches to capture the values of P_0 to P_4 and the erroneous word and its address.

One possible firmware algorithm would be as follows: Upon detection of an error, as indicated by one or more of the lines P_0 to P_4 going HIGH, the values of P_0 to P_4 are latched, and at the same time the address of the erroneous word and the erroneous word itself are latched. The microprocessor is then vectored to a firmware routine in read-only memory (ROM) where there is virtually no chance of soft errors. A lookup table is provided, such as Table 2. A base address is established for the beginning of the table (in this case we use 1000 hex). The value of the pointer word P_0 to P_4 is added to this address, and the resultant address is used to retrieve the appropriate corrector word. The corrector word is EXCLUSIVE ORed with the erroneous word, and the incorrect bit is inverted. The corrected word is then rewritten into memory, and normal processing is resumed.

For example, suppose we correct the 8-bit word used in the previous example in this manner. The procedure is shown in the flowchart of Fig. 8. The

TABLE 2 **Function of the Pointer Word** *(When the pointer word (P_0 to P_4) is added to the base address 1000 (hex), the location of the corrector word is determined. The word at that location is EXCLUSIVE ORed with the erroneous word, thus inverting the erroneous bit. For example, if bit D_2 is in error, the pointer word is numerically equal to 6. This value is added to the base address 1000, to give address 1006. The word at this address, when EXCLUSIVE ORed with the erroneous word, inverts bit D_2, thus correcting it.)*

Address (hex)	Corrector word (binary)	Bit content
1000	0000 0000 0000 0000	
1001	0000 0000 0000 0000	H_0
1002	0000 0000 0000 0000	H_1
1003	0000 0000 0000 0001	D_0
1004	0000 0000 0000 0000	H_2
1005	0000 0000 0000 0010	D_1
1006	0000 0000 0000 0100	D_2
1007	0000 0000 0000 1000	D_3
1008	0000 0000 0000 0000	H_3
1009	0000 0000 0001 0000	D_4
100A	0000 0000 0010 0000	D_5
100B	0000 0000 0100 0000	D_6
100C	0000 0000 1000 0000	D_7
100D	0000 0001 0000 0000	D_8
100E	0000 0010 0000 0000	D_9
100F	0000 0100 0000 0000	D_{10}
1010	0000 0000 0000 0000	H_4
1011	0000 1000 0000 0000	D_{11}
1012	0001 0000 0000 0000	D_{12}
1013	0010 0000 0000 0000	D_{13}
1014	0100 0000 0000 0000	D_{14}
1015	1000 0000 0000 0000	D_{15}

erroneous word is stored in some CPU register, e.g., accumulator A. The pointer word is retrieved from its latch and stored in another CPU register, accumulator B. The address of the lookup table (1000 hex) is retrieved and the pointer word added to it, giving a resultant address 1006. The corrector word at 1006 is fetched (only the lower 8 bits in this case) and EXCLUSIVED ORed with the erroneous word stored in accumulator A. This inverts bit 2, and the corrected value returns to memory.

3.7 An 8-Bit Hardware/Firmware Hybrid Circuit

We now illustrate an application of the hardware/firmware hybrid. Refer to the block diagram in Fig. 9. The operation is as follows: The address bus selects an 8-bit CPU data location and a corresponding 4-bit Hamming data location in the memory blocks. During a write into memory, the Hamming circuitry generates a 4-bit Hamming word from the 8-bit CPU data and stores it in the Hamming memory while the 8 bits of the CPU data are stored in CPU

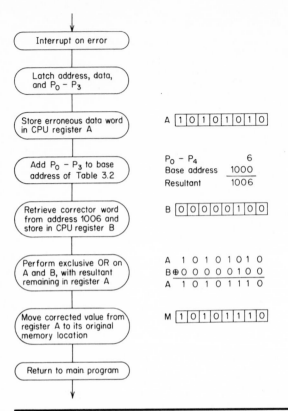

FIG. 8 *Flowchart for the firmware correction algorithm. On an interrupt due to an error, the address of the erroneous word and its pointer word are latched. The correction then proceeds as outlined in the figure.*

memory. During a read from memory, the Hamming circuitry compares the Hamming and CPU memory data. If there is an error, the interrupt circuitry senses that one or more of the output parity lines P_0 to P_3 are HIGH and latches the current address, CPU data, and Hamming output data into their respective latches. An interrupt is sent to the CPU, which retrieves the data from the latches, corrects it, and then rewrites it into memory, all via the program stored in ROM. In addition, a simple overall parity of the Hamming and CPU data is taken to detect double errors.

Figure 10 shows the hybrid circuit in more detail. During a write into memory, the H_0 to H_3 and H_p lines are disabled from memory by tristate buffer M and grounded by tristate buffer N. Each parity chip G through J then sums the parity of the pertinent CPU data, with its respective Hamming bit set equal to **0**. Note, however, that chips K and O sum the total parity of D_0 to D_7 and H_0 to H_3, whereas chips G through J solve the Hamming equations P_0 to P_3. P_p is the simple overall parity. The parities P_0 to P_3 and P_p are enabled to memory by buffer P.

During a read from memory, the parity lines P_0 to P_3 and P_p are disabled from memory, and Hamming lines H_0 to H_3 and H_p are disabled from ground and enabled to memory. The parity chips can now sum the parity of the appropriate data and Hamming bits for equations P_0 to P_3 as well as the overall parity P_p.

For example, during the previous write into memory, if the parity of the data bits in chip G was **1**, this value was stored in memory as H_0. It is now summed with the CPU memory data (which has odd parity, assuming no errors) to give an even parity, or **0**, for P_0. Likewise, chips H through J solve the equations for P_1 to P_3, and chips K and O provide the overall simple parity P_p.

On the other hand, if there is an error, one or more of the parity outputs go to **1** and there is an output from gate Q. This output is enabled to the microprocessor via a timed interrupt circuit that also sends an enable strobe to the latches B through E, causing the address, data, and parity bits to be trapped. Also, the write ($\overline{WR}$) line is disabled to protect the memory from inadvertent modification when an error has been detected. This strobe remains LOW until

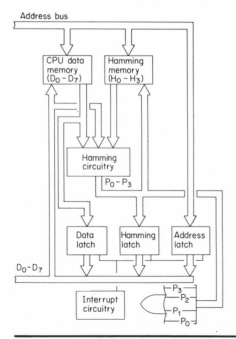

FIG. 9 *This block diagram of the hardware/firmware circuit outlines its operation. No decoders or* EXCLUSIVE OR *gate arrays are required. However, there are latches for CPU data, Hamming data, and the address of an erroneous bit. Any of the lines P_0 to P_3 going HIGH will cause an interrupt, as well as latch the above-mentioned data.*

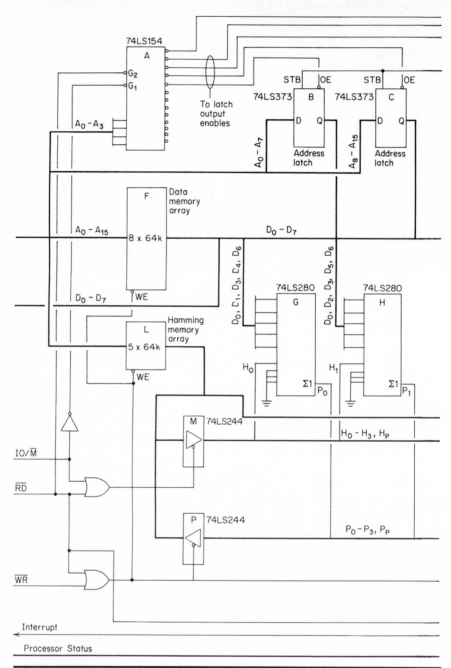

FIG. 10 Detailed schematic of the hardware/firmware circuit. The parity chips G through J solve the Hamming equations, and chips K and O sum the overall simple parity. If there is an error, the output of the gate Q is enabled by the timed interrupt circuit which causes the latch strobe-out line to go LOW. This captures address, data, and parity in latches B through E and also interrupts the microprocessor. When an error has been detected, gate R prevents further writing into memory until the error has been corrected. However, gate R does not protect the internal registers of the CPU.

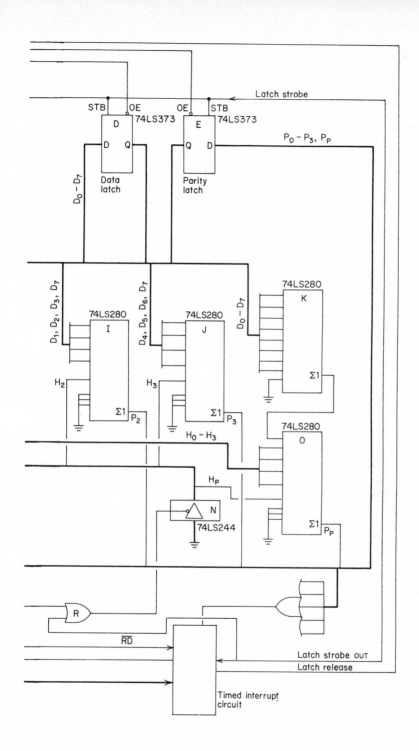

it is released by a strobe from the 4-to-16 line decoder chip A. This chip is addressed as an I/O port.

After the interrupt, the microprocessor is vectored to the previously described firmware routine, which reads the data from the latches, which in turn are each output-enabled by chip A. The firmware then corrects the data and writes it back into memory (provided there was only one error). After this, the latch strobe from the timed interrupt circuit is released and the circuit itself is reset. No details of the timed interrupt circuit are specified here because they are dependent upon the timing signals from the particular processor, the access time of the memory array, and the propagation time through the parity chips. Time must be allowed for the data to stabilize prior to enabling the interrupt, or false interrupts will occur.

The software must be organized into security blocks because data in the internal registers of the CPU may be modified by an error. Thus, return points must be available for restart after an error correction.

3.8 Summary

The practical aspects of Hamming code theory were presented as the code applies to 8-and 16-bit microprocessors and microcomputers.

Two basic approaches to applying error correction to microprocessors were discussed: hardware/firmware and real-time. The first approach is slightly faster than the real-time one if the overall parity is not checked because of different propagation times through the correction circuitry. The correction program must be stored in a memory array that is much more reliable than the memory array being checked because an error in the correction program could produce catastrophic results. Furthermore, very careful organization of the software into security blocks is needed to ensure that any erroneous OP code fetches cause no damage prior to correction. On the other hand, the real-time approach has propagation delays that could necessitate adding WAIT states to a fast processor, thus slowing it down. In applications such as telecommunications, disrupting a control processor at random times to correct errors could cause considerable difficulties.

Finally, several problems encountered with error correction in 16-bit machines were pointed out, along with an approach to solving them.

REFERENCES

1. May, T. C., and M. H. Woods: "Alpha Particle Induced Soft Errors in Dynamic Memories," *IEEE Electron Devices ED-26,* January 1979, p. 2.
2. Yaney, D. S., J. T. Nelson, and L. L. Vanskike: "Alpha Particle Tracks in Silicon and their Effect on Dynamic MOS ROM Reliability," *IEEE Electron Devices ED-26,* January 1979, p. 10.
3. Ziegler, J. F., and W. A. Lanford: "The Effect of Sea Level Cosmic Rays on Electronic Devices," *1980 IEEE International Solid-State Circuits Conference Digest of Technical Papers,* Philadelphia, Pa., February 1980, pp. 13-15.
4. Lin, S.: *An Introduction to Error Correcting Codes,* Prentice-Hall, Englewood Cliffs, N.J., 1970.

5. Wakerly, J.: *Error-Detecting Codes, Self-Checking Circuits and Applications*, Elsevier North-Holland, New York, 1978.
6. Hamming, R. W.: "Error-Detecting and Error-Correcting Codes," *Bell System Tech. J.*, Vol. 26, April 1950, p. 147.
7. Becher, W.: *Logical Design Using Integrated Circuits*, Hayden, New York, 1977.

ACKNOWLEDGMENTS

The author would like to express his thanks to John Cocking, Dinesh Joshi, Marcus Maranhao, Geoff Stagg, Graham Wisdom, and Dr. Santanu Das for their helpful comments and suggestions. Also, he would like to thank Gabe Pettner for his work in the testing laboratory, and Dr. J. Woo for his computer simulation of the hardware/firmware circuit.

CHAPTER FOUR

A Microprocessor-Controlled Color TV Receiver

Kaare Karstad

*RCA Corporation, Solid State Division,
Somerville, New Jersey*

INTRODUCTION

Until recently, the number of user-controllable features on TV sets
was quite limited because of technical and economic reasons.
Channel selection and indication were by mechanical means, and
the remaining features were restricted to sound and picture control.
With the advent of the varactor diode, electronic tuning via the
voltage-variable capacitance of a diode became common. Electronic
control opened the way for today's channel and program selection
from a keyboard and station number shown either on- or off-screen.

In most cases the control electronics has been standard medium-
scale integration (MSI) circuits or custom MSI/LSI tailored for
specific functions. The availability of the microprocessor will allow a
large degree of flexibility in implementing new and interesting
features in TV receivers. Several models with microprocessor control
have already been discussed in the literature[1-3] and promise
numerous useful and sophisticated features not previously possible.

This chapter describes a microprocessor-controlled color TV receiver with a large number of features and options. Not all the features will be commonly found in the average receiver for some time. Nevertheless, this design, based upon the 1802 (an 8-bit complementary MOS (CMOS) microprocessor), illustrates the possibilities of applying the stored-program concept to implement a variety of ideas. Microprocessor control offers a modular design approach: Essential functions such as tuning and station selection are implemented first; other features are added or existing ones modified for various models or markets. Important new features can be brought quickly to the marketplace simply by program changes or additions without a long-range custom LSI development phase.

The design also highlights the close coupling between software and hardware and how several real-time events are processed by the 1802, orchestrating all three modes of I/O techniques: programmed mode, interrupt, and direct memory access (DMA).[4]

ORGANIZATION OF THE MATERIAL

An overview of the system's functional operation is first presented, with its major features highlighted. This is followed by a discussion of the software approach required and implemented to meet the system specifications.

Next is a more thorough discussion of the major functions, with representative tasks described in detail, bringing out where appropriate the close interrelationship between hardware and software.

The end of the chapter summarizes the operational specifications, commands, and their implementations within the entire TV controller.

4.1 Overall Functional Operation

Tuning Control and Preprogramming As indicated in Fig. 1, an all-electronic tuning system is implemented with frequency synthesis. A phase-locked loop (PLL) selects the correct local oscillator (LO) frequency for a specific channel and keeps the receiver tuned irrespective of time and temperature changes in the tuner.

The superiority of the closed-loop approach to tuning is discussed in detail in Sec. 4.5, *Tuning and Program Selection.* Using this method, any number on the keyboard from 1 to 99 is translated into a 14-bit code that sets the PLL to regulate on a constant LO frequency, correct for the channel in question.

A read-only memory (ROM) table translates the key depression into the correct bit code for the PLL according to international channel allocations. This 14-bit code places the LO on the exact allocated frequency within any channel and permits direct fine tuning over the whole channel. The traditional reason for automatic fine tuning (AFT) is eliminated by the exact-frequency-

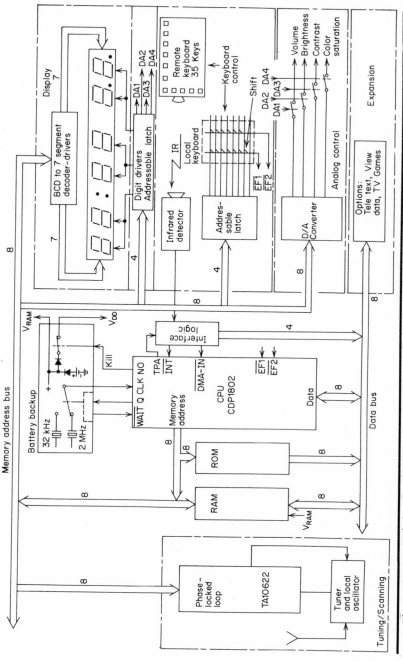

FIG. 1 The user interacts with this television controller via a local 2 × 12 keyset or a 35-key remote unit sending infrared pulses. The display and feedback are on a 6-digit display showing clock and program. Exact tuning is through a PLL. Scanning, preprogramming of channels, events, and analog values are some of the major features. A battery backup system keeps a clock running and/or stored information intact in case of power failure.

synthesis approach, but some users desire it in fringe areas for improved picture quality. In some areas there is also a need to tune in nonallocated channels for cable TV and master-antenna TV (MATV) systems. Fine tuning is implemented in 25-kHz steps for VHF and 100-kHz steps for UHF.

An important feature of this design is preprogramming of channels. In the remaining discussion we distinguish between programs and channels, as commonly practiced in Europe. For example, in one geographic area a program denoted number 1 may be allocated to channel 4 but to a different channel in another region. In this design 16 storage locations are allocated for 16 different programs. Any program can be stored in any of these locations and assigned to any channel. Tuning is accomplished by merely entering a number between 1 and 16 into the keyboard.

This preprogramming technique requires the channels to be known. For the more general case when the channels are not known, a scanning mode is available. After the SCAN key is pressed, the search starts at the present channel and stops at the first higher channel available on the air. If the scan mode is terminated, the frequency channel is automatically assigned to the currently chosen program number. Each push of the SCAN button makes the tuning system search for the nearest higher available carrier. If no station is found, the scan "wraps around" and stops on the frequency from where the search started.

In addition to the channel scan, a program scan is also part of the tuning system. This scan searches the 16 prestored programs. The scan starts at the current program and stops at the nearest higher program number on the air. Off-the-air stations are quickly bypassed, and valid stations are given enough time to lock up. A wrap-around feature is also part of this scan mode.

Display and Keyboard Control   Channel and program numbers are shown on a 6-digit light-emitting diode (LED) off-screen display; the display format is shown in Fig. 2. For a while on-screen display was popular. However, a dedicated off-screen display is a simpler solution because it can be on permanently and does not distract the viewer's attention from the screen.

Six digits is the optimum design for permitting continuous display of clock and program number. This is the normal or prioritized display mode. Upon request from the keyboard, both channel and program numbers are shown; the channel number displaces the clock display. In the scanning mode, the channel frequencies assigned to program numbers are automatically displayed.

Clearly, the presence of a real-time clock permits event programming, i.e., a certain program can be automatically turned ON or OFF at a specific time. A 6-digit display is sufficient for easy programming of events or for listing events that are already programmed.

The local keyboard with 12 keys and a SHIFT key can handle 24 tasks (see Fig. 3). The basic tasks required are program selection, scanning, analog controls (up/down), MUTE, ON/OFF, and setting the clock.

The master keyboard has 35 keys (Fig. 4) and communicates with the

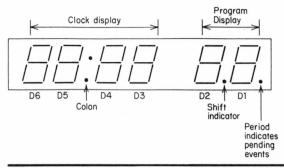

FIG. 2 *Six-digit display format which is nonentry mode shows clock and program numbers and also indicates whether a programmed event is pending.*

SAT▼ 7	BRT▼ 8	CON▼ 9
CON▲ 4	NORM 5	VOL▼ 6
VOL▲ 1	SAT▲ 2	BRT▲ 3
TIME P	MUTE 0	SBY
	SHIFT	

FIG. 3 *Local keyboard with shift key handles 24 functions.*

receiver over an infrared link. Each depressed key generates a 7-bit unique code as a pulse-position modulation (PPM) pulse train.[5] A specific distance between pulses is defined as a **0** bit; a **1** bit is another defined distance. This pulse train is an asynchronous event with respect to any other task and is processed by the DMA channel. Hence this random real-time event is given required priority.

The analog values of volume (VOL), brightness (BRT) contrast (CON), and saturation (SAT) are changed continuously up or down while the appropriate key is held. A 6-bit word in memory, providing 64-step resolution, is generated at a predetermined rate and incremented or decremented using these keys. A sample-and-hold multiplexing technique allows one output port to serve 4 different channels.

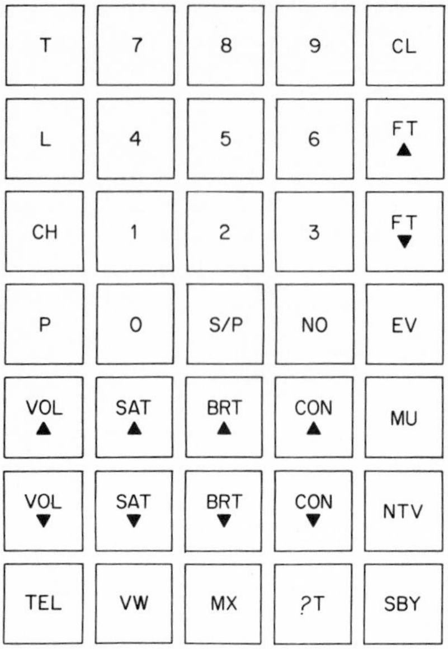

T	7	8	9	CL
L	4	5	6	FT ▲
CH	1	2	3	FT ▼
P	0	S/P	NO	EV
VOL ▲	SAT ▲	BRT ▲	CON ▲	MU
VOL ▼	SAT ▼	BRT ▼	CON ▼	NTV
TEL	VW	MX	?T	SBY

FIG. 4   *Remote keyboard with 35 keys operates an infrared communication link using a CMOS transmitter chip.*

Event Programming   A 6-digit display and a 24-h clock allow a user to pre-program and monitor events from the current time to 24 h into the future. An arbitrary number of memory locations (eight in this design) are reserved for event programs. A user, while watching the display, simply keys in the time for the TV to turn on (or change channels if already on) and the program number to select. This can be repeated until the list is full, which is indicated by the display flashing 9s. There are no restrictions on the sequence of entering events. The software orders the list in time sequence so that the event nearest in time is always on top of the list. The software checks once each minute to see if an event is to be activated. If so, the event is executed and erased from the list, and the next event is moved to the front of the list. If an event is pending, one of the decimal points is illuminated. When the event is executed, the decimal point blinks until a viewer acknowledges by pushing any key. If no acknowledgment is received within 5 min, the TV turns itself off.

What was described may be termed a "one-time" event. One can also program an event to automatically repeat every 24 h or turn off a program at a specified time.

The programmed information (time, program number) can be listed on the display by a LIST button (L) on the keyboard with an indication if it is a one-time, OFF, or repeat event. If the list is empty or exhausted, flashing 8s are displayed.

Expansion   The software's modular structure makes it possible to add options by connecting additional ports to the data bus and adding segments of code to the software. Two options of considerable future interest are Teletext[6] and Viewdata[7]. For instance, if a key marked TELETEXT is depressed, the software checks for the existence of this option. If the option is present, from this moment certain keys are redefined and execute different tasks from the normal TV (NTV) mode. The NTV mode is recalled by the NTV key. Another option is the video interface system (VIS), which also is Teletext-compatible. This system is built around two LSI CMOS chips and offers a variety of formats for displaying and modifying data under software control with either National Television System Committee (NTSC)- or phase-alteration line (PAL)-compatible output signals.[8]

Battery Backup   Loss of stored channels and event data as a result of power failure cannot be tolerated. The problem is solved by a battery backup scheme. Because of the all-CMOS circuitry for logic and processor, this scheme can be implemented with low-capacity nickel-cadmium cells.

A two-level backup system maintains the clock for about a week, after which the central processing unit (CPU) and the system shut down. The random access memory (RAM), which stores channel information, is powered by the nickel-cadmium cells for approximately 3 months.

4.2 Basic Software System Approach

Many tasks must be performed in this real-time controller application. Most of these tasks have strict requirements that must be observed: The software must multiplex the 6 display digits, multiplex 4 analog channels, update the clock, monitor the two keyboards for action, and execute whatever task is requested by a keyboard.

The clock must be updated regularly so its display will appear accurate. The display must be refreshed at a rate high enough to avoid flicker, i.e., at least 50 to 60 Hz. The analog control outputs must also be refreshed steadily at a rate high enough to maintain a dc signal without excessive large-filter time constants. The keyboards must be checked often enough to catch any random key depressions. Whenever a command is received (fine tuning, scan, mute, and so on), it must be immediately processed and executed. Certain tasks, such as volume up/down, require software to support continuous depression of a key for any possible length of time.

These overlapping and partially conflicting specifications are resolved by an interrupt-driven system together with a DMA channel for the remote keyboard.

A pulse train derived from the CPU clock interrupts the software program every 4 ms (see Fig. 5). The INTERRUPT routine, which must be executed frequently and regularly, is divided into three groups in order to distribute the load. Each time the INTERRUPT SERVICE routine is called, a test is made

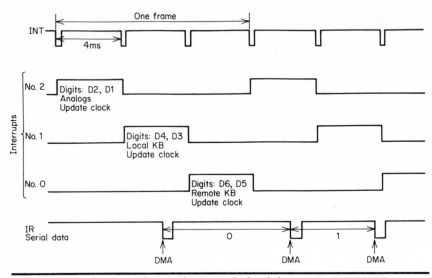

FIG. 5   *The system is interrupt-driven with a time-multiplexed, three-section INTERRUPT-SERVICE routine. Remote infrared control pulses are received in real time via DMA without interference with normal processing.*

to determine which is next for service. Three cycles comprising a complete frame are sequentially serviced, and after 12 ms a full INTERRUPT SERVICE frame repeats.

The 6 digits are grouped in pairs, to reduce the multiplex rate and provide twice as much time between interrupts. Refresh rate for the display is now 83 Hz—well above the critical flicker rate.

The sequence of events are as follows: An interrupt occurs. The last digit pair is turned OFF and the next pair is turned ON. The 4 analog channels are multiplexed and refreshed, and the clock is updated. Control next returns to the MAIN program. At the next interrupt, the last digit pair is turned OFF and the next one ON. The clock is updated again, but in this cycle the local keyboard is also scanned for key closure. At the third interrupt the last digit pair is handled, and the SERVICE routine monitors if a character is being received from the remote keyboard and processes the command. Once more the clock is updated and the MAIN program resumes execution.

All the urgent tasks are thus served regularly and frequently. The clock is updated every 4 ms, and every 12 ms the display and the digital-to-analog (D/A) channels are refreshed. Both keyboards are monitored, and if a key closure occurs, preprocessing is performed, providing data upon which the MAIN program can later process.

A key closure on the remote keyboard generates a string of pulses varying widely in length. How can these irregular-length pulse trains, which occur randomly, be received without tying up the processor and neglecting other real-time events? The problem is solved by feeding the pulses into the DMA input. Thus the information is conveyed to the CPU through a cycle-stealing process without slowing or interfering with the CPU's current operation.

The INTERRUPT SERVICE routine in each 4-ms time-slot may vary in length according to which cycle is on. The length also depends upon how much of the clock UPDATE routine is required at a specific moment. Nevertheless, during the major part of the time-slot, the processor is idle and available for background processing in the MAIN program.

4.3   Descriptions of Major Functions

Routine MAIN   When control returns to MAIN in each time-slot, the program simply checks to see if a command was received from one of the keyboards. If so, that task is executed. If no command was received, the CPU is essentially idle until the next interrupt occurs. In most cases the free time in one of the three cycles is ample for processing any task in MAIN. If not, the next interrupt simply postpones the background processing for a later time-slot. (This is not apparent to the user.)

The flowchart for MAIN, Fig. 6, clarifies these points. An interrupt can occur at any time in MAIN. Most of the time MAIN loops through the first five branch tests if no keyboard command is received. A few other tests are also regularly made. Every minute a search is made for pending event programs, such as: (1) was an event executed but not acknowledged, (2) has ac power failed, or (3) is no station on the air?

UPDATE *Routine for the 24-Hour Clock*   Four locations in RAM are assigned to hold the 4 clock digits. As shown in the flowchart in Fig. 7, at every interrupt register CNT is incremented. Later, in the UPDATE routine, the counter is tested and the Update buffer is loaded with the new time if 1 s has elapsed.

The Display buffer, another buffer in RAM, contains binary-coded decimal (BCD) data for the 6 display digits. The UPDATE routine transfers data for the 4 clock digits from the Update buffer to the Display buffer; the two buffers are shown in Fig. 8. The UPDATE flowchart in Fig. 9 describes the transfer of data between these two buffers.

The UPDATE routine begins by checking to see if the TV receiver is ON. If so, then register CNT is tested to see how many interrupts have occurred. It is reset after 250 interrupts. Because interrupts occur precisely every 4 ms, register CNT is reset once per second.

Two of the CPU's 16-bit registers are assigned as pointers: register DPTR points to the Display buffer, and register AUX points to the Update buffer. These pointers are initialized, as shown in Fig. 8. The first test determines if we are in ENTRY mode, which is a state where the display is needed to verify use of the keyboard in executing certain commands. For instance, if the display is used for setting the clock or selecting programs, transfer of data from the Update buffer to the Display buffer must be inhibited for the duration of the command. An ENTRY mode flag bit is therefore tested. In the ENTRY mode the colon is also turning on and off every second to remind users that they are

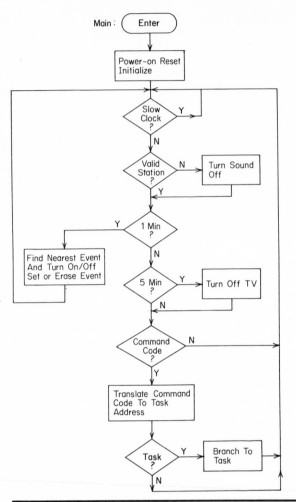

FIG. 6   *The MAIN program normally loops in a short section where it is continually watching for a keyboard command. If one occurs, the appropriate task is called and executed. MAIN also searches once each minute to see if a programmed event calls for action. If the television brings on a programmed event, the user has 5 min to acknowledge. If no station is turned on, sound is automatically muted.*

in an ENTRY mode. Notice that a user has the option of turning off the clock display. If key T on the keyboard is pushed, this changes the AUX pointer, which transfers a hex digit F to the Display buffer. F is not decoded in the hardware decoder and blanks the display. Another key depression toggles the display back ON.

Three more flag bits are found in the UPDATE routine for proper time sequencing of some other routines. If the TV has been scheduled to turn itself on or off at a certain time or change program, an acknowledge (ACK) flag is

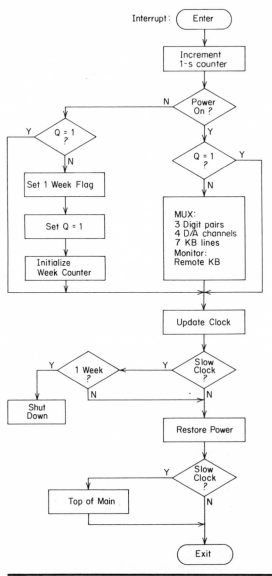

FIG. 7 *The INTERRUPT SERVICE routine increments the second counter and updates the clock. It also multiplexes the display and the analog values and scans and monitors the keyboards. If ac power fails, the CPU switches to a low-frequency clock and battery power.*

set upon execution of the task. The flag bit is tested once each second. If true, the period in the display is complemented and starts blinking on and off each second. The viewer has 5 min to acknowledge by pushing any key and thereby resetting the flag. If not acknowledged, the TV turns itself off after 5 min. Hence, a counter is initialized in the event section and incremented and

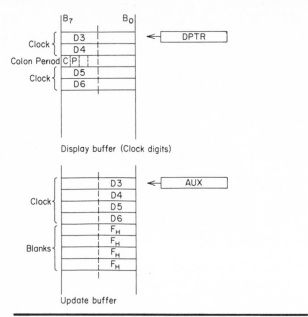

Display buffer (Clock digits)

Update buffer

FIG. 8 *Part of an INTERRUPT SERVICE routine updates four RAM locations and transfers the data into the clock digit locations in the display buffer at every interrupt.*

tested every minute in the UPDATE routine. Once each minute a 1-min flag is set. The 1- and 5-min flags are tested in the MAIN program, as shown in Fig. 6. If the 5-min bit is true, the ON/OFF routine is called, and if the 1-min bit is true, a call is made to a SEARCH routine, which scans the entries in the event list.

From this point on, the actual updating takes place. Each digit is fetched from the Update buffer, and the buffer is incremented, replaced, and tested for overflow of the digit. Notice that the 24-h clock increments from 23:59 to 00:00.

Data Formatting for Multiplexing Display, D/A Channels, and Keyboard Scanning The configuration of the data in the Display buffer, Fig. 10, is closely related to the hardware scheme shown in Fig. 12. Segment data for a digit pair is fed from two separate CD4511 latch/decoder circuits. An 8-bit addressable latch CD4099 selects the digit pair or the D/A channel to be sampled. Another addressable latch provides scan address for testing key closures on the local keyboard. The required 16 bits of data is assembled in one 16-bit CPU register and outputted over the memory address bus with just one instruction. Four locations in the Display buffer store the 6 bits of D/A data, which is outputted before the D/A channel is sampled. The latched data is smoothed by a simple R/2R network; no great precision is required.

The 16 bits of data required to control the hardware in Fig. 12, that is, the two addressable latches and the two 4-bit to 7-segment latch/decoder drivers, is assembled by software into one of sixteen 16-bit scratchpad registers in the CPU. The appropriate data to build this 16-bit data output word is fetched from the Display buffer. The ability to output 16 bits of data with one output instruction in an 8-bit microprocessor in unique to the CDP1802 and described in detail elsewhere[9]. Accordingly, when register OUTRE1 is assigned as a data pointer, the 16-bit content goes out over the address bus. The most significant byte (MSB) is then latched by pulse TPA, and the least significant byte (LSB) is latched by pulse TPB during the execution phase when the N1 select line is true (see Fig. 11).

We discussed earlier how the interrupt load was split into three time slots. Figure 13 shows how data are assembled in register OUTRE1 as the three cycles progress. The figure should be read from the top down as time progresses. After the first interrupt occurs in cycle 2, data D2 and data D1 are fetched from the Display buffer and loaded into the high-order byte of the out register, as shown. In this cycle, the keyboard is not scanned, so bits 4 through 7, address, and data are all 0. Bits 0 to 2 are set to the digit pairs' address **010**. A **1** in bit 3 position turns the digit pair ON, and a **0** turns the pair OFF. The keyboard address and digit pair data remain constant while the 3 least significant bits are incremented, thereby permitting the D/A channels to be multiplexed.

In cycle 1, after digit pair D4 and D3 has been turned ON at address **001**, the keyboard scan address is incremented seven times to test for key closures. When data has been written into the addressable latch, data stays latched until it is changed by another write command. The output data for the D/A converter, colon, and period are also handled by register-based output instructions from OUTRE2 and is fetched from the Display buffer. See Fig. 10.

The software section of the INTERRUPT routine that interacts with the hardware in Fig. 12 is detailed in Fig. 14. The program turns OFF the last select line for a digit pair and tests if it was cycle 0. If it was cycle 0, a new frame of events is about to be repeated, and the display pointer is reset to the top of the Display buffer. Segment data for the next digit pair are outputted and the pair is selected. If the interrupt starts cycle 2, the four D/A channels are sampled in a burst mode, after which the UPDATE routine terminates. At the next interrupt (cycle 1), the program turns on the next digit pair and scans the local keyboard. Finally, at the third interrupt (cycle 0), the remote keyboard routine is sequenced.

Scanning the Local Keyboard A key depression on the local keyboard is translated into a command code and stored in memory for the MAIN program to process. The keyboard is monitored in the INTERRUPT routine once during each cycle 1.

Referring to the flowchart in Fig. 15, the sequence of events is as follows: An output line from the addressable latch (CD4099 in Fig. 11) is activated, and the CPU tests the first flag line (EF1) for key closure. The output line is active HIGH, pulling the flag line HIGH if a key along its row is active. For example, if key number 4 is pushed as EF1 is tested (defined as row 0), then a possible key closure is identified and marked as key number 4 + 0 = 4.

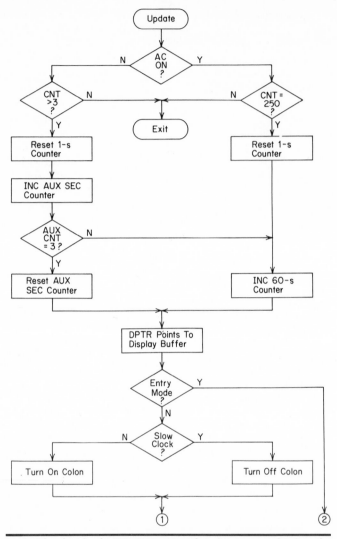

FIG. 9   *Flowchart for the UPDATE routine. The software moves data from the update buffer to the display buffer and updates minutes and hours for a 24-h clock.*

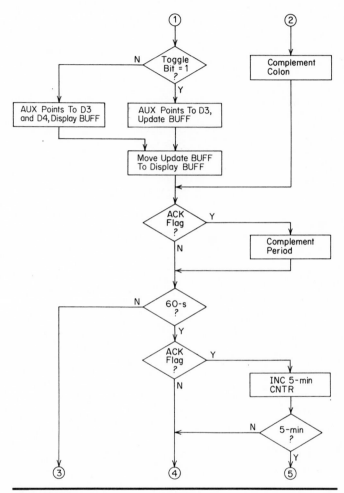

FIG. 9 (Cont.)

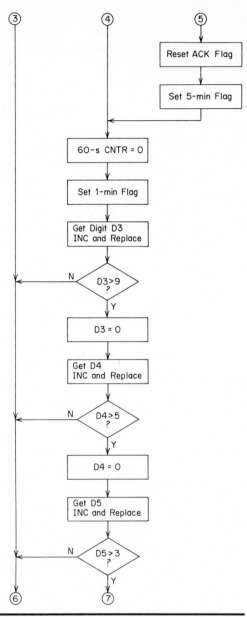

FIG. 9   *(Cont.)*

4-16

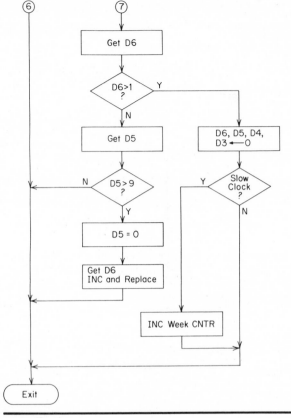

⑥ ⑦

FIG. 9 *(Cont.)*

Next, the CPU tests line EF2 (defined as row 7). If key 11 is depressed, it will be identified as key number 4 + 7 = 11. The key number is used as an address pointer to a ROM table storing the actual command code for that particular key. Because the local keyboard has 12 keys but 24 functions are possible, a shift-key depression must also be verified. If the shift key is down, 12 is added to the table address, effecting a jump to the second part of the table containing the shift commands. The keyboard scan repeats every 12 ms. If key closure is detected, a DEBOUNCE routine allows 36 ms to verify a valid key depression. The last action of the routine is to move the command code into a storage location. This same location is shared by a command that may have originated with the remote keyboard.

There are two important flags in the keyboard scanning routine: KDA and KREP. Flag KDA (data available local keyboard) is set every time a key closure is detected and verified. The flag is reset in the appropriate task after it has been executed. But we are concerned with two types of command. For instance, VOLUME UP must be executed for the duration of the key depression,

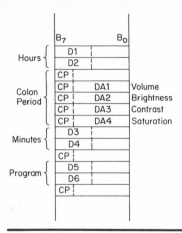

FIG. 10   *Configuration of data in the display buffer: six clock digits, colon, period, and four analog values.*

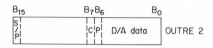

FIG. 11   *Output data for Secam/Pal bit, colon, period, and an analog channel are formatted in the 16-bit outregister (OUTRE2).*

whereas ON/OFF is a one-time command. In the latter case, the key may be held down for a while, although the task should be executed only once. This dilemma is solved by implementing another flag bit, KREP (key reported local keyboard).

Entry of PPM Data via DMA

Signal definitions   The PPM data are generated by a CMOS transmitter chip SAB 3011.[5] Each command word is packaged as a number of pulses with different time intervals (see Fig. 16). A 1 bit is represented by 7.1 ms; 0s have 5.1 ms between pulses. Each word has 6 data bits and 1 start bit equal to **0**, although the transmitter can be programmed to send a **1** as a start bit. A keypad connected to the transmitter chip can then generate 2×64 different commands. In this pulse train each character is repeated with an interword distance of 14.3 ms for as long as the key is depressed. In all cases a minimum of two words is transmitted. Each pulse is really a group of narrow pulses because the transmitter modulates the IR diode with narrow high-current pulses achieving large transmission range and high noise immunity. The time intervals defined are valid for a crystal frequency of 4 MHz driving the transmitter chip. Other numbers can be obtained by changing the crystal frequency.

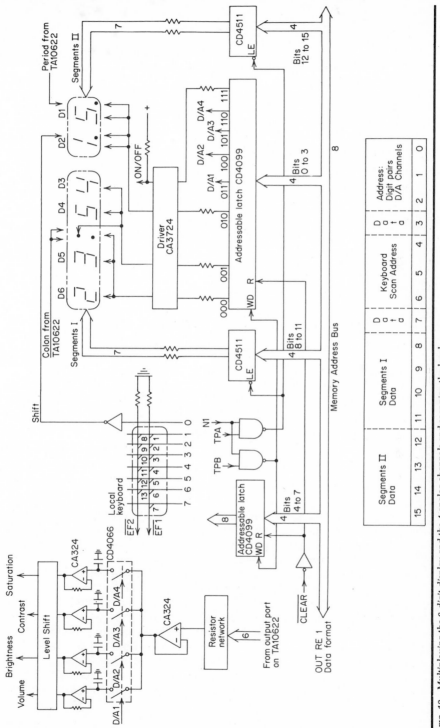

FIG. 12 Multiplexing the 6-digit display and the 4 analog channels and scanning the local keyboard are accomplished with a compact 16-bit data format. The 8-bit CDP1802 outputs the full data word over its 16-bit memory address bus with only one instruction.

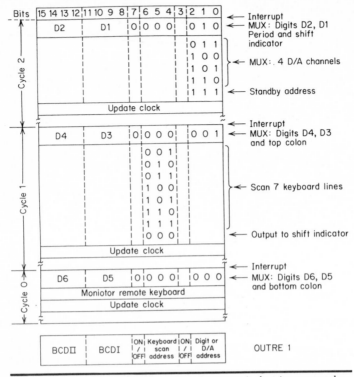

FIG. 13   *Data formatting in OUTRE 1 as time progresses in the 3 interrupt cycles. BCD data is fetched from the display buffer and the digit pairs are turned on and off at their selected addressses. Keyboard scanning is handled in the same data word.*

The interface logic   The interface to the microprocessor is shown in Fig. 17. This logic controls a PLL, which is described in Sec. 4.5, *Tuning and Program Selection.* The circuitry measures the time interval between IR pulses and inputs the result to RAM. The time base for the measuring counter (CD4520) is a 0.1-ms pulse providing good resolution for the 5.1- or 7.1-ms intervals. The trailing edge of each IR pulse, after detection and amplification, generates a DMA-IN request[4]. The CPU then responds with a DMA cycle that resets the DMA REQUEST READY line, thus enabling the circuit for the next pulse. The IR pulse also enables the 8-bit counter and strobes the high nibble of the count into a 4-bit latch (CD4076). During the DMA cycle, when the input port is enabled to the bus, the CPU issues a write pulse (SC1) that writes the content of the port into RAM. At the end of the DMA cycle, the counter is reset and starts counting again until arrival of the next IR pulse. At this point the count is read and the sequence of events repeats. This DMA technique ensures that the random pulses automatically transfer their bit

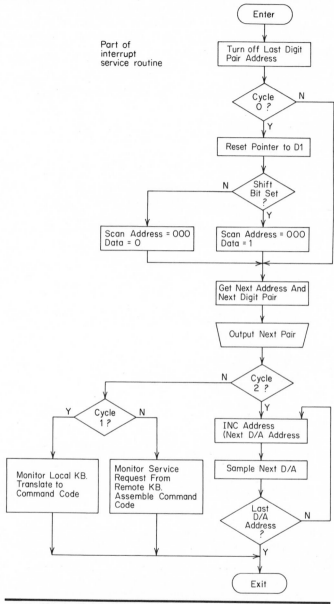

Part of
interrupt
service routine

Enter

Turn off Last Digit
Pair Address

Cycle 0 ?

Reset Pointer to D1

Shift Bit Set ?

Scan Address = OOO
Data = O

Scan Address = OOO
Data = 1

Get Next Address And
Next Digit Pair

Output Next Pair

Cycle 2 ?

Cycle 1 ?

Monitor Local KB.
Translate to
Command Code

Monitor Service
Request From
Remote KB.
Assemble Command
Code

INC Address
(Next D/A Address

Sample Next D/A

Last D/A Address ?

Exit

FIG. 14   This detail of the INTERRUPT SERVICE routine shows time-division multiplexing in 3 cycles to distribute the real-time load.

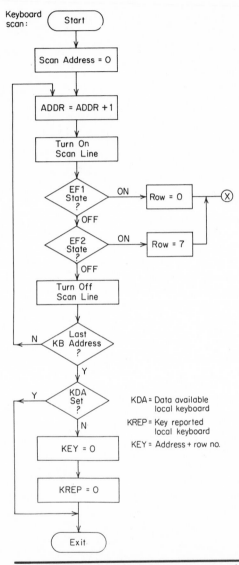

FIG. 15   Flowchart for KEYBOARD SCAN routine which is part of the
INTERRUPT SERVICE routine. Twelve keys and a shift key are
checked for contact closure, and the key number finds the
corresponding command code in a lookup table. KDA = Data
Available Local Keyboard, KREP = Key Reported Local Keyboard,
and KEY = Address + Row No.

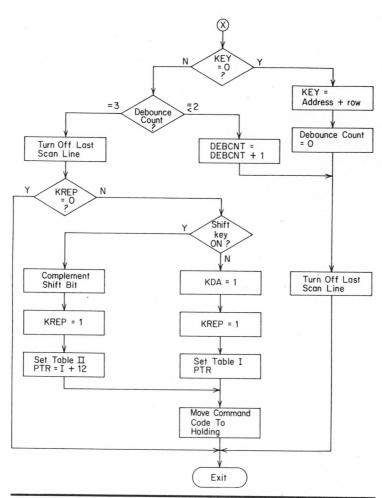

FIG. 15   (Cont.)

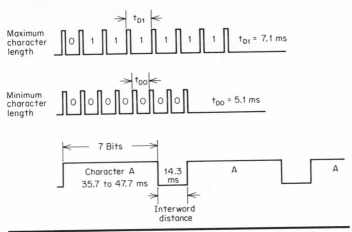

FIG. 16   The PPM data word has 7 bits. The distance between pulses signifies whether the bit is a **0** or a **1**. Each data word in the same command repeats, with at least 2 words being transmitted for redundancy.

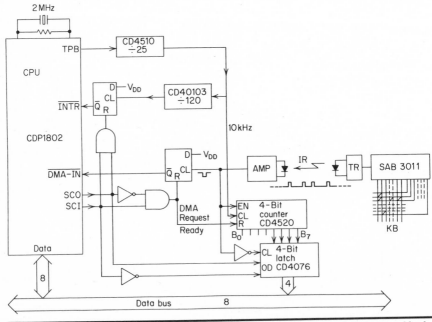

FIG. 17   The logic interface measures the interval between pulses in the command character and loads the count automatically into RAM via DMA. An infrared link carries the information from the transmitter chip.

information into RAM without interfering with the CPU and its normal program execution.

Only the 4 most significant bits from the 8-bit counter are read. If the counter operates for 5.1 ms, the counter reaches a state of 33 (hex). Counter operation for 7.1 ms generates an output state of 47 (hex). Thus, as shown in Fig. 18, a **0** bit is indicated by a 33 (hex) state, and a 47 (hex) signifies a **1** bit. We see that B_6 of the count directly gives the correct answer for the data bit. The system is therefore insensitive to innacuracies in the IR pulse positions. A ± 10 percent variation from the nominal values can be tolerated without affecting B_6. Hence only the upper nibble is transferred into RAM.

Software processing   A unique feature of the CDP1802 8-bit processor is its built-in DMA pointer, which is automatically incremented at each DMA cycle. The pointer is initialized to the top of an 8-byte buffer in RAM. After one PPM character has been received, this buffer is filled as shown in Fig. 19, and the command code is found in the B_6 column.

The flowcharts (Figs. 20 and 21) describe how the software monitors program reception of the data and repacks it into a byte. Upon proper reception and verification, a data available (DA) flag is set, indicating a command code was received and stored. The MAIN program tests this flag.

The program sequence under discussion is part of the INTERRUPT SERVICE routine and is entered every 12 ms. A test is first made of the DMA pointer's address. If the pointer has moved from its rest position, at least one IR pulse has been received. Next, test for overrun since conceivably the pointer has moved too far (e.g., because of noise pulses). A check of the last buffer address indicates if the character is complete. If so, a first CHAR flag bit is tested. Characters are transmitted continuously with an interword interval. Therefore, proper command code can be verified by comparing two characters. Assume a received character was the first in a string. The buffer information is then extracted and stored in location HOLDF, whereupon the first CHAR flag is set. The DMA pointer is reset to the initial position, and the program exits from interrupt. Later, another character fills the DMA buffer. Because the first CHAR flag is set, the information is reassembled and stored in a second holding location R(N). During all this time, a software counter (interdigit timer) makes sure the DMA pointers stay in the rest position. If this interval is small (24 ms here), the two characters belong to the same pulse stream and are compared. A character match is final approval, and a DA flag is set. The command code is found in location HOLDF.

Another flag (REP) is also set to help the MAIN program distinguish between a single command such as ON/OFF or a continuous command such as an analog value moving up or down.

Although the system must recover from possible overrun, it is also conceivable that the DMA pointer could get stuck before a valid character is complete. To guard against this, a 3-bit pass number sets a limit of 60 ms, just above the time for a maximum-length character plus interword distance. Measured intervals above the limit reset the system.

Code		Number of pulses counted (hex)	B_7	B_6						B_0
Start	0	33	0	0	1	1	0	0	1	1
LSB	1	47	0	1	0	0	0	1	1	1
	1	47	0	1	0	0	0	1	1	1
	0	33	0	0	1	1	0	0	1	1
	1	47	0	1	0	0	0	1	1	1
	0	33	0	0	1	1	0	0	1	1
MSB	1	47	0	1	0	0	0	1	1	1

Ignored by hardware

Correct answer

FIG. 18   *This example shows how the correct bit information from the remote keyboard is given directly by B_6 in the CD4520 counter.*

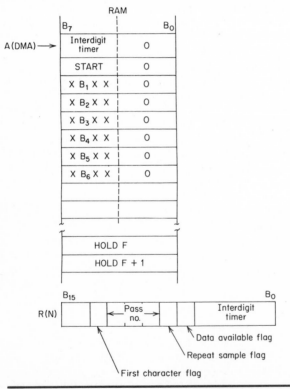

FIG. 19   *The DMA pointer is automatically incremented for each DMA cycle thereby loading successive RAM buffers with numbers corresponding to the time between infrared pulses. The 16-bit CPU register R(N) holds flag bits to aid in processing.*

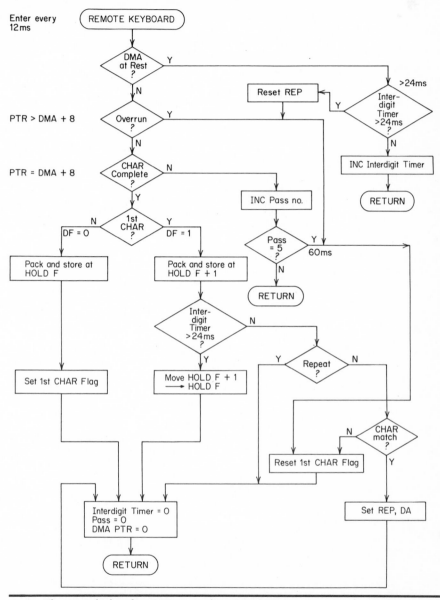

FIG. 20 The remote keyboard routine is a part of one INTERRUPT routine entered at regular intervals. The program tests for number of bits, overrun, and hang-up and verifies proper characters. Each command is stored and the DA flag is set.

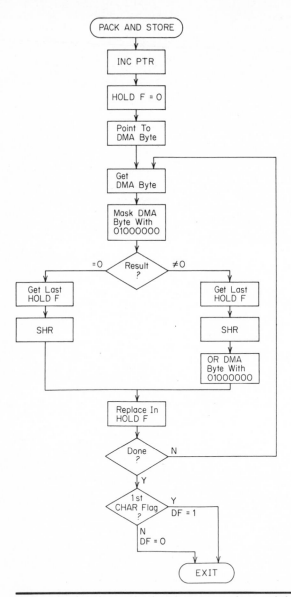

FIG. 21   *Flowchart showing details of the routine used to repack the bits in the buffer into a proper command code.*

4.4 Task Handling

The Real-Time Executive   The TV controller is designed to handle a number of tasks such as turning the TV ON or OFF, muting, program selection, and program scanning. The various tasks are located as segments of code in the MAIN program. These tasks are all initiated by pressing keys on either keyboard. The tasks must be executed in real time, i.e., when a user issues a command. This section describes the program structure and its implementation in response to a command.

When a user hits a button on the keyboard, the INTERRUPT SERVICE routine detects and encodes this event into a 7-bit command code that is stored in a known RAM location. If the remote keyboard is used, the command arrives already encoded. Whether in local or remote keyboard, the command is stored in the same location, irrespective of its origin. A short module in the MAIN serves as a dispatcher or an executive and effects a jump of the program counter to the desired task routine.

The keyboard interrupt command is functionally implemented as shown in Fig. 22. There is a list of commands together with their binary representation

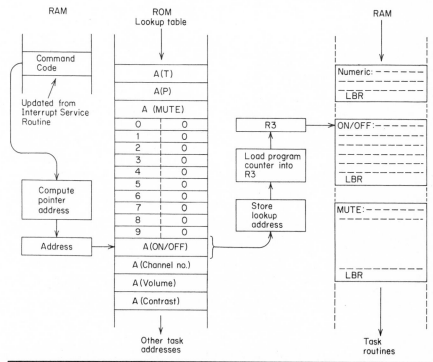

FIG. 22   *The individual task routines are found by using the received command code as a pointer to the task routine's address. LBR = long branch return to top of MAIN.*

defined by the designer. One such code is placed in a RAM location by the INTERRUPT SERVICE routine and is used to compute an address to a lookup table in ROM. This table stores the addresses for the various tasks. The 2-byte task address is next loaded into the program counter, forcing a jump to the task routine. At the end of the routine, the program makes a long branch (LBR) back to the beginning of the MAIN program.

The task is called as shown in Fig. 23. The standard call and return technique (SCRT) with its register assignments is implemented in the software. For details, see Ref. 10.

In the SCRT, registers R4 and R5 are dedicated program counters for CALL and RETURN routines. When a call is made, the current value of the MAIN program counter R3 is saved in register R6.

A variant on the SCRT is used in the executive design. As seen in the flowchart, the lookup address is stored in register R6. When a RETURN (SEP R5)

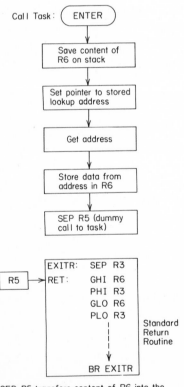

FIG. 23   The task is called when its lookup address is loaded into the program counter R3 by executing a subroutine RETURN. SEP R5 transfers content of R6 into the program counter R3.

is executed, it performs a dummy call to the task, although we are executing a RETURN sequence. This causes the content of R6 to be loaded to R3, the MAIN program counter. The program branches at the end of the RETURN and picks up R3 as program counter, which then jumps to the task routine. As mentioned, at the end of all task routines, the program branches to a single address at the top of MAIN, where the search for a possible new command code starts all over.

Any code found in the assigned RAM location is considered a command and is executed. However, from an operational viewpoint, this controller design distinguishes three types of commands:

1. Type 1 is the *numeric command*, which is simply a BCD number entered into the clock display. It is generally followed by one or more BCD numbers that are shifted into other digits of the clock display, just as digits are entered into a calculator display. Numeric commands always require a terminating nonnumeric command (e.g., the T key). In the latter case, entered digits are transferred into the Update buffer, thereby setting the clock.

2. Type 2 comprises *analog commands*, such as volume or fine tuning. These are also executed immediately but are stand-alone commands. They do not require an interpretive terminating command as the numerics do.

3. Finally, the *function command*, such as ON/OFF, is executed directly, and the command T builds compound commands. Examples of this type of command are setting the clock or event programming.

A pictorial representation of how the commands are sorted, by interpreting the command code, is shown in Fig. 24 and discussed in the *Event Programming* part of this section. Illustrative examples of the various command types are treated in the next few subsections.

Numeric Task Assume that the MAIN program determines there is a numeric command code present by testing the KDA and RDA flags. The program counter then points to the beginning of the numeric task shown in Fig. 25. Assume also that no other keys were previously hit. Two flags are then set. If the numeric flag is true, it indicates that at least 1 numeric digit has already been pushed on the keyboard. The ENTRY mode flag is tested in the UPDATE routine in the interrupt service section. If the flag is set, the UPDATE routine complements data for the colon every second. A blinking colon is a reminder that one is in an ENTRY mode.

Next, the clock display is entered to 0s, then the numeric number is entered into the least significant digit of the clock display. When the numeric command has been executed, the DA flags, KDA/RDA, are reset and the program counter returns to the top of the MAIN program.

If another numeric button is pressed, the digits in the clock display are moved one position to the left to make room for the new digit, which is entered in the least significant position. After each exit from the numeric task, the software is still in the ENTRY mode, where it remains until some other task resets the ENTRY mode flag. When this flag is reset, the colon stops blinking.

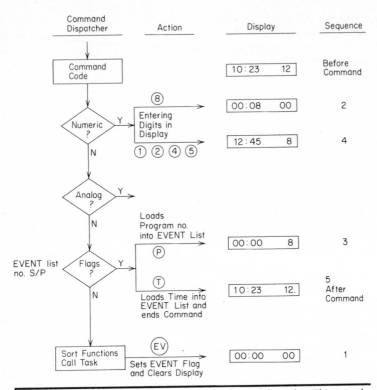

FIG. 24   *Compound commands are filtered by the command dispatcher. This example shows the sequence of steps in event programming EV 8P1245T, i.e., program number 8 is set to turn on at time 12:45.*

Analog Task   The same routine handles a total of eight tasks: volume up or down, brightness, contrast, and saturation; Fig. 26 shows this routine.

When the analog task is called, the display pointer is loaded with the address of DA1 (volume) in the Display buffer. On the first pass through the routine, a delay counter is set. The value of this delay determines the speed with which the analog value is ramped up or down. The command code is next fetched, to determine which of the four analog variables are to be executed, and the display pointer is advanced accordingly. Note that the command code was already examined once and found to be an analog type. The command codes are assigned so that all up commands have a **0** in their least significant bit and the down commands have a **1** in the same bit position. This allows the same task routine to handle eight different functions. As indicated in Fig. 26, a volume command is bypassed if the TV set is already muted.

The program checks if the delay has expired. If not, the delay exits after setting an analog flag bit. The flag is tested in the INTERRUPT SERVICE routine and each interrupt decrements the delay counter if the analog flag is true.

After determining if the command is up or down, the value in the Display buffer is fetched and either incremented or decremented. After resetting a number of flags, including DA (KDA and RDA), the program branches back to the top of MAIN.

If the analog button continues to be held down, the task is entered over and over for the duration of the key depression, and the function is ramped up or down.

At the bottom of Fig. 26, note that there are stop limits for the 6-bit analog values that they cannot pass.

Function Tasks The final category of simple tasks are the function tasks. Some examples are ON/OFF, MUTE (T), and SCAN PROGRAMS (P). To illustrate, look at the T task in Fig. 27. The T task simply toggles the clock display ON

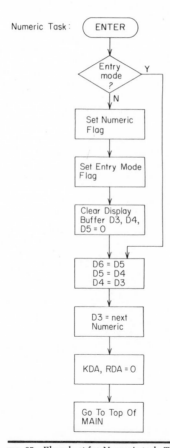

FIG. 25 *Flowchart for Numeric task. The clock display is cleared and a digit entered in the least significant position. Subsequent entries are shifted left.*

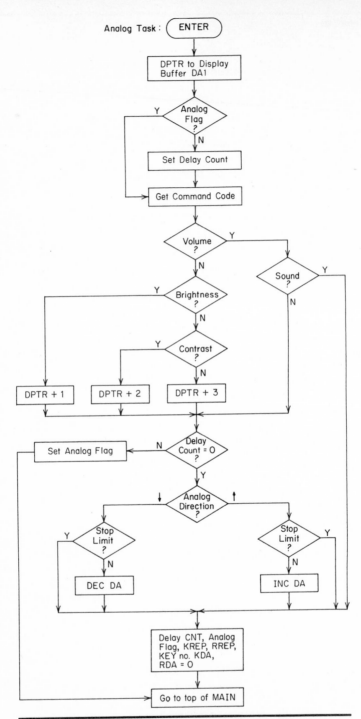

FIG. 26   Flowchart for Analog task. This routine handles eight different functions, i.e., it controls all four analog values either up or down. The delay count sets the ramping speed.

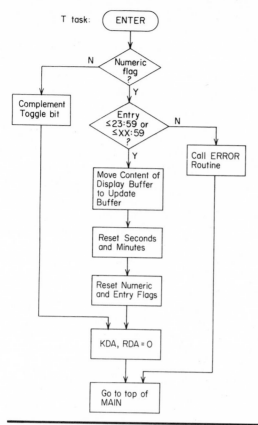

FIG. 27   *The T task sets the clock by moving the content of the display buffer into the update buffer. This routine is also used to toggle the clock display* ON *or* OFF.

and OFF. The 2-digit program display is unaffected. If no numeric key has previously been hit and we push the T key, the task simply complements a bit called the toggle bit. The bit is tested in the UPDATE routine at every interrupt, and if the bit is true, the content of the Update buffer is loaded into the Display buffer. If the bit is false, the pointer is displaced and the fetched data, hexadecimal F, is decoded as a blank. Hence, alternate depressions turn ON or OFF the 4-digit clock display.

Compound Tasks   We now look at how various types of simple commands are combined into compound commands to execute compound tasks.

Setting the clock   Numerics followed by the T command set the clock, for example, 1234T. The numerics are entered and executed first by the numeric task as described earlier and shown in Fig. 25.

At this stage the numerics are simply entered into the Display buffer and a numeric flag bit is set. Setting the clock requires that the numerics are terminated with a T command. Because the numeric flag is true, the T task, Fig. 27, does not toggle the clock display—it moves the content of the Display buffer into the Update buffer. The seconds and minutes are reset to zero and the routine exits to the top of MAIN after resetting the appropriate flag bits. Resetting the ENTRY mode flag stops the colon blinking as a visual confirmation that the command is terminated. Illegal clock entry calls an ERROR routine, which displays blinking eights for 3 s, after which the display and the state of the machine revert to its preentry state.

Event (EV) programming   A good example of a complex command is EV 8P1245T. After execution, the TV set will turn on or switch to program number 8 at the time 12:45. Event programming is a linking of two compound tasks 1245T and 8P. As stand-alone groups, they perform the specific tasks of setting the clock and selecting program 8. When the two groups are combined and preceded by the EV command, a new task is executed.

The sequence of events is best understood by studying how the command dispatcher (Fig. 24) filters the commands. Refer to the flowcharts shown in Figs. 28 and 29 for details of this sequence.

EV is a function command whose main task is to set a bit called event flag. The task also clears the display to 0 digits and invokes the ENTRY mode, indicated to the user by a blinking colon. Digit 8 is next entered into the least significant clock digit by the numeric task. The next command is P, which

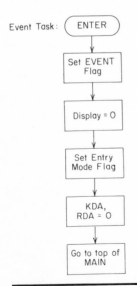

FIG. 28   *The principal function of the Event task is to set an event flag which is required in order to reinterpret the P and T commands in the event programming mode.*

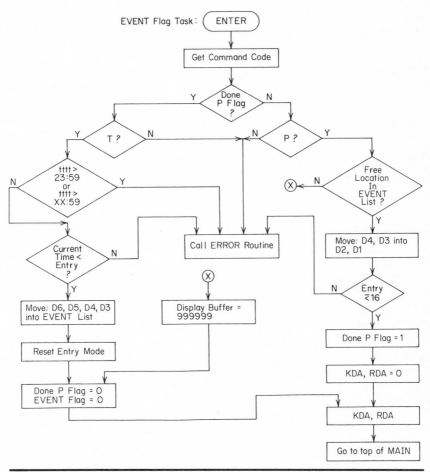

FIG. 29   *When the event flag is set, memories terminated with P and T are filtered into the EVENT FLAG routine. P loads program number and T loads time into the event list. The routine also checks for illegal entries and full list.*

normally selects program 8 if just 8P is executed. But because the command chain was initiated with EV, which set a flag, the P command is filtered into the EVENT FLAG routine (Fig. 29). This task loads program number 8 into an event list in RAM and also into the program locations of the display. The clock display is cleared again for new entries. Next, the time digits 1245 are entered by the numeric task into the clock display. The display at this stage shows 12:45 8, verifying what a user wants to enter into the event list. The colon is still blinking. Command T terminates the sequence. Normally, after a sequence of digits T sets the clock, but in this case the command is trapped in the EVENT FLAG routine and loads the numbers into the time part of the event list. The program in the display, before the EV command is saved. The program is enabled to transfer data from the Update buffer into the Display buffer. When T terminates the compound command, the original display is restored. However, if the list was empty, a period is displayed to indicate that there is now a programmed event in the list. The flowchart for the EVENT FLAG routine shows that before entering an item, the list is scanned for free locations. If the list is full, blinking 9s are moved into the display until a user clears the command.

The EVENT FLAG routine tests for four error conditions. Program numbers higher than those the design is implemented for cannot be entered, nor can illegal times. The order of the P and T commands are fixed; any violation calls an ERROR routine that places blinking 8s in the display for 3 s, after which the system reverts to its precommand state. For proper event programming, the time entry must be greater than current time.

No restrictions are otherwise imposed on programming events. The entries can be made out of time sequence. The software orders the entries so that the one nearest in time always is at the top of the list.

Leading zeroes need not be programmed; they are blanked in the program display if they are erroneously entered.

4.5   Tuning and Program Selection

The Phase-Locked Loop (PLL)   A prescaler ($\div$ K) in the closed-loop circuit divides the outputs from the local oscillator (LO) by 64 for VHF and 256 for UHF. See Fig. 30. The prescaler output, now within the frequency range of CMOS circuitry, feeds a 14-bit divide-by-N counter, the output of which is compared with a reference frequency f_{ref}. The output from the phase detector is filtered, amplified, and applied to the varactor diode tuning the LO. The LO frequency is therefore measured, and whatever control voltage is necessary to force the frequency to the correct value for a selected channel is generated by the loop. At phase lock, when the inputs to the phase detector are the same frequency, the LO frequency is

$$f_o = KN\, f_{ref} \tag{1}$$

The divide-by-N counter is programmable and under software control, which allows software selection of any VHF/UHF channel.

In a PLL system, the channel spacing, F_c, or resolution is nominally equal to the reference frequency. If a prescaler is required, as here, the value of the reference frequency must be reduced by a division K. Hence

$$f_{ref} = \frac{F_c}{K} \tag{2}$$

A low-pass filter is employed in PLLs to remove time-variant components from the LO control voltage. Otherwise the reference frequency and its harmonic output from the phase detector may be of sufficient magnitude to cause unacceptable FM modulation of the tuner LO.

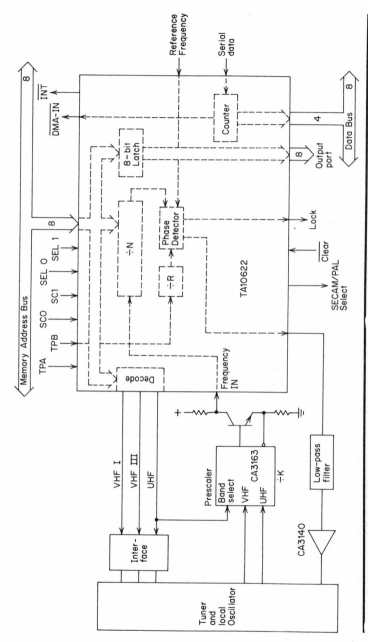

FIG. 30 Precise tuning and station selection is done with a PLL. The loop is controlled by a CMOS LSI chip which contains a divide-by-N counter, band-select outputs, a phase comparator, and reference frequency dividers.

Equation 2 brings out an inherent problem with simple PLLs employing prescalers. Good resolution or small channel spacing requires a low reference frequency, and a low reference frequency requires good filtering of the phase-detector output. This slows down the loops' settling time. Design considerations covering loop dynamics, noise, and filter designs are well-covered in the literature.[11]

The reference frequency in this design is 390.625 Hz, which with the chosen prescaler gives a channel spacing of 25 kHz for VHF and 100 kHz for UHF. This is a good compromise between narrow channel spacing and acceptable lock-in time. This reference frequency is derived from a CPU crystal oscillator with a frequency of 2 MHz. For maximum design flexibility, a separate input (DIRECT REF) on the frequency-synthesizer chip TA10622 permits a wide range of referency frequencies to be applied. The chip also provides an in-lock signal that is HIGH when the loop is in lock and LOW all other times. If the signal is monitored by the CPU, it provides a means for dynamically varying the time constant of the low-pass filter during the acquisition period. The data format for channel selection is a 16-bit word, as shown in Fig. 31. The 2 most significant bits are decoded to select one of three bands (two for VHF and one for UHF). The remaining 14 bits is the binary representation of the N-number for a specific channel; 14 bits gives sufficient resolution to implement fine tuning. The LO frequencies can be placed as close as 25 kHz for VHF, which provides for easy selection of any official channel in the world as well as unassigned channels used in cable TV and MATV installations.

The 16-bit channel-selection data is outputted over the 8-bit memory address lines, with only one instruction using register-based output[9]. Except for the ECL prescaler, low-pass filter, and operational amplifier, all circuitry for the PLL is integrated on one CMOS chip. The interface logic for handling a remote keyboard transmitting PPM pulse trains is also included on the chip.

The PLL system differs fundamentally from the open-loop analog system commonly employed in TV receivers using varactor tuning. In the latter case a predetermined voltage is applied to the tuner with the expectation that the generated frequency will be correct. With no feedback, as in the PLL system, time and temperature changes in components affect the frequency. Automatic compensation for differences in tuner characteristics is not possible using the open-loop analog circuit.

Fine Tuning   Although a PLL system sets the frequency to an exact predetermined value, at times fine tuning (FT) is desired, for example, when locating unassigned channels.

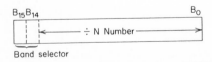

Band selector

FIG. 31   *Band and channel frequency information is contained in a 16-bit data word sent over the memory address bus.*

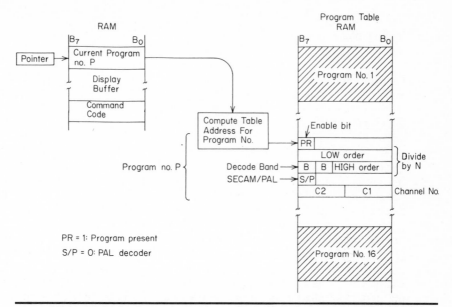

FIG. 32   *Timing information for 16 programs is stored in RAM. Each group contains an enable bit, control bits for the PLL, the PAL/SECAM decoder, and the assigned channel number. PR = 1: program present. S/P = 0: PAL decoder.*

Fine tuning is a function task, as defined earlier, but its structure is similar to an analog task. Fine tuning up or down is implemented in 25-kHz steps for the duration of a key depression.

A RAM table is maintained to store tuning information for a certain number of programs (16 in this design). Each block in the table can store (see Fig. 32): the 14-bit divide-by-N number, 2 bits for decoding the band, 1 bit defining PAL or sequential with memory (SECAM) decoding (for European systems), the FCC or CCIR channel number assigned to the program slot, and an enable bit to indicate if something is programmed into this particular table location.

The first problem upon entering the program sequence in the task routine is to determine which N-number in the RAM table should be modified. As shown in Fig. 32, a byte located near the Display buffer is always updated with the currently active program number. Hence, the address can be computed to the correct table location. Assume that FT was just called. Refer to Fig. 33. A delay count is set, and the program exits to the top of the MAIN after setting an analog flag bit. This is similar to the analog tasks, where the delay counter determines the up/down ramping speed. The counter is decremented in the UPDATE routine every 4 ms if the analog flag is true.

On the next pass through the FT task, the command code is examined for up or down information. The N-number is fetched from the table and incremented or decremented by 1, after which an output instruction loads the PLL with the new N-number. Preceding the load command, a bit is tested in the table to determine if there is an entry. Finally, the new N-number is replaced in the table, and the routine exits after resetting all relevant control flags. The described sequence of events are repeated as long as the key is active.

Program Selection, Preprogramming, and Scanning   It is useful to reemphasize the distinction between channels and programs, to avoid confusion. A ROM table contains the binary codes for 99 frequency channels, which are the official channels for any country allocated by CCIR[12,13]. This design has another table in RAM, which stores tuning information for 16 programs. The program, or network, a receiver sees depends upon the receiver's geographic location: The same program may be received in different areas on different frequency channels. Hence, it is desirable to be able to preprogram a certain channel to a specific program number. Tuning is then later done by simply selecting a program number.

We now discuss four different modes of tuning. The *command pp*^{p} selects directly program number pp. A *P command* not preceded by numerics scans from the current program number to the next higher one with a valid station assigned to that program number. A *command ccCH* assigns the frequency channel cc to the program number currently selected. A *CH command* without preceding digits scans from the frequency channel assigned to the currently selected program up to the nearest channel on the air. In both scanning modes, there is a wrap-around feature that halts the scanning where it started if none of the program slots were preprogrammed or no stations were on the air.

The preprogramming command ccCH is convenient when the channel frequency is known. When this is not the case, the channel scan CH allows a user to search for a station and assign it to a program number.

We describe in some details only the CH task that covers two functions: direct assignment (ccCH) and scanning (CH).

Direct assignment—ccCH   Refer to the flowchart in Fig. 34. Assume that 29 has been entered by the numeric task as the first step in assigning channel 29 to whatever program number the TV is displaying (for example, program 8). The CH task is entered upon terminating the command with CH. We are not in the scan mode, and the numeric flag is already set. A pointer address is then computed to the correct table entry in RAM for the currently selected program number 8. Next, the content of D4 and D3 in the Display buffer (the number 29 just entered) is moved into channel number locations C2 and C1 in the RAM table. From the channel number another address is computed in the ROM table, which stores the divide-by-N number for channel 29 and its 2 bits defining the band. The 16 bits are copied into the RAM table, and the PR bit is set to indicate an entry is present in this RAM section. It remains for the task to reset the control bits and turn the sound ON again before returning to the top of the MAIN program. Just prior to hitting the CH key, a user sees 00:29 8 on the display, which verifies that channel 29 is assigned to program number 8. When CH is pushed at the end of the task, the ENTRY mode flag is reset, which restores the clock display (XX:XX 8) and stops the colon from blinking.

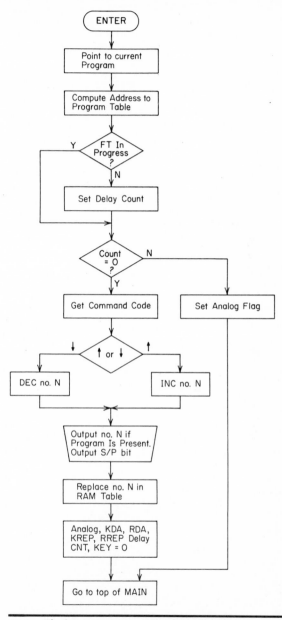

FIG. 33   The fine-tuning routine (FT task) handles frequency increments in 25-kHz steps up or down. Ramp speed is set by a delay constant.

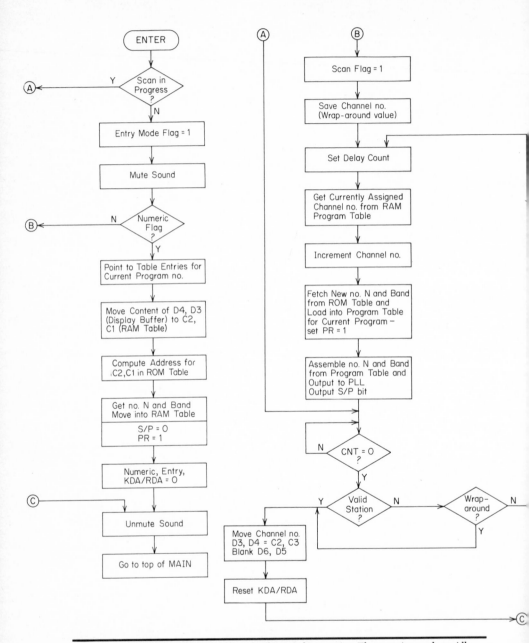

FIG. 34 Channel assignment (CH task) can be direct or by scanning. The scanning mode rapidly bypasses stations off the air and has a wrap-around feature. Sound is muted during search and lock-in.

Channel scan—CH   Let us proceed under the assumption that we want to assign a different channel to the current program selection 8 but we do not know the channel number. The scan mode is invoked simply by pressing the CH button. Upon entering the CH task the first time, the scan mode is not yet recognized, but the ENTRY mode flag is set and sound is muted as described earlier. However, the numeric flag is false this time, and the program branches to a scan sequence. A scan flag is set, and the current channel number 29 from which the channel scan starts is saved. A delay count is loaded that determines the scan rate. Knowing the current program number 8, the task addresses the RAM table and fetches the current channel number 29, which is incremented by 1. The new channel number 30 addresses the ROM table, from which it transfers both the divide-by-N number and band into the RAM program table for program 8.

An output instruction takes the same information after it is assembled (in a 16-bit register) and loads it into the PLL system. The program now waits a predetermined time for the PLL to acquire lock, after which it tests if a valid station is on the air. Assume that channel 30 is not present. The program loops back and loads the PLL with channel 31 and again tests for a valid station. Before each channel search, the incremented value is compared with the start value of 29. After channel 99, the count wraps around to 1, and if no stations are present, the system stops on return to channel 29. However, if channel 30 is transmitting, the digits 30 are moved into the D4 and D3 positions of the display and D6 and D5 are blanked. The task now resets the control bits, turns the sound back ON, and returns execution to the top of MAIN.

At this point, a viewer reads on the display 00:30 8, with the colon blinking, indicating that the scan mode is operating. If a viewer keeps the button down or presses it once more, the channel scan continues as described because the scan flag is still true. A user has the option of using the CLEAR button, which resets the scan flag that terminates the scanning mode and restores the normal clock display XX:XX 8.

With a PLL system, preprogramming of channels or events can be done at any time—no stations have to be on the air. It is possible to preprogram TV sets even before they are sold, provided they have a battery backup system for the controller.

4.6 Battery Backup

A battery backup system is implemented to avoid losing prestored channel programs and event programs during power failure. The outage may last from seconds to hours or for an indefinite period if a user unplugs the ac cord. Because of an all-CMOS system, continuous operation is possible using only four small nickel-cadmium rechargeable cells (see Fig. 35).

A two-level battery mode is implemented. If the CPU senses a power failure, the nickel-cadmium cells automatically take over and run the whole system for approximately 1 week (refer to the flowchart in Fig. 7).

To conserve power, when the CPU detects a power failure, it automatically

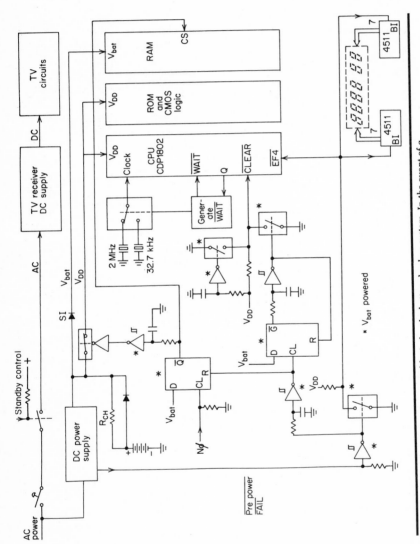

FIG. 35 This diagram shows the control logic for the battery backup system. In the event of a power failure the system switches to a 32-kHz crystal and maintains time and stored information for one week. Longer outages shut down the system but the battery operates the RAM for several months.

switches from the 2-MHz crystal to a low-frequency (32 kHz) crystal. The switching takes place during a few milliseconds WAIT state that the CPU enters upon detecting power failure. If power is not restored within the predetermined number of days, the CPU kills itself after shutting down the whole system (except for the RAM storing user-programmed information). The remaining battery power is sufficient for approximately 3 months. If power returns before 3 months, operation resumes as normal, with stored information intact.

The slow-clock mode works satisfactorily because during absence of ac power, the software only updates the clock at each interrupt that occurs 60 times slower. Essentially the same UPDATE routine is used (see Fig. 9), except in slow-clock mode a Branch instruction sets a new limit for the number of interrupt pulses required to measure 1 s. The software also ignores all code except update clock and testing for presence of ac.

When in the slow-clock mode, the counter limit for 1 s becomes a noninteger number. If the test is for four pulses, the clock runs slightly fast because the correct number must be 4.0959 pulses. This error can be corrected to an acceptable value by subtracting 1 s at every 43 pseudoseconds.

Details of the control logic are shown in Fig. 35. A prepower fail signal must be available from the power supply, with a few milliseconds lead time. The flag input EF4 on the CPU monitors this signal. When it goes true, the CPU generates a $\overline{WAIT}$ signal, permitting automatic and glitch-free switchover from a 2-MHz to a 32-kHz crystal oscillator.

There are several types of automatic power-on reset. If the preassigned time limit for the system be UP, one of the CPU's lines (Nø) triggers a flip-flop that inhibits RAM and after a time delay disconnects battery power from the rest of the system. Only RAM with stored program and event information remains under power.

4.7 Summary of Implemented Functions and Commands

The operating specifications for the TV receiver are summarized in Table 1; all simple and compound commands are listed and explained. While reading this section, refer to the 6-digit display in Fig. 2 and the two keyboards in Figs. 3 and 4.

TABLE 1   Summary of keyboard commands and operating specifications

Commands	Action
Numerals: 0 to 9	First numeral is entered in D3; D4 to D6 become 0s. The colon blinks, succeeding numerals are entered in D3, and previous entries are shifted left.

TABLE 1 *Summary of keyboard commands and operating specifications   (Continued)*

Commands	Action
Set clock: tttt^T	Numerals are entered as above. Command T stops colon from blinking, after which the clock begins running at newly set time. Entries must be $\leq$ 23:59 or $\leq$ XX:59. Leading zeros need not be entered.
Program selection: pp^P	Numerals are entered as above, and the colon starts blinking. The P stops the colon from blinking. The program number appears on D1, D2; the clock display reappears on D3 to D6. The program is selected. During selection, the sound is muted, but it is gradually restored after P is pressed. Entries > 16 trigger error mode. If the TV was OFF, this command turns it ON. If program no. 0 (that is, 00P) is selected, the TV turns OFF and goes to standby.
PAL/SECAM select S/P P	Colon blinks after S/P and stops blinking after the second P is depressed. Afterward, a program selection (pp^P) selects PAL or SECAM mode. The selection toggles between the two modes.
P	The colon blinks and D1, D2 show the nearest higher program number that is programmed and transmitting. D3, D4 show the assigned channel number for the locked-in program number. Program locations are rapidly skipped if they do not contain programs or if the assigned channels are off the air.
P.P.P . . .	At each depression of P, the action above is repeated while showing the next higher program and its assigned channel number. This manual scan mode has a wrap-around feature that quickly returns to the lowest preprogrammed channel after the highest channel is bypassed. To leave the scan mode, press CL (clear): The clock display will reappear and the colon will stop blinking. During scanning the sound is muted, but it is gradually restored if a station is detected.
Preprogramming of channels: (a) Channel known: ccCH	Channel number is entered in D3, D4 and the colon blinks. The CH part of the command stops the colon from blinking, causes the clock display to reappear, and assigns channel cc to the current program number.
(b) Channel scan: CH	At the first CH command the colon blinks and the channel scan starts at the current channel and stops at the first valid channel on the air. The channel number is displayed in D3, D4.
CH.CH.CH . . .	At each depression of CH the above action is repeated. Press CL (clear) to exit scan mode, after which the colon will stop blinking, clock display

TABLE 1 *Summary of keyboard commands and operating specifications (Continued)*

Commands	Action
	will reappear, and the last channel found will remain ON. Sound is muted during commands but is gradually restored after channel is found.
Preprogramming of events: (a) One event: EVpp^{P}tttt^T	Event (EV) starts the colon blinking and clears the display. The pp entry is shown in D3, D4. Pressing P transfers the program number into D1, D2. The tttt entry is then displayed on D3 to D6. When T is pressed, the colon stops blinking, the old clock and program display reappears, and the new preprogrammed data is stored. If this is the first preprogrammed event, the preprogramming indicator turns ON.
(b) Repeat event: S/P EVpp^{P}tttt^T	The action is similar to above, except the colon starts blinking when S/P is pressed.
(c) Off event: EV 00^{P}tttt^T	This command will turn OFF the TV at the assigned time tttt.
Listing: List	Pressing L causes the colon to blink, and the nearest event in time is displayed in the 6 digits. Eact depression of L displays the next stored event. The end of the list is indicated by an all-8s display. CL (clear) will restore normal display. OFF items in the list will be indicated by 0s in D1, D2. Repeat items in the list will be indicated by a blinking program number (D1, D2).
Cancel events: List item	To cancel a listed entry, press NO and the display will show 0s. Listing can continue as before, or exit is possible by using CL (clear).
Acknowledge: Any key	The period will blink after any automatic turn-on. Any key except ON/OFF can be used to acknowledge that someone is watching the TV. This causes the blinking period. If no acknowledge is provided, within 5 min the TV turns OFF.
Fine tune: FT ↑ or FT ↓	The command is active for the duration of the key depression. The last value is automatically stored. The FT steps are 25 kHz for VHF and 100 kHz for UHF.

Analog controls:
  Brightness ↑ or ↓
  Color Sat. ↑ or ↓
  Contrast ↑ or ↓
  Volume ↑ or ↓
	These commands are active for the duration of a key depression. The software has limit stops such that any value can not go below zero or above its maximum.

Store users' value: S/P NTV	After this combination of keys is pushed, the colon stops blinking and the four analog values active are stored. These can later be recalled by pressing NTV.

TABLE 1 Summary of keyboard commands and operating specifications   (Continued)

Commands	Action
Clock display: T	This key toggles clock display ON or OFF.
What channel? S/P CH	The colon blinks and the channel number is shown in D3, D4 for current program. CL returns display to normal operation.
Clear: CL	Four functions are performed with this key: 1. It can acknowledge an automatic turnon. 2. It will return control to a previous mode. 3. It allows an escape from an error mode before a time-out. 4. It is used to return from LISTING, SCAN, or WHAT CHANNEL.
Mute: M	This key toggles the sound ON or OFF. The sound ramps between levels.
On: ON/OFF	When the TV is turned off the program display is blanked. OP is used for this command. The last selected program is again displayed when the TV is turned on.

REFERENCES

1. Kleiman, A.: "Programmable Color TV," *Radio Electronics*, May 1977, p. 49.
2. Baum, W.: "Farbfernsehgerät mit Microprocessor—Steuerung," *Funkschau*, Heft 17, 1977, p. 61.
3. Mokhoff, N.: "Consumer Electronics—Intelligent Television Receivers," *IEEE Spectrum*, January 1980, p. 64.
4. "User Manual for the CDP 1802 Microprocessor, MPM-201," RCA Corporation, Solid State Division, Somerville, N.J., March 1980.
5. Data Sheet SAB 3011, Valvo Corp., Hamburg, Germany, 1978.
6. "Teletext—The LSI Solution," Mullard Technical Information TP1606, London, England, 1977.
7. Fedida, S.: "Viewdata," *Wireless World*, vol. 83, no. 1494, February 1977, p. 32.
8. Data Sheets for CDP 1869 and CDP1870, RCA Corporation, Solid State Division, Somerville, N.J., 1979.
9. "Register-Based Output Function for RCA COSMAC Microprocessors," App. Note ICAN—6562, RCA Corporation, Solid State Division, Somerville, N.J., 1979.
10. "User Manual for the CDP1802 Microprocessor, MPM-201," RCA Corporation, Solid State Division, Somerville, N.J., March 1980, p. 61.
11. Gardner, F: *Phase-Lock Techniques*, Wiley, New York, 1966.
12. *Funkschau* 1975, "Norman für Schwarzweiss-und Farb-Fernsehen" Funktechnische Arbeitsblätter - DK 621.397.13:389.6 FS 01 Schwarzweiss- und Farb-Fernsehen, 1975 Heft 7, p. 75, and 1975 Heft 9, p. 55 (2 issues).
13. *World Radio TV Handbook*, vol. 31, 31st ed. Billboard Publications, New York, 1977.

CHAPTER FIVE

Microcomputer Data Acquisition Module

Vincent C. Negro

U.S. Department of Energy,
New York

INTRODUCTION

It is often necessary to record analog and/or digital signals. The analog signals generally come from some kind of transducer or sensor that produces an output voltage which varies (usually linearly) as some input parameter (temperature, pressure, current, and so on) changes. Two common measurement examples are the temperature in an industrial process or the weather-related barometric pressure. The digital signals might come from counting items on a conveyor belt, electronic pulses from various equipment such as nuclear-particle detectors, or an outdoor rain-gauge monitor (tipping-bucket type). The type of instrument most often used to record analog signals is a strip-chart recorder, and digital signals can be recorded by a variety of electric or electromechanical counters and an associated printer. If the interest in the signal is short-term or as a gross operational check, the aforementioned instruments are probably adequate. However, if detailed analysis is required, the strip charts must be examined manually, which is a tedious and error-prone procedure.

Analysis of voluminous printer output data is also tedious. To eliminate manual analysis, analog and/or digital signals (data) should be recorded in a manner that permits real-time computer analysis. The microprocessor is an effective tool for doing this.

5.1   Signal Handling

The analysis of any analog process first requires the conversion of data to a digital format. This can be done with an analog-to-digital converter (ADC), but the process presents some problems. One problem is the resolution of the ADC. For many applications, 8 bits will suffice, but others may require 10, 12, or even 16 bits. Because the data bus for most microprocessors is 8 bits, a 10-bit or more ADC requires a latch for the higher-order bits and software overhead to handle the resulting double-precision words. In addition, an analog multiplexer is probably required, which adds complexity and more software overhead. Because of these considerations, this chapter discusses the use of voltage-to-frequency converter (VFC) techniques instead of ADCs.

The VFC can be thought of as an ADC with a single-line serial output instead of a multiline parallel output. The pulses on this serial output must be counted. If the pulses are counted every second, a typical VFC has a resolution of 1 part in 10,000, which is better than 13 bits of binary resolution. If more resolution is required, VFCs with a resolution of 1 part in 100,000 are available at an additional cost of only $20; this resolution is better than 16 binary bits (1-s count). Another advantage of VFCs is that noisy signals are effectively filtered by the inherent averaging. Because the VFCs require no microprocessor control and produce only a single-line (count) signal, they are separate from the microprocessor module and will not be discussed further. Therefore, the inputs to the microprocessor module will be counting inputs.

The maximum frequency from the VFCs is 100 kHz, but pulses from nuclear detectors must also be counted. The Poisson distribution of these pulses dictates that the counters must be able to resolve pulses 1 μs apart. Therefore, the counter must be specified to handle inputs of 1 MHz or greater.

5.2   System Overview

The module called Clever Counter (shown in Fig. 1) is housed in a narrow enclosure known as a one-wide nuclear instrument module (NIM)[1]. The NIM system is a flexible and efficient method of busing power and other signals to several modules contained in a common enclosure known as a NIM bin. For our purposes it is sufficient to say that the Clever Counter module derives its power from a NIM bin. The NIM system is not discussed further in this chapter.

Timers, Counters, and Time-of-Year (TOY) ***Clock***   The data acquisition module contains 5 independent counting channels. Each channel consists of a 6-decade counter and a 6-decade timer. The timers are programmable and can

FIG. 1   *Front panel of the Clever Counter described in this chapter. It is packaged in a nuclear instrument module (NIM).*

be preset from 1 s to 1 million s (about 11½ days). The counters can accommodate transistor-transistor logic (TTL) level pulses at counting rates to 7 MHz. If desired, the user can gate any counter or any combination of counters by enabling the external gate inputs. These inputs are located on the rear of the module, as shown in Fig. 2. At the end of the preset time, the contents of the counter and the preset time are recorded on a cassette tape and, optionally, on a printer. In addition to the counters and timers, there is a programmable time-of-year (TOY) clock that is updated every second. The contents of the TOY clock are also recorded whenever any timer reaches the preset time. During a power failure, a small on-board battery maintains the operation of the TOY clock.

Display   During operation, a user can observe the status of the active counters, timers, and TOY clock on two alphanumeric displays. The upper display (see Fig. 1) indicates the function (e.g., DAY, HOUR, SEC), and the lower display indicates the numerical value. Pressing the DISPLAY button activates this function, which causes a sequential display of counters, timers,

FIG. 2   Rear view of the Clever Counter NIM.

FIG. 3   A pocket entry unit for programming the Clever Counter.

and TOY clock. If constant monitoring of a particular counter/timer is required, it can be "frozen" in the display.

Self-Starting In case of a power failure, all current information in the counters and timers is lost, but, as mentioned, the backup battery maintains the function of the TOY clock. When power is restored, the unit will program itself with values set in memory (EPROM) and initiate operation without operator intervention. Thus, data acquisition is lost only during the power outage. The duration of the power outage can be determined from observing the TOY clock information recorded just prior to, and immediately following, the power outage.

***Pocket* TTY** Figure 3 is a photograph of the pocket TTY[2] used for programming the module. It is connected to the module via the RS232C connector located in front of the module (see Fig. 1). This method prevents accidental program modification caused by brushing against a control or from unauthorized personnel moving the switches. The TTY is light and portable and can be used to set up several modules. This technique also avoids dedicating a terminal for the programming function. If hard copy is desired, a printer is used instead of the pocket TTY.

External Control On the rear of the module (Fig. 2) is a switch that selects internal or external operation. This switch, in conjunction with the two jacks labeled BUSY and RESUME, can be used to synchronize the counter and timer of channel 1 with external equipment. In the external position, when timer 1 has reached the preset time, a signal on the BUSY jack appears that can be used to initiate a cycle in external equipment (e.g., index to another position). While the external equipment is operating, counting in channel 1 is suspended. At the end of its cycle, the external equipment produces a resume pulse that restarts data acquisition on channel 1. None of the other counter/timer channels are affected while the external equipment cycles.

Cassette Recorder When any timer reaches its preset time, information is recorded on a Phillips-type magnetic cassette. To optimize data retrieval, the information is recorded twice, and each record contains a checksum character. During data analysis, the host computer uses this checksum character to ascertain the validity of the record. If an error is found, the duplicate record is used.

5.3 Detailed System Description

Very Large-Scale Integrated Circuits (VLSI ICs) From the beginning of this design, it was decided to use VLSI as much as possible, mainly to substantially reduce wiring complexity. The original Clever Counter[3] has almost 1000 connections and requires automatic wiring performed by an outside vendor. In

FIG. 4 Original breadboard Clever Counter using MSI integrated circuits.

FIG. 5 Prototype Clever Counter using VLSI integrated circuits.

addition to being expensive, automatic wiring requires tables to generate the wiring program. The preparation of these tables is uniquely demanding, tedious, and boring! By using VLSI, the number of connections has been reduced by a factor of 5, to about 200. This permits the wiring to be done in house. Most small facilities should be able to do this wiring by using printed circuit or wire-wrap techniques. The 200 connections are reduced another 25 percent by using the EPROM version (MC68701) of the Motorola MC6801[4]. Figures 4 and 5 compare the original Clever Counter with a prototype of the VLSI design and illustrate the dramatic reduction in part complexity. Besides reducing wiring complexity, the VLSI design has capabilities that the original Clever Counter lacks, namely, display, cassette recorder, an additional counting channel, and the ability to self-start. One final point should be stressed: A system with 200 connections is much less prone to failure than a system with 1000 connections.

Block Diagram   Figure 6 shows a simplified block diagram of the system. The Motorola MC6801 microprocessor is configured such that port 4 is the upper address lines (A_8-A_{15}), and port 3 is the multiplexed data lines and lower address lines (expanded multiplexed mode). An 8-bit latch separates the lower address lines, A_0-A_7, from the multiplexed lines, but the data lines remain multiplexed (starred notation $D_0^*-D_7^*$). To properly define the data lines and avoid bus conflicts, the enable (E) signal from the microprocessor must be used as part of the decoding signal [usually chip-select (CS)] for the auxiliary circuits.

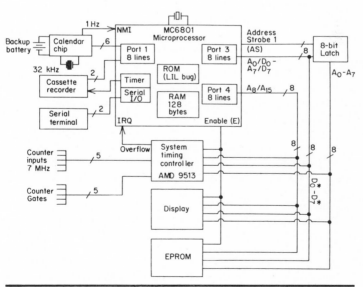

FIG. 6   *Simplified block diagram of the Clever Counter.*

The Advanced Micro Devices—AMD9513—system timing controller (STC) is configured as five 4-decade binary-coded decimal (BCD) counters. Each counter represents the 4 least significant decades (LSDs) of the overall 6-decade counter. The 2 most significant decades (MSDs) are implemented by a word in random-access memory (RAM), which is updated when the 4-decade counter overflows. This is done by gating all the overflow lines from the counters into a common microprocessor interrupt signal (IRQ). The software routine servicing this interrupt polls the AMD9513 to identify the interrupting counter and updates its associated 2 MSDs in RAM. Placing the low-order decades in hardware external to the microprocessor allows the system to resolve pulses less then 0.2 μs apart, which is well beyond the capability of the microprocessor alone. If future applications require more than 6 counting decades, additional decades are easily added with software. The five counter gates shown in Fig. 6 can be software-configured to gate the counter inputs in a variety of ways, which are discussed in the description of the AMD9513.

The 1-Hz signal that updates the calendar chip is also used to update the timers and TOY functions which are controlled by the MC6801. This is done by tying the 1-Hz signal to the nonmaskable interrupt (NMI) of the MC6801. Not shown in the block diagram is additional gating that inhibits the NMI signal when reading or writing the calendar chip.

Port 1 of the MC6801 supports the calendar chip and the cassette recorder. The cassette recorder requires an additional clock signal that is obtained from the built-in timer of the MC6801.

The built-in serial input-output (I/O) of the MC6801 requires only level shifters to support a serial terminal. Also, the MC6801 contains a monitor debugging aid in read only memory (ROM) and 128 bytes of RAM; these are discussed in the following description of the MC6801.

5.4 Major LSI Integrated Circuits

Motorola MC6801 Microprocessor The MC6801 microcomputer[5-12] may be considered an entire family of processors, all of which have been integrated into one common design. This family of devices has unique characteristics, such as eight-mode operation, four ports, expanded multiplexed, partial decode, mask options, expanded nonmultiplexed, and so on.

Figure 7 is a block diagram of the MC6801. Much of its versatility stems from its ability to operate in eight different modes. Each mode offers different configurations of memory (internal and/or external), I/O lines, and address size. The mode is selected by the logic levels present on pins 8 to 10 during the rising edge of the reset pulse. A detailed description of all the modes is not feasible here, so only the mode in use (expanded multiplexed) for this system is discussed; the others are mentioned briefly.

In all modes, ports 1 and 2 are available. Port 1 is an 8-bit port whose individual bits may be configured as inputs or outputs. Port 2 is a 5-bit port whose individual bits may be configured as inputs/outputs or used for the timer and

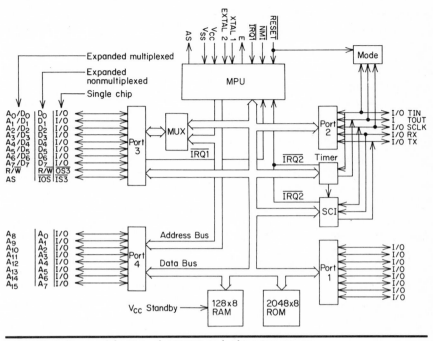

FIG. 7 *Block diagram of the Motorola MC6801 single-chip microcomputer.*

serial I/O operations (see Fig. 7). Note, however, that one line of port 2 is either the timer output or an input (no output). Also common to all modes is the location 0000–001F of the internal registers that are used to configure the ports.

Test modes 0 and 4 can be used to test internal memory and ports 3 and 4. Mode 7 is the single-chip mode and provides internal memory (RAM and ROM), with ports 3 and 4 available for I/O. In this mode, port 3 also has "handshake" ability via OS3 and IS3. If a small amount of additional memory (up to 256 bytes) is required, mode 5, expanded nonmultiplexed, can be used. In this mode, port 3 is configured as a data bus, and port 4 is configured as the lower-order address lines (A_0–A_7). If all eight address lines are not required, the remaining lines can be used as inputs. This is known as partial address decode. To accommodate larger amounts of external memory, expanded multiplex (modes 1, 2, 3, or 6) must be used. In these modes, port 3 is a multiplexed data bus and lower-order address bus; port 4 is the upper-order (A_8–A_{15}) address bus. The differences in these four modes are in the internal memory configuration: mode 3 has no internal RAM or ROM; mode 2 has only internal RAM; and modes 1 and 6 have internal RAM and ROM. In addition, mode 6 has partial address-decode capability. When used, the internal 2K ROM occupies hex-locations F800–FFFF, and the internal RAM (128 bytes) occupies hex-locations 0080–00FF.

For the Clever Counter system, modes 1 and 2 are used, mode 1 to test and modify software routines under control of the built-in ROM monitor (MC6801-L1); in operation, mode 2 (no internal ROM) is used so that the outboard EPROM memory can replace the internal ROM and reside at F800 through FFFF. This facilitates using either the MC6801 (ROM) or the MC68701 (EPROM). Of course, if the software routines in the outboard EPROM are written in position-independent code, it would not be necessary to put the EPROM at F800 through FFFF, but the instruction set of the MC6801, unlike the MC6809, does not readily support position-independent code.

As mentioned, port 3 functions as a time-multiplexed address/data bus in the expanded multiplexed modes. Address information is valid on the negative edge of the address strobe (AS) signal. This signal is used to control the 8-bit latch that provides A_0–A_7 and is shown in Fig. 6. The data bus is valid while the enable (E) signal is HIGH. This signal is used as part of the decoding logic that generates CS for the bus-connected circuits.

Other hardware features of the MC6801 are discussed in Sec. 5.5, *Interfacing between Major Parts of the System*, and the expanded instruction set and control registers are discussed in Sec. 5.6, *Software Overview*.

System Timing Controller—AMD9513 The AMD9513 STC,[13,14] like the MC6801, has a large variety of operating modes. Figure 8 is a block diagram of the AMD9513. The interface (lower left) is bus-oriented and can be configured to either an 8-bit or 16-bit data bus. Normally, the microprocessor's least significant address line is connected to the command, $\overline{\text{data}}$ (C/$\overline{\text{D}}$) line of the STC. Then, when $A_0 = 0$, a data register can be written or read, and when $A_0 = 1$, either the COMMAND register is written or the STATUS register is

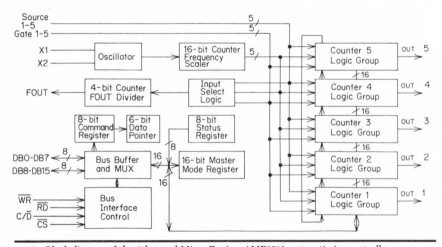

FIG. 8 Block diagram of the Advanced Micro Devices AMD9513 system-timing controller.

read. Five bits of the STATUS register reflect the state of the counter outputs (overflow). Thus, in the Clever Counter application, reading the STATUS register shows which counter(s) has overflowed. The microprocessor then uses this information to update the appropriate high-order decades in memory. Because most of the registers in the STC are 2 bytes wide (16 bits), information on byte transfer is required. This is also done by a bit in the STATUS register known as the byte pointer. When this bit is a **1**, the least significant byte (LSB) is transferred (written or read) next, and when it is a **0**, the most significant byte (MSB) is transferred next.

The COMMAND register permits direct control over each of the five general counters and, by setting the DATA POINTER register, controls which register is accessed by the data port. Some of the commands that are executed by the COMMAND register are arming and disarming the counter(s), loading and saving the counter(s), and setting or resetting the counter(s) overflow output. Special functions such as MASTER-RESET and selection of 8- or 16-bit data bus width are also done via the COMMAND register.

Although there are almost 450 bits available for control and operation of the STC, only two locations of address space are required. This is largely achieved with the DATA POINTER register, whose value, set via the COMMAND register, determines which of 19 (eighteen 16-bit, one 8-bit) registers is accessed by the data port for read-write operations.

The AMD9513 provides four modes of automatic sequencing of these 19 registers, permitting rapid access by the host processor. For example, if the automatic sequencing mode, known as hold cycle, is selected and the DATA POINTER register is initially set (via the COMMAND register) pointing at the HOLD register of counter 3, then the sequence is as follows each time the data port is accessed: 3—LSB, 3—MSB, 4—LSB, 4—MSB, 5—LSB, 5—MSB, 1—LSB, . . . , 3—LSB, and so on. Figure 9 shows the logic associated with each counter. The host microprocessor can read or write all the registers, but the counter itself is never directly accessed. Each counter can be programmed to count up or down and to count in binary or BCD by setting the appropriate bits in the COUNTER MODE register. This register also selects any 1 of the 16 counter inputs shown. The TCN-1 is the output (overflow) from the adjacent lower-numbered counter. When this input is selected, the counters are effectively concatenated. The five FREQ (frequency) inputs from the 16-bit frequency scaler (Fig. 8) are useful for waveform generation applications but are not used in the Clever Counter. The remaining 10 inputs [5—SRC (source), and 5—gate] can be used as counter inputs. In addition, the gate inputs can be used to gate the counter input. The gating selected (e.g., active HIGH, active LOW) is controlled by additional bits in the COUNTER MODE register.

The HOLD register can be used to read the counter without interrupting the counting process. Also, both the HOLD and LOAD registers can be used to preset a value in the counter (modulo control). Counters 1 and 2 have additional registers and logic that permit time-of-day operation and can "flag" when the counter contains a value of special interest (e.g., alarm condition).

Additional details about the STC are presented in Secs. 5.5 *(Interfacing between Major Parts of the System)* and 5.6 *(Software Overview)*.

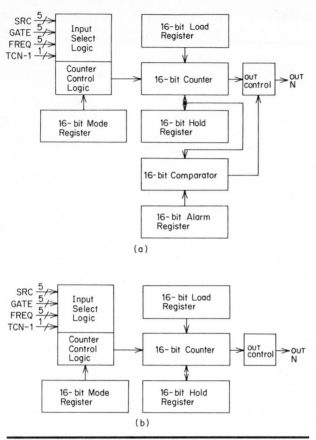

FIG. 9 *Two types of programmable counters in the AMD9513 system-timing controller: (a) Counter logic groups 1 and 2; (b) Counter logic groups 3, 4, and 5.*

***Alphanumeric Intelligent Display*™** The Litronix DL-2416 is a 4-digit, 16-segment (plus decimal) alphanumeric Intelligent Display.™ By combining several technologies, such as CMOS large-scale integration (LSI) integrated circuits (ICs) monolithic light-emitting diode (LED) displays, and plastic immersion optics, the DL-2416 dramatically reduces the support hardware normally used in display applications. This display stores the ASCII coded signals it receives, then translates and displays these signals as alphanumeric characters without any external support hardware.

Figure 10 is a block diagram of this display system. Data in ASCII code is taken from the seven data lines and stored in RAM. The system then repeatedly sequences through the RAM, translating the ASCII data into 17 lines that drive the LED display. To the host microprocessor, the DL-2416 looks like a write-only memory. Once the ASCII data is written, the microprocessor is free to perform other functions.

Clock and Calendar The NEC μPD1990C is a serial I/O calendar and clock chip contained in a 14-pin dual in-line package (DIP). Using CMOS LSI, this device indicates the month, date, day of week, hour, minute, and second. In the event of a power failure, continued calendar operation can be maintained by a small backup battery. The current consumption is typically only 20 μA.

Figure 11 is a block diagram of the μPD1990C. Note that this is not a bus-oriented part, so interfacing it to a microprocessor is not as straightforward as interfacing the previously discussed parts. The three command inputs, C_2, C_1, and C_0, select the various test and operating modes, as shown in Table 1. The calendar is initially set by entering the register shift mode and serially shifting 40 bits (ten 4-bit words) of data via the data-in pin. Each 4-bit word is input with the least significant bit (LSB) first (that is, 1, 2, 4, 8). The input order is second $\times$ 1, second $\times$ 10, minute $\times$ 1, minute $\times$ 10, and so on, as indicated in the time counter in Fig. 11. Once the ten 4-bit words have been entered, the time set mode is used to latch this value in the time counter. To read the calendar, the time read mode is used to transfer the contents of the time counter to the SHIFT register, and then the register shift mode is used. The data is read from the data-out pin. The first bit available is the LSB of the least significant word (second $\times$ 1).

Note that when the register hold mode is used, a 1-Hz signal is available at the data-out pin. This feature is used in the Clever Counter as the time base for the TOY and the timers. In addition to the 1-Hz signal, there are three TP modes in which 64-, 256-, and 2048-Hz signals are available at the TP pin.

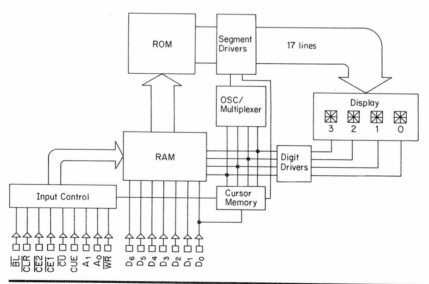

FIG. 10 *Block diagram of the Litronix DL-2416 alphanumeric intelligent display.*

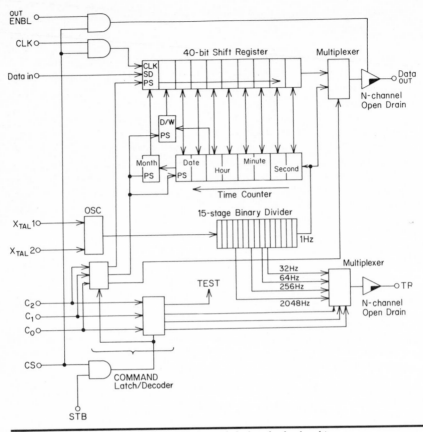

FIG. 11   Block diagram of the NEC μPD1990C serial clock and calendar chip.

TABLE 1   Test and operating modes of the UPD1990C clock and calendar device

Group	C_2	C_1	C_0	Function	
0	0	0	0	Register hold	Data out = 1Hz
	0	0	1	Register shift	Data out = [LSB]
	0	1	0	Time set	Data out = [LSB]
	0	1	1	Time read	Data out = [LSB]
1	1	0	0	TP = 64 Hz set	
	1	0	1	TP = 256 Hz set	
	1	1	0	TP = 2048 Hz set	
	1	1	1	Test mode set	

NOTE: Groups "0" and "1" hold their functions independently.

5.5 Interfacing Between Major Parts of the System

Interfacing to the 6801 When interfacing bus-oriented parts to a microprocessor, there is a strong temptation to connect the read-write line of the microprocessor to the read-write line of the part and to generate the CS by decoding one or more microprocessor address lines. Although this may work with some memory parts, it is not feasible here for two reasons: (1) In many parts CS controls the tristate logic of the data bus. Therefore, if the microprocessor's address lines are used to generate CS, there would be a bus conflict on the multiplexed lines of the MC6801. (2) In the AMD9513, the read ($\overline{RD}$) line controls the tristate logic of its data bus. If this line were directly connected to the $\overline{RD}$ line of the MC6801, the same bus conflict would result because the timing of the $\overline{RD}$ and address lines of the MC6801 is the same. In addition to bus conflicts, an interface that works with *typical* timing specifications may result. Then, when a part is replaced or the system is duplicated, errors appear. To avoid these problems, it is best to design an interface by carefully studying timing relationships.

Timing Relationships of the MC6801 Figure 12 shows the timing relationships for the MC6801 in the expanded multiplexed mode. The lower-order address lines (A_0–A_7) do not originate in the MC6801 but are derived from port 3 using an external 8-bit latch (Fig. 6). The latch is a "transparent" type of D flip-flop. This means that while AS is HIGH, the latch outputs will follow the inputs, but when AS goes LOW, the outputs are latched. The AS signal loads this latch with the timing indicated in Fig. 12.

Because data information is multiplexed, the enable (data strobe) signal (E) *must* be used for all data transfers. Before E goes LOW, the data is valid for a minimum of 225 ns (t_{DSW}) during a write operation and must be held valid (by the device being read) for a minimum of 80 ns (t_{DSR}) during a read operation. Note that after E goes LOW, the minimum hold time for R/$\overline{W}$, A_8–A_{15}, and data (write) is 20 ns (t_{AH} and t_{HW}), and the hold time for data (read) is 10 ns (t_{HR}). Because of the latch, the hold time of A_0–A_7 is extended ($\approx$ 75 ns).

Having briefly discussed the timing of the MC6801, we now consider the interface requirements of each device connected to the MC6801.

Interfacing the AMD9513 STC To interface the AMD9513 STC, the pertinent signals are $\overline{CS}$, C/$\overline{D}$, read ($\overline{RD}$), write ($\overline{WR}$), and data. Figure 13 shows the timing relationships for these signals. Note that $\overline{CS}$ must be present during the rising edge of both $\overline{RD}$ and $\overline{WR}$. Because $\overline{CS}$ does not control the tristate logic ($\overline{RD}$ does), the address lines of the MC6801 can be used (after decoding) for $\overline{CS}$. This will meet all the timing requirements on $\overline{CS}$ for both R/W operations. If the data strobe (E) and the R/$\overline{W}$ of the MC6801 are gated with some logic, the resulting signals can be used for $\overline{RD}$ and $\overline{WR}$ of the AMD9513. Figure 14 shows the complete interface. The two gates to which the E signal is applied are low-level Schottky (74 LS) because their maximum output delay for a **0**-to-**1** transition is 15 ns, whereas the maximum delay for a standard (74) gate

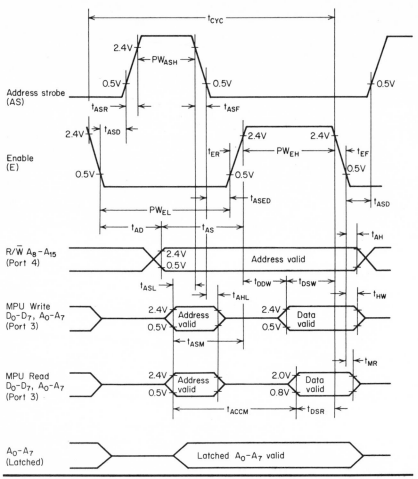

FIG. 12 *Timing relationships for the MC6801 in the expanded multiplexed mode.*

is 22 ns. This latter figure might cause problems, particularly if the decoder delay is small because the minimum hold time (t_{AH}, Fig. 12) of the address lines generating $\overline{CS}$ is 20 ns. Therefore, a gate delay of 22 ns might remove $\overline{CS}$ before the end of $\overline{WR}$ or $\overline{RD}$, violating the timing specified in Fig. 11. The latched address line A_0 meets all the requirements for the C/$\overline{D}$ line.

***Interfacing the TMS2516* EPROM**   Figure 15 shows the timing relationship for Texas Instruments' TMS2516 EPROM. Because $\overline{CS}$ controls the Hi-Z mode of the data bus, the data strobe E of the MC6801 must be used as part of the decoder generating $\overline{CS}$. The other decoder inputs will be address lines. For a read operation, the MC6801 requires that the data be valid for a minimum of 80 ns (t_{DSR}, Fig. 12) and have a hold time of 10 ns (t_{HR}, Fig. 12). The timing is now checked to see that these figures are met. The minimum hold time of the

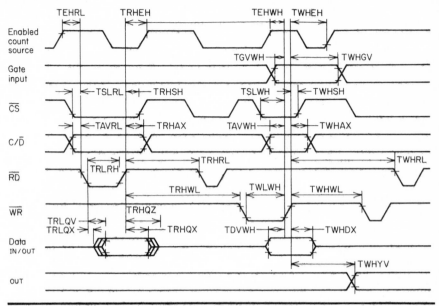

FIG. 13 Timing waveforms for the AM9513 system-timing controller.

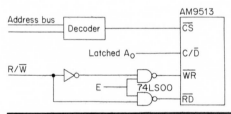

FIG. 14 Interface circuitry between the MC6801 microcomputer and the Am9513 system-timing controller.

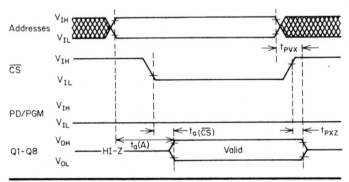

FIG. 15 Read-cycle timing for the Texas Instruments TMS2516, a 16-kilobit EPROM device.

EPROM, t_{PXZ}, is 10 ns and is measured from the trailing edge of $\overline{CS}$. Because E is used to generate $\overline{CS}$, $\overline{CS}$ lags E by the delay in the decoder. Therefore, the minimum data hold time, measured from the falling edge of E, is 10 ns plus the decoder delay, so the hold-time requirement is met. The maximum access time, $t_a(A)$, from address to data is 450 ns for the EPROM. The minimum time from valid address to valid E, t_{AS}, is 210 ns minimum (Fig. 12). Because the minimum width of E is 450 ns, data is valid for:

$$450 - (450 - 210) > 80 \text{ ns}$$

so the maximum $t_a(A)$ meets the read-data requirement. The other EPROM access time that must be checked is $t_a(CS)$, which is 150 ns maximum. Because $\overline{CS}$ lags E by the decoder delay (T_D), the appropriate expression is

$$E - T_D - t_a(CS) > 80 \text{ ns} \qquad \text{or} \qquad 450 - T_D - 150 > 80 \text{ ns}$$

Therefore, T_D must be less than 220 ns, which is easily met by commonly used decoders.

Interfacing the Litronix DL-2416 Display   Figure 16 shows the timing relationship for the DL-2416 display. If the R/$\overline{W}$ and E lines of the MC6801 microprocessor are gated, the resulting signal can be used to drive the $\overline{WR}$ line of the display. This will meet the requirements for the address setup time, t_{AS}, and the data setup time, t_{DS}, but will not satisfy the data hold time, t_{DH}. In addition, the gating delay of E, which previously relaxed the hold-time requirement for a read operation, now, because data is not delayed, increases the hold-time requirements for a write operation. Assuming a 74LS gate, the minimum hold time required is t_{DH} + 15 or 65 ns, whereas the hold time available is only 20 ns (t_{HW}, Fig. 12). Keep in mind that these are worst-case requirements; the author has tested these displays successfully without modifying the

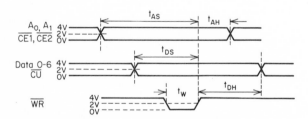

Switching Characteristics of the DL-2416 at 25° C

Symbol	Parameter	Units min
t_W	Write pulse	200 ns
t_{DS}	Data setup time	100 ns
t_{DH}	Data hold time	50 ns
t_{AS}	Address setup time	300 ns
t_{AH}	Address hold time	0 ns
t_{CLR}	Clear time (see text)	15 ms

FIG. 16   *Timing waveforms of the Litronix DL-2416 alphanumeric intelligent display.*

hold time. However, to avoid problems, the hold time must be modified. This can be done by latching the display's data lines, just as the lower-order address lines are latched. The signal E is used to control the latch, resulting in a hold time greater than 450 ns. The latched data is then used for both displays. The remaining display lines are straightforward; both chip enables, CE1 and CE2, are tied together and driven by an address decoder, and the digit selects, A_0 and A_1, are driven by the latched address lines A_0 and A_1.

Interfacing the NEC Calendar Chip As mentioned, the NEC μPD1990C is not a bus-oriented part. Figure 17a shows its timing relationships. This timing is very slow compared to the MC6801 bus timing (Fig. 12), so the I/O lines of port 1 are used for this interface. To reduce the number of I/O lines required, some functions are not used. Referring to Fig. 11, the output enable OUT ENBL,

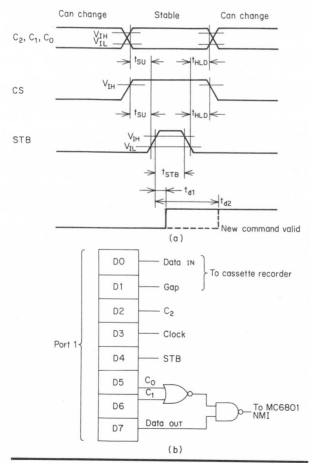

FIG. 17 Interfacing the NEC μPD1990C serial clock and calendar chip: (a) command input timing diagram; and (b) connections to generate the nonmaskable interrupt (NMI) from the inputs to this device.

and CS lines are tied high, and because the TP output is not used, the command line controlling TP, C_2, is connected to ground. This reduces the number of I/O lines required to six. Two of these lines, Data OUT and Data IN, are connected to the MSB and LSB of port 1, respectively, to simplify the program shifting requirements. To send the calendar a byte of data, the following sequence is used: output through LSB, shift right, output through LSB. . . . To receive a byte of data, the following sequence is used: input from MSB, shift right, input from MSB. . . . The shift operations are performed on a data word, not on port 1 lines because logic levels on the remaining port 1 lines must be maintained. The remaining four calendar lines, clock, STB, C_0, and C_1, are connected to port 1, as shown in Fig. 17b. When the command lines C_0 and C_1 are both zero, a NOR gate enables the 1-Hz signal appearing on Data OUT of the calendar to drive the NMI of the MC6801. Thus, the NMI is disabled automatically when the calendar is read, written, or shifted (see Table 1) and enabled only when the signal out of Data OUT is 1 Hz.

Because the calendar is a CMOS part operating with 2.5V, 100-K resistors are required in series with all its active inputs. In addition, a pull-up resistor (to + 5V) is required on its Data OUT signal.

Interfacing the Cassette Recorder   The cassette recorder is an incremental write-only type manufactured by Memodyne.[15] Three signals—clock, data, and gap—control data writing. The recording format is such that 2 gap bits and 4 data bits are required for each BCD digit.

Each positive transition of clock (CLK) writes either 1 bit of gap or 1 bit of data. If the gap signal is a **1**, a gap (no flux change) is written; if it is a **0**, data is written. The data signal shares the LSB of port 1 with the calendar, and gap is connected to port 1 bit 1, as shown in Fig. 17.

The Clock signal requires a 100-Hz square wave that is obtained from the built-in timer of the MC6801. This timer consists of an 8-bit control and status register, a 16-bit free-running counter, driven by the system clock (E), a 16-bit output compare register (OCR), and a 16-bit input capture register. To generate an output waveform, a software routine reads the counter and adds the desired pulse width (in increments of E). This total is then stored in the OCR. When the free-running counter is equal to this total, an output compare flag, OCF, is set in the timer control and status register (TCSR). At this time, the level set in bit 0 of the TCSR appears on the timer output line. If enabled, an interrupt, EOCI (enable output compare interrupt), will also be generated. The software uses the OCF flag or the EOCI interrupt to toggle bit 0 of the TCSR and reload the OCR. This causes the timer output level to toggle when the next OCF occurs. In addition to generating output waveforms, the timer can analyze input waveforms by using the input capture register along with additional flag and interrupt bits in the TCSR.

Interfacing Serial I/O Terminals   The pocket TTY or serial terminal is used with the built-in serial port of the MC6801. The built-in registers of this port (port 2) are shown in Fig. 18. With the addition of some level shifters, interfacing to an RS232-C device is possible.

The serial port is a full-duplex asynchronous serial communications inter-

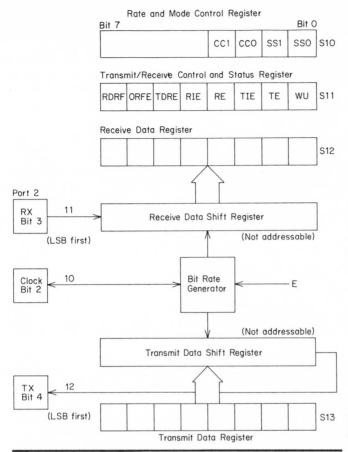

FIG. 18 *Serial input/output circuits on the MC6801 chip.*

face (SCI). The SCI can provide two data formats, mark/space or bi-phase, at selectable data rates. These are controlled by the 4 bits in the rate and mode register (RMR). After setting these 4 bits, transmit and receive operations are controlled by bits TE (transmit enable) and RE (receiver enable) of the control and status register (CSR). With TE set, the transmit line is marking (all 1s) until a byte of data is transferred to the transmit data register (TDR). At that time, a start bit (0), 8 data bits, and a stop bit (1) will be transmitted. When the TDR is empty, bit TDRE (transmit data register empty) is set. In addition to this flag, an interrupt can be generated if bit TIE (transmit interrupt enable) is set. The flag or interrupt is used to request additional data from the controlling software.

For receive operation, bit RE functions like bit TE. The flag and interrupt conditions for receive operation are RDRF (receiver data register full) and RIE (receiver interrupt enable). In addition, if an overrun or framing error occurs, bit ORFE (Overrun framing error) is set. An overrun occurs when a new byte is received while the previous byte is still in the data register. Framing errors are caused by improper synchronization.

Address Decoding for All Peripheral Devices   Decoding is often overlooked. After all, gating several microprocessor address lines to generate a CS signal could not be more straightforward. However, the resulting "don't-care" address states can put an unnecessary overhead on the software and encumber system expansion.

At a Spring 1980 seminar sponsored by National Semiconductor, three CS decoding techniques were considered: *general case, limited decode,* and *no decode.* In the general case, the address bus is compared to one specific address. When there is a match, CS is generated. This case was dismissed quickly because a 16-bit address bus would require a complex part in a 40-pin package to generate one CS signal. In limited decoding, several address lines are used with a gating structure to generate CS. The remaining address lines become don't-care address states. This method is probably the one most often used. The last case, no decoding, uses one address line as a CS for each peripheral device. Although this method is the simplest from a hardware viewpoint, each peripheral device occupies a large section of memory space, rendering this method of limited practical use.

The don't-care address states that occur when using limited decoding are actually required in memory applications. For example, consider a 2K-byte memory. Because A_0 through A_{10} are used to access the 2K memory locations, only A_{11}–A_{15} are required for decoding. On the other hand, consider a 4-digit display whose digits are selected by A_0 and A_1; this leaves 14 address lines to be decoded. In practice, only a few of these lines are actually used. For example, if a system has four displays that start at the hex-address 8000, a good way to decode would seem to be 8XX0 to 8XXF. The X's are don't care states, and the 8 is specified by decoding the four most significant address lines. Because each display requires A_0 and A_1 to specify the digit, A_2 and A_3 ($\overline{A_2} \cdot \overline{A_3}$, $A_2 \cdot \overline{A_3}$, $\overline{A_2} \cdot A_3$, $A_2 \cdot A_3$) are used to specify each of the four displays. In this manner, all addressed are consecutive, which simplifies the software. However, if the system is expanded to eight displays, redesign is required. With consecutive addresses, it is easy to modify the software so that it indexes through eight displays instead of four, but because of the decoding used, implementation is difficult from the hardware viewpoint. It requires that $\overline{A_4}$ must be gated with the A_0–A_3 terms of the four original displays. If these terms were implemented with two-input gates, extensive rewiring must be done. If this is not practical, the addresses of the additional display can be put elsewhere (for example, 9000), but this will require a software patch. Depending upon the system software, it may be easier to rewire instead of reprogram.

Clearly, what is needed is a more flexible scheme for decoding. One promising method involves using an EPROM as a decoder. The EPROM's 8 data lines are used as eight CS signals. To use this method with a 2K-byte EPROM (for example, TMS2516), the $\overline{CS}$ is tied LOW (enabled) and address lines A_{10}–A_0 are connected to A_{15}–A_5 of the microprocessor's address bus. Thus, all address combinations of A_{15}–A_5 are uniquely decoded by the 2K words in the

EPROM. By programming the appropriate 1s and 0s in the EPROM, eight CS signals having only A_4–A_0 as don't care states can be generated. Specifying an address without don't care states for a 4-digit display requires gating the EPROM-generated CS signal with A_4, A_3, and A_2. If an 8K-byte EPROMs is used, it decodes A_4 and A_3 so only A_2 need be gated. This method is much more flexible than limited decoding. In addition, any required changes are done by reprogramming the EPROM as opposed to changing the wiring.

When this method is used, timing must be considered. Suppose an EPROM is used to generate CS for the DL-2416 display. The DL-2416 timing requirements (Fig. 16) show that the maximum EPROM access time from address $t_a(A)$ should be approximately 350 ns. Because the maximum $t_a(A)$ of many standard EPROMs is 450 ns, an A version (for example, TMS27A16) must be used.

5.6 Software Overview

Although here software is discussed separately from hardware, the designer should realize that the two are closely related. For example, recall from the discussion of the calendar interface that specific connections to port 1 were made to *simplify the programming*. Generally, the designer should have a good idea of the software support required *while considering* a particular hardware design to eliminate those designs that seem efficient from a hardware viewpoint but which may encumber the support software.

Because software costs are so high, many methods for reducing these costs have been published. These methods generally involve writing programs in a structured high-level language (e.g., Pascal or C) and storing the generated machine code in position-independent ROMs. Position-independent code allows the ROM to operate anywhere in the memory space. For example, the programs in a 2K-byte ROM would operate the same way whether the ROM was decoded for $(0000-07FF)_{HEX}$, $(F800-FFFF)_{HEX}$, or any other address. Unfortunately, microcomputers such as the Motorola 6800 (and 6801) or the Intel 8080 do not readily support high-level languages such as Pascal.[16] On these machines compilations of even simple arithmetic expressions lead to prohibitive amounts of machine code, and more complex expressions are difficult or impossible to compile. In addition, the instruction set and addressing modes of these machines do not support position-independent code. Because of these difficulties, the software for this application is written at the assembly language level.

Rather than purchase a development system for the 6801, an existing LSI-11-based minicomputer from Digital Equipment Corporation was used in conjunction with a cross assembler. This is more cost-effective than the development system. If another microprocessor is used on the next project, only a new cross assembler is required. Cross assemblers are available from a number of software houses. The one chosen for this application is supplied by Virtual Systems, Inc., and includes a cross assembler, linking loader, librarian, and formatter. The following overview is presented rather than detailed description of how this equipment operates.

The librarian maintains and updates frequently used subroutines or program modules. If one of these subroutines or program modules is desired, only its name is required as input to the cross assembler (for example, JSR LOOP). When the cross assembler output is used by the linking loader, an unresolved external (LOOP) will be present. On command, the loader will then search the library for unresolved externals; when one is found, it is loaded.

The cross assembler is a relocating type. Relocation permits programs to have different memory bounds without being reassembled. However, unlike position-independent code, a relocatable program *must* be reloaded with the linking loader. This output from the linking loader is then used to reprogram the EPROMs to the new memory bounds. The cross assembler also supports a RAM/ROM environment by preceding variables requiring RAM with a DSCT (data section) command and preceding fixed instructions with a PSCT (program section) command. At load time, the linking loader will commit code following DSCT to RAM and code following PSCT to ROM. The user must specify to the linking loader the start addresses of RAM and ROM. After assembling and loading, the formatter uses the output of the linking loader to generate formats suitable for EPROM programmers.

The EPROM programmer used in this application plugs into the bus of the LSI-11. It is less expensive than stand-alone programmers and can use the resources of the LSI-11. This programmer is manufactured by Interplex, Inc., Mountain View, California.

Assembly Programming Style   There is nothing more frustrating than trying to decipher an undocumented software routine. Usually the effort is abandoned, and the routine is completely rewritten at considerable expense. To avoid this problem, documentation is essential.

Any existing undocumented routines should be run through a disassembler, to at least provide rudimentary documentation. As implied by its name, a disassembler's output is the normal input to an assembler. A disassembler for 6800 type machines is found in Ref. 17. For new routines, using an assembler is a good way of documenting, particularly if liberal use is made of the comment field. The style in which the program is written also determines its ability to be understood. Generally, programs that are broken down into a string of short subroutines are easier to understand, debug, and modify.[18] In small routines this may result in longer code, but in complex routines shorter code usually results because the subroutines are used a number of times. In addition, the author has found machine language flowcharts helpful aids in software development.

Machine Language Flowcharts (MLFCs)   Flowcharts are often used with higher-level languages to develop methods or algorithms for the particular application at hand. Each entry in a "box" may represent 10 or more lines of higher-language statements. However, in machine language flowcharts (MLFCs), each box entry represents a single machine-level instruction. The author has found that MLFCs are much easier to follow and understand than assembly level listings.

For example, consider the MLFC that updates the TOY clock shown in Fig. 19. Every second the 1-Hz signal from the calendar chip produces an NMI, which causes the program to vector to the entry point shown in Fig. 19. The TOY data consists of 10 decades as follows: days—4 (2 HIGH, 2 LOW), hours—2, minutes—2, and seconds—2. As indicated, these decades are stored in RAM locations 81 through 85; location 80 holds the counting modulus—60 for seconds and minutes, 24 for hours, and 0 (actually 100) for days. With this information and the MLFC, a person familiar with the microprocessor's instruction set can see at a glance what the routine is doing. It also facilitates changes and additions by a person who did not write the original routine. The following explanation is for those unfamiliar with this particular instruction set.

First, assume that the TOY is such that the seconds are unequal to 59 ($\neq 59$); therefore, all that has to be done is to add 1 s to the current TOY. The index register is first set to 85, after which 60 is stored in 80. The first BSR (sec) indicates a Branch-to-Subroutine to UPDATE. The first instruction of the sub-

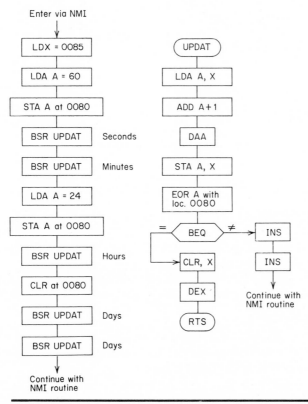

FIG. 19 *Machine language flow chart (MLFC) for the time-of-year (TOY) routine.*

routine, LDAA, X, loads accumulator A via the index (X) register. Because the X register is set to 85, the contents of location 85 (i.e., seconds) are loaded into accumulator A. One is added to A (ADD A) and A is decimal-adjusted (DAA). The decimal adjust is a rather involved instruction, but basically it permits counting in base 10. However, to use it properly, the condition code register (CCR) of the MC6801 must be correctly set. This cannot be done by the 1-byte increment instruction, so the 2-byte ADD A must be used. The updated accumulator A is then stored back in location 85 (STA A, X), and accumulator A is tested to see if it equals 60. Because the ≠59 assumption was made, the updated value is unequal to 60 and the test (EOR-A and BEQ) causes the ≠ path to be followed. At this point the TOY function is complete. However, because the subroutine that does the updating was entered via a BRANCH subroutine (BSR), the stack register was decremented twice to hold a return vector (not used) and must be restored before continuing. This is done with the two INS (Increment Stack) instructions. The NMI routine then continues with its other operations, such as updating the active timers.

If the seconds of the TOY are equal to 59 (= 59), the operation is the same and 60 is initially stored in location 85. However, the test for 60 is now true and the equal (=) branch is taken. This causes location 85 (seconds) to be set to zero (CLR, X). The X register is decremented (DEC) from 85 to 84 (minutes), and a subroutine return (RTS) vectors the program to the BSR (min) instruction. This causes the UPDATE subroutine to be reentered, and minutes are updated. If 60 results, the above repeats, but the RTS returns to the LDA A = 24 instruction. When stored in location 80, this established the modulus for hours. The process is similar for days.

This entire TOY routine uses only 22 instructions and demonstrates how easily the microprocessor handles the mixed units of days, hours, and so on. In fact, this one routine replaces TOY modules implemented with MSI logic and costing $1000.

5.7 Memory Considerations

RAM The MC6801 has an on-board RAM of 128 words located at 80 through FF. To keep the Clever Counter design simple, the software is constrained to use this RAM only. However, during the program development phase, additional RAM was required because the ROM monitor ("Lil-Bug") uses almost all the on-board RAM.

Most of the on-board RAM is used for the counters, timers, and TOY clock as shown in Table 2. The number of RAM words is: TOY—10, timers—15, preset time—15, and high-order counter decades—5. These and other volatile flag and status words are stored in the lower half (80—BF) of the RAM. This portion of the RAM has the ability to retain its information via a backup battery (8 mA maximum). Storing all the volatile data in this area of RAM facilitates retaining this data if required by some applications. It is not implemented in the current version of the Clever Counter.

TABLE 2 *Assignments of all RAM locations (Most of the locations are for counters, timers, and the TOY clock.)*

Address	Content		Address	Content	
0080	60,24,0	⎫	00AF	C65 ⎫	⎫
0081	H day		00B0	C43 ⎬ 3	
0082	L day		00B1	C21 ⎭	
0083	Hour		00B2	C65 ⎫	Complete
0084	Min		00B3	C43 ⎬ 4	Counter
0085	Sec	⎬ TOY	00B4	C21 ⎭	(continued)
0086	H day buffer		00B5	C65 ⎫	
0087	L day buffer		00B6	C43 ⎬ 5	
0088	Hour buffer		00B7	C21 ⎭	⎭
0089	Min buffer		00B8	Sec	⎫
008A	Sec buffer	⎭	00B9	Min	
008B	T65 ⎫	⎫	00BA	Hour	⎬ Calendar
008C	T43 ⎬ 1		00BB	Date	
008D	T21 ⎭		00BC	Mo. & Day	⎭
008E	T65 ⎫				
008F	T43 ⎬ 2				
0090	T21 ⎭		00BD	⎫	
0091	T65 ⎫				
0092	T43 ⎬ 3	⎬ Timers	to	⎬ Working Variables (flags, etc.)	
0093	T21 ⎭				
0094	T65 ⎫		00DF	⎭	
0095	T43 ⎬ 4				
0096	T21 ⎭				
0097	T65 ⎫				
0098	T43 ⎬ 5		00E0	⎫	
0099	T21 ⎭	⎭			
009A	P65 ⎫	⎫	to	⎬ Stack area	
009B	P43 ⎬ 1				
009C	P21 ⎭		00FF	⎭	
009D	P65 ⎫				
009E	P43 ⎬ 2				
009F	P21 ⎭				
00A0	P65 ⎫				
00A1	P43 ⎬ 3	⎬ Preset Time			
00A2	P21 ⎭				
00A3	P65 ⎫				
00A4	P43 ⎬ 4				
00A5	P21 ⎭				
00A6	P65 ⎫				
00A7	P43 ⎬ 5				
00A8	P21 ⎭	⎭			
00A9	C65 ⎫	⎫			
00AA	C43 ⎬ 1				
00AB	C21 ⎭	Complete counter			
00AC	C65 ⎫				
00AD	C43 ⎬ 2				
00AE	C21 ⎭	⎭			

EPROM   As mentioned, the external EPROM must be compatible with the EPROM contained in the MC68701. This requires a 2K-byte EPROM starting at location F800. The 2K bytes are more than adequate for the Clever Counter routines.

The Motorola Lil-Bug Monitor   Lil-Bug is a monitor contained in the MC6801 ROM that is used for program development and debugging. It can load and dump programs via a terminal, read and write memory, read and write registers, and establish and execute breakpoints. Its most noteworthy feature is its ability to trace program operation by executing one instruction at a time. In this mode of operation, the instruction OP code and the contents of the microprocessor's registers are printed on a terminal as each instruction is executed; this greatly facilitates program debugging. Program debugging is also aided by the Branch-Never (BRN) instruction, which is one of the several new MC6801 instructions. This instruction can replace other Branch instructions to reduce, for example, the printout in a trace operation. More detailed operation of the Lil-Bug monitor is found in Ref. 19.

5.8   Program Routines

General   When power is applied to the Clever Counter, a microprocessor reset pulse is generated by a MCG-5* IC. During reset, the states of the three mode-selection pins (8 to 10) are latched into the mode control register. By using diodes from pins 8 and 10 to the reset pin (6) and a pull-up resistor on pin 9, mode 2 (010_2) is latched into the MC6801. In addition, reset clears most of the MC6801's internal registers and starts executing the program located at the address contained in FFFE and FFFF. If an interrupt occurs at this point, it could cause loss of program control if the interrupt vectors to a RAM location whose contents are not yet defined. Generally, it is good practice to inhibit interrupts until the system has completed its initialization routines. Reset, by clearing the registers, particularly the data direction register of port 1, inhibits NMIs. Recall from the calendar chip discussion that the 1-Hz NMI is gated by the C_0 and C_1 outputs from port 1, but clearing the data direction register configures the lines of port 1 as inputs, thereby inhibiting the NMI. Reset also sets the I (inhibit) bit of the CCR, which disables the remaining interrupts (IRQ 1 and IRQ 2).

INITIALIZATION *Routine*   The INITIALIZATION routine starting address is stored in locations FFFE and FFFF. The first function of this routine is to configure the registers of the MC6801. The stack pointer (SP) register is done first. Basically, the stack is a last-in first-out (LIFO) queue in RAM managed by the SP. Each byte "pushed" on the stack causes the SP to decrement, and each byte "pulled" from the stack causes it to increment. During an interrupt, three

*Hi-G Electronics, Windsor Locks, Connecticut.

1-byte registers (accumulators A, B, and CCR) and two byte registers (INDEX and PROGRAM COUNTER) are pushed on the stack; this decrements the SP seven times. The stack must be large enough to accommodate two concurrent interrupts and several nested subroutines (subroutines push the SP twice). Therefore, the stack should have a RAM area of about 30 locations. If enough room is not allotted, the stack will overrun other RAM locations and "bomb" the system. For the Clever Counter, the top of the stack is put at the top of RAM (location 00FF), and all other RAM storage is below 00E0 (see Table 2).

Figure 20 shows the byte address and bit assignments for the MC6801's internal registers. In expanded-multiplexed mode 2, ports 3 and 4 become buses. Therefore, locations 04 through 07 and 0F do not access the registers shown in Fig. 20 but are decoded externally. This permits external hardware emulation of data ports 3 and 4 that respond to the internal data port addresses. If implemented, this allows system expansion (e.g., from mode 7 to mode 2) without changing the routines for the data ports.

The I/O data registers of ports 1 and 2 (02 and 03) are written *before* the data direction registers (00 and 01). This prevents port 1 from sending a 00 code to the calendar, which would enable the NMI. The on-board serial channel is accessed via port 2 and configured by writing 07 in location 10. This sets control bits CCO and CCI (see Fig. 18) for the internal clock source and releases bit 2 for use as a general I/O line. It also specifies NRZ data and sets the baud rate select bits, S1 and S0, for 300 Bd. This assumes that the input clock to the MC6801 is 4.915 MHz. If half this frequency (2.4576 MHz) is used, the baud rate is 150, and so on. At this time the serial channel is disabled by writing 0s to the receiver and transmit enable bits (RE and TE) in location 11.

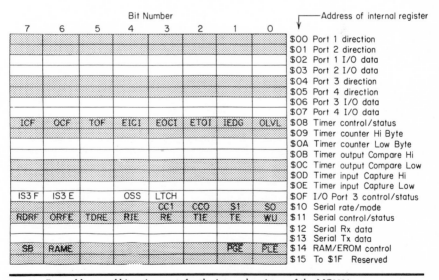

7	6	5	4	3	2	1	0	Address of internal register
								$00 Port 1 direction
								$01 Port 2 direction
								$02 Port 1 I/O data
								$03 Port 2 I/O data
								$04 Port 3 direction
								$05 Port 4 direction
								$06 Port 3 I/O data
								$07 Port 4 I/O data
ICF	OCF	TOF	EICI	EOCI	ETOI	IEDG	OLVL	$08 Timer control/status
								$09 Timer counter Hi Byte
								$0A Timer counter Low Byte
								$0B Timer output Compare Hi
								$0C Timer output Compare Low
								$0D Timer input Capture Hi
								$0E Timer input Capture Low
IS3F	IS3E		OSS	LTCH				$0F I/O Port 3 control/status
			CC1	CCO		S1	S0	$10 Serial rate/mode
RDRF	ORFE	TDRE	RIE	RE	TIE	TE	WU	$11 Serial control/status
								$12 Serial Rx data
								$13 Serial Tx data
SB	RAME					PGE	PLE	$14 RAM/EROM control
								$15 To $1F Reserved

FIG. 20   *Byte address and bit assignments for the internal registers of the MC6801.*

When these bits are enabled, data is transmitted by first checking the status of TDRE—bit 5 of location 11—and then loading the byte to be transmitted in the TDR—location 13; once this is done, the bit-by-bit data transmission proceeds automatically. Similarly, serial data is received by checking the status of receive-data-register full (RDRF—bit 7 of location 11) and then reading location 12. If desired, these two conditions can generate interrupts by setting bits TIE and RIE (transmit and receive interrupt enable). Thus, serial communication is reduced to merely reading/writing two locations as opposed to the hardware and software overhead required to support bit-by-bit data transmission in microprocessors not having an on-board serial port.

The last set of MC6801 registers to initialize are those for the timer function. The 16-bit free-running counter (locations 09 and 0A in Fig. 20) also provides the internal clock for the serial channel. Therefore, writing into these locations must be avoided. The INPUT CAPTURE register (locations 0D and 0E) is normally employed for waveform analysis and is not used in this application. To enable generating an output wave form, bit 1 of port 2's DATA DIRECTION register (location 01) must be set. This allows the value of the timer's OLVL (output level) bit (bit 0 of location 08) to appear at pin 9 of the MC6801.

To generate the 100-Hz clock for the cassette recorder, the value 2FBB is added to the OCR each time the output compare flag (OCF—bit 6 of location 08) is set. The OCF is set when the OCR matches the counter. Also, at this time the OLVL bit is toggled by executing an EXCLUSIVE OR instruction. The value 2FBB assumes a system clock of 4.9152 MHz, which makes the enable pulse frequency 1.2288 MHz (one-fourth of system clock). If desired, an interrupt can be generated when OCF goes true by setting enable output compare interrupt (EOCI—bit 3 of location 08).

5.9 Hardware-Oriented Routines

Initial Setup of Counters   To configure the AMD9513 STC, first issue a MASTER RESET by writing FF into its COMMAND register. This disables all five counters and loads hex-code 0B00 into each COUNTER MODE register and hex-code 0000 in the MASTER MODE register.

Each COUNTER MODE register controls gating (bits 15–13), count source selection (bits 12–8), count control (bits 7–3), and output control (bits 2–0). Initially, all gating is disabled by setting each gating bit to zero. However, Clever Counter provides commands that allow a user to select either high- or low-level gating for each counter. The count source selection bits are set to **10001** for counter 1, **10010** for counter 2, **10011** for counter 3, and so forth. This specifies front-panel input 1 for counter 1, input 2 for counter 2, and so on. It also specifies counting on the falling edge of the input pulse. The count control bits are set to **00111**, which specifies repetitive BCD up-counting. Lastly, the output control bits are set to **010**, which specifies a high output level when the counter overflows. The overall hex-code for COUNTER MODE register 1 is 113A.

For this application, the pertinent bits in the MASTER MODE register are 0–3 and 13–14. Setting bits 0–3 to zero disables both the time-of-day mode and the special comparators (alarm). A data bus width of 8 bits is selected by setting bit 13 to zero. The only bit in the MASTER MODE register that is active is bit 14, which enables (**0**) or disables (**1**) the automatic sequencing of the AMD9513's registers. However, this operation can also be done via the commands available with the COMMAND CODE register and does not require accessing the MASTER MODE register. Therefore, the hex-code 0000 inserted in the MASTER MODE register by the MASTER RESET command need not be changed.

COUNTER OVERFLOW *Routine*   When a counter overflows, the high-order decades associated with that counter must be updated. This is done by the COUNTER OVERFLOW routine. As mentioned, the output control is configured to produce a high level when a counter overflows from 9999 to 0000. This causes interrupt IRQ 1 to occur, which vectors the program to the address contained in FFF8 (MSB) and FFF9 (LSB). These locations contain the starting address of the COUNTER OVERFLOW routine. When an interrupt occurs, the MC6801 sets the I (interrupt) bit of the CCR to inhibit further interrupts. If desired, the routine servicing the interrupt can reset the I bit. This permits interrupts with a high priority to gain control while a lower priority interrupt is being serviced. The I bit has no affect on the NMI, which is an unconditional interrupt. The COUNTER OVERFLOW routine then establishes which counter or counters have overflowed by reading the 8-bit STATUS register of the AMD9513. Bits 1 to 5 of this register contain overflow information for each counter. This information is stored in a flag and used by a subroutine that determines the software decades to be updated by testing the bits of the flag. It also clears the interrupt by resetting the output level of the counter(s) that overflowed.

Other Counter Functions   In addition to handling the counter-generated overflow, other routines provide starting, stopping, clearing, and reading the counters. The AMD9513 provides specific instructions for starting (Arm), stopping (Disarm), clearing (Load), and Hold (used for reading). The following example illustrates the basics involved in the HOLD function (i.e., reading).

This routine reads and stores all the counters while counting continues. It requires that the AMD9513 first be configured as discussed in the earlier *Initial Setup of Counters* part of this section. In addition, a 7F is written to the COMMAND register. This is the Load and Arm command for all five counters. It loads each counter with the contents of its associated LOAD register (0000) and enables counting.

The READ and STORE function (see Fig. 21 for MLFC) starts by writing a BF to the AMD9513 COMMAND register, which saves the contents of each counter in its associated HOLD register. A 19 is then written into the COMMAND register, which allows the DATA POINTER register to access the HOLD register of counter 1. The next read-data operation will transfer the 2 *least significant decades* (LSDs) from the HOLD register of counter 1. These 2

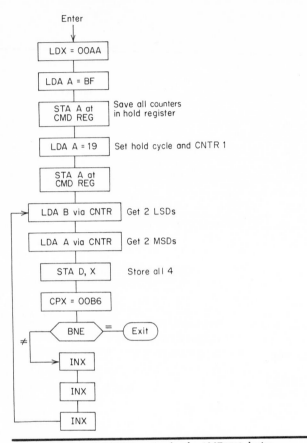

FIG. 21   *READ AND STORE routine for the AMD9513 device.*

decades are stored in the B accumulator of the MC6801. The following read-data operation transfers the 2 *most significant decades* (MSDs) to the A accumulator. The next read will transfer the LSDs of counter 2.

All 4 decades of counter 1 are stored by the STA D, X (store D via index) command. Accumulator D is a concatenation of accumulators A and B. Because the index register is initialized at AA, the two MSDs of counter 1 are stored in AA, and the two LSDs are stored in AB. The routine then tests the index register for the last counter (00B6) and exits if true. If not, the index register is incremented three times to point at storage for the next counter, and the loop is reentered. The index register is incremented three times instead of twice, to skip the location containing decades 5 and 6 that are maintained by software (see Table 2). In contrast, a routine to read the counters of the original Clever Counter is an order of magnitude larger and much more complex. This savings in the new design is due to the usage of VLSI.

NMI *Timers* In addition to maintaining the TOY clock, the NMI routine also updates the active timers, checks them with their corresponding preset time, and inhibits those counters whose timers have reached the preset time. This inhibiting is only temporary. Upon returning from the NMI, the supervisor routine will reinitiate those channels that have timed out and restart them. This reduces the error caused by the time that a counter is active after its preset time has been reached. This technique is perfectly adequate for our applications. For high counting-rate applications it may be necessary to inhibit a counter immediately after updating its timer.

Figure 22 shows the MLFCs for updating and checking the active timers. The flag contains a 1 in each bit position where a channel is active. For example, if channels 1, 3, and 4 are active, then bits 1, 3, and 4 of the flag word are set. The index register is initially set at 008D, which contains the two LSDs of timer 1. Each active timer is determined by shifting the flag to the right and checking the Carry bit. Those timers that are active will set Carry and Branch to the ACTIVE subroutine. Here, registers A, B, and X are temporarily stored by pushing them on the stack, and the UPDATE subroutine is entered. This routine counts in base 10 (note DAA-decimal adjust instruction) and adds one each time it is entered. In going from 99 to 00, Carry is set, causing a branch that loads the next 2 higher-order decades of the timer for updating. After updating, the timer is compared with its associated preset time by the COM-PARE subroutine. The timer and its corresponding preset time are offset by 15 (0F) memory locations using the SBU A, X + F instruction. If the timer matches the preset time, a return to the ACTIVE subroutine is made with Carry set; otherwise, Carry is cleared. Back in the ACTIVE subroutine, the registers are pulled off the stack. Because of the LIFO nature of the stack, they are pulled opposite to the push sequence. If Carry is set, bit 4 of register B is set (ADD B = 10), and a return back to the timer program is made. The index register is incremented to point at the LSDs of the next timer, and register B is again shifted to the left. This moves the bits of *both* the active timers and the timers that have timed-out. When complete, the active timer bits will have been shifted out and replaced by timers that have timed-out. Upon leaving the timer routine, bit 7 of the B register is set (ADD B = 80), thereby specifying the Disarm and Save all selected counters command of the AMD9513. This command is executed by storing register B in the COMMAND register of the AMD9513. Thus, all timers that timed-out have their corresponding counter disarmed and its count information saved. The RTI (return from interrupt) pulls all the registers off the stack and returns to the program that was interrupted by the NMI. The supervisor will use the flag information to initiate writing the contents of the timed-out channels and restart them.

Display Routine This display is extremely easy to program because the display looks like memory. Data to be displayed must be converted to ASCII format and stored in the appropriate display locations. To facilitate this, the two four-character displays are decoded to occupy eight consecutive address locations.

Some of the parameters that are displayed may, depending upon their

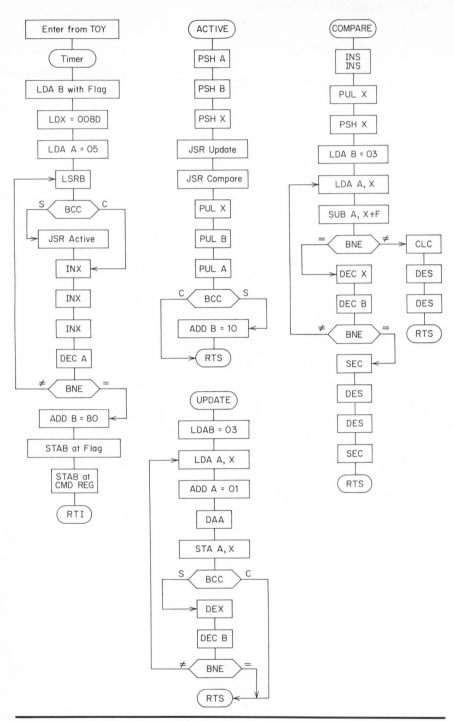

FIG. 22 Four routines for updating and checking the active timers.

value, require six characters. These parameters are preset time (XP), elapsed time (XE), and count (XC). To accommodate these, the two rightmost characters of the upper display are used to display the 2 high-order decades when the overall value exceeds 9999_{10}. Otherwise, these two display characters are blanked, which limits the parameter identification to the two leftmost characters of the upper display. The X in the parameters is 1, 2, 3, 4, or 5, depending upon which channel is selected. The numeral is placed before the alpha character to avoid confusion when reading the data information.

When TOY information is displayed, all four characters of the upper display are available for parameter identification. The upper display shows the sequence DAY, HOUR, MIN, and SEC when TOY information is displayed.

To illustrate how the display is used, the routines that read the TOY and then display are now discussed. For simplicity, only the numeric value (lower display) of the TOY is considered.

In Sec. 5.6, *Software Overview,* in the subsection *Machine Flowcharts,* it was stated that the TOY resides in RAM at locations 81 through 85. These are dynamic locations that are updated by the NMI routine every second. If these are displayed, errors will result because of updating (e.g., seconds changing from 59 to 0) and the several seconds needed for an observer to read the display. Therefore, a sample of the TOY is taken and stored in a buffer. The contents of this buffer are then used for the display. This TOY buffer resides in locations 86 through 8A of RAM (see Table 2). Thus, each buffer location is displaced from its corresponding TOY location by 5.

Figure 23 shows the MLFC for the subroutine, which reads the TOY into the buffer. To prevent reading during an NMI, the Wait for Interrupt (WAI) instruction is used. Program execution stops at the WAI until an interrupt (NMI) is generated and serviced. This ensures that none of the TOY parameters change while it is being read into the buffer. The rest of this subroutine is straightforward. To display the TOY, accumulator A is loaded with HIGH-DAY data and a pointer is set for the third (from right) display character with the LDX = D3 instruction. The subroutine Display 2 is then entered. To keep the correct order of the digits displayed, this routine first puts the MSD in accumulator B, LSD in accumulator A, and converts both to ASCII with the ADD 30 instruction. The STA D, X instruction stores (displays) accumulator A (LSD) in the third (from right) display character and accumulator B (MSD) in the fourth. It then returns to the calling program, where a loop is created for LOW-DAY, HOUR, MIN, and SEC, which are displayed in characters 1 and 2. (Note the LDX = D1 instruction.) The subroutine Pause waits for two NMIs (2 s), thereby allowing time for an observer to read the display. After pausing, the display is blanked by storing a nonexistent ASCII character (00) in it. The several Push (PSH) and Pull (PUL) instructions are used for temporarily storing registers on the stack.

CALENDAR *Chip Routines* The CALENDAR routines (see Fig. 24) consist of CALENDAR SET, which writes the calendar, and CALENDAR READ, which reads the calendar. These use the subroutines COMMAND, which strobes a command into the calendar, and SHIFT, which shifts the calendar 1 bit.

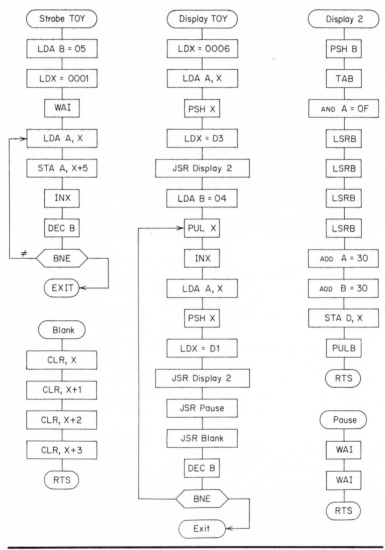

FIG. 23   *Five routines which read the TOY and display the contents.*

The calendar data resides in RAM at locations 00B8 through 00BC (see Table 2). Each word of the first four locations contains two BCD digits corresponding to seconds, minutes, hours, and date. The upper half of the last location contains a hexadecimal digit for month and the lower half a BCD digit for day of week.

To set the calendar, the Julian TOY data is converted by a supervisor routine to month, data, and day of week, which is stored in the calendar locations.

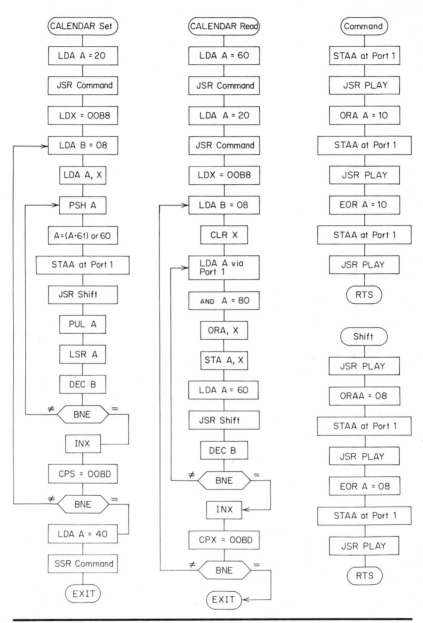

FIG. 24   *Calendar routines which read or write into the calendar chip.*

The CALENDAR SET routine is then entered. The calendar is put in the data shift mode by the first two instructions. This also disables the NMI by removing the zero condition from bits 5 and 6 of port 1. Data is put in the calendar from the LSB of port 1. $A = (A \cdot 61)$ or 60 is used (instead of 01) to ensure that the NMI remains inhibited. Once the data is present in the LSB of port 1, it is shifted into the calendar by the SHIFT subroutine. The data word is then shifted to set up the next bit. After the entire word has been shifted into the calendar, the index register is incremented and the loop is reentered. When the last word has been entered, the time set command is given by the two instructions preceding the RTS. This loads the 40-bit register of the calendar into its internal timer registers.

To read the calendar, the CALENDAR Read routine is entered. Here, the first two instructions load the calendar's internal timer data into its 40-bit shift register. Again, this also inhibits the NMI. The calendar is then put into its register shift mode with the next two instructions. Before storing any data, the memory location is cleared (CLR, X). One bit data from the LSB of the calendar's register is read into the MSB of port 1. This 1-data bit is stripped from the port 1 word (AND $A = 80$) and stored without disturbing previous data (ORA, X and STA A, X). The stored data is then shifted and the next bit is clocked from the calendar's register. After 8 bits, the index register is incremented to the next memory location, and the loop is reentered.

The two subroutines Command and Shift pulse the calendars' strobe and clock inputs, respectively. This is done by setting (ORA A) and resetting (EOR A) appropriate bits in port 1. The several NOPs (no-operation) are used to satisfy the calendar's timing requirements.

Cassette Recorder Routines The MLFCs for writing a word containing 2 BCD digits on a cassette recorder are shown in Fig. 25. The cassette recorder is a Model 201 manufactured by Memodyne and is an incremental recorder that uses a 2-bit gap to separate each word recorded. Records or files are distinguished by longer EOF (end of file) gaps. The recorder is normally configured for an 8-, 12-, or 16- bit data word. However, because the basic data unit of the Clever Counter is a BCD digit, 4-bit data words are used. Therefore, the total bit length of each word, including the 2-bit gap, is 6 bits.

Upon entering these routines, first the 2-bit gap is written by setting the second bit of port 1 and generating two clock pulses. The 4-bit BCD data is then output 1 bit at a time. The gap condition is removed the first time the two instructions AND $A = 01$ and STA A at PORT 1 of the BCD routine are executed. After the first BCD digit is written, another gap is generated, and the BCD routine is reentered to output the second BCD digit. This digit was shifted four times while the first digit was written and is now in position for output.

The Pulse subroutine calls the TIMER subroutine first with bit 0 of the A register set and then with bit 0 reset. This generates a delay followed by a **0**-to-**1** transition on the timer's output and a delay followed by a 1-to-0 transition on the timer's output. This sequence produces one clock pulse. The TIMER subroutine waits until there is a match in the OCF flag and then sets or resets

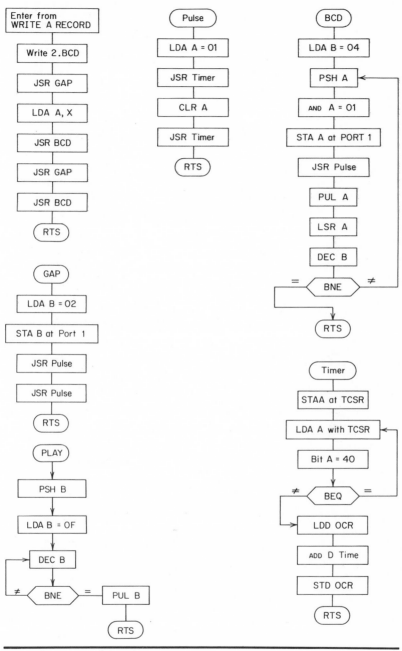

FIG. 25   *Cassette recorder routines.*

the output level, depending upon the value in the A register. The delay time is then added to the OUTPUT COMPARE register and stored. This store in OUTPUT COMPARE register also clears the OCF flag.

At the end of a record, a long gap (EOF) must be generated. Because this is easily done by repeated entry of the GAP routine, it is not shown in Fig. 25.

REFERENCES

1. "Standard Nuclear Instrument Modules," TID-20893, (rev. 4, July 1974. Available from Superintendent of Documents, U.S. Government Printing Office, Washington, D.C. 20402).
2. Pocket Terminal manufactured by G. R. Electronics, Ltd., Fair Oak House, Church Road, Newport, Gwent, United Kingdom. United States distributor: G. R. Electronics, Ltd., Santa Monica, Calif.
3. Negro, V. C., and T. Reiser: "A Micro-Computer Data Logging System," in Samuel C. Lee (ed.), *Microcomputer Design and Applications*, Academic Press, New York 1977, pp. 163–193.
4. Sharon Lamb: "PRObug™—Programming Monitor for the MC68701" Prel. Rept, Motorola NMOS Microcomputer Systems, Austin, Tex.
5. "MC6801 Single Chip Microcomputer Application Manual" (prel.), Motorola MOS Microcomputer Design, Austin, Tex.
6. Bauer, C.: "Timer/Counter Schedules of μC Interrupts—Simply," *Electronic Design*, May 24, 1980, pp. 75–81.
7. "MC6801 Advance Information," Motorola Data Sheet, 1978.
8. Thompson, R., and D. Tietjen: "Distributed Processing Applications Using the MC6801 and the MC68488," IEEE 1979 Electro-Professional Program, sess. 27, Microcomputer Industrial Control Networks.
9. Smith, D. W.: "Microcomputer Can Stand Alone or Join Forces With Other Chips," *Electronics*, Dec. 6, 1979, pp. 143–149.
10. Bauer, C.: "One-Chipper Gives Eight Operating Modes to the Cause of Optimum System Design," *Electronic Design*, Feb. 15, 1980, pp. 118–132.
11. Farrell, J. J. III: "Single-Chip 6801 Offers Versatility—Part 2," *Digital Design*, October 1979, p. 76.
12. Mallon, R.: "A Versatile Single-Chip Microcomputer," *Mini-Micro Systems*, November 1979, pp. 83–90.
13. Kroeger, J. H.: "AMD9513 System Timing Controller Detailed Functional Description," Advanced Micro Devices, Sunnyvale, Calif.
14. "AMD9513 System Timing Controller" (prel. inf.), Advanced Micro Devices, Sunnyvale, Calif, 1979.
15. Memodyne Corporation, Needham Heights, Mass. 02194
16. Forsyth, C. H., and R. J. Howard: "Compilation and Pascal on the New Microprocessors," *BYTE*, vol. 3, no. 8, August 1978, pp. 50–61.
17. Lentz, B.: "6800 Disassembler," *BYTE*, vol. 4, no. 5, May 1979, pp. 104–106.
18. Lewis, J.: "Some Notes on Modular Assembly Programming," *BYTE*, vol. 4, no. 12, December 1979, pp. 222–226.
19. "'Lil-Bug'—Monitor for the MC6801L1," Motorola NMOS Microcomputer Systems, Austin, Tex., 1979.

CHAPTER SIX

Microprocessor-Controlled Lumber Grader

Paul S. Kreager and Lynn E. Cannon

*Washington State University, Computing Service Center, Pullman, Washington**

BACKGROUND INFORMATION

Wood has been the traditional building material for many years because of its varied applications and value within the living environment. About 40 billion board feet of dimension lumber is used in the United States and Canada annually. In recent years, more stringent strength demands have been placed upon wood for use in particular application areas. Laminated beams, for instance, require lumber with fewer defects to maximize strength under tension. Grading operations at the mill are processes of sorting lumber according to estimations of its strength. For many years, lumber has been graded visually, a process not sufficiently precise for today's structural needs. The modern demand for quantity, quality, and application-typed lumber has created a need for a more rapid grading process with increased accuracy. Accurate, high-speed grading allows the mill to use materials efficiently, reduce waste and rejects, and deliver consistent quality to its customers.

*Work done under contract to Metriguard, Inc., Pullman, Washington.

MODULUS OF ELASTICITY

The modulus of elasticity (MOE) of a material provides information directly usable in structural deflection calculations and as a predictor of its strength. Wood has a considerably wider range of MOE values than other building materials, such as metal. Selecting various MOE ranges for wood allows placing lumber in certain application areas. Grading wood at the lumber mill by determination of MOE has thus been the challenge for the electronics age. Not only must MOE be computed accurately and consistently, it must be computed in the rather harsh conditions of the mill. MOE must be determined on-site at the mill, in real time, and in an electrically noisy and physically dirty environment. Finally, to be practical for mill operations, the material properties must be determined nondestructively.

MILL CONDITIONS

The mill conditions require that some thought be given to properly designing the electronic equipment to be placed there. For instance, application of computer technology at the mill should include consideration of the potential soft error problem caused by the electrically noisy conditions. Built-in diagnostics likewise, help the mills's own personnel more effectively analyze the problem. This chapter describes the design of a lumber grading machine and some of the thinking that went into making it a dependable and accurate method for grading lumber.

6.1   Review

In previous work, the authors and J. D. Logan of Metriguard, Inc., described a nondestructive lumber tester that computes MOE by measuring the velocity of a stress wave as it propagates through the material.[1,2] The reader is directed to these references for the basics of MOE and a more in-depth description of that particular method of determining MOE. The work presented here determines MOE differently, by measuring the period of oscillation as the lumber vibrates. Also, this work discusses a more sophisticated handling of computations via a 12-digit floating-point arithmetic processing system. Note that this project began in early 1976; although arithmetic chips are now common, none adequate for the task were available then.

MOE *Calculation* If a piece of lumber is set into vibration and allowed to oscillate, it will do so with a period characteristic of its MOE as shown in Fig. 1. The constant in the MOE equation is set for both the material characteristics and scaling of units, giving millions of pounds per square inch (lb/in^2) as a convenient unit of measurement. For typical lumber and timber shapes, the vibration period ranges from 0.05 to 10 s for a corresponding MOE range of 0.5 to 3 million lb/in^2. The basic problem in determining MOE is data acquisition of weight and the period of vibration; the remaining parameters in the MOE equation are readily obtainable.

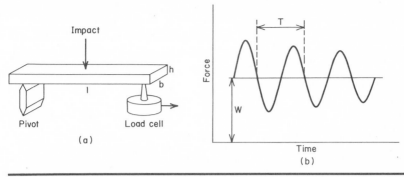

FIG. 1 *Derivation of MOE: (a) W = weight, l = length, b = base, h = height, T = period, k = constant. (b) MOE = $\dfrac{Wl^3}{kbh^3T^2}$ lb/in².*

Construction and experience with the lumber tester gave the hindsight necessary to know that a microprocessor was a realistic tool for solving MOE via measuring the period of oscillation. Previous experience also instilled confidence for increasing the sophistication of the firmware by implementing the floating-point, stack-operated arithmetic processor (described in more detail in Sec. 6.4, *Software*).

6.2 Basic System Design

The general system configuration necessary for grading is shown in Fig. 2. Both the weight and oscillation are obtained from the output of the load cell. Weight is the baseline of the oscillation, and time is derived from the zero crossings. Using this proven configuration[3] as a base, six of the design goals selected were:

1. To also compute density as all information necessary is present. Density is another useful parameter for determining wood characteristics.
2. To provide the ability to average weight and period over 1 to 9 cycles of oscillation for more accurate computation of MOE.
3. To be able to watch MOE, T, and density dynamically as the oscillation dies out.

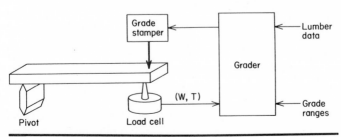

FIG. 2 *Basic system components.*

4. To refresh data in the machine periodically to minimize soft error problems.
5. To provide built-in diagnostic capability.
6. To perform computations within a maximum time limit of 1 s.

The most complicated task in realizing the goals is dynamically tracking the oscillations. During this time the microprocessor must keep track of which half-cycle it is in, save weight and time information for each cycle, control the analog-to-digital (A/D) conversion of weight, and look for false zero crossings and false weight information generated by noise. The worst case—of the period approaching 50 ms—presents no problem because no detailed computations are necessary when tracking the oscillations.

6.3 Hardware Configuration

The resulting overall lumber grading system can be divided into two major sections, as shown in Fig. 3. Housed within the mill operations are the electric and mechanical equipment for handling the lumber under test. Electronics connected to the remote Model 3300 E-Computer system direct the lumber clamps, conveyor, load cell, and grade-stamping operations. A start command is sent to the 3300 system, indicating that a piece of lumber is on the test supports, has been set into oscillation, and is ready for analysis. The 3300 then calculates MOE and selects the proper grade as determined by the operator-selected grading ranges. Grade data is then sent back to the lumber-handling machinery for grade-marking of the lumber. The 3300 itself houses the computer for analysis of the lumber, electronics for determining vibration period and weight from the load cell, and all controls necessary for the operator. The computer is a custom single-board computer (SBC) utilizing a 6800 microprocessor, memory, and all input-output (I/O).

Selection of the 6800 microprocessor was based on (1) experience with the device, (2) availability of software design tools such as an assembler and a simulator, and (3) hand-calculated benchmarks of representative decimal arithmetic routines.

System Operation The control panel in Fig. 4 shows the various features of the system. The operator selects the proper lumber dimensional data, desired grade ranges, weight range, and number of cycles to analyze. The desired mode (single or continuous) is then selected, and the system is ready to start. The operator may display any value shown on the display selector at any time, even during the computation process. For example, MOE can be viewed dynamically as the oscillation dies out. Any errors occurring are flagged by an appropriate console lamp. The operating firmware has many error traps, too many to be conveniently displayed by individual lamps. To handle this, the error-code lamp is illuminated and the numeric display is loaded with a reference number indicating the exact error condition. For example, a random access memory (RAM) failure detected during a test operation will be shown

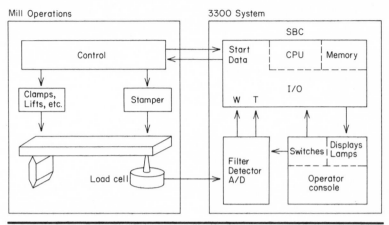

FIG. 3   *Grader hardware configuration.*

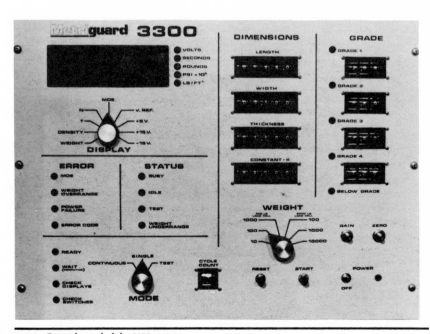

FIG. 4   *Control panel of the 3300 system.*

with an error code indicating which RAM chip in the system failed. The firmware also allows for very complete testing of the console I/O. When in the test mode, RAM and ROM are first checked for proper operation. RAM is tested by writing all values into each location; each value is read back and checked for errors. ROM is tested by adding the contents of a ROM and comparing it to zero. All ROMs are made to sum to 0 by inserting a checksum byte in each ROM, which is determined after compiling the ROM code. Next, the TEST program allows the operator to verify that all displays are functioning. All lamps are first cycled ON and OFF several times, and then the displays are cycled through the 10 digits for visual verification. The final test permits the operator to test any or all console switches. The firmware is structured to look for any switch change and show the new setting on the displays. Switch inactivity for a preset time lapse forces the firmware back to its normal idle state.

6.4   Software

Arithmetic Processing Unit (APU)   Software for the lumber grader was designed for reliability and maintainability, with several programming techniques[4] used to achieve these characteristics. The most significant design feature enabled the software to eventually be run on a multiprocessor system. All arithmetic operations are done by a program called the arithmetic processing unit (APU). The APU was written so that it could either run as a subroutine or as a MAIN program in a separate processor. For this project, however, a single processor was used.

Program Modules   The software was designed in a modular fashion: separate functions were written as separate routines. This allowed each routine to be tested or modified without affecting others. For example, the APU, which is itself a collection of routines, can be tested with a DRIVE program only 13 bytes long.

Self-Documenting Listings   Programming shortcuts were avoided in the interest of a clearly written and easy-to-understand code. The programs are self-documenting; that is, except for flowcharts, the programs are the documentation. This was accomplished by using comments extensively in the source code. The comments completely describe data formats and the function of each routine.

ROM *Usage*   To facilitate self-testing, each of the 14 ROMs contains a checksum byte whose value makes the modulo 256 sum of all bytes in the ROM be 0. The operator can invoke a test procedure which verifies that the sums are still 0. To allow for program changes without having to reprogram all ROMs, several bytes were reserved in each ROM for patches. This technique can save money if ROMs have to be sent out for programming or if fusible-link or mask-programmed ROMs are used.

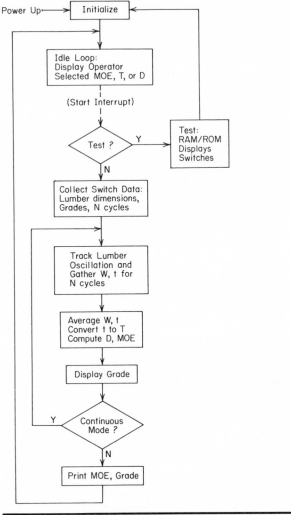

FIG. 5   General system flow chart. Key: t = time, T = period, N = number of cycles, D = density, W = weight, MOE = modulus of elasticity.

MAIN *Program* The MAIN program controls inputs and outputs, performs the computations using the APU for floating-point processing, and does system testing. A general flowchart for the MAIN program is shown in Fig. 5; it does not show the extensive error-checking performed by the program at almost every step or the recomputation of some values, which is done occasionally to minimize the effects of soft errors.

RAM *Usage* The APU is controlled by the MAIN program through the use of common data areas in RAM, as indicated in Fig. 6. These data areas contain the following fields: eight 8-byte fields that form a data stack for floating-point numbers, 9 bytes that form a command stack, 1 byte that is the APU status, and 2 bytes that are used to return an error code for abnormal terminations. In addition to the common data areas, the MAIN program and the APU each have local data areas. All RAM is in base-page to take advantage of the 6800's faster "direct" addressing mode.

Floating-Point Floating-point numbers are represented internally as 8-byte words, with 1 byte each for the exponent and the sign and 6 bytes for the mantissa. See Fig. 7.

The exponent is an 8-bit binary number with a bias of 128. That is, a hexa-decimal value of 80 represents an exponent value of 0, values less than 80 represent negative exponents, and values greater than 80 represent positive

ADDRESS	MAIN	APU	USE
00 – 3F	X	X	Data Stack (Floating-Point)
40 – 57		X	Memory Registers (Floating-Point)
58 – 6F		X	APU Working Registers (Floating-Point)
70 – 78	X	X	Command Stack
79	X	X	APU Status
7A – 8B		X	APU Local Storage
8C – A0	X		General Save Area
A1 – E3	X		Input Data Save Area
E4 – EB	X		Output Data Save Area
EC – FF	X	X	System Stack Area

FIG. 6   *Memory map for RAM.*

Exp.	Sign			Fractional Mantissa			
Byte 0	Byte 1	Byte 2	Byte 3	Byte 4	Byte 5	Byte 6	Byte 7

FIG. 7   *Floating-point data format.*

exponents. Thus, the range of exponent values is from -128 to $+127$. The exponent value indicates the power of 10 by which the mantissa is multiplied to obtain the value of the floating-point number being represented. As examples, a value of 83 means "multiply the mantissa by 1000," and a value of 7C means "multiply the mantissa by 0.0001." This binary exponent format was used to simplify exponent processing. Exponent magnitudes can be compared directly as unsigned integer values. Similarly, when aligning mantissas or normalizing floating-point numbers, the exponents can be incremented or decremented without concern for the sign of the exponent. Also, the detection of overflow or underflow conditions is much simpler than would be the case if either binary-coded decimal (BCD) or signed binary exponent formats were used.

The sign of the floating-point number is represented by 1 byte. A hexadecimal value of 00 indicates a positive floating-point value, and a hexadecimal value of 80 indicates a negative floating-point value. An entire byte was used for the sign to simplify the processing by separating the sign determination from numerical calculations.

The mantissa is a 6-byte field that contains 12 BCD digits, with an assumed decimal point to the left of the high-order digit. A BCD representation was chosen for the mantissa because all input and output of numerical data are in BCD. No conversion of data between BCD and binary is required.

The floating-point numbers are normalized after operations so that the high-order BCD digit of the mantissa is always nonzero. This greatly simplifies floating-point arithmetic, particularly division, and helps maintain the significance of floating-point values.

APU *Operation* To use the APU, the MAIN program places floating-point numbers in the data stack and commands in the command stack. A zero is placed last in the command stack to signify the end of a sequence of commands. The APU is then started by means of a subroutine CALL. The APU performs the operations indicated in the command stack upon data in the data stack. Intermediate results may, if requested, be retained in specified memory registers local to the APU. These retained numbers may be retrieved and used in subsequent operations.

The basic operation of the APU is simple. When activated, the APU saves all register contents, clears the status byte, initializes its command and data stack pointers, and begins processing commands. Command processing consists of decoding the command, setting up the arguments, invoking the appropriate arithmetic routines, and checking for abnormal conditions. When a command of zero is encountered, the APU moves the current result to the top of the data stack, sets the STATUS register to indicate whether the result is positive, negative, or zero, and returns. If an invalid command is detected, an error code is set and return is made via a jump to an error-handling routine. If an arithmetic overflow occurs, the APU status is set and a normal return takes place, with no further processing of commands. If an arithmetic underflow occurs, the APU status is set, the result of the operation that caused the underflow is set to zero, and command processing continues.

APU *Data-Manipulation Instructions*   The APU software performs the following commands:

ADD—replaces the two floating-point numbers currently on the top of the data stack by their sum.

SUB—replaces the two floating-point numbers currently on the top of the data stack by their difference.

MUL—replaces the two floating-point numbers currently on the top of the data stack by their product.

DIV—replaces the two floating-point numbers currently on the top of the data stack by their quotient.

SHIFT—shifts the mantissa of the floating-point number currently on the top of the data stack right 1 digit position and adjusts the exponent appropriately.

ROUNDn—rounds the floating-point number currently on the top of the data stack to n significant places.

STOREn—saves the floating-point number currently on the top of the data stack in memory register n.

FETCHn—retrieves the floating-point number from memory register n and places it on the top of the data stack.

To carry out the operations on the command stack, the APU uses local data storage and a set of utility routines. There are three local floating-point registers (AREG, BREG, and CREG—8 bytes each) for working storage (see Fig. 6). All floating-point operations are carried out on data in these registers. Before an operation can begin, the operand(s) must be moved from the data stack to the appropriate working register(s). The main purpose for performing all operations on data in the working registers is to simplify addressing in the utility routines. It is much easier to handle arithmetic operations on multibyte floating-point numbers if only one possible set of memory locations has to be referenced.

APU *Data Movement and Arithmetic Subroutines*   The movement of data within the APU and the arithmetic computations are performed with a set of local routines. The following routines are used:

MOVE—transfers floating-point data from a specified source to a specified destination within the APU. Accumulator A points to the source, and accumulator B points to the destination.

CLEER—zeros a specified number of bytes. Accumulator A points to the location, and accumulator B specifies the number of bytes to zero.

NORM—normalizes the floating-point number currently pointed to by the index register.

NORMO—normalizes the floating-point number currently in working register CREG.

STORE—moves the floating-point number currently on the top of the data stack to the memory register specified by the command.

FETCH—moves the floating-point number from the memory register specified by the command to the top of the data stack. This is basically a "push" operation.

SHFTIT—shifts the mantissa of the floating-point number in CREG right n places as specified by the command. The exponent in CREG is adjusted appropriately.

RIGHT—shifts the mantissa of the floating-point number in CREG right one place.

ROUND—rounds the floating-point number in AREG to n significant places.

ADDSUB—prepares for the addition or subtraction of the floating-point number in BREG to or from the floating-point number in AREG and places the result in CREG.

AORS—actually performs a floating-point ADD or SUBTRACT.

ALIGN—aligns the mantissa of BREG with that of AREG for an ADD or SUBTRACT.

APUMUL—multiplies the floating-point number in AREG by the one in BREG and places the result in CREG.

APUDIV—divides the floating-point number in AREG by the one in BREG and places the result in CREG.

Example As an example of the floating-point routines in the APU, consider the process of rounding a floating-point number to n significant places. Because the floating-point numbers are all normalized, all significant digits will be left-justified in the mantissa. That is, rounding to, say, 3 significant digits consists basically of truncating the mantissa if the fourth significant digit is less than 5 and truncating and adding one if the fourth digit is 5 or greater. In the APU, this function is accomplished by adding to the number to be rounded to three places a number with a 5 in the fourth-digit position and 0s elsewhere, then truncating the result to 3 significant digits. The routine ROUND accomplishes this, as indicated in the flowchart in Fig. 8, by first creating a floating-point number that when aligned for addition to the number to be rounded will have a 5 in the appropriate position. This number is built using the exponent and sign of the number to be rounded and the value of n indicating the number of significant digits desired in the result. The routine AORS is then invoked to perform the floating-point Add. ROUND then truncates the result, moves the result to the top of the data stack using MOVE, and returns.

6.5 Summary

This project showed that it is possible to place computer technology in the harsh conditions of a lumber mill if sufficient attention is paid to those hardware and software design aspects which relate to reliability and maintainability. Much of the hardware and software for the lumber grader provides

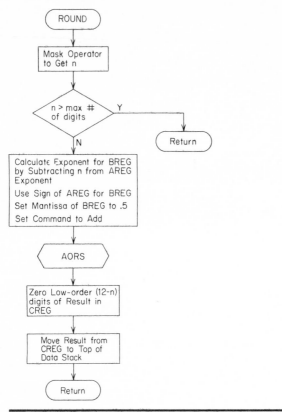

FIG. 8 *Flowchart for ROUND routine.*

confidence that the system is functioning properly and can detect and locate any errors that occur. These design practices should not be limited to systems that will be placed in harsh environments.

REFERENCES

1. Logan, J. D., and P. S. Kreager: "Using a Microprocessor: A Real-Life Application, Part 1—Hardware," *Computer Design*, September 1975, p. 69.
2. Cannon, L. E., and P. S. Kreager: "Using a Microprocessor: A Real-Life Application, Part 2—Software," *Computer Design*, October 1975, p. 81.
3. Pellerin, R. F., and J. D. Logan: Method and Apparatus for Non-Destructive Testing of Beams, U.S. Patent 3,513,690, May 26, 1970 (licensed to Metriguard, Inc., Pullman, Wash.).
4. Cannon, L. E.: "Development of Software for Microprocessors," in R. Chattergy and U. W. Pooch (eds.), *Microprocessors, Microprogramming, and Minicomputers*, Western Periodicals, North Hollywood, California, 1977.

CHAPTER SEVEN

Programmable Video Games

Kam Li

Signetics Corporation, Sunnyvale, California

INTRODUCTION

The first generation of video games has given birth to a new, successful, and highly lucrative business. During the past decade, the growth of this new business has been dramatic: Starting from virtually nothing, the video game industry is now a million-dollar business, and future growth prospects appear limitless. The popular appeal of video games has brought about enormous competition to create better, more exotic, and more stimulating games, and electronic game designers continuously seek better effects and more innovative circuit designs. Consequently, the simpler random logic architecture used in the first-generation games has given way to more complex logic, particularly as the semiconductor industry continues to make significant strides in producing inexpensive large-scale integrated (LSI) microprocessors.

7.1   Components of a Video Game

Before discussing games architecture in detail, let us examine the basic constituents of video games (see Fig. 1):

1. Picture generators: The picture consists of various objects, such as paddles, balls, and players. The background is visually portrayed by tennis nets, court boundaries, and so on. The score is portrayed by numbers, bar graphs, and other devices.
2. Sounds: Sounds include explosions, motor sounds, shots, and even synthesized human speech.
3. Input-output (I/O) accessories: I/O accessories include potentiometers, joysticks, switches, gas pedals, and steering wheels.

Painting the Picture   The standard TV broadcasting system in the United States employs a fully interlaced scan of 525 lines per frame, as shown in Fig. 2. To simplify matters, and because we are not concerned with TV broadcasting, this discussion concentrates on the noninterlaced scheme, where the same field of 262 lines each is repeated.

Figure 3 is a simplified illustration of a noninterlaced screen. To start painting a screen (frame), the electron beam begins at the upper left corner of the cathode ray tube (CRT) and sweeps out a slanting horizontal line ending at the right. The electron beam moves to the right because it is being deflected horizontally by the output of the horizontal oscillator, and the line slants slightly downward because the beam is also constantly being deflected vertically by the vertical oscillator output.

After it scans the first line, the electron beam is repositioned back to the left side, during which time (indicated by the dotted lines in Fig. 3) the screen should be blanked out. After the electron beam has been reset to the left side of the CRT, it sweeps the second horizontal line. Because the electron beam is still being deflected vertically, the second line appears just under the first, and this process continues until the end of the line is reached. At this point, both vertical and horizontal synchronizing pulses occur, and the electron beam is reset back to the left top edge, where it begins to sweep again.

A picture is painted by controlling the intensity of the electron beam. To illustrate how the composite video controls the picture, one picture line is shown in Fig. 4. Notice how the various shades of light and dark portions correspond to higher and lower voltage levels. The edges of the picture are blanked when the blanking pulse is high enough to extend into the black region.

Color   Pictures are painted in color using red, blue, and green guns. Various colors can be produced from mixing various proportions of red, blue, and green with different intensities. In consumer home video games, the various colors are encoded into a single signal before the signal is inputted to the antenna. The technique used is *phase modulation*, whereby the instantaneous color is represented by the instantaneous phase shift of a color carrier in comparison to a reference carrier. In the United States, the color carrier used is

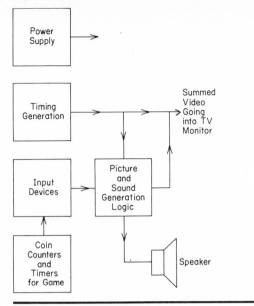

FIG. 1   Components of a video game.

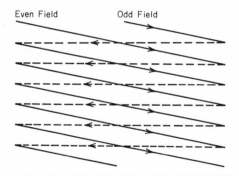

FIG. 2   Interlaced scan. The odd and even fields are swept once per frame.

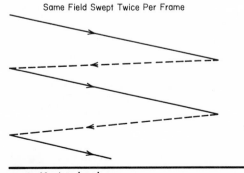

FIG. 3   Noninterlaced scan.

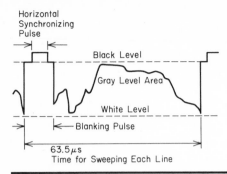

Horizontal
Synchronizing
Pulse

Black Level

Gray Level Area

White Level

Blanking Pulse

63.5 μs
Time for Sweeping Each Line

FIG 4   *Composite video picture of a line on the screen.*

3.58 MHz, and the reference is transmitted during the horizontal blanking period.

Resolution   The resolution of a picture is determined by the rate at which video amplitude levels can change. Higher resolution allows more details to be illustrated. In coin-operated games, the cost of implementing higher resolution is of a lesser concern than in the home consumer games. Another consideration is the bandwidth of home televisions, which limits the effective resolution of video signals to 4 MHz. The following table shows the horizontal image size versus the rate of the changing levels.

Rate of change, MHz	Minimum pulse width of each level, μs	Actual size on 25-in diagonal or 20-in horizontal screen, in
1	1	0.3
2	0.5	0.15
4	0.25	0.075
8	0.125	0.038

Most existing coin-operated machines are built with transistor-transistor logic (TTL) elements operating at 10 MHz or more, which present fairly fine images on the screen. However, home consumer TV games that use existing MOS chips operate at only 4–7 MHz.

Three Dimensions   The three-dimensional concept has been introduced into the video games market in the past several years. This feature is implemented with clusters of lines at various angles to give a pseudo three-dimensional impression. Another method used to obtain the three-dimensional effect is the gradual shading of objects. The latter is a more expensive method and, at present, is rarely used in video games.

Sound Generation   Sound effect is probably the second most important factor in a video game; a player expects an audio response from a corresponding event. Much research has been done in the area of creating various tones and sounds. Primarily, there are two types of sounds: *digital* and *realistic*.

1. Digital sounds are generated by a series of square waves at an audible frequency. The "pitch" of the tone can be varied by the pulse width of the square wave generated, which is sufficient for creating sounds for games like Pong and Hockey. Digital sounds are losing ground to the more sophisticated realistic sounds and synthesized speech (see Fig. 5).
2. For realistic sounds—those that resemble real life—more complex circuitry is required. The fundamental difference is the presence of a white-noise generator, as shown in Fig. 6. The raw-noise waveform generated is then processed and refined to produce more desirable sounds. For example, an explosion sound is produced with a waveform as shown in Fig. 7. The decaying path determines the frequency components.

Many variations of realistic sound have been developed for recent games. Traditionally, consumer-oriented games have used relatively simple circuitry because of the additional cost involved in generating realistic sounds. The increased cost is attributed to additional power supplies, raw-noise generators, RC filters, and amplifiers. However, new developments in LSI technology are making noise generators and even speech synthesis possible.

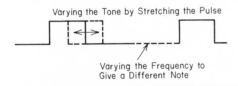

FIG. 5 *Digital noise-pulse waveform.*

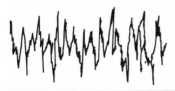

FIG. 6 *Raw noise waveform.*

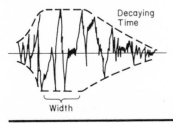

FIG. 7 *Realistic sound waveform.*

I/O *Accessories* Coin-operated video games rely a great deal upon the input accessories. Success of a particular game depends upon how fast the players adapt to the controls. Various accessories like steering wheels, rifles, and gas pedals have been implemented to give that realistic feeling. The most recent adaptation is speech input. However, machines utilizing the speech technology are still in a primitive state and have to be refined before each game. In the home video games, the traditional input has been primarily digital keyboards and potentiometers, but LSI technology has made remote control economically feasible.

Output of video games has primarily been sound and video. In home television games in the United States, the sound is frequency-modulated into the composite video signal at 4.5 MHz before modulating into each channel. In coin-operated games, the sound directly drives a number of speakers to produce realistic effects. Other output accessories, such as lights and digital displays, are also used. The trend toward more complex input and outputs has made microprocessors indispensable.

7.2 *Microprocessor Video Game Architecture*

With the microprocessor, all the picture generation, object updating, and motion are programmed by the microprocessor, thereby eliminating the need for most of the random logic used in earlier designs. The program sets up the rules of the game and controls the screen composition, the sound, and the I/O interface. The type of game determines the complexity of the program and thus the size of the program memory required. Because each game is completely determined by software, the physical form of the memory is an important consideration. If the memory is made up of read-only memories (ROMs), a program contained in a different set of ROMs has to be substituted whenever a new game is played on the system. The substitution can be achieved by using ROM cartridges. Another possibility is to use random access memory (RAM). If RAM is selected, loading of a game program into the RAM is required. This is often done through the use of magnetic tape cassettes. The RAM technique involves a more expensive system because of the cost of RAM; however, its advantage is that it has a bulk serial storage.

Several important benefits are attained with the microprocessor. Most significant is the tremendous amount of development time saved in generating each new game because the same design is used for every different game. Furthermore, malfunctions that may occur at the user level can be corrected just by replacing the ROMs instead of recalling some or all of the boards. In addition, with the microprocessor, a new set of "thinking" games can be implemented.

RAM *Mapping* In microprocessor design there are basically two types of architectures used: RAM-intensive (mapping) and object-oriented. With the RAM mapping technique, every bit of information to be displayed is mapped into a sizable RAM. The finer the resolution, the greater the RAM requirement, and consequently, the more expensive the system becomes (see Fig. 8).

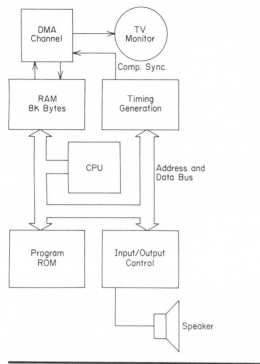

FIG. 8 Microprocessor-controlled video game using the RAM-intensive (RAM-oriented) approach.

Video patterns, such as tanks, cowboys, and planes, are permanently stored in ROMs. During initialization, these data patterns are transferred from ROM and loaded into RAM, where most of the data are stored throughout the game's progress. The initial address in RAM, hence the initial position in which the image will appear, is fixed by the program. As a result, the images always appear in the same location each time the game is started. Some images, e.g., stationary images such as houses or trees, retain their initial address location in RAM for as long as they appear on the screen and are simply read out each frame at the same location. Other images, such as submarines and tanks, are made movable by changing the location of the video pattern in RAM so that the images position on the CRT changes in subsequent frames. Although vertical motion is relatively simple and involves only moving the block of image data up or down in memory, the actual mechanics of moving a complete video image up or down the CRT are more complex. Because it is necessary to retain coherence and smoothness in all motions, each word in the block must move the same number of address units. Also, to prevent a flickering screen, updating the display RAM is always executed during the blanking period.

Horizontal motion is much more complex. Moving blocks of data alone causes a jump from location to location, resulting in jerky or uneven motion. The proper way to obtain smooth horizontal movement requires shifting each word into the next word (see Fig. 9).

Games designed using the RAM mapping technique are generally multi-purpose and can be adapted easily to other games by changing the programs. Most of the burden associated with block movement is controlled by the microprocessor.

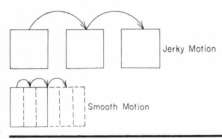

FIG. 9 *A comparison of smooth and jerky motion.*

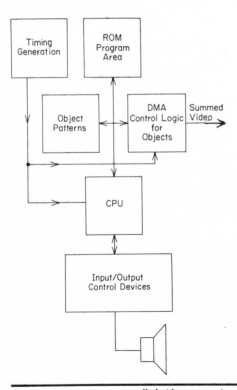

FIG. 10 *Microprocessor-controlled video game using the object-intensive approach.*

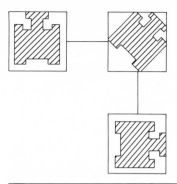

FIG. 11   *A sequence of three patterns for a 90-degree rotation.*

The only limitation is the number of moving objects that can be supervised by a microprocessor. A detailed example is discussed later, in Sec. 7.3.

Object-Oriented Approach   Figure 10 is a block diagram of an object-oriented, microprocessor-controlled game system. Associated with each object is an object pattern and a pair of coordinate registers that specify the location where the object is to be shifted out. A set of master counters and vertical and horizontal counters is also included to indicate where the electron beam is at any given instant. When the coordinate registers match the master counters, the object pattern is shifted out.

Objects can be moved by programming the microprocessor to change the coordinate register pair of the objects. Vertical motion can be achieved by incrementing or decrementing the vertical coordinate register. Horizontal motion is accomplished by incrementing or decrementing the horizontal coordinate. In this way, 2 degrees of freedom are available to each object. Other motions, such as rotation, are performed by more complex means. For example, an automobile with rotation involves several object patterns at different angles. A 90° rotation involves successive displays of several patterns, as shown in Fig. 11.

The object-oriented approach has the advantage of allowing designs using more objects. Also, the motion of the objects is easily controlled; that is, it takes a very small number of program steps to move an object from one place to another, thus saving considerable processor time for more objects. Because RAM requirements are minimal, the system cost is lower.

7.3   Examples of Microprocessor-Controlled Video Games

This section provides detailed examples of microprocessor-controlled video games using the RAM mapping and object-oriented design techniques. Two basic home television games are described; both are adaptable for the European as well as the United States markets. The primary visible difference between the European phase-alternation line (PAL) systems and the United States National Television System Committee (NTSC) systems is the number of horizontal lines in a frame. For the European PAL system, in the interlaced form, the number is 625 as compared to 525 used in the NTSC system.

RAM-*Oriented (Mapping) Approach*   In a microprocessor-controlled video game based upon the RAM-oriented approach, the TV screen is divided into a large dot matrix, with each dot represented by a bit in a RAM. There is a 1:1 relationship between the dots on the screen matrix and the contents of the RAM. In the simple example shown in Fig. 12, each memory bit represents one dot on the screen, and objects can be built up by setting the appropriate memory bits to logic **1**. Such an organization, however, allows only black and white pictures to be generated. Generating various brightness (luminance) levels or various colors requires a number of bits per dot. For example, in Fig. 13 the memory is organized as 3 bits per dot, giving eight colors (or eight luminance levels).

Figure 14 shows a typical games system using the RAM-oriented approach. Notice that the RAM refresh memory acts as a buffer between the microcomputer and the TV interface logic. On the one side, the microcomputer system fills the RAM with the data required to compose a picture. On the other side, the content of the RAM is continually read out (displayed) on the screen. The readout is controlled by the direct memory access (DMA) logic and is synchronous with the television timing.

Actions such as the illustration of objects and their motion and rotation, and score indication and changes in the background must all be implemented by changing the bit pattern at appropriate positions in the RAM. This imposes a heavy burden upon the microprocessor, especially when object motion is involved because it must be performed by repositioning large numbers of individual dots every frame (see Fig. 15).

The total size of the RAM depends upon the number of colors and luminance levels to be used. In this RAM-oriented approach, a matrix of 128 horizontal dots by 96 vertical dots with four colors (2 bits) per dot is used. The

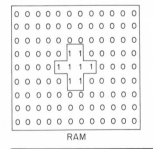
RAM

TV screen

FIG. 12   *One-to-one relationship between memory content and screen picture.*

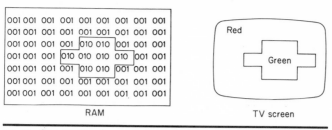

FIG. 13   *Organization of memory to give color and luminance information.*

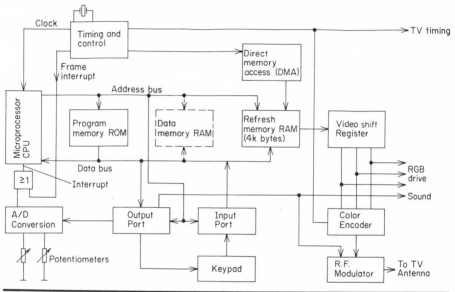

FIG. 14   *Block diagram of a RAM-oriented video-games system.*

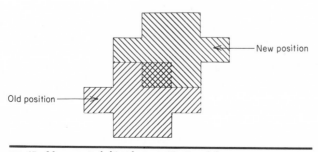

FIG. 15   *Movement of object by repositioning of dots.*

total memory required is then 128 $\times$ 96 $\times$ 2, or 24,576 bits. To simplify the microprocessor interface, the RAM is organized in 8-bit (byte) words. This means a memory of 24,576/8 (3072 bytes) is required. The best way of implementing such a RAM is to use eight high-density dynamic 4K RAMs, giving a total of 4096 bytes. The remaining 1024 bytes are used as a scratchpad memory. The 4096-bit dynamic RAM is probably the least expensive memory component available. It can be used conveniently in this application because the necessary data refresh is performed automatically by continuous reading of the data via DMA logic.

In both the PAL and NTSC systems, each horizontal scan line takes approximately 64 μs. Of this time, the visible portion takes about 52 μs, so each dot in the game matrix takes about 52/128, or 400 ns, requiring a video shift frequency of 2.5 MHz. Vertically, there are 96 dots in the matrix, with 3 TV lines per dot. This means that 96 $\times$ 3, or 288, lines can be painted, which is adequate for the visible portion of a television screen in NTSC and PAL systems. The format of the screen, as a function of the RAM refresh memory, can be built up by dividing the screen into 32 vertical columns, each using 96 bytes of memory (see Fig. 16). Each byte represents four horizontal dots, with 2 bits per dot for color information. The RAM refresh memory is accessed alternatively by the microprocessor address bus and address counters of the DMA logic, as shown in Fig. 17. All the signals necessary to control the DMA logic, the video shift register, and the microprocessor are derived from the timing and control circuit.

An important timing signal is the frame interrupt signal, which synchronizes the microprocessor with the TV frame every 20 ms (16.67 ms for NTSC systems). Within this 20-ms interval, all program functions, such as object motion, rotation, reading of the status of input units, and analog-to-digital (A/D) conversion, must be accomplished. If these functions cannot be completed during this time, changes in the positions of objects can be achieved only every alternate or every third frame.

The RAM-oriented approach provides great flexibility because the entire screen can be controlled and accessed through individual dots. This is an advantage, especially in static games with detailed backgrounds, such as a board game like chess (see Fig. 18). However, all operations on objects must be carried out dot by dot, which requires relatively complex programs and lengthy executions.

In games with moving objects, the operating speed of the microprocessor limits the number of objects and game effects (collisions and so on) that can be supervised. Another disadvantage of the RAM-oriented approach is that the number of components, especially the RAMs for the refresh memory and the TTL circuits for the DMA logic, makes the system rather costly.

Object-Oriented Approach An object-oriented video games system uses dedicated hardware in which small RAM blocks store the object descriptions specified by the game program memory. Each RAM block is, in effect, made up of two parts. The first part stores information on the object, such as its size, shape, and color, and the second part consists of two coordinate registers that

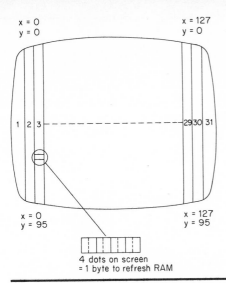

FIG. 16   Television screen as a function of RAM refresh memory.

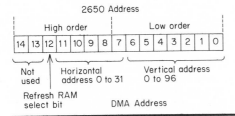

FIG. 17   Address format used in RAM-intensive game.

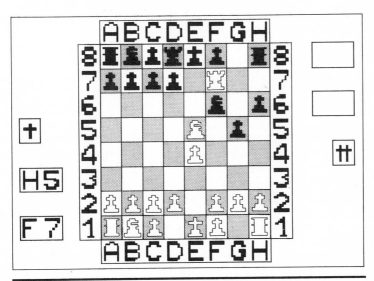

FIG. 18   Chess game display generated by RAM-oriented game system.

determine the horizontal and vertical coordinates of the object on the screen. The contents of these registers are compared with a master horizontal and vertical counter controlled by the timing circuits. When the contents of the coordinate registers and the master counter coincide, the object data are shifted out of the RAM as serial video information (see Fig. 19).

The size and shape data in the RAM determine the dimensions of the object as it appears on the screen. Various sizes are achieved by means of logic that "multiplies" the dimensions of each dot making up the object; the factor by which the size is increased is called the multiplication factor.

Objects can also be duplicated in the same frame as the original by using the horizontal and vertical duplicate registers and letting several objects be generated from a single RAM block. The organization of an object RAM is shown in Fig. 20.

LSI *Required to Support the Microprocessor*   To simplify the game program, special hardware is used to detect video overlay (collision) between objects and between objects and background. Other hardware is required to generate backgrounds, such as field lines and labyrinths, as well as some form of numeric character displays for score indication. All these functions have been implemented on the programmable video interface (PVI), a single LSI chip.

The PVI is a peripheral circuit for use in object-oriented microprocessor-controlled video games. It provides most of the commonly required video game circuits on a single chip. The eight main features of the PVI are:

1. Four object RAMs, each allowing programmable shape, size, color, and position and programmable positioning of object duplicates.
2. Fully programmable logic for background formats (field lines, racetracks, and so on) and screen colors.
3. Score logic with programmable contents, position, and format.
4. Indication of interobject and object-to-background collisions.
5. Programmable sound.
6. Two analog-to-digital converters (ADCs) for interfacing with potentiometers, joysticks, and so forth.
7. Scratchpad memory.
8. Multiple PVIs can be used in parallel to provide more images on the screen.

Figure 21 shows the block diagram of a typical video games system using the PVI. As shown, the PVI serves as a video generator, interpreting the commands of the microprocessor and presenting serial video information to the color encoder and video summer. Typically, the PVI operates at 3.58 MHz.

The microprocessor together with the program memory and key-pad interface operate as a standard microcomputer configuration. A master timing generator, the universal sync generator (USG), provides all the necessary timing signals to control both the microcomputer system and the TV color-encoder circuit. This timing generator is available as a single integrated circuit (IC) in both PAL and NTSC systems.

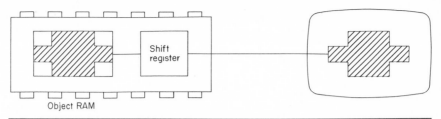

FIG. 19   *Shift of object video data out of RAM.*

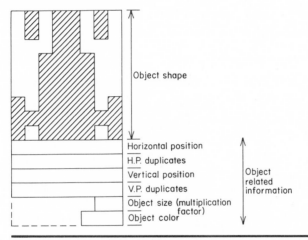

FIG. 20   *Organization of object RAM.*

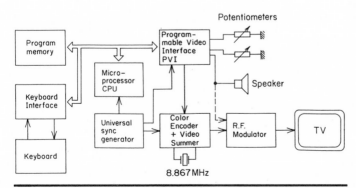

FIG. 21   *Block diagram of object-oriented video-games system using a PVI chip.*

7-15

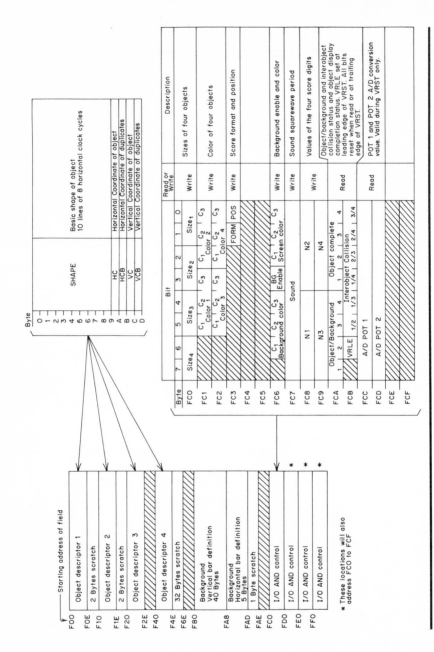

Byte

Byte		Read or Write	Description
0			
1			
2			
3			
4	SHAPE		Basic shape of object
5			10 lines of 8 horizontal clock cycles
6			
7			
8			
9	HC		Horizontal Coordinate of object
A	HCB		Horizontal Coordinate of duplicates
B	VC		Vertical Coordinate of object
C	VCB		Vertical Coordinate of duplicates
D			

Bit

Byte	7	6	5	4	3	2	1	0	Read or Write	Description
FC0	Size₄		Size₃		Size₂		Size₁		Write	Sizes of four objects
FC1	C₁ C₂ C₃ Color 1			C₁ C₂ C₃ Color 2					Write	Color of four objects
FC2	C₁ C₂ C₃ Color 3			C₁ C₂ C₃ Color 4					Write	
FC3							FORM POS		Write	Score format and position
FC4										
FC5										
FC6	C₁ C₂ C₃ Background color			BG Enable	C₁ C₂ C₃ Screen color				Write	Background enable and color
FC7				Sound					Write	Sound squarewave period
FC8	N1				N2				Write	Values of the four score digits
FC9	N3				N4				Write	
FCA	Object/Background 1 2 3 4				Object complete 1 2 3 4				Read	Object/background and interobject collision status and object display completion status. VRLE set at leading edge of VRST. All bits reset when read or at trailing edge of VRST.
FCB	VRLE 1/2 1/3 1/4				Interobject Collision 2/3 2/4 3/4				Read	
FCC	A/D POT 1								Read	POT 1 and POT 2 A/D conversion value. Valid during VRST only.
FCD	A/D POT 2								Read	
FCE										
FCF										

Starting address of field

FOO	Object descriptor 1
FOE	2 Bytes scratch
F10	Object descriptor 2
F1E	2 Bytes scratch
F20	Object descriptor 3
F2E	
F40	Object descriptor 4
F4E	32 Bytes scratch
F6E	
F80	Background Vertical bar definition 40 Bytes
FA8	Background Horizontal bar definition 5 Bytes
FAD	1 Byte scratch
FAE	
FC0	I/O AND control
FD0	I/O AND control *
FE0	I/O AND control *
FF0	I/O AND control *

* These locations will also address FC0 to FCF.

FIG. 22   Internal memory map of the programmable video interface chip.

Operation of the Object-Oriented* LSI *System   The microprocessor "plays" a game by transferring object shape patterns into the RAM blocks of the PVI and then routing the corresponding position codes into the coordinate registers. An object is moved by programming the microprocessor to change the contents of the coordinate register pair in the appropriate RAM block. Vertical and horizontal motion are thus obtained by incrementing and decrementing the vertical and horizontal registers, respectively.

The object blocks in the PVI internal memory store information about the object shape and the positions of the object and its duplicates on the screen. An object and any subsequent movement is positioned by setting VC and HC (the vertical and horizontal coordinates of the object) to the required values in the appropriate object RAM. These 8-bit unsigned values represent the number of TV lines to skip vertically (VC) and the number of clock pulses to skip horizontally (HC) before shifting out the object video. Several duplicates of a given object can be displayed by setting HCB (the horizontal coordinate of the duplicate) to the required value and VCB (the vertical coordinate of the duplicate) to the number of lines to skip less one after the last line of the primary object video.

In the I/O and control section of the PVI internal memory map (Fig. 22), the first 3 bytes control the sizes and colors of the object. The size of an object is defined by a 2-bit code (**00**, **01**, **10**, or **11**) that allows the dimensions of an object to be multiplied by a factor of 1, 2, 4, or 8. Figure 23 illustrates how the duplicate logic operates and how these codes relate to the object dimensions.

Storage of Object Shape   The object shape is described by a 10-byte array known as SHAPE (see Fig. 24). For an object of size code **00**, each byte in the array represents the video display of one TV line for 8 horizontal clock cycles. That is, each bit represents the video display of one TV line for 1 clock cycle. Bits set to logic **1** cause the video to be displayed (in the color defined by the color-code bytes); bits set to logic **0** give no display. Fig. 25 is an example of how the object shape and multiplication factor are related.

Background-Object Generation   The generation of background video is based upon four data structures:

1. Vertical bar definition (320 bits, that is, 40 bytes)
2. Horizontal bar definition (40 bits, that is, 5 bytes)
3. Background color and enable bits
4. Screen color bits

In the PVI internal memory (Fig. 22), the horizontal- and vertical-bar definition bytes are grouped as 45 consecutive bytes. The physical layout of the bars used to compose a background for a game is shown in Fig. 26. There are 16 vertical lines, each made up of bars alternately 2 and 18 TV lines in height, respectively. Each bar is 1 clock cycle wide and separated from the next bar by 7 clock cycles. Therefore, in all, 320 distinct bars can be displayed. By programming a logic **1** into the appropriate bit of a vertical-bar byte, a particular bar can be displayed in the color defined by the background color code.

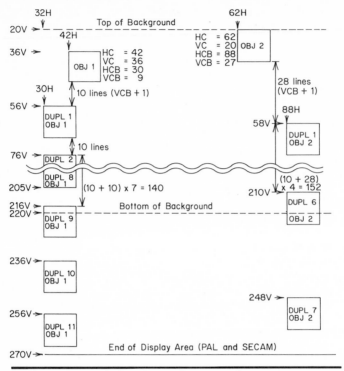

FIG. 23 *Operation of duplicate logic in object-oriented game system.*

Horizontal bars are obtained by extending the vertical bars horizontally to a width of 1, 2, 4, or 8 clock cycles. Each of the five horizontal-bar definition bytes is related to a certain group of sets of vertical bars as follows:

FA8 relates to sets 1 to 4 (F80 to F87)
FA9 relates to sets 5 to 8 (F88 to F8F)
FAA relates to sets 9 to 12 (F90 to F97)
FAB relates to sets 13 to 16 (F98 to F9F)
FAC relates to sets 17 to 20 (FAO to FA7)

Bits 5 to 0 of each of the 5 bytes apply to specific sets of vertical bars. For example, for the first byte:

Bit 0 set 1
Bit 1 top 9 lines of set 2
Bit 2 bottom 9 lines of set 2
Bit 3 set 3
Bit 4 top 9 lines of set 4
Bit 5 bottom 9 lines of set 4

In the next byte, this sequence is repeated for the next four sets of vertical bars, and so on.

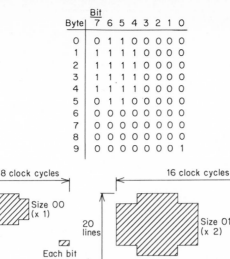

FIG. 24 *SHAPE array and example of relationship between shape and multiplication factor.*

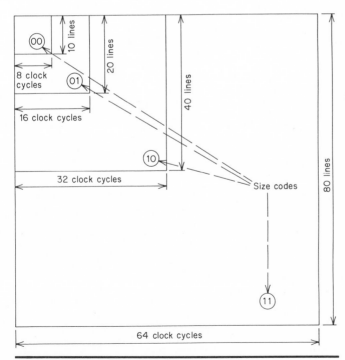

FIG. 25 *Definition of object-size codes.*

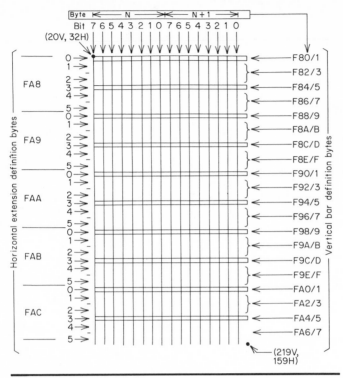

FIG. 26   *Formation and layout of background picture.*

When an appropriate bit is programmed to logic **1**, a particular bar is extended horizontally to a width of 8 clock cycles. When programmed to logic **0**, the width is determined by bits 7 and 6 of the same byte according to the following code:

Bit 7	Bit 6	Horizontal extension (clock cycles)
0	0	1
0	1	2
1	0	1
1	1	4

Figure 27 is an example of background programming. The vertical-bar structure in Fig. 27a is extended horizontally in Fig. 27b according to the horizontal definition byte FA8.

Figure 28 is a typical example of a complete background composition. The screen and background colors are programmed in byte FC6 of the I/O and control section of the PVI internal memory (Fig. 22). The screen color code generates a screen color at places where no background, score, or object video are produced.

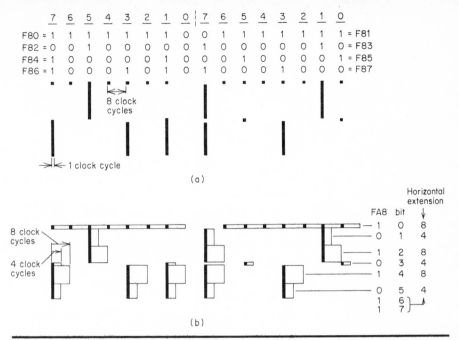

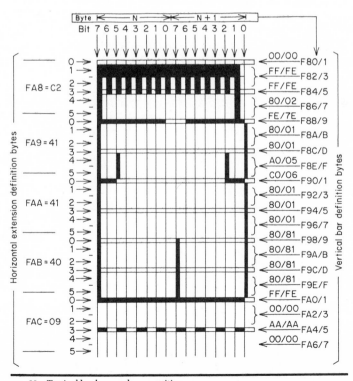

FIG. 27 *Example of background programming: (a) vertical bar definition, and (b) horizontal bar extension as defined by FA8. For clarity, the horizontally extended portions are shown unshaded.*

FIG. 28 *Typical background composition.*

The background enable bit in FC6, when set to logic **0**, outputs a code of 111 on the color outputs for both background and screen color. This allows the color outputs of other PVIs to be wire-ORed in a multiple PVI system in which only one PVI controls the screen and background colors.

Score Display The digits can be displayed as two separate score digit formats or as a single 4-digit field. The format chosen is set by the form bit in byte FC3 of the I/O and control section, logic **0** for 2-digit formats or logic **1** for a 4-digit format (Fig. 22). The position of the score display can be programmed in the POS bit; logic **0** displays the score in the top 20 lines of the background, and logic **1** displays it in the bottom 20 lines. Figure 29 shows the two score formats.

The color-precedence scheme of the PVI is activated in the following order of priority: objects, background, and screen color. As shown in Fig. 22, the 2 bytes at addresses FCA and FCB in the I/O and control section of the PVI memory contain various status bits.

Synchronization of Object-Oriented System The vertical reset leading edge (VRLE) bit and the OBJECT COMPLETE bits, when set, generate an interrupt signal to the microprocessor. The VRLE bit and the interrupt signal are derived from the frame timing signal generated by the timing circuit. This timing signal is produced every 16.67 ms in the NTSC system. The interrupt signal, which generates a fixed-address vector on address 0003 (hex), is used to synchronize the game program with the frame timing signals.

The OBJECT COMPLETE bits are set when the last line of the video display of an object is shifted out to the color outputs of the PVI. An interrupt signal is also generated indicating to the microprocessor that a given object or one of its duplicates has been completely shifted out. This accurately defines the moment for the processor to change the shape and size of an object, the positions of its duplicates, or even its color. With the techniques outlined here, it is possible to simultaneously "paint" to about 80 different objects on the screen using the object blocks of only one PVI.

Many games require the detection of collisions (video overlay) among objects and between objects and background. Collision detection is easily achieved with the PVI by using the arrangement shown in Fig. 30. A 6-bit status word indicates to the microprocessor which two objects have collided. Similarly, collisions between objects and background can be detected. The collision status bits are valid and can be read out during the TV vertical flyback period. They are reset upon readout or at the end of the flyback period.

Audio Output The PVI contains an 8-bit register in which a code n can be written to enable the generation of an audio frequency f_s.

$$f_s = \frac{f_h}{n+1} \qquad n > 0$$

where f_h is the horizontal line frequency generated by the timing circuit. A value of $n = 0$ will inhibit the sound output. A range of different sounds can be obtained by programming different frequencies with different durations.

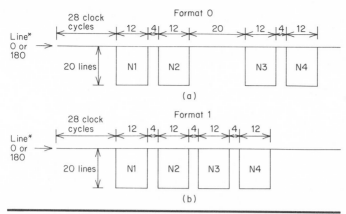

FIG. 29 *Score formats: (a) separate 2-digit fields, and (b) single 4-digit field (*relative to upper left corner of background).*

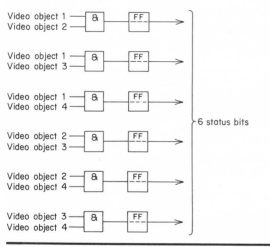

FIG. 30 *Principle of collision detection.*

Human Inputs Interfacing the games system with the players is generally achieved through potentiometers, joysticks, and key-pad switches. With both analog and digital input devices, the PVI is designed to minimize the hardware required.

To interface with potentiometers, the PVI has two potentiometer inputs, each connected to its own on-chip ADC. The converters have an 8-bit resolution, and the digital values can be read out every frame (the principle is shown in Fig. 31). A digital pulse is derived from the analog input signal by means of the level detector. The duration of this pulse (count enable) depends upon the shape of the curve, which in turn depends directly upon the value

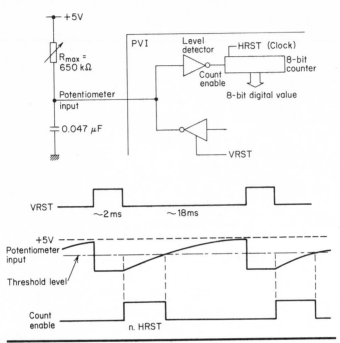

FIG. 31 Analog-to-digital conversion in the PVI chip.

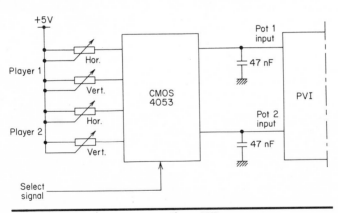

FIG. 32 Use of four potentiometers with one PVI.

of the potentiometer resistance. At every frame (16.67 ms) the potentiometer resistance is monitored and converted to a digital value.

To increase the number of potentiometers in a system (for example, four potentiometers), analog multiplexers such as the CMOS 4053 can be used (see Fig. 32). For key-pad inputs, a special I/O select signal is generated by the

PVI. This signal is derived from the address bus between the microprocessor and the PVI. With two simple standard TTL circuits, matrix key-pad configurations of 32 key positions can easily be achieved. These 32 keys operate as two isolated groups of 16 keys, one group for each player (see Fig. 33).

Clock and Timing Signals The USG provides the timing and control circuits necessary for displaying TV composite video information. It is mask-programmed for the PAL and NTSC TV standards. Both the timing and clock signals for the PVI and microprocessor, and the special TV timing signals for control of the color-encoder circuit, are generated in this circuit from a single master clock input.

In the NTSC version of the USG, the master clock input is the NTSC color-carrier frequency 3.579545 MHz. In the PAL system, the master input frequency is slightly different, namely, 3.54689 MHz, and is derived from the PAL double color-carrier frequency 8.867238 MHz divided by 2.5. This divisor of 2.5 is provided by the PAL color encoder and video summer circuit.

The object-oriented approach to the implementation of video games using the PVI offers a number of advantages for both system hardware and software. Many essential actions, such as the movement, rotation, and enlargement of objects, the detection of collisions, and color changes, can be easily programmed using a small program. In addition, the number of objects displayed is not overly limited by the speed of the system. Empirical results indicate that with a single PVI and a typical 8-bit microprocessor, up to 28

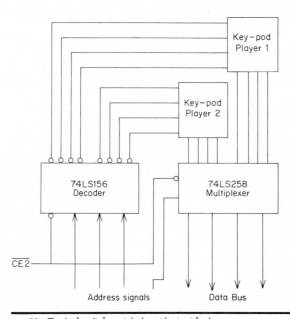

FIG. 33 *Typical switch matrix input/output logic.*

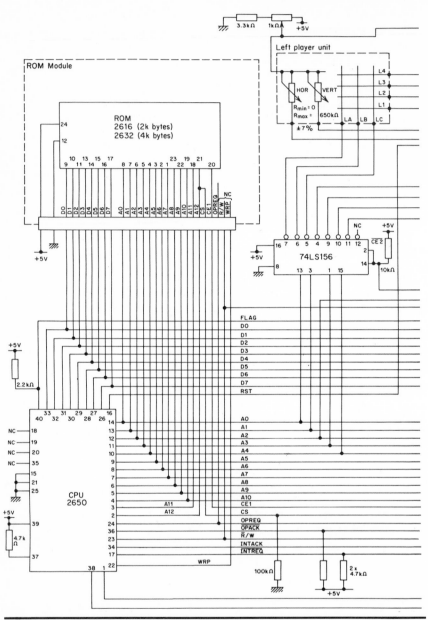

FIG. 34   Typical video-games system using the 2650 microprocessor.

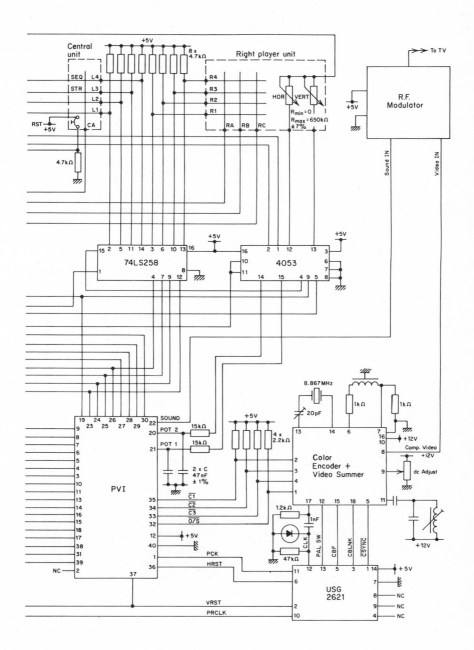

moving objects can be easily programmed. Another key feature is extremely low hardware cost because all the video generation logic and some of the I/O control facilities are all integrated on a single LSI chip.

A typical programmable games system requires only the following components:

Four NMOS LSI circuits
One bipolar LSI circuit
Two medium-scale integrated (MSI) TTL circuits
One CMOS circuit

The complete diagram of a games system using the PVI is given in Fig. 34.

7.4 Game Examples Using the Object-Oriented Approach

A battle involving two tanks is one of the most popular video games; the goal is to shoot and destroy the opponent's tank. The success of the game is largely attributed to the realistic motion and sound and the manner in which the tanks are controlled. The logic of the first game was built entirely from TTL MSI. The following example illustrates how the same game can be implemented using the PVI.

During initialization, all the patterns of the tank and shells are loaded into the four object RAMs. The color, size, and background are set up, and the game begins. The rotation and motion of the tank are controlled by switch inputs to the microprocessor. All inputs are debounced and then decoded to give rotation, acceleration, and deceleration; steady motion; shell motion; shell explosion; blow up of tanks; and scoring.

Using the PVI described earlier, all these functions can be accomplished under software control. When the microprocessor receives an input to rotate the tank, the pattern of the object is updated once every 6 to 10 frames by loading a different image into the SHAPE of the object RAM containing the tank.

The microprocessor controls the motion of the tank by updating its position once every six or seven frames. Angle of motion is determined by the relative frequency of updating the vertical or horizontal position. For example, a 22½° motion is updated once vertically and twice horizontally every six or seven frames. Speed is then determined by the frequency with which the positions of the tanks are updated. The more often a tank's position is updated, the faster it is traveling. Changes in frequency also determine the acceleration and deceleration functions. All these functions are under software control.

When the microprocessor receives a switch-closure input for firing a shell, a shell is painted at the coordinates of the tank's gun. The shell is then directed to move at a faster speed in the direction of the traveling tank. The microprocessor keeps track of the time (in terms of elapsed frames) and explodes the shell after a fixed number of frames. If the microprocessor detects a coincidence of the coordinates of the shell and the opponent tank, the tank explodes. The explosion is portrayed by various explosion patterns every three or six frames.

Objects in the background of the video screen (e.g., mines and walls) are set up by the microprocessor. When a tank runs into a mine, for example, the program again gives explosions of the tank and afterward removes the mine from the screen.

REFERENCE

Li, K.: "Microprocessor-based Video Games," *Electronic Design*, vol. 25, Dec. 6, 1977, p. 84.

CHAPTER EIGHT

Microprocessor-A/D Converter Interfaces

David F. Stout

Dataface, Inc.
Santa Clara, California

8.1 Basic Definition of an Analog-to-Digital Converter (ADC)

An ADC changes an analog input voltage into an n-bit digital word. In effect, the input voltage is quantized into 2^n different digital words, one for each state of the n-bit output word.

Hundreds of different approaches to A/D conversion are published in the literature, but only a few techniques have been successfully implemented in monolithic form. Several of these approaches use an integrator stage and can be classified as high-precision–low-speed devices. The fastest techniques use successive approximation (S/A) and are several orders of magnitude faster than the integration methods. Here we discuss three integration techniques and one S/A technique.

Dual-Slope ADC   The basic circuit for this technique is shown in Fig. 1. The control logic begins each cycle by commanding the input switch to the lower position, where a current proportional to the input voltage

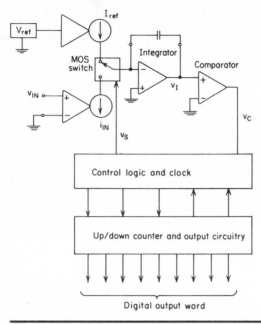

FIG. 1   *A dual-ramp A/D converter uses an integrator with switched inputs and a comparator. (From Ref. 9, with permission)*

is processed by the integrator. Because this current pulls positive charge from the op-amp input, the integrator output slews upward, as shown in Fig. 2. This positive slope continues for a fixed time T_1, as established by the control logic. The peak voltage reached by v_I is proportional to the input voltage v_{IN}. At the end of T_1 (and the start of T_2), the control logic changes the switch to the reference-current input. Because the reference current goes into the integrator, the voltage v_I decreases at a rate proportional to V_{ref}. During T_2 a counter begins operating. When the negative-going ramp crosses zero, the comparator output changes state, causing the counter to stop. The magnitude of the number stored in the counter is therefore proportional to the input voltage v_{IN}.

Note that during T_1 the integration takes place for a fixed time at a variable slope. During T_2 the integration is accomplished at a fixed slope and a variable time. From Fig. 2 observe that the change in capacitor voltage is equal in magnitude during T_1 and T_2. Thus

$$\frac{1}{C} \int i_{IN} \, dt = \frac{1}{C} \int I_{ref} \, dt$$

or $\qquad i_{IN} T_1 = I_{ref} T_2$

If each voltage-to-current converter is linear and their gains are equal, then

$$v_{IN} T_1 = V_{ref} T_2$$

The unknown voltage v_{IN} in terms of the three known or measurable parameters is therefore

$$v_{IN} = \frac{V_{ref}T_2}{T_1}$$

Both V_{ref} and T_1 are constants, and T_2 is proportional to the digital output word. We conclude that the digital output word is proportional to the magnitude of the input analog voltage.

The principal advantages of a dual-slope ADC is its high resolution for a relatively low cost, accounted for by the absence of an on-chip precision resistor network. Dual-slope ADCs in monolithic form are available with up to 14 bits of resolution. Because the input signal is integrated, these converters are nearly immune to noise. They are also highly linear with a guaranteed monotonicity; i.e., missing codes are nearly impossible because of the nature of integration signal processing. The main disadvantage of dual-slope converters is their slow speed: A typical 8-bit dual-slope ADC might require 10 ms per conversion. However, in many applications, such as digital voltmeters, samples are needed only several times per second.

Dual-Slope ADC with Automatic Zero Even though dual-slope ADCs are highly accurate, they can still be improved using automatic-zero circuitry. A dual-slope converter can be considered a two-phase circuit: The first phase is the positive integration of the input signal; the second phase is the negative integration of the reference source. Automatic-zero ADCs typically use three, four, or five phases per complete cycle. The last two phases operate in the normal dual-slope mode. The automatic-zero operations operate just before the positive signal integration.

The multiphase automatic-zero technique reduces the errors caused by off-

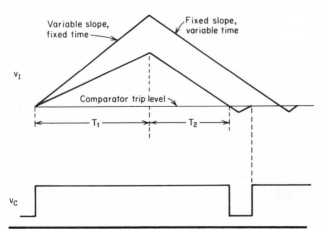

FIG. 2 *Waveforms of the ADC integrator output* v_I *and comparator output* v_C. *(From Ref. 9, with permission)*

set and drift of the integrator and comparator. The ultimate resolution of the ADC is thereby determined by the noise of the system. In effect, the automatic-zero circuitry measures offset errors just a few milliseconds before the dual-slope measurement and stores the resulting error either on a capacitor or in a digital word. If the error is stored on a capacitor, it is then subtracted from the dual-slope measurement in an analog subtractor circuit, i.e., by using the other input to the integrator. If the error is stored in a digital word, it is subtracted from the digital counter output using digital subtraction techniques. In either case the errors are subtracted for the ADC output cycle-by-cycle. In this manner the error-correction circuitry tracks errors as they change with time or temperature.

The Analog Devices, Inc. AD7550 ADC uses auto-zero circuitry to achieve 13-bit resolution with less than 1 ppm/°C gain and offset sensitivity. This chip is advertised as a quadruple-slope device, but before the four phases begin, a setup phase ϕ_o is required. During this time, as shown in Figs. 3 and 4, switch S1 is closed and switches S2 to S4 are open. This applies the full V_{ref} to the integrator negative input, resulting in a negative-going ramp at the integrator output. When the ramp voltage is equal to the comparator's trip voltage, ϕ_1 begins. This trip voltage is at analog ground.

At the initiation of ϕ_1, a digital counter starts, S3 is closed, and all other switches open. This connects the analog ground to the integrator input to determine whether the ADC's negative supply voltage is at analog ground potential. If not, an error voltage (dashed line in Fig. 4) is produced, which is proportional to the difference. This error voltage is stored on the external integrating capacitor.

During ϕ_2 the integrator is connected to V_{ref} by closing S1 and opening all other switches. The output of the integrator falls at a rate proportional to V_{ref} until the comparator trip point is reached. If no errors have been accumulated up to that point, ϕ_2 lasts exactly as long as ϕ_1. If errors are found on AGND or V_{ref} with respect to $V_{ref}/2$, the comparator will not trip exactly T_1 after ϕ_2 begins. The trip-time error T_2 can be a positive or negative number about the ideal trip time if an error occurs. T_2 is stored for use during the final two phases of the cycle.

The main integration phase ϕ_3 takes place with S2 closed and all other switches open. This set of conditions lasts for a fixed time $2T_1$ plus or minus the error time T_2. As shown by the dashed lines, if the error is positive, the time for phase ϕ_3 is shortened. This shorter time effectively reduces the gain of the integrator during ϕ_3.

The final phase ϕ_4 is implemented by closing S1 and opening all other switches. This discharges the integration capacitor at a fixed rate determined by V_{ref}. This phase terminates when the capacitor voltage goes through the comparator trip level. Because of the slope correction during ϕ_3, the counter contents at the end of ϕ_4 will contain a corrected A/D conversion number.

Charge-Balancing ADC   This type of conversion process, like the dual-slope process, requires integration of the input signal, but the similarity ends there. Charge balancing, or quantized feedback as some manufacturers call it, is

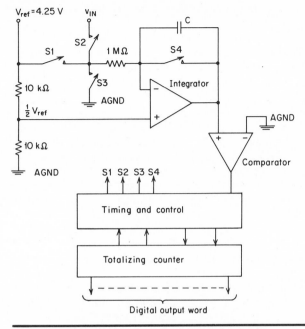

FIG. 3 Simplified schematic of Analog Devices AD7550 A/D converter with 4-phase auto-zero circuitry. (From Ref. 9, with permission.)

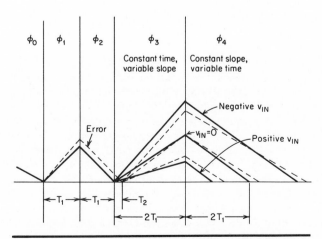

FIG. 4 Integrator output voltage during a complete cycle of the auto-zero A/D converter shown in Fig. 3. (From Ref. 9, with permission.)

becoming the preferred technique for LSI ADCs when high-speed operation is not required.

The dual-slope converter applies an unknown signal to an uncharged capacitor for a fixed length of time and later measures the time required to discharge the capacitor at a constant rate. In a charge-balancing converter, however, there is no fixed charging period; the charging continues as long as required to boost the capacitor voltage past a fixed voltage threshold. Each time this crossover occurs, a reference current is subtracted from the input current. When the capacitor discharges past the threshold, the process repeats. This incremental charge balancing repeats many times until the conversion period is complete. During all the conversion period, the ADC keeps the integrator output voltage near the level of the reference voltage. In effect, the device measures the amount of charge required to balance the charge developed on the integrating capacitor by the analog input. The net time required by the reference circuitry to hold the capacitor voltage near the threshold is therefore proportional to the input voltage. A counter accumulates clock pulses whenever the reference is switched ON. At the end of the conversion period, this counter contains a number proportional to the analog input voltage.

Several variations of the basic charge-balancing technique have been implemented in monolithic form. Figure 5a shows a block diagram of the approach used in the Siliconix LD130 converter. This device uses two reference currents summing into the integrator input, along with a current proportional to v_{IN}. If $2I_{ref}$ is ON 50 percent of the time, the average reference current is zero. These are the operating conditions with zero analog input voltage. With zero v_{IN}, the up-down counter fills to the 50 percent point during each conversion period, indicating the midpoint between $-v_{IN,max}$ and $+v_{IN,max}$. If a positive v_{IN} is applied, $2I_{ref}$ is ON more than 50 percent of the time, to keep the integrator output near the comparator V_{ref}. This causes a faster accumulation of clock pulses in the up-down counter. Likewise, negative v_{IN} voltages create a switch-duty cycle less than 50 percent and a corresponding smaller pulse accumulation in the counter.

***Successive-Approximation* (S/A) ADC** The faster ADC chips use the S/A technique. These devices are typically two or three orders of magnitude faster than ADCs using integration, but during any given year the S/A chips lag behind the resolution of integrating chips by 2 to 4 bits.

As indicated in Fig. 6, the basic components of an S/A ADC are a voltage comparator, a D/A converter (DAC), a successive-approximation register (SAR), and a clock. The SAR enables the bits of the DAC one at a time, beginning with the most significant bit (MSB). As each bit is enabled, the comparator output indicates whether v_{IN} is larger or smaller than the DAC output v_D. If $v_{IN} < v_D$, the bit is turned OFF. If $v_D < v_{IN}$, the bit is left ON. After this test, the next lower-order bit is tested. When all bits have been tested, the conversion cycle is complete and the lines between the DAC and SAR contain the digital output. In most devices an end-of-conversion signal is sent to outside circuitry to flag the availability of a complete output word.

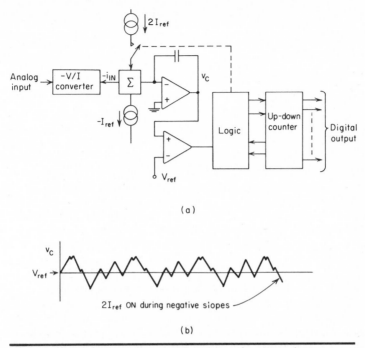

(a)

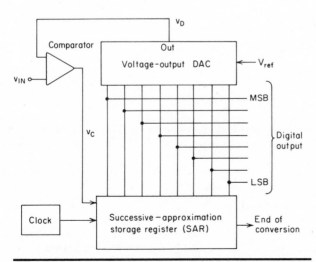

(b)

FIG. 5   *A charge-balancing ADC using both positive and negative reference-current sources: (a) block diagram, and (b) typical waveform on the integrating capacitor. (From Ref. 9, with permission)*

FIG. 6   *The four basic components of a successive-approximation A/D converter. (From Ref. 9, with permission)*

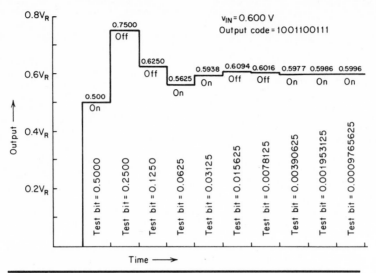

FIG. 7   *Output voltage from the DAC in a successive-approximation ADC if V_{IN} = 0.6 V_R (V_{IN} = 0.600 V; output code = **1001100111**). (From Ref. 9, with permission)*

Figure 7 helps clarify the process just described. Suppose v_{IN} = 0.600 V and V_{ref} = 1.000 V. The DAC first tries 0.500 V and finds v_{IN} larger, so that bit remains ON. The next bit causes the DAC output to be 0.500 + 0.25 = 0.75 V. This is too large, so the bit is left OFF and the SAR proceeds to the third bit. After 10 bits have been tested one at a time, the binary number will be **1001100111**, which is equivalent to the following sum:

$$
\begin{array}{r}
0.5000000000 \\
0.0625000000 \\
0.0312500000 \\
0.0039062500 \\
0.0019531250 \\
\underline{0.0009765625} \\
0.5996093755
\end{array}
$$

Of course, because this example concerns a 10-bit ADC, the ultimate resolution is 0.1 percent, and so we can use only the first 4 digits, that is, 0.5996.

8.2   ADC *Parameter Definitions*

Each manufacturer uses a preferred set of parameters to specify its product. When comparing various ADCs, the designer often has the problem of evaluating devices from several companies when no standard specifications exist between manufacturers. Before parameters with the same name on different data sheets can be compared, the designer must ascertain that the test conditions for each are identical (or at least similar). Perhaps the most surprising result of a perusal of a number of ADC data sheets is that some data sheets specify nearly all the following parameters, but a few data sheets discuss *none.*

Accuracy, absolute   This is also called *gain variance* or *full-scale gain set point.* The ability of an ADC to duplicate the transfer function at full scale as established during manufacture is called the absolute accuracy. This parameter can usually be trimmed by the user.

Accuracy, relative   Same as integral linearity.

Gain drift   This parameter is also called *gain temperature coefficient (gain TC), full-scale drift,* or *full-scale set-point TC.* It is also dependent upon drift of the reference voltage.

Linearity, differential   Figure 8a clearly illustrates the differential linearity (or nonlinearity) of an ADC (only 3 bits of resolution are used, to simplify the drawing). Differential linearity error is the amount of deviation of any quantum step Q from its ideal step size; i.e., it is the deviation in the input analog difference between two adjacent output codes from the ideal value of $FS/2^n$. If an ADC is specified as having a maximum differential linearity error of $\pm\frac{1}{2}$ least significant bit (LSB), the actual size of any quantum step is between $\frac{1}{2}$ and $1\frac{1}{2}$ LSB because the nominal step size is 1 LSB. Figure 8a shows differential linearity errors of $+\frac{1}{2}$ and $-\frac{1}{2}$ LSB. The finite step size Q is sometimes called *quantization error.*

Linearity, integral   As indicated in Fig. 8b, a straight-line transfer function is drawn between the zero input-output (I/O) point and FS I/O point. Integral linearity error is caused by curvature of that transfer function. Thus, integral linearity error is defined as the maximum deviation of the actual transfer

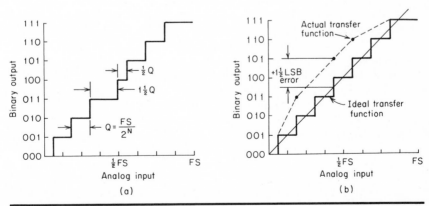

FIG. 8   *Eight-level examples of (a) differential nonlinearity, and (b) integral nonlinearity of an ADC. (From Ref. 9, with permission.)*

function from the ideal straight line. This parameter is specified in LSBs or percent of full scale.

Linearity drift Both differential and integral linearity errors are subject to drift induced by temperature and time. This drift is usually specified in parts per million per Celsius degree (ppm/°C).

Noise The input comparator or input op amp of an ADC are the most likely sources of internal noise. Because the output of an ADC is a digital word, any noise measurement must look for false changes of output states when the input is held constant. The noise, however, is referred to the input because noise has traditionally been an analog quantity.

The noise due to quantization of the analog input into 2^n discrete digital output words is an inherent irreducible source of noise. Because an ADC cannot distinguish an analog difference less than Q (see Fig. 8), its output at any point may be in error by at least $\pm Q/2$.

Power Supply Sensitivity It is desirable for an ADC to maintain a precise transfer function with little dependence upon power supply voltage stability. The power supply sensitivity specifies the effect of changes in power supply voltage on the ADC transfer function. Typically, the effect is tabulated at zero input, midrange input, and/or full-scale input. The parameter units are usually percent per percent, percent full-scale percent, or percent per 1 percent. The data sheet also shows the test setup for this measurement.

Some data sheets also separately specify the effect of the power supply on the internal reference voltage. However, any drift in the reference voltage also shows up as drift in the ADC transfer function. The overall power supply sensitivity parameter should be adequate for most applications.

Resolution The nominal resolution of an ADC is the relative value of the LSB, namely, 2^n. It is expressed as 1 part in 2^n, as a percentage, in parts per million, or simply by n bits. Useful resolution is the smallest uniquely distinguishable change in the transfer function for all operating conditions, i.e., over time and temperature. For example, a 12-bit ADC may have a useful resolution of only 10 bits when all errors are summed together.

Symmetry ADCs that handle both positive and negative analog inputs have the additional problem of characterizing uniformity of response on both sides of zero. The symmetry parameter is specified at the full-scale positive and negative inputs. Each input should produce the exact same digital output word, except for the sign bit. Any error is characterized in terms of LSBs or percentage of full scale.

Zero Drift Most ADC devices can be trimmed at zero and full scale. The gain drift specifies the stability of the full-scale set point. At the other end of the scale, the zero-drift parameter characterizes the stability of the zero set point.

8.3   Two Examples: Interfacing an ADC with a Microprocessor

Software control of ADCs provides a wide range of application possibilities to systems designers. The two applications discussed utilize the Teledyne 8700 incremental charge-balancing ADC. In the first application (Sec. 8.4), which utilizes the 6800 microprocessor, converted samples are averaged and compared with other data stored in software via the free-running mode. Program control depends upon the outcome of each averaged sample compared with previous averaged samples. This particular program was developed for a system requiring precise determination of the amplitude of a noisy signal. The peak measurement in a given time interval is stored and its magnitude used to control the program direction. The second application (Sec. 8.5) shows how this same ADC could interface with an 8080 microprocessor via the interrupt mode of operation.

8.4   Free-Running Averaging ADC

As indicated in Fig. 9, the A/D chip interfaces with the microprocessor data bus through two 80C95 hex CMOS tristate buffers. Each time the address decoder generates a negative pulse on UP or UP + 1, each buffer transfers the ADC outputs to the data bus.

***Free-Running or Clocked* ADC**   The A/D output data are not valid unless the data-valid line is HIGH. Figure 10 shows that this condition does not exist for about 1.25 to 1.8 ms after the initiate conversion (IC) line is pulsed by the microprocessor. This is called the *clocked mode* because the ADC remains idle until the microprocessor requests a conversion. The software must be written so that the output data are not read until the valid line has gone LOW and returned to the HIGH state. If the output data are read within 1 ms after the rising edge of IC, the data will be old.

If the ADC is used in the *free-running mode*, as in this example, the sampling interval of the microprocessor must be greater than 1.8 ms to ensure independent samples. Assume that this circuit is part of a large system controlled by a single microprocessor. The ADC is only one device of many being sampled periodically. Assume that the sampling interval of any particular device is 10 ms minimum. This ensures independent samples of the ADC because only one of every six converter samples will be utilized.

Obtaining Valid* ADC *Data   As shown in Fig. 11, the ADC must be sampled only when valid is HIGH. One approach is to read the valid line just before reading the converter. If valid = **1**, the measurement is made. Otherwise valid is reread until it indicates that a complete conversion is available for transfer to the microprocessor. However, this approach has a basic problem. After valid is read, it takes 5 to 10 μs for the microprocessor to decide if valid = **1**

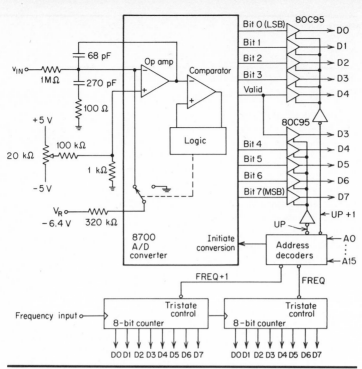

FIG. 9   An A/D converter controlled by a microprocessor. (From Ref. 9, with permission.)

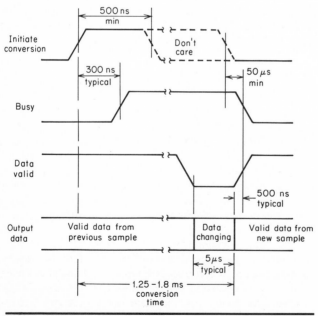

FIG. 10   Timing waveforms for the 8700 A/D converter operating in the clocked mode. (From Ref. 9, with permission.)

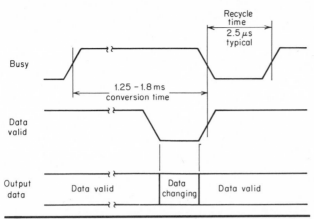

FIG. 11 *Timing waveforms of the 8700 A/D converter operating in the free-run mode. (From Ref. 9, with permission.)*

and make the decision to read the ADC data. During this 10-μs interval the A/D data can start changing. A better approach is to read the data and the valid line simultaneously using a Load Index Register (LDX) instruction.

The LDX instruction is 5 μs long, assuming a 1-MHz clock. The 16-bit index register is loaded in two 8-bit bytes during the fourth and fifth microseconds (see Motorola 6800 data sheet). Suppose we load 4 bits of the ADC data along with the valid bit during the fourth microsecond. On the fifth microsecond we load the other 4 data bits along with the valid bit again. If both readings of the valid bit are HIGH, the data word has a 100 percent probability of being correct. The software then combines the two halves of the data word and processes the result.

Software Description The flowchart and program listing of the microprocessor-controlled ADC subroutine are shown in Fig. 12. Follow both the listing and the flowchart as the subroutine is described. The subroutine computes the average of 256 samples from the ADC. An 8-bit counter labeled N keeps track of the sample number. As the subroutine is entered, N is checked to see if it is **0**. If so, a previous 256 average has been completed and a new average is to be started. This is done by clearing out SUM1 and SUM2, that is, the 16-bit register holding the sum of the samples. Each new sample is added to SUM1. Whenever SUM1 overflows, SUM2 is incremented. After 256 additions into SUM1, the 16-bit register represented by SUM2 and SUM1 contains the total number. The average sample is merely the total divided by 256. This could be obtained by shifting the 16-bit total of the right eight places, but this division is not required if we use the upper 8 bits directly; i.e., SUM2 is the average value of the 256 samples.

The 16-bit index register is loaded with 8 bits of data and the valid bit (twice), as shown in Fig. 13. After the index register is loaded, it is immediately

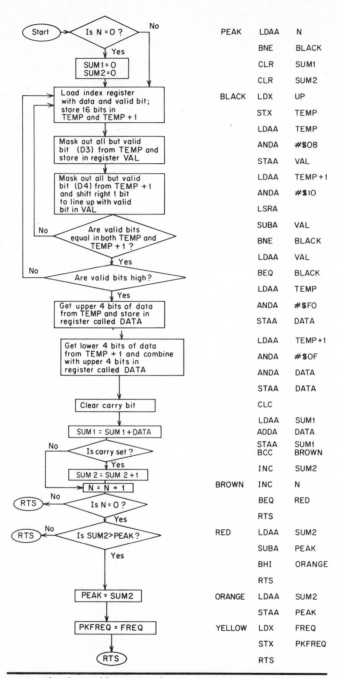

FIG. 12   Flowchart and listing of a subroutine to average an input voltage
over 256 samples, compare with previous peaks, and store another variable
which identifies the location of the peak. (From Ref. 9, with permission.)

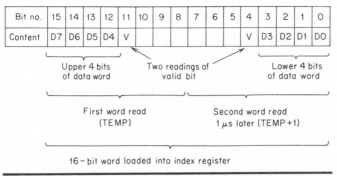

Bit no.	15	14	13	12	11	10	9	8	7	6	5	4	3	2	1	0
Content	D7	D6	D5	D4	V							V	D3	D2	D1	D0

Upper 4 bits of data word   Two readings of valid bit   Lower 4 bits of data word

First word read (TEMP)   Second word read 1 μs later (TEMP + 1)

16 – bit word loaded into index register

FIG. 13 Arrangement of data and valid information loaded into the 16-bit index register. (From Ref. 9, with permission.)

stored in TEMP and TEMP + 1. Register TEMP contains the valid bit (D3) and the upper 4 bits of the data word (D4 to D7). TEMP is loaded into the A accumulator, where the data word is removed by ANDing with $08. If valid is HIGH, D3 will be HIGH. The result is stored in a register called VAL. Register TEMP + 1 is next loaded into the A accumulator. This register contains the valid bit again (D4) and the lower 4 bits of the data word (D0 to D3). The data word is masked out by ANDing with $10. The result is shifted right one place so that the valid bit is in the same bit position as the valid bit in TEMP. Now subtract the VAL register from accumulator A. If both valid bits are HIGH, the result is **0** and the program continues. If one of the valid bits is LOW, accumulator A will contain a nonzero number. In this case the program returns to black, where the A/D sample is read again. The program also returns to black if both valid bits are LOW.

If both valid bits are HIGH, the program reconstructs the 8-bit data word by using a $FO mask on TEMP and a $OF mask on TEMP + 1. The results of each masking are combined and stored in a register called DATA. This register is next added to the SUM1 register. If the SUM1 register overflows, register SUM2 is incremented on count. Counter N is also incremented at this time and tested for zero content. If N ≠ **0**, the subroutine is finished for this loop of the MAIN program (256 passes through the subroutine are required for each averaged sample). If N = **0**, the averaging is complete and SUM2 contains the average of all 256 A/D conversion samples. This average (SUM2) is compared with PEAK (the largest average found at some earlier time when this subroutine was utilized). If SUM2 ≤ PEAK, the subroutine is terminated. If SUM2 > PEAK, SUM2 replaces PEAK. Another variable is also recorded to identify the time (or some other identifier such as operating frequency) where this new PEAK occurred. In the author's system the A/D conversion was performed on the automatic gain control (AGC) of a sophisticated receiver and PKFREQ was the tuning frequency where the peak AGC occurred. This subroutine facilitated automatic tuning of the receiver.

8.5   *Software-Initiated* ADC

This section describes a method of interfacing an 8-bit Teledyne 8700 ADC with the 8080 microprocessor using the interrupt mode of operation. The system provides one ADC sample for one initiate conversion (IC) signal from the microprocessor. Because the conversion requires over 1 ms to perform, the microprocessor proceeds with other calculations while the ADC responds to the IC command. When conversion is complete, an interrupt (data valid) is transferred to the microprocessor and the 8-bit converter output is read.

The data-valid output is normally HIGH, indicating that the converter output lines are valid, except for approximately 5 μs before the end of the conversion time, when these outputs are updated (see Fig. 10). The output latches maintain the data from the previous conversion while the next conversion is being performed. The initiate conversion input line allows the ADC to be operated under system control. A positive-going pulse at least 500 ns long causes the conversion to begin.

Communications between an 8080 microcomputer system and the outside world are via I/O ports addressed by the address bus. I/O instructions utilize 8-bit addresses that simultaneously appear on both the upper 8 bits and the lower 8 bits of the 16-bit address bus. In addition to the 24 address and data lines, the 8080 system communicates with the ADC via a set of control signals called $\overline{\text{IN}}$ and $\overline{\text{OUT}}$. As shown in Fig. 14, data-bus buffering and the generation of $\overline{\text{IN}}$ and $\overline{\text{OUT}}$ are performed with the 8228 chip. A logic LOW on the $\overline{\text{IN}}$ line enables the input port corresponding to the address on the address bus at that time. The $\overline{\text{OUT}}$ line performs a similar function for data coming out of the microprocessor system.

The conversion is started on command of the 8080 using the IC input of the 8700. When the conversion is complete, the 8700 requests an interrupt. The INTERRUPT SERVICE routine transfers the current data from all working registers to the stack memory, and the A/D input port is read. Another IC command is issued and the cycle repeats.

In most microprocessor systems the data bus is shared by many devices, such as memory and I/O ports. If the 8228 bidirectional bus driver-receiver is used, the data-bus information is inverted throughout the system. The 80L98 inverting buffers are provided at the ADC outputs to invert the data-bus lines, boost their power level, and provide a three-state capability. Thus, the 8700 is electrically removed from the 8080 system data bus when its input port is not selected.

Each port of the microprocessor system is assigned an address. Either the upper 8 bits or the lower 8 bits of the address bus must be decoded for each port. In Fig. 14 the output of the 7430 gate is LOW only when address lines $\overline{A}_o$ to $\overline{A}_7$ are all LOW. This corresponds to an I/O port having an address of FF (hex). This same port address is used for input or output to and from the 8700 ADC. The IC pulse is generated using the $\overline{\text{OUT}}$ instruction to output port FF twice. On the first $\overline{\text{OUT}}$ instruction, 80 (hex) is loaded onto the data bus. The D flip-flop FF2 sees the 80 inverted to a LOW state on data bus line $\overline{D}_7$, and the flip-flop $\overline{Q}$ output latches into the HIGH state. A second output instruction,

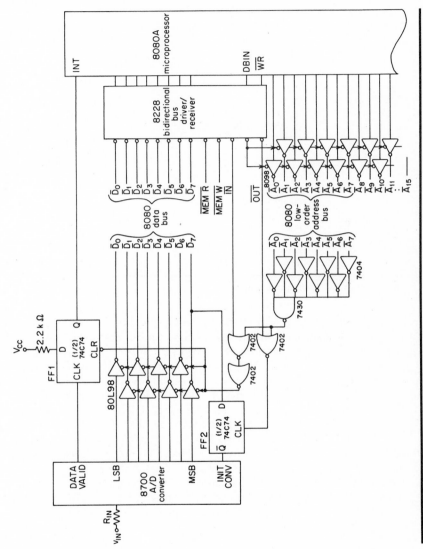

FIG. 14 Digital interface of an 8700 A/D converter and an 8080-based microprocessor system. See Fig. 9 (p. 8–12) for the analog connections to the 8700. [From Ref. 9, with permission.]

TABLE 1 *Program listing of 8700* ADC INTERRUPT SERVICE *subroutine*

START	MVI	A, 80H	Initiate conversion:
	OUT	FFH	output HIGH level
	MVI	A, 0	then
	OUT	FFH	output LOW level
	RET		
INTERRUPT	PUSH	B	
	PUSH	D	
	PUSH	H	
	PUSH	PSW	
	IN	FFH	
	MOV	B, A	
	MVI	A, 80H	
	OUT	FFH	
	MVI	A, 0	
	OUT	FFH	
	POP	PSW	
	POP	H	
	POP	D	
	POP	B	
	RET		

SOURCE: From Ref. 9, with permission.

sending zero to the same port, clears the flip-flop $\overline{Q}$ output and removes the IC signal. Because each output instruction requires approximately 5 μs, this will be the approximate width of the IC pulse. After this pulse is issued, the microprocessor is free to perform other tasks while the ADC performs its conversion.

When the 8700 completes the A/D conversion, the data-valid line goes HIGH. This signal triggers FF1, clocking a logic HIGH from the D input onto the microprocessor interrupt-request (IRQ) line. The INTERRUPT SERVICE routine is initiated when IRQ goes HIGH. The microprocessor is directed to read the 8700 data at input address FF (hex). This action causes the $\overline{\text{IN}}$ line to go low, which in turn activates the 80L98 buffer and clears FF1. After the ADC data has been read and stored in memory, the microprocessor system is free to issue another IC command whenever needed.

Table 1 shows the software program to operate the 8700 ADC.

REFERENCES

1. Guzeman, D.: "Interfacing the 8700 A/D Converter with the 8080 Microprocessor System," Teledyne Semiconductor App. Note 8, August 1976.
2. Zuch, E. L.: "Interpretation of Data Converter Accuracy Specifications," *Computer Design*, September 1978, p. 113.
3. Henry, T.: "Successive Approximation A/D Conversion," Motorola App. Note AN-716, 1974.
4. Sheingold, D. H., and R. A. Ferrero: "Understanding A/D and D/A Converters," *IEEE Spectrum*, September 1972, p. 47.

5. Ritmanich, W.: "Buffer Improves Converter's Small Signal Performance," *Electronics*, Sept. 29, 1977, p. 100.
6. Evans, L.: "Building Blocks Take the Problem Out of A/D Converter Designs," *EDN*, Aug. 5, 1976, p. 68.
7. Kime, R. C., Jr.: "The Charge-Balancing A/D Converter: An Alternative to Dual Slope Integration," *Electronics*, May 24, 1973, p. 97.
8. Grandbois, G., and T. Pickerell: "Quantized Feedback Takes Its Place in Analog-to-Digital Conversion," *Electronics*, Oct. 13, 1973, p. 103.
9. Stout, D. F., and M. Kaufman: *Handbook of Microcircuit Design and Application*, McGraw-Hill, New York, 1980, p. 25-1.

CHAPTER NINE

Microcomputer Applications in Telephony

Donald K. Melvin

Intel Corporation, Santa Clara, California

9.1 Digital Switching Systems

Microcomputers Speed Digital Evolution of Telephony Early large-scale integrated (LSI) microprocessors, and more recent VLSI central processing units (CPUs) and single-chip microcomputers, have affected the circuit designs and system architectures of virtually every segment of telephone system plant now being planned and developed for the rapidly evolving digital telecommunications network in North America, Europe, Japan, and several other countries. This chapter deals primarily with the application of microcomputers and other microcircuit components that are based upon LSI and VLSI technology in digital switching and transmission systems for telephony. Both public exchange and private branch exchange (PBX) switching systems as well as high-feature customer switching systems (CSSs) are discussed.

The telephone industry in many countries is in the process of converting and upgrading its telephone facilities from electromechanically switched, analog transmission circuits to digitally switched, digital transmission circuits. This trend permeates the telephone central-office plant, the interoffice transmission systems that connect them, business telephone switching systems, and essentially all categories of customer-station apparatus.

Telecommunications systems, however, typically require long design cycles, large software-development efforts, high-volume production quantities over a long production cycle, and upward compatibility of new systems with systems previously installed. LSI technology is making dramatic advances in the complexity of function, reduction of cost per function, density per function, and performance of system components. Software is also becoming increasingly important in supporting the use of microprocessors and signal processors. Standard LSI product families benefit from the increasing learning-curve/cost reduction impact of combined, cumulative usage in the telecommunication and electronics industries.

In digital telephone systems, once the analog voice signals are digitized, the processing and control functions can be performed by digital hardware used in common by manufacturers of computers, data systems, telephone switching systems, transmission systems, and many other types of digital systems. This mass application of commonly used components helps improve system economies and thus benefits both the equipment operators and the end users by providing improved services at reasonable costs.

This chapter reviews just a few of the many possible telecommunications-system applications of microcomputers, memory devices, and other computer peripherals as well as special telephone-oriented LSI devices, including pulse-code modulation (PCM) codecs and voice-channel filters. The rate of transition from analog to digital telephony has rapidly increased as the various key elements needed for digital switching and transmission systems have become available. This digital conversion has created a fast-moving digital revolution within the telephone industry. LSI implementation has also supported international efforts to standardize switching and transmission system-performance parameters.

Telephone Switching System Categories The implementation methods used in various central-office and private automatic branch exchange (PABX)* telephone switching system architechtures can be categorized as (1) *electromechanical* (using relays), (2) *semielectronic* (electronic control of a relay-implemented switching network), or (3) *fully electronic*. We will not consider the first two architectures here because they are not the major types of systems now being developed.

Fully electronic switching systems may be further classified by the method of switching used. *Space-division* switching uses one or more matrices of solid-state switching devices; *time-division-multiplex* (TDM) switching uses TDM transmission highways that carry samples (usually digitally encoded) of in-progress conversations. In large systems, interhighway gates may be used,

---

*The term PABX is currently used interchangeably with PBX. The letter A was originally added to differentiate an automatic (dial) PBX from a manual (operator) PBX.

or high-speed store-and-forward circuitry may be used to couple digital code groups between various digital highways. This latter switching network circuitry is referred to as a *digital interchange*, on a *time-slot interchange* (TSI).

TDM switching systems may also be subcategorized according to the TDM transmission technique used: pulse-amplitude modulation (PAM), delta modulation (DM or ΔM), and pulse-code modulation (PCM). Each subcategory is being used in recent switching systems. However, PCM is now most frequently used in new switching systems because of its compatibility with standard digital transmission systems used in North America and abroad and its inherent high-quality, low-noise capabilities when used on long-distance circuits. Descriptions of each digital modulation method are found in textbooks dealing with digital transmission.[1,2]

When studying digital switching systems (which connect to the public switched network) for development and production in the foreseeable future, it is sufficient for our purposes to narrow the scope of consideration to fully electronic, TDM switching systems using PCM digital coding techniques. Within this category, systems are produced that are based upon either the *centralized* concept, where all switching functions for a local central office are located at one facility, as shown in Fig. 1, or the *decentralized* or *distributed* concept, where remote line groups serve remote clusters of customers at a distance from the serving host or base-unit office, as shown in Fig. 2 and discussed in Sec. 9.5, *Distributed Switching System Architectures*. Traffic may

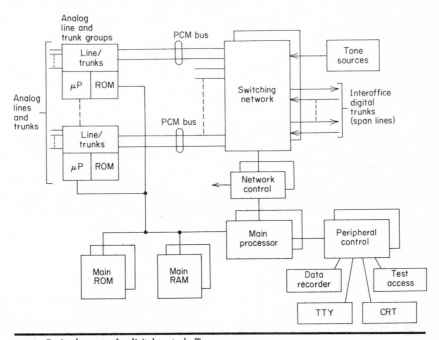

FIG. 1   *Basic elements of a digital central office.*

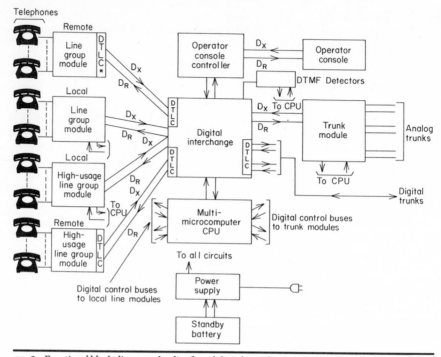

FIG. 2   Functional block diagram of a distributed digital switching system DTLC (digital transmission line controller).

also be remotely concentrated so it may be served over just a few lines, compared with the number of telephones being served. That is, only as many transmission paths need be provided as there are expected simultaneous calls during the busy hour of a defined busy day.

In large switching systems, say, over 2000 lines, combinations of time and space-division switching techniques may be used, and in many variations, depending upon the system size and features. The architectures and techniques just described are used in both local central-office applications and PABXs as well as in some key telephone systems;[3] automatic call distributors (ACDs) as used in large reservations centers to assign calls to attendants based upon priority of call receipt, and in large trunk-switching (tandem) telephone exchanges.

The Transition from Space to Time-Division Switching   Before digital technology matured, most telephone switching systems were electromechanical; essentially all switching functions were performed by relays and other special switching mechanisms such as Strowger step-by-step two-motion switches, X-Y two-motion switches, crossbar switches, or reed-relay (or solid-state equivalent) switch matrices, latching-code switches, or other similar devices.[4,5] Because voice paths switched through these electromechanical systems were isolated from one another only by the space that separated adjacent circuits, the term *space-division* was applied to include this whole category of switching systems.

In space-division systems, a conventional 2-wire analog telephone line is usually extended metallically into a battery-feed circuit that can be used for one call at a time by a large number of lines which have access to it and by other similar battery-feed circuits. In effect, the analog telephone instrument superimposes the relatively low-voltage ac voice signals on the dc line (nominally 20 to 100 mA), which is supplied by the battery-feed circuit (frequently from a 50-Vdc exchange battery) in the switching system. At the battery-feed circuit, the ac voice signals are again separated from the dc path and, after being routed through the system switching network, coupled into the other-party battery-feed circuit.

In digital switching systems, this method of shared battery-feed circuits is replaced by a one-per-line battery-feed method as discussed in Sec. 9.7, *A Digital PABX*.

The Digital Trend in Telephony   The plan for digitizing voice circuits as close to the customer's telephone as is economically feasible is now gradually being implemented. Having a digital *coder* and *decoder* (codec) at the first subscriber-line interface with digital switching or transmission facilities allows the removal of subsequent A/D and D/A conversions and their associated 2- to 4-wire conversion (hybrid) requirements as used at junctions between 2-wire space-division switching systems and 4-wire interoffice multiplex (carrier) transmission facilities. This can result in the integration of switching system multiplexed digital voice *transmission highways* (serial digital buses) with interoffice digital transmission lines (spanlines). In a digital switching system, conventional channel-bank requirements (see Sec. 9.4 *Voice Digitization*) can be essentially eliminated, and digital interoffice trunks can originate and terminate on switching system digital transmission highways that use span-line–compatible digital formats. This trend will ultimately lead to elimination of many of today's analog interoffice trunks.

Another long-range goal of the telephone industry is digital transmission, telephone-to-telephone. The introduction of LSI devices such as the codec (see Sec. 9.3, *Per-Line Codecs and Channel Filters*), PCM channel filters (sec. 9.3), and microcomputers and their various peripherals (see Sec. 9.7) is speeding the evolution of an "all-digital" system goal, which will be approached asymptotically with time.

Microcomputers Used for Programmable Control of Telephone Switching System Functions   The development of the microcomputer as a small, powerful, programmable, and versatile tool for digital switching system design engineers led to the creation in the mid-1970s of many new digital switching systems. Microcomputer-controlled PABXs have since been produced by several major manufacturers of telephone switching systems. In the United States, independent (non-Bell) manufacturers have introduced microcompu-

TABLE 1 *Digital* PABXs

Manufacturer	Code	Year introduced	Max. line size
Collins	CVS	1974	512
Digital Telephone	D 1200	1974	1,024
Jeaumont/Schneider	TLC 10	1974	1,200
Rolm	CBX	1975	800
Northerm Telecom	SL1	1975	7,600
General Telephone & Electronics (GTE)	GTD	1976	4,500
SAT	Telecom 200	1976	10,000
American Telecom	Fetex 400	1976	400
Wescom	580	1977	3,000
Stromberg-Carlson	DBX	1978	960
Nippon Electric Co.	NEAX 22	1978	12,000
(for B.P.O.)	CDSS 1	1978	120
Swedish Tele Adm.	A 345	1978	7,600
Plessey	PDX	1978	800
Oki	KC 270	1979	1,500
Ericsson	ASDP 162	1979	600

TABLE 2 *Digital local switching systems*

Manufacturer	Code	Year introduced	Country	Max line size (1000s)
CIT-Alcatel	E-10	1970	France	30 (E-10B)
Stromberg-Carlson	DCO	1977	United States	28
Northern Telecom	DMS 10	1977	Canada, United States	7.5
ITT-BTM-FACE	System 12	1977	Belgium, Italy	12
SIT-Siemens-SCELT	PROTEO	1978	Italy	30
Vidar	ITS 4/5	1978	United States	12
ITT-North Electric Co.	DSS 1	1978	United States	28
Nippon Electric Co.	NEAX 61	1979	United States	100
Northern Telecom	DMS 100	1979	Canada	100
Plessey-STC-GEC	System X	1980	United Kingdom	50
GTE-AE	No. 5 EAX	NA	United States	150
Western Electric	No. 5 ESS	NA	United States	NA

ter-controlled digital PABXs and digital tandem (also called transit, intermediate, trunk-switching or class 4 offices) and digital local or end offices (class
5), or combinations of these. Bell System now operates several toll-tandem
number 4 electronic switching system (ESS) offices. In the early 1980s, Bell
System plans to introduce its local (class 5) digital number 5 ESS, See Tables
1 to 3 for the manufacturers of these systems and the countries in which a
number of digital switching systems were introduced.

Most of these switching systems are microcomputer-controlled to some

TABLE 3   Digital switching intermediate offices

Country	System	Manufacturer	Size	Control*	Status
Italy	SINTEL 1	TELETTRA	250	WL	Lab exp. 1966
Japan	DEX-T1	NTT	192	WL	Lab exp. 1967
United Kingdom	Empress	BPO	192	WL	Field exp. 1968
Australia	1ST	APO	192	SPC	Field exp. 1971
United Kingdom	Moorgate	STC	394	WL	Field exp. 1971
Netherlands	DTX 500	NETH. PTT	1.1K	SPC	Lab exp. 1972
France	E 10	CIT	72K	SPC	Service 1975
United States	No 4 ESS	WE	107K	SPC	Service 1976
United States	IMA 2	Vidar	1.4K	SPC	Service 1976
Italy	SINTEL 3	TELETTRA	14.4K	SPC	Field exp. 1976
Italy	PROTEO	SIT-Siemens	16.3K	SPC	Field exp. 1976
Netherlands	PDX	Philips	23K+	SPC	Field exp. 1976
W. Germany	EWS-D	Siemens	63K	SPC	Lab exp. 1976
Sweden	AXE	LME+	32K	SPC	Field exp. 1976
United States	No. 3 EAX	GTE-AE	60K	SPC	Service 1976
United States	DTT-200	Collins	1.5K	SPC	Lab exp. 1977
United States	DMS 200	Northern Telecom	60K	SPC	Field exp. 1977
United Kingdom	System-X	4 Manufacturers	32K	SPC	Lab exp. 1978
United States	DTM	Stromberg-Carlson	4K	SPC	
Japan	NEAX 81A	NEC	13.4K	SPC	Lab exp. 1977
France	MT 20	Thompson-CSF	65K	SPC	Service 1979
Japan	FETEX 100T-Toll	Fujitsu	60K	SPC	Lab exp 1979
Japan	HTX-Toll	Hitachi	60K	SPC	Lab exp. 1978
Japan	NEAX 611TS	NEC	60K	SPC	Service 1979

*WL = wired Logic; SPC = stored-program control
+Ericsson Telephones—Australia (trial in Italy)

degree and use digital transmission techniques.[6] Prior to the availability of microcomputers, most new electronic telephone switching systems were designed around space-division switching (usually using reed relays for switching voice paths) and custom computer-controlled architectures with stored-program control (SPC). Early TDM switching systems with SPC in which voice channels from lines and trunks (interoffice circuits) are sampled and converted into PAM, PCM, or ΔM signals for switching purposes, appeared on the market on a limited basis until the cost-effective microcomputer became available.[7,8]

9.2   Time-Shared Transmission Paths and Control Functions

Digital Voice Transmission   In North America, Bell System's T1 digital interoffice multiplex transmission standard,[9] which specifies PCM transmission parameters, to a large degree became the de facto design basis for digital switching system interface compatibility. In Europe, CCITT* recommenda-

*CCITT is the International Telegraph and Telephone Consultative Committee and is affiliated with the International Telecommunications Union, Geneva, Switzerland.

tions G711 and G732 have been used similarly.[10] Although some variation of these digital transmission system standards does occur within switching system designs produced by different manufacturers, the 8-kHz sampling rate of voice channels, the 125-μs frame period, and the 8-bit companded PCM coding methods (μ law primarily for North America and A law primarily for Europe) have been nearly universally adopted, thus permitting LSI codec and channel-filter standardization to a large degree. (See Sec. 9.3 for definition of companding laws.)

The LSI codec reduced to only a single semiconductor chip per voice circuit a major portion of the complex circuitry previously needed at the analog voice-circuit interface with a digital switching system. Furthermore, at least one type of LSI codec can perform additional time-slot switching and TDM functions, along with A/D and D/A digital conversion. (See Ref. 11 and Sec. 9.6, *Line Group Architectures.*) These additional digital functions can allow even further reduction of line-interface-circuit complexity. However, not all systems required codecs with this on-chip time-slot memory that provide the on-chip channel-switching capability. In some applications, each codec may be required to maintain a fixed time-slot relationship to all other codecs in a group, as discussed in Secs. 9.4 and 9.6.

Considering first the public switched telephone network, a major development effort today is the design and production of digital local and tandem central-office switching systems. These systems are primarily being designed around the capabilities of LSI microprocessors and single-chip microcomputers, which lend themselves well to distributed control architectures, as discussed in Sec. 9.5.

The LSI CPU and single-chip microcomputer may be applied to permit groups of lines, interoffice trunks, or switching network sections to be controlled separately by individual computers, so that catastrophic system outages can be avoided by distributing control functions throughout a switching system. Centralized controls, where required, are duplicated, but design complexity is minimized by the use of standard LSI CPU devices.

In-Service Performance—The Real Criteria for LSI Applications   The final proof of a digital switching system design is the quality of service provided to the users and the reliability and cost effectiveness of the design. The serviceability of the system by the maintenance personnel must also be considered in the total cost effectiveness of the system design.

In general, the simpler the design, the fewer the components, and the more easily the circuitry can be understood by the maintenance personnel, the more satisfied the user and the operating company will be once the digital switching system is cut over to service.

Careful selection of repetitiously used system components, such as microprocessors, codecs, filters, and other related devices used in analog line and trunk interface circuits, is a very important factor for long-term customer (user and operating personnel) satisfaction. The high-density, high-quality, and uniform performance properties of LSI technology, when appropriately used in telephone switching, transmission systems, and terminal apparatus, provide the means for accomplishing high-quality in-service performance and use microcircuit technology to its greatest advantage.

The Impact of LSI ***on Telephone Switching System Architectures*** Telecommunications-system development engineers have clearly seen the major turning point in system hardware development and architectures since the microprocessor and special LSI telecommunications devices became available. New LSI-equipped circuits and products will likely ultimately replace most of the major electromechanical telecommunication systems hardware developed to date. This conversion is a major challenge because the existing electromechanical systems are so extensively used throughout the world.

As shown in Table 4, from a system designer's point of view, new digital switching systems based upon LSI-implemented circuitry will have radically different characteristics compared with earlier electromechanical, space-division, analog (class 5) switching designs. Although there may be some variation from the entries for certain existing system architectures, the table is representative of typical in-service systems.

Gradual Microcomputer "Design-In" Following the introduction of the microprocessor to industrial applications, it was several years before its usefulness in telephone systems was fully appreciated. Prior to the availability of microprocessors, telephone switching system designs were based upon common control techniques, with wired logic and circuit redundancy for reliability. As progressively more powerful 8-bit and then 16-bit models of the microprocessor became available, such as Intel's 8080, 8085, 8086, and 8088 and similar products from other semiconductor manufacturers, design aids were developed that simplified programming techniques and provided more convenient interface access.[12]

A number of telephone switching system architectures had been proposed as early as the mid-1960s, but they were not economically feasible until low-priced memory and control and logic functions later became available through LSI technology. The distributed switching system architecture, which utilizes digital remote-line modules (RLMs) to provide central-office or PBX types of service at some distance from the central exchange, evolved around LSI technology. These RLMs are connected to a central host exchange by digital span lines for centralized voice-path switching, control, routing, billing, access to long-distance circuits, and so on.

Microcomputer control is also being applied to telephone systems such as PABXs, key telephone (multiline) systems, line concentrators, central-office switching systems, and a variety of related test equipment and service monitoring systems. Typical microcomputer system applications include common control or CPUs for PABXs, line-group control for central offices, remote-line concentrators, and distributed multiprocessor control applications in central-office systems. Also, single-chip microcomputers are being applied in electronic high-feature telephones, electronic-key telephone instruments, and other business telephone systems.[13]

TABLE 4   *Comparison of some analog and digital switching system architectural differences*

System function	Type of switching systems	
	Analog space-division	Digital time-division
Voice path through system	2-wire (transmit and receive over same path)	4-wire (separate transmit and recieve channels)
2- to 4-wire conversion location	At each interoffice trunk interface	At each analog line and trunk interface
Digital encoding and decoding (codec function)	At each digital trunk interface	At each analog line and trunk interface
Voice-path bandwidth limiting filters	At each multiplexed interoffice trunk interface	At each analog line and trunk interface
Control	Common (centralized)	Distributed
Telephone-line battery-feed circuit (during conversation)	In shared-resource circuitry (selector, connector, junctor, etc.)[4,5]	At each analog subscriber-line interface
Ringing-signal application and trip circuit	In shared-resource circuitry (connector, junctor, etc.)[4,5]	At each analog subscriber-line interface
High-level signal access to telephone line for testing, howler, coin-collect/ refund, and so on	By manual patch and/or shared-resource circuitry (test connector, pay station repeater, etc.)	At each analog subscriber-line interface
On/off hook (supervision detection for call initialization (seizure signal)	At individual, per-line relay or electronic equivalent	At each analog subscriber-line interface
Rotary-dial pulse detection	In shared-resource circuitry (registers, selectors, connectors, junctors, etc.)	Same per-line circuitry as for line supervision (above)
Tone-dial (DTMF)* signal detection	In shared-resource circuitry (DTMF registers)	In shared-resource circuitry (DTMF registers)
Special services, e.g., pay station coin-collect/refund, party-line selective ringing, automatic number identification (ANI) of parties on a party line	In shared-resource circuitry	At each analog line interface

*DTMF is dual-tone multifrequency signaling, as produced by a tone-dial or other signal generator.

9.3 Per-Line Codecs and Channel Filters

The Codec—Key to Digital Telephony The LSI codec was the first major class of microcircuit devices specifically developed for mass application throughout the telephone industry. The industry's potential need for millions of codecs annually spurred the effort to reduce both the basic codec and devices performing related functions to a single, mass-producible, and reliable solid-state device.

A/D conversion as provided by the codec allows many existing, general-purpose LSI devices to be used to control or handle digitized voice signals. Once voice or other analog signals are converted by a codec into a standardized digital format, switching, routing, and other processing can then be accomplished by various digital microcircuit devices that are also used for the other mass markets of digital computers, industrial control, and data processing. Microcomputers and various semiconductor memory and logic devices can be used to perform the switching, routing, and multiplexing functions required for telecommunications applications (see Sec. 9.7).

PCM-Codec Functions Each codec converts analog voice signals, which arrive at the switching system via an analog subscriber line or analog trunk, into bursts of digital codes, and vice versa for transmission in the reverse direction. Digitally encoded voice signals *within a digital switching system* are transmitted by interleaving the 8-bit code bursts, which carry one direction of transmission for one conversation along with similarly produced code bursts from other codecs, over shared transmission buses or *digital transmission highways*. A shared controller may assign time intervals (slots) on a transmission highway as required to handle traffic demands.

Any one conversation on a digital transmission highway is represented by two 8-bit code bursts, one for each direction of voice transmission, and the code bursts usually occupy an assignable increment of time on periodic basis. The period of time occupied by each 8-bit code burst is thus known as a *transmission time-slot*.

For example, each PCM codec has four leads or pins assigned to handle voice transmission, as shown in Figs. 3 and 4 (see Refs. 11, 14, and 15). Two leads carry analog voice frequencies in and out of the codec (for example, VF_X and VF_R, respectively), and two carry digital equivalents of the voice signals, one each for inward and outward digital transmission (D_X and D_R, respectively). Analog voice signals from the customer's telephone arrive via battery-feed circuitry, a 2- to 4-wire hybrid, and channel-filter circuitry[16,17] at a codec on lead VF_X (voice frequency, transmit direction). Furthermore, coded data received on lead D_R is converted into voice or other analog signals by the codec and applied on lead VF_R for transmission via the filter, hybrid, battery-feed circuitry, and subscriber line to the telephone receiver. (See Fig. 4 and Sec. 9.7.) Loop supervision (on- or off-hook signals) may be transmitted via lead SIG_X, and ringing control signals via lead SIG_R in some applications.

Codecs used in systems requiring either fixed or variable time-slot assignments can be strobed in the assigned time-slot by external control circuitry.

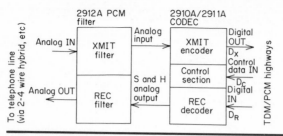

FIG. 3   Simplified interface of the Intel 2912A PCM filter with the Intel 2910A/2911A codec.

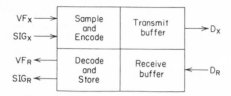

FIG. 4   Basic codec functions and lead designations.

However, for those systems where codec-variable time-slot assignments are required, on-chip time-slot memory is provided in some codecs to reduce line-board complexity and unburden the line-group control circuitry of the responsibility of remembering and strobing time-slot data once per frame period for all codecs in a line or trunk group.

A Per-Line Versus Shared Codec in Switching System Applications   Two basic types of codec configurations, and thus two basic types of analog line and trunk interface architectures, have evolved as a result of the introduction of both per-line and shared codecs.

The *shared* codec used for switching system line and trunk interface circuits is a group of integrated circuits (ICs) that may exceed 24 IC device packages and are shared by a number of analog line or trunk circuits (usually eight) to perform the A/D and D/A conversions and companding actions required for all (eight) circuits.

The LSI shared-codec concept is a carryover from discrete-component shared-codec designs used in many early PCM channel-bank designs for interoffice digital carrier systems, such as Bell's D-type terminals and equivalents for T1 carrier systems. However, these discrete-component channel-bank shared codecs usually serve 24 or 30 (in Europe) voice circuits (see Sec. 9.4).

The *per-line* codec is based on a newer, more versatile design concept that spreads the conversion and control functions over a line or trunk group instead of concentrating them in a few components, thus greatly improving system reliability.

The decision as to whether the per-line or shared-codec architecture is most appropriate for any given *switching system* application should be based upon an in-depth analysis of the overall effect each approach will have on the system. The codec selection should be based upon at least the following 11 factors:

1. Cost
2. System reliability
3. Compatibility with future digital subscriber lines
4. Unburdening of common-control circuitry
5. Noise reduction on conversion paths
6. Space considerations
7. Power consumption
8. Circuit complexity
9. External component considerations
10. System architectural considerations
11. In-service performance

Extra logic functions are sometimes also built into the single-chip codec to further simplify common circuitry, reduce system costs, and enhance reliability. Instead of having one high-speed codec provide A/D and D/A conversions for several lines, per-line codecs allow distribution of functions to each chip, thus more than doubling system reliability. If a codec should fail, only one circuit is affected; if a shared codec fails, several circuits could lose service.

National and International Transmission Standards Met by LSI Codecs

Standardization of the basic parameters of digital transmission, to meet national and international specifications, is one benefit of using LSI devices in the transmission path of switching, transmission, and terminal equipment. The analog-to-digital and digital-to-analog converters (ADCs and DACs) in telephone system voice paths depend upon a nonlinear coding/decoding technique to reduce quantizing noise and give more faithful reproduction of low-amplitude analog signals for a given number of coding bits (8) than is achieved with linear coding techniques.

The D3 and D4 channel banks (see Ref. 9 and Sec. 9.4), for instance, require toll-quality performance, signal dynamic ranges of approximately 72 dB, and signal-to-distortion ratios of about 4 dB. To achieve this with an 8-bit code word, a nonlinear encoding technique is required for the A/D conversion. Similarly, the decoder must restore the signal to its linear range when converting back from digital to analog.

Voice-Path Companding

In digital telephony, two considerations are particularly important to transmission system designers: (1) the dynamic range of analog signals transmitted over a digital voice channel and (2) the PCM bit rate needed to maintain that dynamic range with a minimum distortion level. The dynamic range is determined from speech characteristics and differences in power losses over long lines compared to short lines.

Typically, a 72-dB dynamic range is needed with distortion levels about 40 dB below the signal to accommodate the range and clarity of speech for toll-grade transmission. This dynamic range requires at least 12 code bits for a linear A/D conversion. On the other hand, the PCM designer likes to have a minimum number of bits per time-slot so that more time-slots can be transmitted at a given transmission-line bit rate. T1 carrier uses 8 bits per time-slot rather than the 12 bits mentioned, and 8-bit encoding is a near-worldwide practice for digital voice transmission.

A compromise involves the use of compression and expansion of the signal (companding) during the A/D conversion process; the companding allows the 8 bits to represent the full 72-dB dynamic range and maintain a relatively constant signal-to-distortion ratio.

With linear encoding, where uniform quantizing steps are used, the quantizing error percentage is greater for small signals than for large signals. This degrades the relative signal-to-noise ratio for small signals. Thus, it is desirable to use an increasing number of quantum steps of decreasing size as the analog-signal amplitude decreases so that the percentage error remains relatively constant over the expected range of amplitudes. This may be accomplished by using either a complementary nonlinear encoder/decoder arrangement or a linear encoder/decoder preceded by a compressor and followed by a complementary expandor. LSI codecs now employ the former method, which is in effect the application of an instantaneous compandor.

Figure 5 illustrates uniform quantizing levels on the left (linear A/D) and nonuniform quantizing levels (compression) on the right for two different signals. Observe that although the quantized large signal appears about the same with or without compression, the quantized small signal is much better defined when using the nonuniform quantizing levels. In quantitative terms, the signal-to-quantizing distortion ratios are equalized for large and small signals when the compression system is used.

When the coder/decoder transfer characteristics are combined, the resulting analog-in versus analog-out curve shows the quantization steps as a function of signal amplitude, as in Fig. 6. Tables 5 and 6 show the transfer characteristics of the mu (μ)- and A-law decoders.

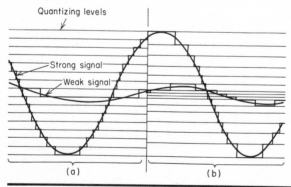

FIG. 5 *Voice compression through the use of nonuniform quantizing levels: (a) without a compandor, and (b) with a compandor.*

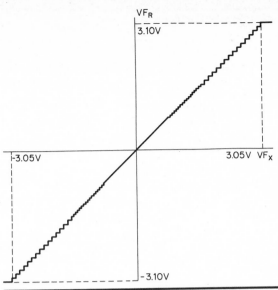

FIG. 6 Total transfer function for a signal going through both the coder and decoder of a codec.

TABLE 5 μ-Law decoder transfer characteristics

Chord	Step size normalized to full scale	Chord endpoints normalized to full scale	Step size mV	Step size as % of full scale	Chord endpoints in dB down from full scale
0	2	30	0.769	0.025	−48.55
1	4	93	1.539	0.05	−38.73
2	8	219	3.078	0.1	−31.29
3	16	471	6.156	0.2	−24.63
4	32	975	12.31	0.4	−18.32
5	64	1983	24.62	0.8	−12.15
6	128	3999	49.25	1.6	−6.06
7	256	8031	98.5	3.2	0

TABLE 6 A-law decoder transfer characteristics

Chord	Step size normalized to full scale	Chord endpoints normalized to full scale	Step size mV	Step size as % of full scale	Chord endpoints in dB down from full scale
0	2	31	1.538	005	−42.28
1	2	63	1.538	0.05	−36.12
2	4	126	3.075	0.1	−30.10
3	8	252	6.150	0.2	−24.08
4	16	504	12.30	0.4	−18.06
5	32	1008	24.60	0.8	−12.04
6	64	2016	49.20	1.6	−6.02
7	128	4032	98.41	3.2	0

μ- and A-Law Coding for Telephony   In telephone transmission systems, two methods of companding are typically used: μ law for the United States, Canada, Japan, and the Philippines, and A law for Europe and elsewhere. Both μ and A law represent particular implementations of incremental linear approximations to logarithmic compression curves. Mathematically stated, the compression curves are approximations to the following equations:

μ law

$$F(x) = \text{sgn}(x)\,\frac{\ln(1 + \mu|x|)}{\ln(1 + \mu)} \qquad 0 \le |x| \le 1$$

A law

$$F(x) = \text{sgn}(x) \left[\frac{1 + \log_{10}(A|x|)}{1 + \log_{10}A} \right] \qquad \frac{1}{A} \le |x| \le 1$$

$$= \text{sgn}(x) \left[\frac{A|x|}{1 + \log_{10}A} \right] \qquad 0 \le |x| \le \frac{1}{A}$$

where x = input signal
  $\text{sgn}(x)$ = sign of input $(+$ or $-)$
  $|x|$ = absolute value of x (magnitude)
  μ = 255 (defined by AT&T)
  A = 87.6 (defined by CCITT)

Codecs designed for telephone transmission applications use 8 bits per time-slot to specify the amplitude as an incremental linear approximation to these log curves. The $\mu = 255$ law uses a 15-segment approximation, whereas the A law uses a 13-segment curve. The 8-bit digital code has a sign bit, 3 bits for chord selection, and 4 bits for step selection within the chosen chord.[11,16]

Several other forms of distortion arise in digital transmission paths as a result of coding processes. These forms include harmonic distortion, which may be caused by overload or poor compander tracking, and foldover distortion, which may occur if the high-frequency channel cutoff is set at too high a value.[11]

Signaling Via the μ-Law Codec   Signaling to and from digital switching system analog line and trunk interface circuits can be accomplished via the codec signaling channels (when provided) and thus via the transmission highways to the microcomputer system in the associated control circuitry (see also Sec. 9.7, via separate signaling highways that are multipled to all line and trunk interface circuits from the control system as shown in Fig. 18, or by both methods.

The most basic signaling *toward* the line circuit (from the line-group control CPU) is for ringing control, and signaling *from* the line circuit (toward the same CPU) is for loop-current status, i.e., loop-supervision signals that may indicate an off-hook condition, rotary-dial pulses, or a disconnect (on-hook) condition. Other signals are also required in some systems, such as calling-party identification, party-line selective-ringing control, PABX trunk control, pay-station coin-collect/refund, and busy lamps.

Analog trunk circuits in a PABX are similar in some ways to analog line circuits but do not supply battery feed (i.e., for the PABX end of a trunk to a central office). They detect inward trunk-seizure signals and provide outward trunk-seizure or trunk-answer signals.

PABX trunks can be one-way outward, one-way inward, or two-way. Two-way trunks must have special circuitry—a _ground-start circuit_—to avoid call collisions when a trunk is seized from opposite ends at the same time. This function requires special and different circuitry at each end of the PABX trunk as well as signaling channels via the trunk-interface circuits to the controlling CPU.

These added signaling functions require additional signaling capacity that may be derived by multiplexing from a codec signaling channel or provided by separate, multiplexed, trunk-circuit backplane signaling buses. This is only one example of added signaling complexity in trunk circuits that the system must accommodate.

In many analog line and trunk interface circuit applications, 4 signaling channels in each signaling direction handle the signaling needs. In a few high-feature line interface circuits, 8 signaling channels in each direction suffice.

Usually μ-law codecs provide optional signal-channel availability; A-law codecs do not. In North American telephone practice, the eighth bit of μ-law codec-assigned time-slot is borrowed every sixth frame ($6 \times 125\ \mu s = 750\ \mu s$), resulting in a 1.333+ kb/s signaling channel in each direction. Eighth-bit signaling channels are shown relative to the other time-slot bits in Fig. 7, and the transmit and receive signaling leads SIG_X and SIG_R, respectively, for the codecs in Fig. _8a, b._

This signaling-channel bit rate can be further subdivided into two 666.66+ b/s signaling channels, or four 333.33+ b/s signaling channels, depending upon the needs of the application. Sampled signaling data is usually transmitted over these signaling channels.

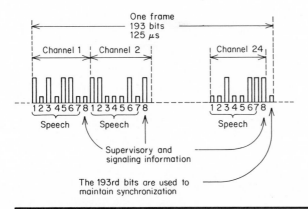

<small>FIG. 7</small>   _The T1 PCM carrier format._

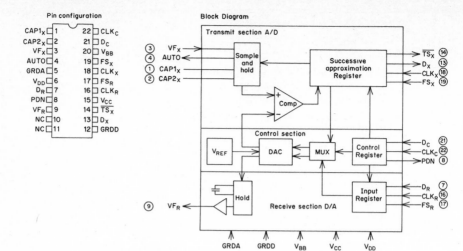

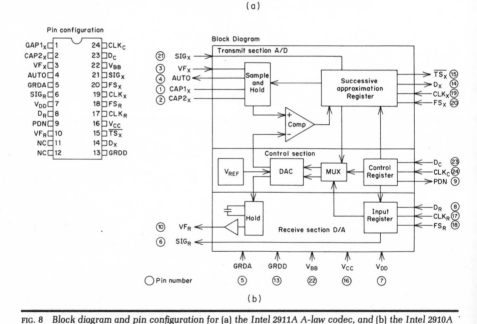

FIG. 8   Block diagram and pin configuration for (a) the Intel 2911A A-law codec, and (b) the Intel 2910A μ-law codec.

Pin Names for (a)		Pin Names for (b)	
CAP 1$_X$ CAP 2$_X$	Holding Capacitor	CAP 1$_X$ CAP 2$_X$	Holding Capacitor
VF$_X$	Analog Input	VF$_X$	Analog Input
VF$_R$	Analog Output	VF$_R$	Analog Output
D$_R$ D$_C$	Digital Input	D$_R$ D$_C$ SIG$_X$	Digital Input
D$_X$ $\overline{TS_X}$	Digital Output	SIG$_R$ D$_X$ $\overline{TS_X}$	Digital Output
CLK$_C$ CLK$_{X\%}$ CLK$_R$	Clock Input	CLK$_C$ CLK$_X$ CLK$_R$	Clock Input
FS$_X$ FS$_R$	Frame Sync Input	FS$_X$ FS$_R$	Frame Sync Input
AUTO	Auto Zero Output	AUTO	Auto-Zero Output
V$_{BB}$	Power (−5V)	V$_{BB}$	Power (−5V)
V$_{CC}$	Power (+5V)	V$_{CC}$	Power (+5V)
V$_{DD}$	Power (+12V)	V$_{DD}$	Power (+12V)
PDN	Power Down	PDN	Power Down
GRDA	Analog Ground	GRDA	Analog Ground
GRDD	Digital Ground	GRDD	Digital Ground
NC	No Connecton	NC	No Connection

When eighth-bit signaling is subdivided into two signaling channels per direction of transmission, the two channels are referred to as A-channel and B-channel signaling, or simple A and B signaling. This latter method is frequently used in some channel-unit codec applications in digital channel banks, for interoffice signaling (see also Sec. 9.9, *Digital Subscriber Lines, Common Channel Signaling Throughout the Digital Network*).

The Single-Chip, Per-Line Filter for PCM Systems Transmit and receive channel filters are required with per-line LSI codecs to limit the signal bandwidth on the analog circuits to and from the codecs. The Intel type 2912 PCM line filter shown in Fig. 9, for example, can be used with each codec in switching system and channel-bank applications. The filters can be powered up or down under programmed control via the associated per-line codec, such as Intel's type 2910A (μ-law companding) or 2911A (A-law) codecs.[17,18]

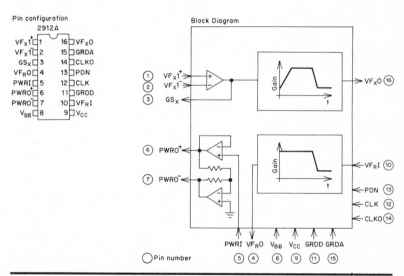

FIG. 9 *Block diagram and pin configuration of the Intel 2912A PCM filter chip. Each device contains two filters.*

Pin Names

VF_xI^+ VF_xI^-	*ANALOG INPUTS*
GS_x	*GAIN CONTROL*
VF_xO	*ANALOG OUTPUT*
VF_RI	*ANALOG INPUT*
VF_RO	*ANALOG OUTPUT*
PWRI	*DRIVER INPUT*
$PWRO^+$, $PWRO^-$	*DRIVER OUTPUT*
CLK	*CLOCK INPUT*
CLKO	*CLOCK SELECTION*
PDN	*POWER DOWN*
V_{CC}	*POWER (+5V)*
V_{BB}	*POWER (−5V)*
GRDD	*DIGITAL GROUND*
GRDA	*ANALOG GROUND*

Each analog line and trunk interface circuit, in a digital switching system or in a carrier system channel bank, usually requires separate transmit- and receive-direction channel filters. This is true whether a shared- or single-channel codec architecture is used. Having the A/D interface circuitry architecture configured for one codec for each channel filter in first-generation PCM systems makes later conversion to combined filter codec simple.

The line filter in Fig. 9 is a monolithic IC device that includes both the transmit- and receive-direction filters and is packaged in a 16-pin dual-in-line package (DIP). This and other similar filters for this application are designed to be compatible with the CCITT recommendation G712 and AT&T's D3 and D4 channel-bank specifications.

The transmit filter in Fig. 9 rejects the 50- to 60-Hz signals characteristic of low-frequency commercial power source interference (hum) that might be induced or otherwise coupled onto telephone circuits. The filter also provides for gain adjustment in both directions of transmission under external control. It can interface with either a transformer or electronic type of 2- to 4-wire hybrid and to type 2910A or 2911A codecs.

The availability of per-line codecs and filters and microcomputer control subsystems opened the way for fully electronic, fully digital switching and transmission systems. These and other LSI system components are now impacting the telephone industry as it converts to digital technology.

9.4   Voice Digitization

Digital Voice Transmission in* TDM *Systems   Even before LSI technology made digital switching and interoffice-transmission techniques economically viable at essentially every level of the national network, as it now appears to be doing, early digital systems were developed that were based upon discrete-component-circuit implementation.

The research in the late 1950s that led to Bell System's T1 interoffice exchange carrier system proved that 24 interoffice analog trunk circuits, carrying 24 two-way conversations, could be sampled, encoded, and time-division-multiplexed in such a way that one pair of twisted-pair copper wires in each direction of transmission could reliably carry all 24 conversations between exchanges. During this same period, similar 30- and 32-channel systems evolved in Europe.

The CCITT, desiring to standardize digital transmission specifications for interoffice trunks, published recommendations for two standards that describe digital transmission parameters. One is based upon Bell System's T1 exchange carrier system, the other upon the European 30-channel digital multiplex system.

Table 7 summarizes the two digital transmission standards now recommended by the CCITT for carrier-system applications. Many aspects of these standards have since been adopted for digital transmission paths within a switching system and were the basis for establishing switching system compatibility with digital interoffice transmission facilities. Refer to Fig. 10 for the

TABLE 7 *Comparison of international digital transmission standards*

CCITT recommendation number	Primarily used in	Digital line bit rate, Mb/s	Time-slots per frame	Voice channels	Companding law used
G.732	Europe	2.048	32	30	A
G.733	North America	1.544	24	24	μ

CCITT- recommended PCM transmission-line format for Europe and elsewhere, which operates at a 2.048-Mb/s line bit rate.

In most digital transmission systems that carry voice traffic, PCM encoding methods are used, so that all signals are transmitted as binary **1**s or **0**s.

Unlike analog signals, the digital pulses used in PCM transmission, after becoming distorted by noise and the effects of the transmission medium during transmission, can be completely regenerated by transmission-line repeaters along the route between the transmitting and receiving terminals. Span-line repeaters are spaced at a nominal 6000-ft (1800-m) separation for 22-gauge exchange-grade telephone cable.

The T1 span-line signal is described as a 1.544-Mb/s bipolar 50 percent duty-cycle pulse train. That is, there are 1,544,000 bit periods of 648 ns each, and each bit period carries one binary digit (bit) of information that has the value of **1** if the pulse is present and **0** if the pulse is absent. The 50 percent duty-cycle factor indicates that the time between two adjacent **1** bits is ideally the same as the duration of each bit (324 ns). *Bipolar* refers to the alternating character of pulses, as shown in Fig. 11.

On a T1 span line, the binary information is carried by the presence or absence of the pulses, *not* by their polarity. Bipolar line transmission is used because the bipolar mode eliminates any dc component and concentrates the energy content of the bit stream at one-half the bit rate (772 kHz). Nevertheless, the power spectrum of this signal covers a broad frequency range, with significant energy components extending from 20 kHz to 1 MHz.

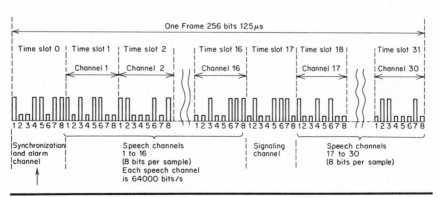

FIG. 10 *CCITT-recommended PCM format for Europe and several other countries.*

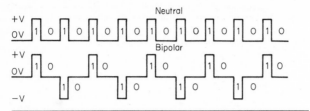

FIG. 11   *Format of a bipolar PCM spanline compared to the T1 spanline which uses the neutral format.*

Digital Transmission Systems and Channel Banks   As the national telephone networks evolve from the analog transmission and electromechanical switching era into the digital era, digital span lines will interface directly with digital switching systems without the need for any A/D or D/A conversions at the digital trunk/digital switch interface.

When digital trunks interface with an analog switching system, a *channel bank* provides the necessary A/D and D/A conversions as well as channel-filtering and multiplexing functions. In North America, Bell System's type D3 and D4 channel banks are frequently used at these digital trunk interfaces with analog switching systems. These are just two of an evolutionary progression of D-type channel banks—designated D1 through D4—that have several variations for accommodating data and wide-band signal transmission instead of, or in addition to, digitized voice transmission between central offices.[19]

9.5   Distributed Switching System Architectures

High-Speed Time-Shared Operation Versus Low-Speed Duplicated Switching System Functions   In the early days of telephony, the industry goal was to eliminate individual lines between a telephone and several other telephones connecting to it and instead have one pair of wires connect the phone with a central office that could give it access to many other telephones. This also permitted removal of the *local battery* that was once required in each telephone and replacing it with one large *common battery* in the central office that serves all telephones in that exchange. Simplification of the telephone to just the transmission devices, ringer, and the calling device (dial) that activates the centralized switching equipment by remote control was a result of this goal. A basic electromechanical local central-office switching "unit" size was limited to about 10,000 lines.

Today, many of these earlier basic system concepts are changing. Fundamental to this change is the fact that new microprocessor-controlled and solid-state switching devices can operate so rapidly, compared to their electromechanical forerunners, that switching functions which were formerly served by highly duplicated equipment to meet large system traffic demands can now be performed sequentially by high-speed, time-shared devices. Thus, the entire switching system architecture must change to optimize the use of new solid-state devices.

The introduction of LSI technology has further ensured that virtually all major categories of electronic-circuit applications in telecommunications will be impacted by some type of upgrading redesign. Typical telecommunications-circuit categories in which LSI devices are already finding heavy application include:

1. Centralized and distributed switching system control functions
2. A/D conversion (and vice versa) for voice paths in switching and transmission systems
3. Signal processing and filtering
4. Temporary, semipermanent, and permanent digital memory
5. Switching system ancillary functions such as digital line synchronization, signaling, routing, billing, maintenance, testing, alarm reporting, digital tone and announcement generation, among many others
6. Remote-line concentration, switching, and multiplexing
7. Digital terminal devices, including single-line telephones, key (multiline) telephones, data terminals, transaction terminals, and many other types of digital terminal devices
8. Digital, regenerative repeaters for digital interoffice transmission circuits (span lines).

Distributed Digital Switching Systems for Local Exchanges Digital switching and transmission systems and digital customer lines and terminal devices now being installed in the switched public network in many countries indicate the trend of conversion to digital technology. Digital interoffice transmission systems that usually multiplex 24, 30, or more voice circuits over two twisted-wire cable pairs, called spanlines, commonly use transmission bit rates of 1.544 or 2.048 Mb/s, respectively, or nominally double these bit rates for twice the number of voice paths.

A digital switching system may not only interface *directly* with digital interoffice spanlines but also with digital lines from RLMs without the requirement for A/D or D/A conversions at the switching system interfaces, although these can be provided when necessary for analog system interfaces.

Figure 12 is a block diagram of a typical digital local (class 5) switching system, using a modular system architecture and distributed control. Switching systems having this basic architecture have been in the planning stages since at least the mid-1960s but did not become cost-effective until the introduction of LSI devices with appropriate reliability, capability, and programmability. The introduction of the microprocessor was primarily the deciding factor that prompted LSI-based designs of distributed switching systems.

Random access memory (RAM), read-only memory (ROM), the per-line PCM codec, and the per-line voice channel filters completed the list of most required components to make digital distributed switching systems a practical reality today.

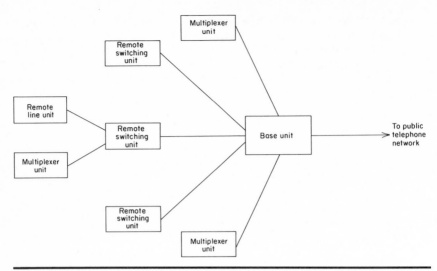

FIG. 12   *Block diagram of a class 5 local digital switching system, based on a distributed system architecture.*

In Fig. 12, the lines connecting the multiplexer or remote switching units with the host switch or base unit or connecting a remote line unit or multiplexer unit with a remote switching unit are all digital. They may carry up to 24 or 30 digitized voice paths, or multiples thereof, depending upon the span-line bit rate, the number of digital lines used to serve traffic demands and provide a satisfactory grade of service to the system users, and the signaling methods used. In Fig. 12, each remote unit shown served by the base unit can directly serve a group of subscriber lines.

With this distributed architecture, which is the basis of many digital switching systems, all similar customer terminals (telephones, data sets, and so forth) can have the same system features and service offerings available to them, regardless of the type of remote service unit(s) involved or their distance from the base unit.

9.6   Line-Group Architectures

Distribution of Line Groups and Control Functions   The term *distributed switching system* can imply a modular switching system in which parts of that system, i.e., RLMs, controlling base units, multiplexers, and so on, are distributed throughout the geographic area served by the system. Distributed switching also implies distribution of control functions throughout the system such that all control is not concentrated in one part of the system alone, as in earlier common-control switching system architectures.

Modular digital switching system design also allows concentration, digitization, and multiplexing to take place relatively near the customer's premises, so that shared-usage (multiplexed) lines may be used between a base unit or host switch and an RLM, thus greatly reducing cabling requirements between clusters of customers and the serving central-host switch. For example, four exchange cable pairs could serve several hundred telephone subscribers using a remote switching unit of a distributed switching system instead of serving just four main-station telephones, with each pair dedicated to one conventional telephone, as is commonly the practice.

Distributed control can also imply that small controllers reside in the system line groups of one complex and powerful common controller serving an entire central office. Because each system module requires only a limited amount of control power, a VLSI CPU can be appropriately applied in a distributed-control switching system architecture.

Generally, a typical 8- or 16-bit microcomputer system with a multiple-lead two-way bus from a single-chip CPU to external memory and peripherals and just a few thousand bits of RAM and ROM, a few dozen I/O ports, and a cycle time of a few microseconds adequately provides all control functions in a remote line unit or remote switching unit serving several hundred lines of a distributed switching system.

The various functional block diagrams for the modules used in a distributed switching system such as the one described are shown in Figs. 13 to 17. The basic interface, switching network, and control functions are shown in Fig. 13. This relationship carries through the entire system design, and various system modules incorporate this architecture and/or provide a portion of it.

The control portions of the diagrams in Figs. 13 to 17 heavily incorporate LSI microcircuit technology. Included are 8- or 16-bit CPU chips, RAM, EPROM, ROM, I/O devices, and other peripherals. The subscriber-line interface circuits incorporate LSI codecs and channel filters on a one-per-line basis.

Figure 14 is the block diagram of the base or host unit. All lines shown carry digital signals. The facility's interface unit terminates lines, interoffice trunks, and digital spanlines and brings all digital bit streams into synchronism with

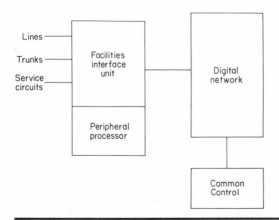

FIG. 13   A basic block diagram of a class 5 digital switching system.

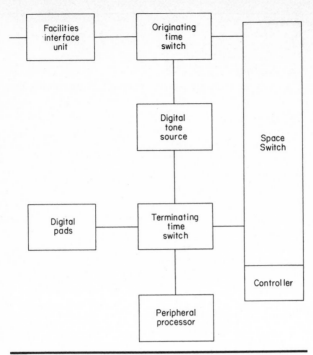

FIG. 14 *Block diagram of a digital switching system base unit.*

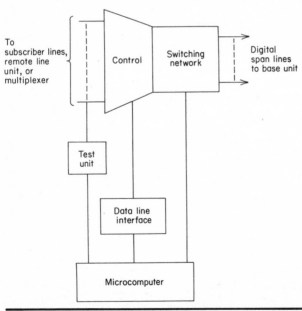

FIG. 15 *Block diagram of a digital switching system remote-switching unit.*

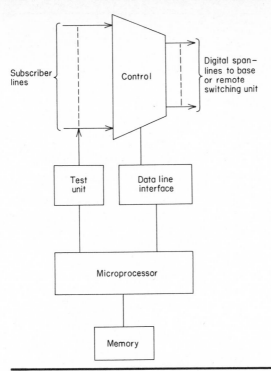

FIG. 16 *Block diagram of a digital switching system remote-line unit.*

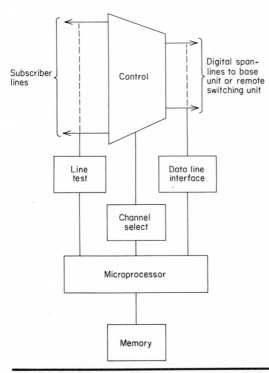

FIG. 17 *Block diagram of a digital switching system multiplexer unit.*

the base unit clock. Combinations of time and space-division switching techniques are used. In this example, call-progress tones and various other supervisory and signaling tones may be digitally generated.

Voice-transmission levels may also be adjusted for compatibility with a national switched network loss/level transmission plan. Either gain (digital amplification) or loss (digital attenuation) can be provided by converting 8-bit digital code groups from one code to another by a digital memory lookup table, thus allowing different level values to be obtained, depending upon the lookup memory data accessed for a given voice path through the base unit. Figure 14 shows the digital level control function as *digital pads*. Other system architectures may add voice-path gain or loss in the line and/or trunk interface units: this may be done on either an analog or digital basis, depending upon voice-path noise and delay and dual-tone multifrequency (DTMF) signaling receive-level-adjustment considerations.

All voice paths through a system of this type are usually in 8-bit PCM code groups that use the nonlinear μ-law (in North America and Japan) or A-law (in Europe and some other countries) companding methods. The 8-kHz sampling rate and 125-μs frame period are industry standards for systems that interconnect with national and/or international digital transmission networks.

Remote Switching Unit   A remote switching unit, such as the one shown in Fig. 15, can provide line concentration and local switching, thus permitting efficient assignments of spanline time-slots because local-to-local connections can be completed via the remote switching unit and need not occupy spanline time-slots during a local-to-local line conversation. Each remote switching unit usually utilizes a shared, separate (common-channel) control-data link to and from the base unit to set up and disconnect voice paths and may also provide digital data paths between digital customer terminals.

Because a direct dedicated physical pair of wires may no longer be used in this type of system between the customer terminal equipment and a centralized testing facility, a remote test unit has to be included at remotely located equipment facilities. This unit tests and may convert into a digital format the results of the tests; the results may be transmitted over the digital spanlines to the centralized test equipment.

Remote-Line Unit   A remote-line unit block diagram is shown in Fig. 16. This unit, like the remote switching unit, may have many line interface circuits, each of which may include an LSI per-line codec and channel-filter chip. However, the remote line unit does not include the local line-to-line switching capability; it therefore gives in-use lines access to available time-slots on the spanlines that interconnect it to an associated remote switching or base unit.

Remote Multiplexer Unit   A digital multiplexer unit as shown in Fig. 17 simply provides a digital channel or time-slot on a spanline for each line connected to the multiplexer unit. Thus it is generally a nonconcentrating unit, usually having fixed time-slot assignments for each codec in each line inter-face circuit. It does, however, include a line interface circuit for each cus-tomer line it serves, to provide the usual BORSCHT line functions required in digital switching system telephone-line interface circuits (see Sec. 9.7 and Ref. 6).

Alternatively, a remote multiplexer unit may assign spanline time-slots as traffic demands, but have as many available time-slots as there are lines served, thus providing nonblocking (nonconcentrating) operation. When this is done, a similar hardware design can serve either a nonconcentrating mul-tiplexer function or a concentrating switching unit function.

Combinations of Line Groups Comprise Digital Class 5 Switching System Figure 2 depicts a representative functional block diagram of a dis-tributed digital switching system. Various-sized line groups are shown; each line group utilizes one transmit-receive highway pair (or spanline).[20]

When a line group is collocated with the central digital time-slot inter-change in this example, the transmit and receive highways may be in phase with the system clock, so that the digital interchange can function synchro-nously with the line-group transmission highways. However, in large systems this may not always be true.

In small systems, or in PABXs, two transmission-line pairs (one pair for each direction of transmission) are appropriate for each line group. However, in larger telephone system applications, multiple highway pairs are fre-quently required for system reliability and improved traffic-handling capacity.

When the line groups are remotely located with respect to a central digital interchange, it is necessary to adjust the phase of digital bit streams received over the highways from the line groups so that they are put into phase with the digital interchange timing base. A digital transmission-line controller (shown in Fig. 2 as DTLC) provides phase adjustment and dc line feed for spanline repeaters (if required) to extend the lines over several miles from the central host.

In a distributed switching system such as the one shown in Fig. 12, the call-completion (switching) capability between stations served by the same remote line unit is frequently required when the line group is large, serves customers who have a high community interest, and/or is a great distance from the serv-ing host, say, 10 mi (16 km) or so. With this approach, a remote switching unit assumes some of the internal switching complexity of a PABX or community dial office (CDO). Outgoing dial signals may be monitored, and if a call is for another party served by the same remote switching unit, the transmission path to the central-office host may be dropped out and the calling path completed locally within the remote switching unit. Alternately, dialing may be detected centrally and instructions for a remote local-to-local connection transmitted to the remote switching unit line group via a signaling path.

Line-Group Sizes Many digital switching system architectures today are based upon distributed-control techniques. One microprocessor-based control system may provide most control functions for a group of line and/or trunk interface circuits. Line groups served by one microcomputer control system may vary from a few to 256 lines in practical systems, with usual group sizes being 8, 12, 16, 24, 48, 96, 128, or 256 lines in μ-law codec-implemented systems or 8, 16, 30, 32, 60, 64, 120, 128, 240, or 256 lines in A-law codec-implemented systems produced by various manufacturers. Some larger line-group sizes are also occasionally used, such as 512, 768, 1024 lines, and so on. The line-group size depends heavily upon the speed of the group controller CPU and whether per-line or shared controllers are also included on each line board. Multiple line groups, such as those just mentioned, may be collocated and used in single, large line-group applications. Figure 18 shows an example of a line group for digital switching system remote-line-unit architecture.

A line group for a class 5 distributed switching system or a PABX or CSS may have many similarities. To simplify the description of the functions of a digital switching system, a small PABX is now described, to illustrate the interactions between line and trunk interface circuits and their shared microcomputer control system.

Using the PCM Codec As a Microcomputer-Controlled Switching Device
Some PCM codecs can be both a transmission and switching device, with switching done directly on the PCM highways, i.e., when microcomputer control of on-chip time-slot memory is a codec feature. The ability of some per-

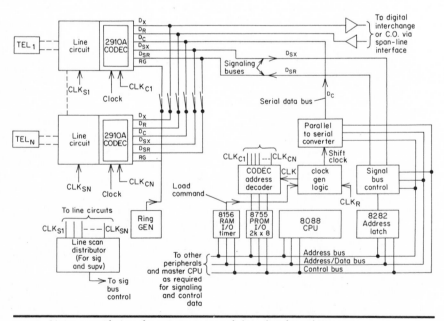

FIG. 18   Line group with time-slot assignment controls for a digital switching system.

line codecs to perform computation of multiplexing time-slots allows them to be readily used to implement concentration, local-call completion, conference-call setup, and other services. Time-slot assignment otherwise would be performed for many codecs by a control subsystem, thus further burdening that subsystem's software program and hardware design.

The optional on-chip memory logic functions also provide the benefits of component standardization by making the codec more versatile. They allow the same codec chip to be used in central-office switching, PABX, RLM, key telephone, automatic-call and digital systems.

Software has become the key to orderly expansion of digital systems and evolution of services. Today most equipment manufacturers are using, or plan to use, microprocessor-based control subsystems to achieve these benefits at low cost.

Some codecs operate in either a fixed time-slot mode or under the command of a microcomputer or other programmable line-group processor. Codecs equipped with a microcomputer control mode are, in a way, able to perform as an "intelligent" peripheral of the processor.

The codec *microcomputer mode* unburdens a line group controller because one microprocessor, dedicated to a small group of lines (up to 256, for example), can contol multiple codecs with less software overhead than would otherwise be required. It can also reduce the high-speed time-slot memory requirements because this memory is on the codec chip instead of in the group controller or distributed throughout the line group. In turn, more of the maximum throughput and memory capacity are available for system expansion and for implementing new subscriber services by software enhancements.

To control multiple codecs, the line-group controlling microprocessor simply issues commands and addresses (assigns time-slots) to the per-line codecs. Assignments may be changed dynamically between calls or during call setup. Time-slots may be assigned independently for each transmission direction, and codec operations for each direction may be synchronous or asynchronous. Also, individual codecs may be activated or switched to an inactive, power-down mode.

The codecs perform the operations required to put PCM data onto, or take data off of, the PCM highways or transmission lines at the proper times. Each active chip may compute its own time-slots and perform its own PCM conversion, multiplexing, and demultiplexing operations. Each codec can also handle its own internal power-down operations as well as power down other associated circuitry.

For conventional telephone switching system economy and versatility, more subscriber lines can be served, and thus more codecs can have access to a switching system highway or spanline than the normal digital highway voice-path (time-slot) capacity. One application is in RLMs that may be located miles from the digital host office.

Very substantial savings in copper wire requirements result from the use of remote multiplexing, concentrating, and switching. For example, a single T1 spanline linking a(n) RLM to its digital host may serve up to about 100 codecs and subscribers—not just 24—and the transmission line serving the remote unit can be just a twisted-wire pair in each direction. Nor are 100 codecs the limit. To improve traffic-handling capacity, North American system designers have started to go from 24- to 48-channel highway architectures within switching systems. Similarly, in Europe 30- and 60-channel highways (or 32 and 64 channels) are used.

The concept of serving more telephones than there are voice paths between a(n) RLM and a central-office host is based upon the probability that not more than a certain percentage of telephones in a given served group will be active at a given time. A study of the calling habits of groups of various telephone users reveals that in many residential applications not more than 25 to 30 percent of the subscriber lines may ever be simultaneously active.

In business applications, the percentages may be higher, and when data is transmitted over the telephone network and the average call-holding times rise, the percentage may closely approximate 100 percent usage during peak periods. For this reason, line (traffic) concentration may be useful in some applications and not in others. Correspondingly, codecs may require variable time-slot assignments in some RLM applications and fixed time-slot assignments in others, where concentration is not needed because of the high-usage nature of the lines being served.

9.7 A Digital PABX

A Microcomputer-Controlled Small Digital Switching System The typical digital PABX described here incorporates many switching and transmission control elements as well as line scanning, signaling, and supervision and is thus representative of the kinds of tasks that can be performed by a microprocessor in a practical system line group.

Figure 19 shows the functional block diagram of a small digital PABX that uses PCM transmission within the system and digital switching techniques. This digital PABX is a 100-port microcomputer-controlled telephone switching system that uses T1-compatible transmission highways (one for each direction of speech transmission), with a serial 24 time-slot, 8-bit per time-slot internal digital transmission format. One microcomputer control system can comfortably handle 100 lines with simple line-interface circuitry. More lines are possible if the system service features are limited to the more basic ones.[6]

The codec (as described in Sec. 9.3) is used for A/D and D/A conversion in each line and trunk circuit. The PABX may use a stored-program CPU for shared (line-group) control functions, including assignment of time-slots on the digital transmission highways and all call-processing functions, such as rotary-dial pulse registration, ringing control, and trunk signaling.

All analog signals received over the connecting analog lines and trunks are converted into digitized equivalent signals to facilitate TDM switching of the digitized voice and signaling samples between various time-slots on the transmission highways. The time-slots are computer-assigned as required by the traffic, to interconnect calling and called lines and trunks.

The time bases for the shared-control CPU and the digital transmission highway may be different and asynchronous to each other. The microcom-

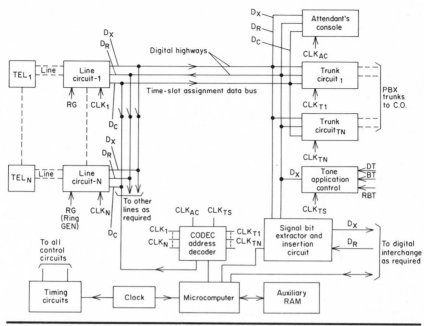

FIG. 19 *Block diagram of a small digital PABX.*

puter control system may operate from its own internal time base, whereas the transmission highways operate at a 1.544-Mb/s bit rate or at another standard digital transmission bit rate for telephone systems, such as 2.048 Mb/s in Europe, or at multiples of these bit rates, and so on.

The serial highways are multipled to other line and trunk circuits and to an attendant's console control and a tone-application control. These highways are the transmit data highway (D_X) the receive data highway (D_R), and the computer data highway (D_C). Highways D_X and D_R are the 1.544-Mb/s transmission highways, and they need not operate in phase with each other. In a small PABX, such as that in Fig. 19, with just single transmit and receive highways, the highways may be operated synchronously. Highway D_C carries computer-generated data for time-slot assignment to the codecs and thus operates at a rate determined by the computer. The codec may operate with either a on- or off-chip-generated time-slot clocking pulses, although the former is shown in this example. Both transmission highways (D_X and D_R) carry bit streams having a 125-μs frame period (for 8-kHz sampling of each voice channel). Each frame is composed of twenty-four 8-bit time-slots, plus one frame-synchronization bit, totaling 193 bit per frame.

Each 8-bit time-slot carries digitally encoded amplitude samples for one direction of transmission of one conversation. The telephone line, trunk, and so forth assigned to a given transmission-highway time-slot may change from moment to moment under computer control. In this example, each port has a variable assignment rather than a fixed time-slot assignment on the transmission highways. Thus the highway time-slots can represent active conversation paths or "links."

Transmission Path Through the Digital Switch In a digital PABX or class 5 office, a digital transmission path through the system may typically include the following nine basic circuit functions, in various combinations:

1. Analog line interface circuit
2. Digital line interface circuit
3. Hybrid (2- to 4-wire conversion)
4. Transmit and receive channel filters
5. Codec (digital coder and decoder)
6. Digital transmission highways
7. Digital interchange
8. Analog trunk interface circuit
9. Digital trunk interface circuit

Most of these functions are potential product areas for LSI technology; however, considerable architectural changes over electromechanical and nondigital electronic switching systems are required to optimize the impact of newer microcircuit technology. Thus, along with the use of digital hardware is the potential for computer-like system designs that result in new feature offerings to the user, improved transmission on long-distance calls, shorter call-setup times, faster trouble-diagnosis times, and so on.

Analog Telephone-Line Interface Circuit Figure 20 shows a block diagram of an analog telephone-line interface circuit for a digital switching system such as PABX or class 5 office. This is a single-party plain old telephone service (POTS) line circuit that serves a conventional telephone line equipped with telephones such as Western Electric Company's type 500 or similar units with high-voltage electromechanical ringers and either rotary or TOUCH-TONE®-type* dials. These telephones also have automatic varistor compensation for adjusting sidetone (your own voice heard in your receiver) and transmitter current (efficiency) as a function of line current and must be accommodated by any new line-circuit battery-feed design.

The telephone industry has coined the acronym BORSCHT, which here refers to all the basic functions required in a digital system analog line interface circuit. These per-line functions are:

B battery feed
O overload protection
R ringing
S supervision
C codec and channel filters
H hybrid
T test

*TOUCH-TONE® is a registered mark of AT&T.

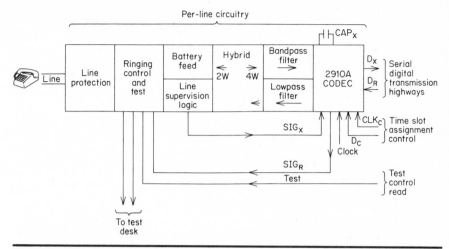

FIG. 20   Block diagram of an analog telephone line interface circuit for a digital switching system. Borscht: B, Battery feed; O, Overhead Protection; R, Ringing; S, Supervision; C, Codec and Channel Filters; H, Hybrid; T, Test

Referring again to Fig. 20, the *line protection* circuitry protects the line circuit from damage caused by overload currents or high-voltage transients on the telephone line due to lightning or electrostatic coupling from other sources or from power line or other induced or conducted currents, and so on.

The *battery-feed* circuit provides a balanced dc talk-battery supply to the line as line current for telephone sets (which usually use a carbon transmitter and require a nominal 20 to 100-mA line current). This battery-feed circuit must provide a low dc impedance for coupling the battery to the line (nominally 400 Ω) and an ac terminating impedance that matches the characteristic impedance of the telephone cable, nominally either 600 or 900 Ω, in series with 2.16-μF capacitance. In practice, a more precise match is required during conversations.

The line *supervision* logic is circuitry that monitors the line loop current and, when detected above a certain threshold (approximately 15 mA), produces a logic level **1** for signaling the line-group CPU that this line is engaged. This circuit also repeats rotary-dial loop pulses (when required) to the CPU in the same manner as for off-hook supervision.

Ringing control circuitry applies interrupted high-voltage ringing signals to the telephone line, to ring a called telephone. This circuitry usually applies ringing from a common ringing generator (norminally 20 Hz, 105 V) by means of a relay or other switching circuit that removes the normal battery-feed circuit while applying the ringing voltage to the line. Also, this circuit provides the circuitry for ring trip, i.e., disconnecting and locking out the ringing voltage once the call has been answered. Some systems generate the ringing signal and ringing interruption cadence individually in each line interface circuit. Other ringing frequencies and voltages are also used for party-line selective ringing schemes and other applications.

Test circuitry usually consist of a test relay that, under control of the line-group CPU, transfers the line to a test circuit which extends the line to a test desk or other test facility.

The line *hybrid* is circuitry used at the transition between 2- (two-way) or 4-wire (separate transmit and receive) operations. Digital transmission is unidirectional in nature, so separate transmit and receive paths are necessary for bidirectional communication. The line hybrid (formerly accomplished by a multiwinding transformer) must prevent or substantially reduce the coupling between the one-way receive and one-way transmit paths (*trans-hybrid loss*) to prevent undesirable echoes or sidetone effect in the connecting telephones. These hybrids are used between the 2-wire battery-feed circuit and the 4-wire (equivalent) channel filter.

Hybrids usually have four sets of terminals: 4-wire transmit, 4-wire receive, 2-wire line, and balancing network. The hybrid is usually balanced for maximum echo cancellation (and return loss) by closely balancing the hybrid balancing-network impedance against the 2-wire line impedance. Adaptive balancing or echo-canceling techniques may also be used to enhance the performance of the hybrid, reduce the critical nature of network balance, and give improved trans-hybrid and return loss over the entire channel bandwidth for all line lengths to be accommodated.

When a codec is used to encode and decode digital signals, channel filters are required to limit the bandwidth of the voice channels. In the transmit direction, the bandpass is nominally 180 to 3400 Hz, according to AT&T's D3 channel-bank-compatibility specification[9] and a comparable CCITT specification.[10] Also, the receive-channel filter is a low-pass filter that passes frequencies below nominally 3400 Hz. The channel filters must be compatible with the codec analog interfaces (see Sec. 9.3).

Battery-Feed Methods in Common-Battery Switching Systems Conventional methods of supplying *talking battery* from a single *common battery* to all lines and telephones in an exchange require some form of isolation to prevent voice, switching, and dialing transients from coupling, via the battery, between lines. This is usually accomplished by feeding direct current to the subscriber line via dual series inductors, usually in the form of a retard coil (choke), a repeat coil (transformer), or a dual-winding relay. The calling and called telephones in any conversation are independently battery fed, and the calling and called lines are ac-coupled only. The inductive battery-feed circuit blocks ac signals from being applied to the battery, and the ac voice signals pass easily between local calling and called lines via the ac-coupling circuit. Figure 21 shows a typical battery-feed circuit for a digital switching system.

Switching transients and other noise are also blocked from the conversation path by the battery-feed transformer inductance. The impedance of the exchange battery is very low, frequently a small fraction of 1 Ω.

In digital switching systems where line battery feed is supplied per line rather than one per conversation path, an inductorless method of battery feed, with resistance battery feed and operational amplifiers to compensate for

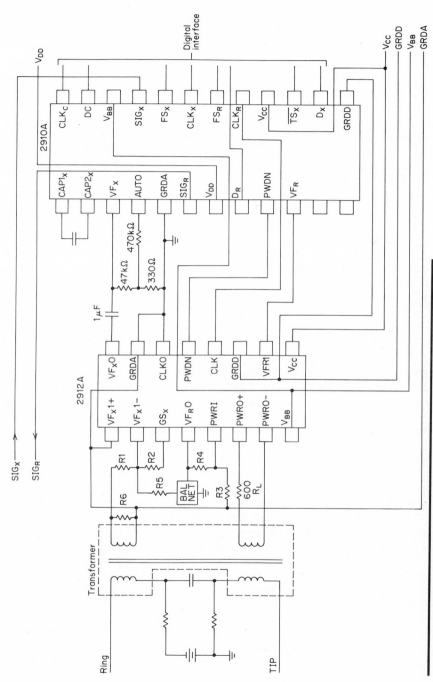

FIG. 21 An analog line interface circuit using transformer battery feed, with resistor hybrid, 2912A filter, and 2910A codec.

transmission losses caused by the battery-feed resistors and to perform other line-driving functions, is sometimes used. LSI devices may be used in line circuits that will compatibly function with conventional telephones in essentially all situations in the same way as the inductor-type battery-feed circuits. Various other battery-feed methods are also used; they are based upon dc-dc converters or miniature ferrite-core transformers with reverse-bias windings to reduce transformer dc saturation.

The line battery-feed function is required on a per-line basis in digital switching systems because the digital time-division path through the system cannot transport the direct current required for line battery feed or the high-voltage ringing, test, or coin-collect/refund signals, and so on. In analog space-division systems, the function is embodied well within the shared portion of the switching system.

Line-interface-circuit components must also be selected and/or designed to withstand the rigors of electrical exposure to outside cable plant. That is, induced or conducted high-voltage transients or steady-state currents or voltages above normal line voltages must be limited by protective devices to prevent line-circuit-component damage.

High-voltage signals for the line are usually applied by means of a "high-level access" or "test" relay per line. Thus, the digital voice path is used to transmit only relatively low-voltage ac signals within the telephone voice-frequency spectrum and amplitude limits of the system.

Equivalent 4-Wire Service   Conventional analog telephones use a single pair of copper wires for the line that connects them with a switching system. Voice transmission conducted over the line in both directions simultaneously provides *full-duplex* operation. However, in digital systems, separate paths are provided for each direction of digital code transmission because each direction must be processed separately. This type of transmission, in which a separate path is provided for each direction of transmission, is known as *4-wire* operation, and each path carries *half-duplex* transmission; the two paths together carry the *full-duplex* transmission as required for a conversation path.

Digital transmission highways in a switching system and digital subscriber data links (lines) may not use 4 physical wires for full-duplex digital transmission. Regardless of the number of wires used, however, the separate-path operation is known as an *equivalent 4-wire* facility.

The present *antisidetone* circuits used in analog telephones to cancel a local talker's voice signals from the telephone receiver circuit can be eliminated in an equivalent 4-wire digital telephone. Future digital customer lines, or fiber-optic subscriber loops, will also help bring about the equivalent 4-wire digital telephone set (see Sec. 9.9).

Both end-to-end digital transmission and separate common-channel interoffice signaling (CCIS) systems as described in Sec. 9.9 can bring improved performance and new services to the telephones of the future. With high-speed CCIS capabilities nationally, such new features as displays of the number of a calling telephone at a called station, storage of numbers of callers to a telephone in a person's absence, or selective answering of desired calls only

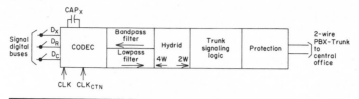

FIG. 22   *A two-wire analog trunk circuit for a small digital PABX.*

become technically feasible, but much remains to be done before 4-wire sub-scriber loops or common-channel signaling become a widespread reality throughout the public switched network.

Analog* PABX *Trunk Interface Circuits   Figure 22 is a block diagram of an analog trunk circuit that interfaces a PCM-PABX with a conventional two-way, PBX trunk from a central office. In this circuit, the codec, filters, and hybrid are basically the same as those used in the line circuits. The trunk signaling logic provides ground-start circuitry (to prevent call collisions), trunk-loop closure, loop pulsing, and ringing detection circuitry. Both inward and outward supervisory signals may be transmitted to the PABX central con-trol microcomputer via the codec signaling leads or special signaling buses that are multipled to each analog trunk interface circuit. One-way trunks are similarly implemented.

Solid-state implementation of most of this circuitry can be achieved using some high-voltage devices as well as varistors and diodes to protect the cir-cuitry against ringing voltages, switching transients, and other potentially haz-ardous voltages and currents. A protection specification being adopted by some manufacturers states that analog line and trunk circuits must be pro-tected against transients of one thousand volts at one ampere for one millisecond.

PABX *Signaling Via the Codec*   The basic function of the codec is to provide a means for encoding transmit-direction voice signals into a 64-kb/s bit stream and decoding a similar received bit stream into voice frequencies; in the North American μ-law version it also optionally provides per-channel sig-naling means.

Signaling information is transmitted in the eighth bit once every sixth trans-mission frame by borrowing the eighth bit from the least significant position of the 8-bit code used for PCM channel transmission. Actually, when the sig-naling channel is provided, the voice channel uses 7⅚-bit encoding of the voice signal over several transmission frames instead of the full 8-bit coding.

When up to 24 similar codecs may be simultaneously active on the same transmission highway, the highway bit rate may be T1-compatible,* i.e., it may operate at 1.544 Mb/s. Some codecs may handle bit rates up to twice this speed, so that up to 48 codecs may be active simultaneously on one pair of transmission highways. This arrangement makes it compatible with existing

---

*T1 is AT&T's designation code for the North American digital transmission-line standard, as discussed in Sec. 9.4, *Voice Digitization, Digital Voice Transmission in TDM Systems.*

24-, 30-, or 48-channel system architectures or any other desired configuration of codec-per-line groupings from 1 to 48. The 24- and 48-channel systems usually use μ-law codecs such as Intel 2910A or an equivalent, and the 30-channel system usually uses the A-law codecs such as Intel 2911A or equivalent. (See Sec. 9.3 and Ref. 6)

Dynamic Time-Slot Assignment in Example **PABX** The application of the codec in a digital PABX, as described here, must be capable of dynamically changing its internally stored channel time-slot assignments under control of a microcomputer which serves that line group. Time-slot assignments need not remain fixed as they are in carrier-system channel-bank applications; they can be changed for each call or for tone assignments, conversation, or conference modes of operation. This provides a PABX architecture that uses as many highway time-slots as maximum simultaneous call requirements dictate rather than one fixed time-slot per line or codec because time-slots need be assigned only when required.

Digital Transmission Highways Within **PABX** The terms *transmit* and *receive* indicate transmission direction relative to a local telephone. Figure 23 *a, b* shows the time-slot protocol of highways D_X and D_R, respectively, in the representative PABX. On D_X, the odd time-slots TS-1 through TS-19 may be *calling-party-transmit* time-slots, and the even time-slots TS-2 through TS-20 may be *called-party-transmit* time-slots. Similarly, on highway D_R, the odd time-slots TS-1 through TS-19 may be *called-party-receive* time-slots, and the even time-slots TS-2 through TS-20 may be *calling-party receive* time-slots. In this small typical PABX, where no time-slot interchange is required, digitized voice samples on highway D_X are coupled back to highway D_R unchanged and in the same time-slots. Signaling data bits (the eighth bit in each time-slot every sixth frame) are modified by the *signal bit extractor and insertion* circuit shown in Fig. 19.

Signaling bits on the transmit highway D_X relate to line and trunk supervision and rotary-dial pulse transmission; signaling bits on the receive highway D_R relate to ringing control for the lines and signaling and supervision for the trunks and attendant's console. In practical systems, signaling is sometimes transmitted by separate highway bits or digital links with the CPU, to permit full 8-bit voice-path encoding to meet toll-grade transmission objectives.

Because two time-slots are required on each transmission highway for each conversation, the related time-slots involved in the same conversation are sometimes referred to as a *link*. Thus the system described here is a 10-link system. A practical small PABX might, for example, have usage requirements of 90 lines and 10 trunks, 40 lines and 8 trunks, or 20 lines and 6 trunks but be limited by link capacity.

Other system architectures could use all time-slots for links, with none dedicated to tone assignment or scanning. A 30-channel CCITT-standard digital transmission format (or multiples thereof) could alternatively be used for additional trunking capacity in PABX and similar RLM applications in large distributed switching systems.

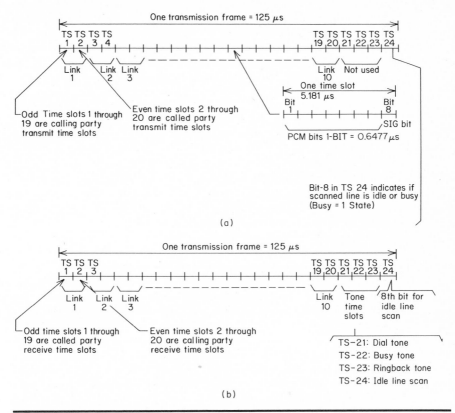

FIG. 23   Transmission-frame formats: (a) transmit highway D_X, and (b) receive highway D_R.

The 2.048-Mb/s CCITT-standard digital transmission format usually requires an A-law companding codec (as described in the first subsection of Sec. 9.4) and could be used for all line, trunk, tone-application, and attendant's console interface circuits instead of the North American T1-standard μ-law codec described here. With the T1 format, each transmission time-slot contains 8 bits, which has a duration of 0.6477^+ μs. Thus the period of one time-slot is 5.181^+ μs.

PABX *Call-Progress Tones* Figure 24 shows one method of applying three of the call-progress tones (i.e., dial, busy, and ringback tones) to the system transmission highways. The tones can be either generated digitally and applied to the receive highway D_R by gates or generated by analog circuits and then compressed and digitized by using the transmit side only of a codec. With this latter method, test jacks can allow the analog tones to be monitored, or they may be used for other analog applications without the need for digital signal decoders. The tones shown are those recommended for use where they may be heard over international circuits and are the same as tones used in many new systems currently being produced in North America.

With the T1 highway format there are 24 time-slots per frame, thus allowing 24 simultaneous voice paths per highway. In the PABX shown in Fig. 19, 3 of the 24 time-slots (see Fig. 23b) are permanently assigned to call-progress tones, as shown in Table 8.

Also, to simplify the per-line circuitry, the idle-line scanning function is performed by a computer-assisted technique that uses time-slot 24 on the receive highway D_R, also shown in Fig. 23b.

With 20 time-slots left for encoded voice transmission, the highways will serve up to 20 active telephones, or 20 percent of the ports in a 100-port system. If the number of ports is reduced, the grade of service can be improved. If the number of ports is reduced to 20, the system becomes nonblocking; i.e., all calls can be processed without abnormal delay.

For higher-grade service capabilities, all 24 time-slots can be used for links, the CCITT-standard 30-channel (2.048-Mb/s) transmission standards may be adopted, or the codecs may be connected for 48-channel operations, i.e., at a 3.088 or 3.152-Mb/s bit rate. In these cases, dedicated time-slots for call-progress tones or idle-line scanning, as described here, need not be used. Scanning can be handled independently of the codec and the tones can be supplied from special tone ports. See Sec. 9.8, *Analog Signal Processing*, for another method of general-purpose call-progress-generation using an analog signal processor.

PABX *Attendant's Console* A block diagram of an attendant's console for a small digital PABX is shown in Fig. 25; there are two sets of interfaces with the central control:

1. Serial-data highways:
   D_X transmit-data highway
   D_R receive-data highway
   D_C computer-data highway
2. CPU I/O ports between the PABX central processor and the buttons, lamps, and other console circuits

The PABX CPU assigns transmit and receive time-slots to the attendant's console codec(s) via highway D_C. A two-way voice path is established between the attendant's telephone and a local telephone or trunk via the assigned time-slots on transmission highways D_X and D_R.

The console tone ringer may be keyed ON by signals received via lead SIG_R of the codec, as a function of lamp and button signals where attendant action is required, or as determined by signals received from CPU ports and button states.

Lamp signals from the CPU are demultiplexed to drive lamp drivers and lamps, and button-state signals are multiplexed to transmit their states to the CPU over attendant-console data buses. Indications of *headset-plugged-in* and *listening key operated* are transmitted over codec signaling channel SIG_X and/or the CPU data leads of the attendant's console.

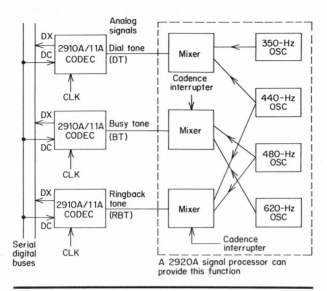

FIG. 24 Call-progress tone-generator circuit using codecs for analog tone digitization.

TABLE 8 Call-progress-tone time-slot assignments

Time-slot	Tone	Abbreviation
21	Dial	DT
22	Busy	BT
23	Ringback	RBT

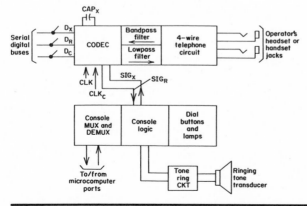

FIG. 25 Block diagram of attendant's console for a small digital PABX.

PABX Microcomputer Control System   Figure 26 is the functional block diagram of a typical LSI CPU. When used in an application such as a small, conventional PABX, one microprocessor can typically handle all central control functions for several hundred lines.

Peripherally interfacing with the microprocessor via address and data buses are a number of memory, I/O, and control devices, such as:

1. PROM: This semipermanent memory is for storing central control function instructions and class-of-service data (feature and service assignments) for lines, trunks, and other ports. (Approximately 4 kbytes of PROM are required for systems of up to about 256 ports, depending upon system features.)
2. RAM: This memory is used for the temporary storage of such call-processing data as

   - Present line status
   - Previous line status
   - Time-slot status/assignment
   - Call-sequence state
   - Dial pulse count
   - Dialed-digit counter
   - Dialed number
   - Trunk status
   - Source/destination address
   - Destination/source address
   - Special-feature status and sequence
   - Stack data for the microprocessor

   Figure 26 also shows the CPU interfaces, and Fig. 27 shows a microcomputer control system for a small PABX.

3. Programmable peripheral interface (8255A): This chip provides the interface between external controlling devices and signals and the computer's parallel-bidirectional data buses. These I/O ports can be used to accept and produce line and trunk signaling data, for transmission to and from all analog line- and trunk-interface circuits, and so forth.
4. I/O driver/terminator interface: This is conventional transistor-transistor logic (TTL) I/O circuitry for driving output circuits and terminating input circuits at the computer system interface.
5. Programmable communications interface (USART)* (8251A): This device provides an interface between the computer buses and teletype interfaces or RS-232C data line or terminal interfaces. This permits direct teletype, data line, or terminal interfacing with the system CPU. Thus, system behavior can be monitored or changed readily via local remote terminal devices. The USART accepts data characters from the CPU (8085, 8086, or 8088) in parallel format and then converts them into a continuous

---

*Universal synchronous/asynchronous receiver/transmitter chip.

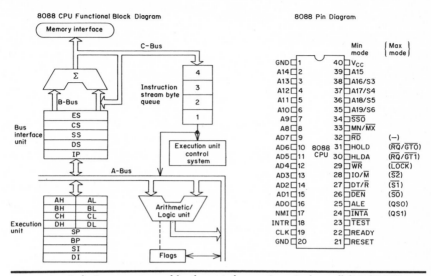

FIG. 26 *A typical microprocessor used for the central processing unit of a small digital PABX.*

serial-data stream for transmission to a data line, data terminal, or tele-type. The USART can simultaneously receive serial-data streams and convert them to parallel-data characters for the CPU.

6. RS232C interface: This interface consists of inverting drivers that drive standard RS232 data lines, a CRT display, or a data coupler from signals produced by the 8251A USART, and vice versa.

7. Multi-Master bus arbitration logic (8289): This chip allows the computer system to share a common system bus with other master devices, such as other CPUs or DMA (direct memory access) devices, thus sharing common memory and I/O resources. This device synchronously arbitrates all system requests for use of the system bus with respect to the bus clock.

8. Programmable interval timers (8253): These timers can be used for many timing functions but are well suited for generating microcomputer inter-rupt signals that cause the computer to momentarily stop its processing action and scan line- and trunk-port signaling leads. For example, a 10-ms interrupt signal can be produced by the timers, causing the CPU to scan a different idle-port signaling lead every 10 ms. This interrupt func-tion could also be accomplished under software control but use of the interval timers allows precise control without accidental changes of the interrupt signal with software changes. Upon line seizure (off-hook con-dition), the 10-ms interrupt rate produces an average dial-tone delay of 0.5 s in a 100-port PABX or remote switching unit. The worst-case dial-tone would be 1 s and that would occur in about 1 percent of the calls.

9. In other CPU peripherals, a number of the functions mentioned are com-bined so that a three-chip set can provide essentially all the computer functions described here.

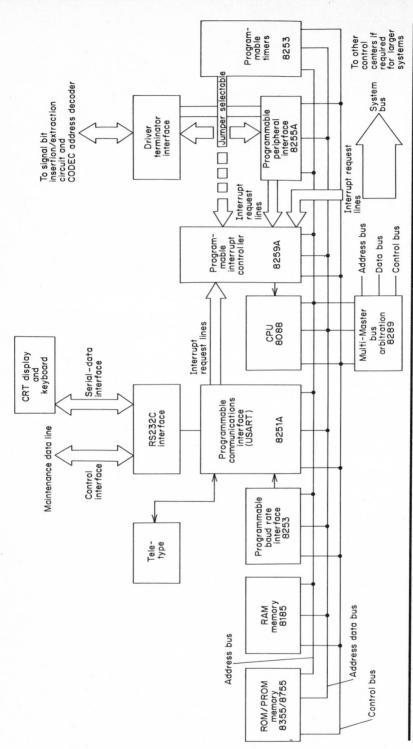

FIG. 27 A microcomputer control system for a small digital PABX.

9.8 Analog-Signal Processing

An LSI *Processor for Analog Signals* Many analog-signal-processing requirements are found in telephone switching systems; the two most obvious are for tone generation and detection. Generation of the call-progress tones, i.e., the dial, busy, ringback, and other tones, can be accomplished either by an analog method or digitally. Tone detection such as for detecting TOUCH-TONE®-type* dial signals, i.e., DTMF signals, also may require analog-signal processing.

Single-chip LSI signal processors may be programmed to frequencies as required for these two telephony applications; the signal processor functions somewhat like a combined microcomputer and programmable analog-signal filter. The same type of signal processor can be programmed for use in a wide variety of applications.

Historically, complex signal-processing problems have been solved in one of three ways: (1) using linear semiconductor circuits requiring passive components, which usually set the performance limits of these systems via their tolerances and temperature coefficients; (2) processing digitized analog signals with a high-speed arithmetic processor, where speed/bandwidth is generally set by multiple capabilities (The decision to use this approach to solve a signal-processing problem is usually set by the price of such a computational system.); and (3) more recently, using custom analog ICs. The third approach is generally more cost-effective and accurate than the other two, but is hampered by its lack of flexibility and nonstandard product status.

The analog-signal processor has been developed to eliminate most of the problems associated with the three described signal-processing implementations. The first such LSI product was Intel's 2920 signal processor, which includes, on one N-channel metal-oxide semiconductor (NMOS) substrate, a high-speed, high-precision microprocessor, a 9-bit analog acquisition system, and a user programmable, erasable programmable read only memory (EPROM) for controlling operations of the digital and analog subsystems. By combining an on-chip analog acquisition system and a specially configured processor on the same silicon substrate, the device is applicable for use in major analog subsystems. The processor architecture is oriented toward real-time processing of digitized analog signals and can implement functions such as filters, oscillators, and limiters as well as various nonlinear functions. A user programmable on-chip EPROM provides firmware.

The signal processor is well-suited to simulate complex analog subsystems such as tone receivers, frequency sources, and modems. The personality of the device is determined by the code sequence set in the EPROM. Any changes are accomplished by erasing the EPROM with ultraviolet light and reprogramming it to a new data pattern.

Signal-Processor Architecture Figure 28a shows a block diagram of the 2920 signal processor in the run mode, as an example.[21,22] In this diagram, the chip

*TOUCH-TONE® is a registered mark of AT&T.

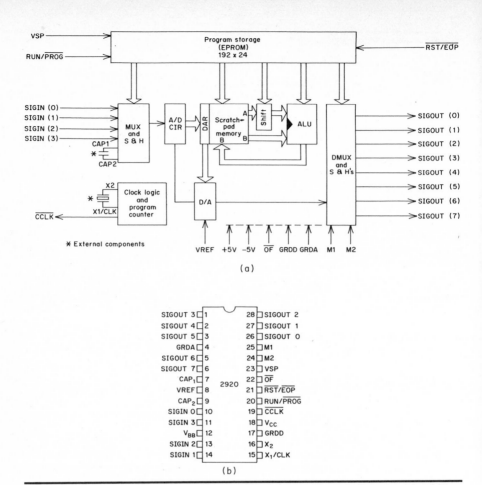

(a)

SIGOUT 3 □ 1   28 □ SIGOUT 2
SIGOUT 4 □ 2   27 □ SIGOUT 1
SIGOUT 5 □ 3   26 □ SIGOUT 0
GRDA □ 4   25 □ M1
SIGOUT 6 □ 5   24 □ M2
SIGOUT 7 □ 6   23 □ VSP
CAP₁ □ 7   22 □ $\overline{OF}$
VREF □ 8   21 □ $\overline{RST/EOP}$
CAP₂ □ 9   20 □ RUN/$\overline{PROG}$
SIGIN 0 □ 10   19 □ $\overline{CCLK}$
SIGIN 3 □ 11   18 □ V_{CC}
V_{BB} □ 12   17 □ GRDD
SIGIN 2 □ 13   16 □ X_2
SIGIN 1 □ 14   15 □ X_1/CLK

2920

(b)

FIG. 28   The Intel 2920 signal processor: (a) functional block diagram (shown in the run mode), and (b) pin configuration.

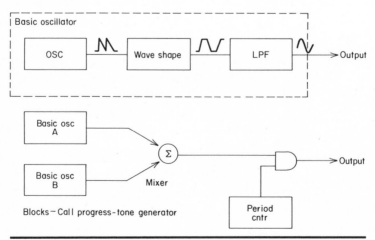

FIG. 29   The Intel 2920 signal processor used as a generator of call-progress tones.

has been divided into three major subsections: EPROM; arithmetic or digital processor; and the analog I/O conversion portions.

Both the analog I/O conversion circuits and the digital processor are controlled by the contents of the EPROM. The analog portion of the chip includes four input terminals, an input multiplexer, a sample and hold circuit, a D/A converter, a comparator, a data register, provision for the S/A A/D algorithm, an output demultiplexer, and eight buffered outputs, each with sample and hold. The data register is a link to the digital processor as well as for the A/D and D/A conversions. The run mode pin configuration is shown in Fig. 28b.

The architecture of the processor was selected for use in real-time signal-processing applications. It includes a two-port scratchpad RAM, a binary scaler, and an arithmetic and logic unit (ALU). To enable communication with the analog portion of the chip, access to the analog data register appears in the address range of the RAM.

The EPROM has provision for up to 192 instructions of 24 bits each. Programs contain no Jump instructions, except for a Jump from the end back to the beginning. Within one program pass, inputs may be sampled and digitized; structures such as filters, multipliers, rectifiers, and limiters may be simulated; and results may be delivered to the output via the DAC.

Generation of Call-Progress Tones by LSI *Analog-Signal Processor*   Figure 29 shows a tone generator with an interrupter used for producing call-progress tones in telephone switching systems. The generator follows the form of a relaxation oscillator converted to a sine-wave approximation. A low-pass filter is implemented to cancel undesirable harmonics that could result in output "aliasing." The basic tones of 350, 440, 480 and 620 Hz are created and then combined to give the appropriate frequency combinations listed in Table 9.

Because the analog-signal processor can operate with an external crystal, the generator's frequencies can be designed to yield better than 1 percent accuracy. Since they are digitally implemented, problems with component aging and drift may be avoided.

TABLE 9   **Call-progress-tone-generator signals produced by a single-chip analog-signal processor**

Frequencies	Tone	Comments
350 Hz + 440 Hz	Precise dial	Continuous
480 Hz + 620 Hz	Busy	0.5 s ON, 0.5 s OFF*
480 Hz + 620 Hz	Reorder	0.2 s ON, 0.3 s OFF*
440 Hz + 480 Hz	Continuous ringback	2 s ON, 4 s OFF*
440 Hz + 620 Hz	Preemption	Continuous†
480 Hz	High	Continuous†
440 Hz	Call-waiting	Continuous†

*Programmable
†Interrupted off-chip as required (Ref.2).

Some tones require a periodic interruption. For this function, constants located in the RAM address field are scaled to the proper precision and used to increment a location in scratchpad RAM. This counter function can then be used by the on-chip logic operations to generate a tone enabling/disabling function.

9.9 Digital Subscriber Lines

Subscriber Data Links Many digital switching systems now being designed and implemented for use in the public switched network may also be adapted to switching digital data between units of digital customer terminal apparatus, when end-to-end bit integrity can be guaranteed where needed, within the switched digital network, with an acceptably low bit-error rate.

These digital terminals may be digital telephones, digital data terminals, or combinations of the two (see Sec. 9.10, *Voice/Data Services*). Such digital terminal lines interface with digital switching systems via digital line-interface circuits, which are similar in function to the present analog versions but do not need the A/D conversion provided by the codec. Loop synchronization, supervision, and signaling requirements have to be provided by digital line-interface circuits.

As the digital telephone network evolves in North America and elsewhere, it will gradually supplant the existing analog network, probably on a widespread basis, sometime after the year 2000. During this transition period, interconnection between the analog network and the digital network must be provided so that all similar customer terminals, analog and digital, can communicate with each other as appropriate.

In Europe, North America, and Japan, standards are being established for providing digital customer loops by means of two-conductor lines of the type now used for today's analog telephone lines.[23-25] one method for rapidly reversing the digital transmission direction of the subscriber's line, bursts of digital codes are first transmitted from a digital telephone or other digital terminal device to the switching system interface circuit, and then a moment later, after line transients have died down, a burst of digital codes is transmitted in the reverse direction. This technique is sometimes referred to as *ping-pong digital transmission*. Line bit rates of 64, 80, 96, 128, 144, 152, 160, and 320 kb/s and others have been suggested by various design groups throughout the world. No widely accepted standard exists as yet for digital subscriber loops, but various standards groups, including the CCITT, are now addressing this issue.

Another method proposed for 2-wire digital loop transmission uses data hybrids at each end of the subscriber loop to prevent data bit streams that are traversing the line in both the transmit and receive directions from interfering with each other. This method permits continuous (full-duplex) digital transmission in both directions over the 2-wire subscriber line.[23-25]

Interchangeability of system line-interface boards within some digital switching systems will allow analog telephone ports to be quickly changed over to digital subscriber-line ports. Replacing the analog telephone with a new digital telephone and removing bridge taps and any nondigital attachments from the line could then permit a line-by-line digital conversion in a digital switching system service area.

Because digital subscriber terminal devices for providing telephone and/or data services can be served over copper twisted wire pairs in exchange cables, by optical-fiber lines, or by coaxial cable, microwave, or other radio links, the general term *subscriber data link* (SDL) becomes appropriate since it is not restricted by transmission medium or digital bandwidth limitations and is thus a generic term replacing the former subscriber loop terminology.

High-Feature Line Interface Circuits   In a distributed-control digital switching system, groups of line-interface circuits (up to 256 or more, for example) may be controlled by a single microcomputer control system, depending upon features, speed of response requirements, and system architecture. As line-interface-circuit features are added and line-board shelf backplane simplification goals are sought, a higher degree of control bus multiplexing is evolving, and a shared line-interface controller per line board or even per individual line circuit becomes a viable design approach.[26,27]

To achieve a higher degree of crossoffice-path availability and improve line-group reliability, each line-interface circuit is sometimes given access to two or more digital transmission-highway pairs within the switching system. This can be achieved by highway-select gates that are enabled by the line controller or via a time-slot interchange elsewhere in the system. Figure 30 shows a representative line-board controller for serving all line circuits on one line board. This diagram is not representative of any particular system; it is an *example* of the control functions required on a typical line board because there are numerous line-interface-circuit architectures.

Shared line-group controller functions may include:

1. Detection of off-hook logic level when a call is originated and the multiplexing of that signal to a higher-order computer system to initiate a call sequence.
2. Control of power application to line-interface-circuit components that are to be powered-down when the line is idle.
3. Assignment of transmit and receive highway time-slots on the controller-designated highways.
4. Selection of the transmission hybrid balancing network component values, when required to reduce voice-path echo by optimizing hybrid balance.[28]
5. Selection of appropriate transmit- and receive-channel transmission levels, including gain or loss as required for a given call. (This level control is provided elsewhere in some system architectures.)
6. Control of the application of the ringing signal to the line.
7. Detection of customer answer signal and ring trip.

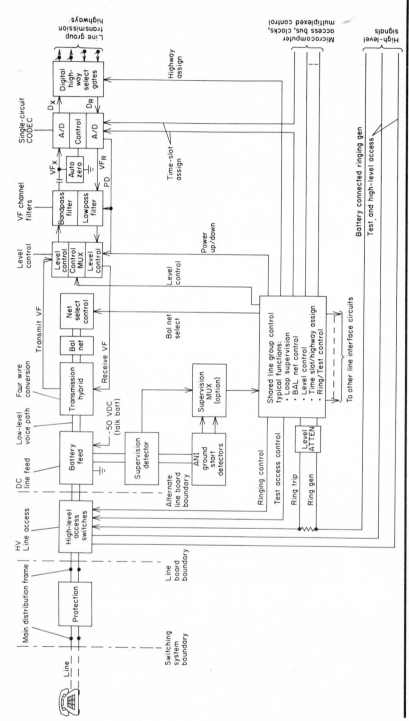

FIG. 30 Functional block diagram of an analog line interface circuit for digital switching systems, using a shared line-group control.

8. Control of multiparty-ringing-frequency selection.
9. Detection of automatic number identification (ANI) signals and pay-station coin-control signals when appropriate.
10. Detection of PBX trunk ground-start signals when appropriate.
11. E & M signaling lead accommodation for analog trunk-interface circuits.

These functions are duplicated for each line-interface circuit served by the controller. Initial discrete-component controllers have occupied at least one-third of the line-board space and have prevented the desired 8-line interface-circuit-per-board architectures from being implemented on a practical line-board size in a number of cases.

As digital SDLs become standardized, the high-feature line-interface-circuit controller functions can also serve digital line-interface circuits.

The shared line-board controller or the individual line-circuit controller can function in conjunction with an additional on-board microcomputer for even higher feature content or processing power (such as code conversions) or with a line-group controlling microcomputer not included as part of a line board. The on-line board controllers are themselves microcomputer-like circuits or LSI devices specifically designed and/or programmed to control all line-interface functions, such as those described for Fig. 30, plus additional functions for digital line-interface control.

Common-Channel Signaling Throughout the Digital Network Common-channel signaling, a method of transmitting signaling information for a group of trunks by encoding it and transmitting it over a separate data channel using TDM transmission techniques, is now being adopted in North America. One signaling technique, long used in many T1 digital transmission systems, borrowed the eighth bit of an 8-bit PCM code group (byte) representing 1 voice channel, once every six frames, for signaling use. This meant that the coding scheme for digitized voice required a 7⅚-bit encoding method when averaged over several frames.

The adoption of a CCIS plan in North America can lead to *full 8-bit PCM encoding* of voice samples, thus improving speech-path performance somewhat as this plan is implemented. Extending common-channel signaling concepts to the digital subscriber terminal also permits full 8-bit encoding of digitized voice samples in digital subscriber terminals and telephones. Thus more than 8-bits are usually required in each digital channel-transmission frame period to handle both digitized voice and signaling requirements.

A single voice path might, for example, require a 64-kb/s (8 bits per word × 8-kb sampling rate) transmission rate in the switched digital network. Two extra bits for signaling, parity, or synchronization would result in an 80-kb/s-data rate in each direction of transmission on subscriber lines.[29] Even higher subscriber loop bit rates will be required when Viewdata, Videotex, or other similar CRT display-based services are provided along with voice communication (see Sec. 9.10).

Adoption of 4-wire subscriber lines, coaxial cable, or optical-fiber lines can vastly expand the digital bit rates and service loop lengths beyond the limitations of today's copper twisted-wire-pair telephone lines that are being used first for digital transmission to the home and business office. Optical-fiber trunks are presently being used to a limited degree to extend large numbers of lines and trunks to large businesses and hotels.

9.10 Voice/Data Services

Integration of Voice and Data Services in an International Network The implications of a switched digital network being available to many users in several countries are far-reaching. For example, new markets are quickly evolving in the areas of "wired households," which will combine telephone, CRT text, and data display; meter reading; burglar alarms; TV-response voting; household-useful information retrieval from centralized computer banks; energy-consumption control; video games; message recording, retrieval, and display; automated home bill payment and bank fund transfer; and many other similar or derived services.

For the business office, the automated electronic office introduced during the 1980s depends upon digital communications links with other offices and computer data bases via telecommunications networks.

The combined voice/data high-feature terminal (HFT) is evolving into much more than just a high-feature business telephone system or business computer. This product area is being attacked from opposite directions by PABX and business telephone system manufacturers on one hand, and office equipment, word-processing machine, and business computer manufacturers on the other. The common denominator is the LSI component manufacturer, who is attempting to develop widely used universal LSI chips for both sides of the development task.

The business office environment calls for a special combination of functional communications requirements that mixes telecommunications, digital display, text editing, information storage and retrieval (local and distant), graphic display, language translation, mathematical computation, accounting, data collection, documentation, storage, and much more. Again, the LSI component content in equipment for each application is high and provides a large, potentially new market for semiconductor manufacturers, telephone equipment manufacturers, and business computer and terminal manufacturers.

Integrated Services Digital Networks (ISDN) As the switched digital network (SDN) evolves in North America and similarly elsewhere, it will gradually supplant much of the existing analog network and terminal apparatus. During this transition period, interconnection between the analog network and the digital network must be provided so that customer terminals, analog and digital, may readily communicate with each other, although there will have to be some limitations.

The coexistence of analog and digital national networks that must be interconnected accentuates the need for end-to-end-connected switched transmission-level adjustment and other signaling requirements and influences the design of switching system line- and trunk-interface circuits. Fortunately, presently available LSI devices can be used for microcomputer-controlled interface performance adjustment.[30]

Not only is the switched digital network being implemented in North America to handle digital telephone traffic, it is also being prepared to ultimately include the capability to handle switched digital data transmission customer-to-customer. This is an international trend, with European countries somewhat ahead of North America in their implementation of an integrated services digital network (ISDN). End-to-end bit integrity throughout the telecommunications network is the goal desired to make an ISDN serve a wide variety of terminal devices. System component reliability heavily influences this goal, and new LSI devices in the control and transmission path can help achieve this goal.

Studies conducted on ISDNs under the auspices of the CCITT encompass local networks and the subscriber interface. The idea of using the same digital communication network for different services has steadily gained momentum, particularly in North America, Europe, and Japan.

Since the introduction of specialized data transmission and switching systems, predominantly based upon *packet switching* techniques, these specialized data networks have evolved from the point-to-point modem-equipped link over multipoint leased-line networks toward data networks with intelligent concentrators and terminals. The inertia of enormous existing investments in the telephone plant has impeded fast introduction of nationwide digital telephone systems. However, the effort to define universal interfaces for the new data networks in the form of CCITT recommendations X.21 and X.25 as well as new procedures for data transmission in the form of high-level data link control (HDLC)[31] have shown that the concept of a very simple customer "digital socket" for a multitude of services is not easily achieved. As a result, development of digital telecommunication networks that integrate the transmission and switching of a number of services is evolving internationally, in the form of ISDN.

Telephony is still regarded as the dominant telecommunication service for a long time to come. The backbone of the ISDN consists of a basic transport (i.e., switching and transmission) system for digital signals, designed so that its characteristics are adapted to the requirements of several services without unduly raising the cost of the basic telephone service. The agreed basic feature of the ISDN is the circuit-switched 64-kb/s time-slot, with the option to switch multiple slots a future possibility. Switching as few as a single bit per frame (i.e., an 8-kb/s time-slot) is also being considered for serving some specific applications on subscriber data links in North America.

The characteristics of the different services are common insofar as they are determined by the basic transport system (e.g., call-setup time, grade of service). The specific characteristics of a particular service are determined by the properties of the user terminal equipment and/or higher level procedures. Also, centralized facilities not usually involved in telephone connections are accessed and charged on a per-call basis. This means that the switching and transmission functions of the ISDN may be used to access special facilities such as packet switches at strategic locations.

For services that cannot be realized economically using the basic facilities of the ISDN, either partially integrated solutions (e.g., transmission) or separate specialized networks are foreseen.

The plans for the introduction of digital telephony necessarily vary considerably from country to country. Because large investments have been made in the present telephone plant, with special emphasis on the local network, continued use of present subscriber lines for digital transmission is a prerequisite.

Voice/Data Terminal Equipment For Home and Business In Europe, Japan, and North America, the switched digital network being planned and implemented will carry both digitized voice and sampled or digital data over switched transmission paths. High-feature voice/data terminals have evolved concurrently for optional connection to the switched digital network. Computer-based communications terminals, which include CRT displays, keyboards, modems, telephones, memory modules, remote control, and telemetry capabilities, are based upon applications of microcomputers, RAM, ROM, bubble memories, and other LSI devices.

Even before digital lines are widely extended to business offices or homes, microcomputer-based, combined voice/data HFT equipment is evolving. In the business office, a combination of business computer and PABX functions are merging into sophisticated voice/data systems, linked between offices both nationally and internationally via an ISDN or its forerunners, on a switched basis. In the home, the combined voice/data HFT is evolving, in some ways, as an outgrowth of the home computer combined with high-feature telephone apparatus.

Teletext, Videotex, and Viewdata Service offerings that provide televised print or CRT character display in the home or office, have appeared internationally under various service names, such as Viewdata (United States), Teletext (Britain), Prestel (Britain), Viewtron (United States), Telidon (Canada), Telset (Finland), Bildschirmtext (West Germany), Ceefax (Britain), Oracle (Britain), Antiope (France), and Captain (Japan).

These services provide selectable alphanumeric and graphic displays via a CRT monitor or TV set equipped with a special decoder. These terminals can display virtually unlimited amounts of information at the touch of a key-pad device, such as news, sports results, stock-market prices, classified advertising, weather, traffic reports, reviews, radio and television logs and reviews, real estate listings, job-hunting information, travel schedules, cooking, gardening and crafts advice, and home-study courses in a wide range of subjects. The TV screen also can become an encyclopedia and dictionary, display messages for an electronic mail and message service, and serve as a convenient way to communicate with the deaf. Two-way capability, when available, can allow voting, public-opinion polling, retail buying and selling, banking and credit transactions, game playing, and home computing.

The generic names of the facilities that bring these services to the end-user terminal are Teletext and Videotex or Viewdata. Teletext is older, having been pioneered by the British Broadcasting Corporation in the mid-1970s, and is now in full operation in Great Britain. It is simple and inexpensive to operate and free to the consumer, except for the cost of the decoder. It is transmitted along with the normal TV signals and uses a portion of the TV vertical blanking signal. Teletext enables the viewer to choose from hundreds of "pages" of printed material that are continually being broadcast along with regular TV programs and stored within the special TV set until requested by the user.

By comparison, Viewdata is a complete, two-way "transactional" device that allows the user to send and receive printed messages and purchase products. Also, Viewdata's capacity is theoretically unlimited, compared with Teletext's current ability to broadcast, in Britain, a menu of several hundred pages.

As with Teletext, the British were the pioneers of Viewdata, which is called by the brand names Prestel in Great Britain and Viewdata in the United States. Viewdata uses telephone lines instead of over-the-air transmission. A viewer can place a call to a Viewdata computer in which is stored, for easy retrieval, a wide range of information and services. The viewer is charged for the telephone call and for many of the pages that appear on the TV screen of the specially equipped set connected to the telephone by an adapter.

The ability to provide Viewdata-type service internationally over either analog or digital trunks and subscriber lines is foreseen and is impacting telecommunications system designs described in this chapter.

REFERENCES

1. AT&T Co.: *Telecommunications Transmission Engineering*, 2d ed., vol. 1: "Principles," chap. 8, Bell Telephone Laboratories, Murray Hill, N.J., 1977.
2. ITT Corp., *Reference Data for Radio Engineers*, 6th ed., Sams, Indianapolis, 1977, chap. 23.
3. Melvin, D. K.: LSI Applications in Telephone Instruments, *Proceedings of the National Electronics Conference*, vol. 32, 1978, pp. 261–266.
4. Martin, James: *Telecommunications and the Computer*, Prentice-Hall, Englewood Cliffs, N.J., 1976, chap. 19.
5. Joel, A. E., Jr.: "Electronic Switching: Central Office Systems of the World," *IEEE Communications Society*, IEEE, New York, 1976.
6. Melvin, D. K.: Microcomputer Applications in Telephony, *Proceedings of the IEEE*, vol. 66, no. 2, February 1978, pp. 182–191.
7. Melvin, D. K.: "A Fully Electronic Automatic Telephone Exchange Using Time-Division-Multiplex Technique," *General Telephone Technical Journal*, vol. 6, no. 4, April 1959, pp. 94–115.
8. Depp, W. A., and M. A. Townsend: "Electronic-PBX Telephone Switching System (ESS-101)," *IEEE Transmission Communications*, vol. Com-83, July 1964, pp. 329–331.
9. "Digital Channel Bank Requirements and Objectives," A.T.&T. Co. *Technical Reference Publication 43801*, December 1978.
10. International Telecommunications Union (CCITT) Sixth Plenary Assembly, *Orange Book*, vol. III-2: "Line Transmission," Geneva, Switzerland, 1976.
11. "Data Conversion, Switching and Transmission Using the Intel 2910A/2911A Codec and 2912 PCM Filter," Intel Corp., app. note AP-64, December 1979.
12. Intel Corp.: *Component Data Catalog*, Santa Clara, Cal., 1980, chaps. 6 and 7.

13. Melvin, D. K.: Trends in the Use of LSI/VLSI Technology in the Telephone Industry, *Digest of Papers, COMPCON-80*, Feb. 25–28, 1980, pp. 21–24.
14. Huggins, J. M., M. E. Hoff, and B. M. Warren: "A Single-Chip NMOS Codec for Voice," *1978-IEEE International Solid-State Circuits Conference Digest*, February 1978, pp. 178–179.
15. Melvin, D. K.: "LSI Codecs Accelerate Digital Implementation," *Telephony*, vol. 195, no. 13, Sept. 25, 1978, pp. 68–76.
16. Hoff, M. E., Jr., J. M. Huggins, and B. M. Warren: "An NMOS Telephone Codec for Transmission and Switching Applications," *IEEE Journal of Solid-State Circuits*, vol. SC-14, no. 1, February 1979, pp. 47–53.
17. Gray, P. R., and D. Senderowicz: "A Single-Chip NMOS Dual-Channel Filter for PCM Telephony Applications," *1979-IEEE International Solid-State Circuits Conference Digest*, Feb. 16, 1979.
18. Ohara, H., S. F. Sando, P. R. Gray, and D. Senderowicz: "First Monolithic PCM Filter Cuts Cost of Telecom Systems," *Electronic Design*, vol. 27, no. 8, Apr. 12, 1979, pp. 130–135.
19. A.T.&T. Co.: *Telecommunications Transmission Engineering*, vol. 2: "Facilities" chap. 21, Bell Telephone Laboratories, Murray Hill, N.J., 1977.
20. Abate, J. E., L. H. Brandenburg, J. C. Lawson, and W. L. Ross: "The Switched Digital Network Plan," *Bell System Technical Journal*, September 1977, pp. 1297–1320.
21. Hoff, M. E., Jr. and M. A. Townsend, "Single Chip NMOS Microcomputer Processes Signals in Real-Time," *Electronics*, vol. 52, no. 5, Mar. 1, 1979, pp. 105–110.
22. Townsend, M., and M. E. Hoff, Jr.: "An NMOS Signal Processor for General Purpose Applications," *National Telecommunications Conference Record*, November 1979, pp. 25.2.1–25.2.6.
23. Meyer, J., and T. Roste: "Field Trials of Two-Wire Digital Transmission in the Subscriber Loop Plant," Norwegian, Telecommunications University of Trondheim-Norway, *ICC '79*, vol. 1, pp. 2.5.1–2.5.5.
24. Seidel, H., R. K. Even, and R. A. McDonald: "Digital Transmission Capability of the Loop Plant," Bell Telephone Laboratories, *ICC '79*, vol.1, pp. 2.1.1–2.1.7.
25. Komiya, R., N. Inoue, and Y. Inoue: "Time-Shared 2-Wire Digital Transmission System for Subscriber Loops," Y-ECL-Japan, *ICC '79*, vol. 1, pp. 2.4.1–2.4.5.
26. Huggins, J. M.: "Analog LSI Components for the Line Card," *Proc. of the National Elect. Conference 1979*, vol. 33, pp. 128–129.
27. Melvin, D. K.: "LSI Helps Telephones Go Digital," *IEEE Spectrum*, vol. 17, no. 6, June 1980, pp. 30–33.
28. Falconner, D. D., and K. H. Mueller: "Adaptive Echo Cancellation/ACC Structures for Two-Wire, Full-Duplex Data Transmission," *Bell System Technical Journal*, September 1979, pp. 1593–1616.
29. Svensson, T.: "Two-Way Digital Communication on Two-Wire Subscriber Lines at 80 KBIT/S," *ICC '79*, vol. 1, pp. 2.6.1–2.6.5.
30. Kundig, A.: "Problems and Prerequisites with the Development of Service Integrated Digital Networks," *ICC '79*, vol. 1, pp. 3.5.1–3.5.5.
31. International Telecommunications Union (CCITT) Sixth Plenary Assembly, *Orange Book*, vol. viii.2: "Public Data Networks," Geneva, Switzerland, 1976.

CHAPTER TEN

A 32-Channel Digital Waveform Synthesizer

Ceasar Castro and Allen Heaberlin

Casheab, San Diego, California

INTRODUCTION

People have long been interested in music synthesis, not only to duplicate existing instruments but to generate new, totally different musical sounds. Much success has been obtained using either expensive specialized equipment or general-purpose computers. Special purpose computers usually cannot generate music in real time because it takes more time to generate the music than to hear it. With recent low-cost technological advances, a real-time synthesizer is now available. This chapter describes the Casheab music synthesizer, beginning with the synthesizer design philosophy, followed by a brief discussion of some synthesis techniques and ending with an in-depth look at the hardware and software design.

10.1 Synthesizer Design Philosophy

Complexity and Cost Tradeoffs   Our goal in designing the Casheab synthesizer was to offer sophisticated performance at a reasonable price. This goal was implemented by making the hardware fast but simple and putting much of the complexity into software, which affords maximum flexibility because software can be updated and changed easily. The goals of sophisticated performance and reasonable price are somewhat exclusive, so we had to make some compromises. One compromise was in the number of channels. In this approach the complexity is roughly proportional to the number of channels. Thus a small number of channels was implemented to allow both lower-speed circuitry and data multiplexing. A modular design was implemented so that more identical synthesizer modules could be used to increase the number of channels.

We first talk about the performance requirements in designing the synthesizer: the capabilities of the synthesizer, the number of channels, sampling rate, and so on. Next we discuss the hardware and software requirements. Finally, we cover piano-organ keyboard input for the synthesizer.

Performance Requirements   Fundamental to the synthesizer design were performance capabilities. First, the synthesizer had to be capable of generating at least 25 different tonal frequencies. This figure was considered a lower bound because it is desirable to produce many more. Since humans have 10 fingers and 2 feet, the maximum number of notes one can play is 12. Having a minimum of 25 possible tonal frequencies ensured that at least two tonal frequencies could be generated for each note. Secondly, there had to be a minimum of four waveforms or tonal sounds generated at one time. Third, there had to be envelope or amplitude control to allow tremolo and transient effects such as attack and decay. This control also had to be programmable. Fourth, the frequency had to be specified accurately, in at least 16 bits, to allow close frequencies to be used for the same note, providing a chorus effect. This frequency control also had to be programmable. Finally, the waveform sample word length had to be at least 12 bits, giving an SNR (signal-to-noise ratio) of 72 dB, and the number of samples specifiying the waveform had to be at least 1000, to enable waveforms to be accurately specified.

Hardware Goals   This design aimed at several important hardware goals. First, no nonstandard technology was to be used, such as emitter-coupled logic or special-purpose chips that are difficult to find. Basically, we wanted the design to use standard off-the-shelf integrated circuits (ICs) such as transistor-transistor logic (TTL) metal-oxide semiconductors (MOS). Second, the design, especially the controller, had to be simple. Difficult troubleshooting problems were avoided by utilizing a simple design to provide simple maintenance. Next, the design had to use a reasonable amount of power—about 10 W maximum. Finally, a medium number of ICs, less than 100, were used to fabricate the synthesizer on two S-100 cards.

Software Design Philosophy   A critical part of the design was software, which was designed with certain guidelines. First, to try to keep the synthesizer hardware to a minimum, the design had to be software-oriented, not only to provide simple hardware design but to increase performance potential. Because a large part of the sophisticated processing is in the software, there is a potential for increased performance using the new 16-bit microprocessors, which have better instruction sets and are faster. In addition, the microprocessor had to completely control the synthesizer, to provide maximum flexibility when modifying and changing the synthesized sounds produced by the system. In essence, in the Casheab synthesizer all the high-speed data processing is done by the synthesizer card, and all the general bookkeeping and control by the microprocessor.

Interfacing to a Keyboard   Finally, because the purpose of the synthesizer is to generate musical sounds, some input device controlling which sound or notes to produce was necessary. Apart from a disk file, the obvious selection was a piano or organ keyboard, which appeared to be the ideal real-time input since the synthesizer is considered an instrument and should be played like one. In addition, the interface had to be under interrupt control because under software polling or other noninterrupt methods little software time could be devoted to other synthesizer software functions.

In general, the synthesizer should meet our original ideal and be reasonably priced yet offer high performance and flexibility.

10.2   Synthesis Techniques

The Casheab synthesizer can implement three types of synthesis: (1) direct digital, in which a recursively generated phase is mapped into a waveform; (2) digital harmonic, in which each harmonic has its frequency and amplitude directly controlled; and (3) frequency-modulated (FM) generation, in which an oscillator's phase is modulated.

Direct Digital Synthesis (Phase Accumulation)   This approach has been discussed in other papers[1,2] and is similar to Snell's[3] approach. In this design (see Fig. 1), a tonal frequency phase is generated recursively by using an accumulator. The accumulator continuously adds a digital word, corresponding to the phase shift between cycles, to obtain successive tonal phases. The waveform memory converts the phase, using the waveform memory as a lookup table, to a waveform sample. The phase is the input address to the memory, and the memory word is the waveform value. Additional address lines select which waveform to generate. At the memory output, the multiplier scales the output by multiplying by a processor-defined scaling value. By controlling this value, the synthesizer implements attack and decay envelopes and also tremolo effects. The circuitry can produce many channels by making the memory a multiword accumulator, i.e., memory and adder rather than register and adder. Control becomes more complicated because the circuitry is shared among different channels. In this case, all the waveforms are summed at the output and this sum is converted to an analog voltage in a digital-to-analog converter (DAC).

This approach is entirely digital, with much of the tonal-generation process easily controlled. The frequency is specified by the word in the frequency-control random access memory (RAM), the waveform produced is the waveform memory, and the amplitude specified by another RAM word. Thus all the above can be controlled from a microprocessor merely by the processor writing into the RAMs.

This approach is computationally simple. To generate an output for each channel, three requirements are necessary: (1) an addition to generate the phase, (2) a memory access to find the waveform value, and (3) a multiplication to implement envelope functions. Also, a summation must be performed over all channels. A logical microprocessor function is envelope generation because envelopes tend to change slowly. The full resources of the microprocessor system (i.e., main memory or disk storage) are available for any slow process.

Digital Harmonic Synthesis (Additive Synthesis)[4] In this approach a processor separately controls each harmonic's amplitude and frequency. Generally, a piecewise linear function is used by the synthesizer to approximate the amplitude and frequency variation. The implementation has fantastic potential for duplicating waveforms and should be able to generate almost any desired waveform. This approach requires an amplitude- and frequency-controllable sine-wave generator for each tonal harmonic. This is a significant hardware requirement because there may be 10 or 15 required harmonics. In addition, because the amplitude and frequency must be specified for each harmonic, a significant amount of control must also be provided. This is difficult for common 8-bit microprocessors (6800, 8080, or Z-80). Thus this approach offers high performance but, unfortunately, high hardware and control requirements. The Casheab synthesizer implements digital harmonic synthesis by first loading a sine wave into the waveform memory. The processor, which is not part of the Casheab synthesizer, must control each harmonic's amplitude and frequency. Because the Casheab synthesizer offers either 16 or 32 channels, only one or two waveforms can typically be generated.

FM Generation[5] In the FM generator approach, a sine wave (or possibly other function) modulates the phase of an oscillator. The phase is then converted to a sine wave, usually by table lookup. If the ratio between the modulating and carrier frequencies is an integer, a harmonic spectra is generated. By changing the ratio between the "modulation" and "carrier," different spectrums can be generated (see Fig. 2). This approach is fundamentally simple because few calculations are required and harmonic-rich waveforms can be generated easily. One objection to this method is somewhat subjective. Because the spectrum is not controlled directly but through a Bessel function, it is difficult to relate the arguments "modulation index" (Fig. 2b) and frequency ratio to the generated spectrums. This it may be difficult to implement a specific tonal waveform if the parameters have not been obtained. Also, if the waveform produced is not band-limited to half the sampling rate, aliasing will occur, which will introduce distortion as spurious frequencies are generated. For a large modulation index the problem becomes severe. The only practical way to correct this problem may be to reduce the spectrum generated by ensuring that the spectrum does meet the Nyquist criteria. Another,

Frequency Control
Word (FCW)

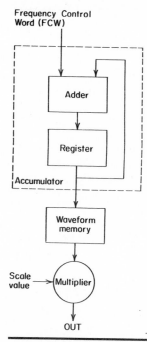

FIG. 1   *Simplified block diagram of the direct digital
synthesis technique for generating multiple musical
waveforms.*

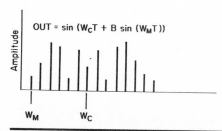

$$OUT = \sin(W_C T + B \sin(W_M T))$$

FIG. 2   *Frequency spectrum showing sidebands generated with the FM
synthesis technique.* OUT $= \sin[W_c T + \beta \sin(W_M T)]$

even less attractive option, is the increase the sampling rate. Thus the
approach does have potential but also some pitfalls. The Casheab synthesizer
implements FM synthesis by adding one channel's output to another channel's phase rather than accumulating the output directly. Each channel has an
enabling bit for FM synthesis. Two channels are required to implement 1 FM
channel.

10.3   Synthesizer Hardware Design

Overall Description   The synthesizer is implemented on two printed circuit cards: a controller card (CTR-10) and a synthesizer card (SYN-10). The frequency generator, waveform memory, and weighting section are located on the synthesizer card. The controller card contains the accumulation section, DAC, timing generator, and computer interface (see Fig. 3). The frequency generator determines the phase at each sample point. This phase directly depends upon the frequency-control word (FCW) provided by the processor. The frequency generator recursively generates the newest phase by adding the FCW to the previous phase. The phase is then passed to the waveform section. Here the phase is "mapped" into the waveform: from the phase the waveform sample value is determined. The waveform is then passed to the weighting section, where a processor-controlled value is used to scale or multiply the waveform value. From the weighting section on the SYN-10 card the signal is passed to the controller card (CTR-10). Here these values go to the summer section, obtaining the summed output of the 32 tone generators. This output is converted from a digital number to an analog voltage in the DAC. In addition, the controller contains two support circuits: the timing generator, which generates all the proper sequencing signals, and the computer interface, which allows the processor to write into the synthesizer.

As described earlier, an important goal of the design was complete processor control over tone generation. In this design the processor *does* have complete control over the synthesizer by writing into all controlling RAM locations. First the processor controls the frequency of each tonal-frequency oscillator by writing the FCW into the frequency-generator RAM. Second, the processor is able to select the waveform number by programming the waveform number in the waveform-selection RAM. Finally, the processor can select the scaling values for tone generation. Because all the functions are processor-controlled, they can change with time. However, if a standard 8-bit processor, such as the 8080, is used, updating all tone generators may be limited to once every 2 ms. The most important processor input is the waveform; by controlling the parameters and waveforms, the processor completely specifies the tonal waveform.

The interface between the synthesizer and processor is a memory map interface such as that used in the Motorola 6800 and Digital Equipment Corporation PDP-11. A 256-byte address space specifies the FCW, waveform number, and weight. Obviously, if separate input-output I/O addresses had been devoted for each, I/O space would have been severely restricted. In addition, if the waveform memories had utilized RAM or ROM, memory space would have been restricted because each waveform is 1K by 12 bits and would have required 2K bytes of addressing space (assuming 8-bit words). With multiple waveforms, the waveform memory space easily could have become very large. Instead, all waveforms are entered through a common port. As the data is entered, an internal counter is incremented, providing the address for the waveform RAM. Another port (memory address) zeros the counter and specifies which waveform memory is to be loaded. Thus all synthesizer controlling data is loaded into a 256-byte region.

The Synthesizer Card   The frequency generator, waveform memory, and weighting section are located on the synthesizer card.

Frequency generator   The frequency generator (see Fig. 4) generates the phase for each tonal generator. The generator is composed of an FCW RAM, a phase RAM, and an accumulator. All calculations are performed using two 8-bit words. Before tone generation, the processor loads the FCW RAM with the 2 bytes, specifying the FCW for each tone generator. The processor writes into the FCW RAM by accessing the computer interface on the controller

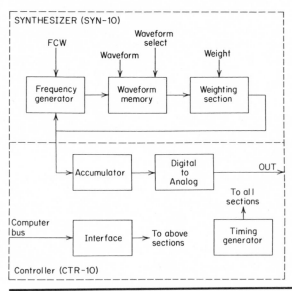

FIG. 3   *Block diagram of the double-board music synthesizer discussed in this chapter.*

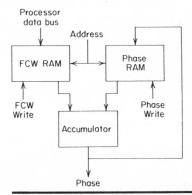

FIG. 4   *A frequency generator which uses digital phase accumulation.*

card. If the FCW RAM is selected, an FCW write signal is generated, which will allow data on the computer data bus to be written into the FCW RAM when an available slot appears. (See "The Controller Card," below.) This value is added to the previous tone-generator's phase in two 8-bit additions, obtaining the new sample period phase. The frequency generator uses two memory reads and two memory writes for one processing cycle (i.e., about 1.75 μs to generate the phase. See the subsection, "Timing-Generator," for a description of a processing cycle.) The most significant 10 bits of the phase is sent to the waveform section.

Waveform   The waveform section (see Fig. 5) consists of either a 4K or 16K word by 12-bit memory. There are different types of operations using this memory. The primary cycle is the *waveform generation cycle*. The phase from the frequency generator is used in conjuction with a waveform-select RAM output as the memory address, and the waveform value is read out. The next type of memory cycle is a *processor write cycle*. The address comes from the internal word counter, and the written data comes from the processor data bus. In this cycle the processor loads the waveform memory and then the internal counter is incremented. The third type of cycle is the *refresh cycle*. Here a memory read is performed, with the address coming from the refresh counter. At the conclusion of this cycle, the refresh counter is updated. This refresh operation occurs every 16 processing cycles.

The memory uses 16-pin 4K or 16K dynamic memory chips. These chips require the address to be multiplexed in conjunction with two separate clocks: row address and column address strobe. These clocks are used for multiplexing the address to the memory chips. Although memory fetch is required by the synthesizer once every processing cycle, a spare memory cycle is available every processing cycle. The synthesizer can use this cycle to either refresh memory or to write new data. The refresh has precedence. If the processor attempts to write data and the synthesizer is not ready, a wait is asserted until the synthesizer is available and completes the cycle. It is anticipated the memory may be loaded under DMA control, which will allow the waveform to be loaded as the note is initiated.

Weighting   The weighting section generates scaled samples from the waveform memory output. This allows the synthesizer to implement attack, decay, tremolo, and other amplitude effects (see Fig. 6). First the data is converted from parallel to a 12-bit serial word. Then a serial multiplier (25LS14) multiplies the waveform sample by the scaling value from the weighting memory. The output is sent to the accumulation section on the controller card.

The Controller Card   As stated, the controller contains the accumulation section, DAC, timing generator, and computer interface.

Accumulation section   The accumulator sums the output of up to four synthesizer cards in a 25LS15 serial adder (Fig. 7). The accumulator sums all channels, that is, all 32 channels for the 32-channel mode and all 16 channels for the 16-channel mode. This sum is a digital word representing the sample

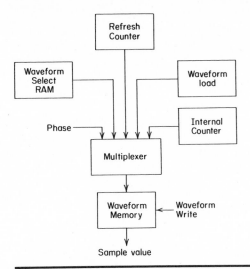

FIG. 5 *The variable-frequency waveform-generation portion of the digital synthesizer.*

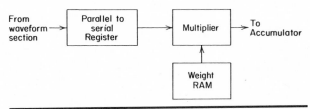

FIG. 6 *The weighting section of the synthesizer, where attack and decay are implemented.*

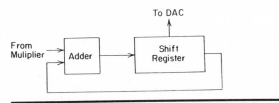

FIG. 7 *The accumulator section of the synthesizer, where all notes are combined before being sent to the DAC.*

value at the sample time. The accumulation word length is 26 bits, to allow up to 64 channels to be summed before encountering possible overflow problems.

DAC A shifter network in the DAC circuit converts the word from the accumulator to two separate words corresponding to a floating-point numeric representation: a 12-bit "mantissa" and a 4-bit "characteristic" (see Fig. 8).

This provides greater dynamic range. The characteristic value represents the shifted value and is used to scale the output. The mantissa represents the data value. The shifter derives the mantissa value by shifting the word until either a sign change is detected in the word or a programmable upper bound is reached. Concurrent with this, a counter is incremented that counts the number of shifts and generates the characteristic. These two words are latched into holding registers at the next output sample clock. The processor can specify a word corresponding to the maximum places shifted; this number corresponds to the maximum anticipated amplitude.

Both the DACs used are 12-bit, multiplying. However, in the scaling DAC only the most significant 4 bits are used. The output of the scaling DAC is the reference input of the mantissa DAC. Because this input is both positive and negative, the DACs must be wired in the four-quadrant mode, requiring two op amps. As the DACs change value, glitches are generated at the output. Hence a sample-and-hold has been added after the DACs. When the outputs are stable, the sample-and-hold samples the DAC output and holds it until the DAC generates the next sample.

Timing generator   A clock, operating at half the master oscillator frequency, generates the timing signals by successively clocking the read-only memory (ROM) output into a holding register (see Fig. 9). Part of these signals determine the next ROM address and consequently the next timing signals. Because the ROM and register cannot be clocked at the full oscillator rate, another register is clocked out of phase with the first holding register. This provides full-rate timing signals but from half-rate clocking. To obtain some signals, logic gates selectively combine signals from the two registers. Because the ROM is 32-word and the synthesizer requires only 14 words, the ROM can store another program.

The basic synthesizer processing cycle is divided into two parts (see Fig. 10): phase generation and waveform generation. For phase generation the synthesizer is divided into a lower-byte phase calculation and an upper-byte phase calculation. Each cycle is further divided into two subcycles. During the first subcycle the phase and FCW data are read and the next phase is calculated. During the next subcycle this phase is written back into the phase RAM, and a previous output can also be added to the phase. This allows the synthesizer to implement FM synthesis and other FM effects.

For waveform generation, the synthesizer cycle is also divided into two parts. During the first part the waveform sample value is determined from the phase and the waveform select value. During the second half the controller can refresh the dynamic memory or, alternately, the processor can write a new waveform byte into the waveform memory. Refresh has precedence.

Obviously, both the synthesizer and computer may want to access the memory simultaneously. In this approach, the synthesizer always has priority. The synthesizer allocates time-slots to the computer when the synthesizer is not accessing the memory. At the time the computer starts a write cycle, the synthesizer asserts a WAIT and the computer waits until the data is written. For dynamic memory there is usually one time-slot during the second half of the

From
Accumulator
Shifter
network
Multiplying
DAC
OUT
Digital to
Analog
converter

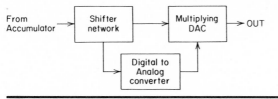

FIG. 8 *The dual D/A converter section of the synthesizer.*

ROM
16-MHz
OSC
÷2
Register
Register
Timing signals

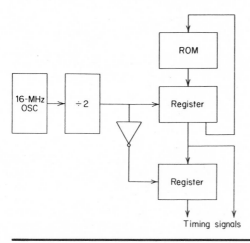

FIG. 9 *The oscillator and master timing circuit for the synthesizer.*

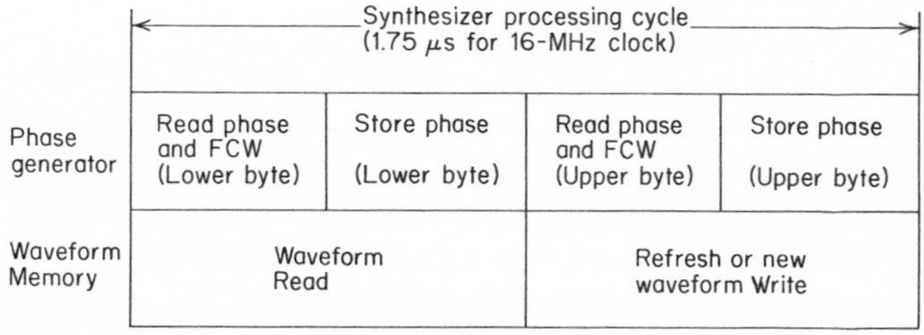

Synthesizer processing cycle
(1.75 μs for 16-MHz clock)
Phase
generator
Read phase
and FCW
(Lower byte)
Store phase
(Lower byte)
Read phase
and FCW
(Upper byte)
Store phase
(Upper byte)
Waveform
Memory
Waveform
Read
Refresh or new
waveform Write

FIG. 10 *Details of the four-section synthesizer processing cycle.*

processing cycle. When a refresh is performed, the computer must wait until the next cycle. For the FCW, waveform select, and weight RAM there are two-time slots during each processing cycle.

Computer interface As far as the computer is concerned, the synthesizer is a write-only memory (see Fig. 11). The write cycle is started by the computer generating an address and status signals (SMEMR, SIN, and SOUT). These

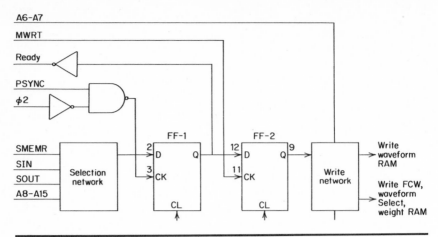

FIG. 11   *The computer interface for the music synthesizer.*

signals must be valid while PSYNC is positive and when phase 2 goes positive. At this time, the selection-network output is clocked into FF-1 (flip-flop 1). If the selection network determined a valid selection, the Ready line to the computer is pulled down. After the data bus has valid data, the computer asserts MWRT. This enabling signal is clocked into FF-2 and causes the controller to write data into memory during the next available time-slot. The cycle is terminated immediately after this event when FF-1 and FF-2 are both cleared, releasing the Ready line.

10.4 Software

The method used to generate music is simple and straightforward, basically consisting of two programs: SCORE and PLAY. Using the CP/M editor, a music file is created. The music is written via a simple notation system. The music file is compiled by a BASIC program (SCORE.BAS). The SCORE program generates a play file from the music file; the play file is then played by an assembly language program (PLAY.COM). The PLAY program performs other tasks besides playing the music: It sets up timing, manipulates tables, and loads timbre waveforms. The timbre waveforms are programmable, so they must be created. They are generated by a frequency-to-time fast Fourier transform program (FFT.BAS) or a second program called WAVEFORM.COM.

The PLAY program has been written to play each note either with or without attack and decay envelopes. With an attack and decay, the software can handle about 16 channels; with no attack and decay, the software can handle all 32 channels. The PLAY program expects the attack-envelope data, decay-envelope data, and timbre waveform to be one file. The attack and decay envelopes can be generated with a simple BASIC program or WAVEFORM.COM. The timbre waveforms are generated by the FFT program or WAVEFORM.COM. Program PIP is used to concatenate the attack/decay and timbre files into one file.

The following sections present a discussion of each program. The *Synthesizer Program* part discusses the software aspects of the synthesizer. The *Attack- and Decay Envelope* section covers the requirements of the attack and decay data and the methods used to generate the attack/decay file. The FFT section considers the FFT program and the timbre waveforms. The WAVE-FORM *Program* section discusses the WAVEFORM program and how it is used to generate attack and decay data and timbre waveforms. The SCORE *Program* section explains the SCORE program and provides details on how to create a music file. Finally, the PLAY *Program* section deals with the PLAY program and all its commands; it also gives step-by-step directions on how to fetch and play a piece of music.

The Synthesizer Program The synthesizer is a memory-mapped device. Table 1 shows the addressing scheme used. The synthesizer is shipped with the address set at F800 (this can be changed). The synthesizer occupies a 256-byte memory space (F800 to F8FF).

TABLE 1 **Memory assignments for FCW, *weight, waveform,* and FM parameters**

Channel	FCW	Weight	Waveform	FM
1	F800 LSB 01 MSB	F842	F882	F881 (Phase for channel 3)
2	F802 03	F844	F884	F883 (Phase for channel 4)
3	F804 05	F846	F886	F885 (Phase for channel 5)
4	F806 07	F848	F888	F887 (Phase for channel 6)
.	.	.	.	.
.	.	.	.	.
.	.	.	.	.
30	F83A 3B	F87C	F8BC	F8BB (Phase for channel 32)
31	F83C 3D	F87E	F8BE	F8BD (Phase for channel 1)
32	F83E 3F	F840	F880	F8BF (Phase for channel 2)

Timbre waveform = F8C0; Timbre load = F8C2; DAC scale = F8C3

The FCW, used to control the frequency of a channel, is 16 bits long and requires 2 bytes of memory for each channel. For channel 1 the FCW is addressed at F800 and F801, with the least significant byte (LSB) at F800. The decimal value of the frequency control word is given by

$$FCW = 65536 \frac{F_n}{F_s}$$

where F_s = sampling rate = $F_c/28\ N = 16 \times 10^6/28 \times 32 = 17.857$ kHz
  F_c = master clock frequency (16 MHz)
  F_n = frequency of note
  N = number of channels (16 or 32 in this chapter)

Table 2 presents FCWs for the equally tempered scale. To generate middle C in channel 1, load 960 (03C0 hex) into F800 and F801 (C0 hex into F800 and 03 hex into F801).

Amplitude control requires 1 byte for each channel. The scale is from 0 to 255, where 0 generates a zero output and 255 generates maximum output for that channel. For channel 1, the amplitude weight address is located at F842. Note that the weight addresses are all even numbers and that channel 31's amplitude address is located at F87E, whereas channel 32's amplitude address is at F840.

Waveform selection is accomplished by loading a waveform number at the appropriate address. For the SYN-10/16, a channel can use any 1 of the 16 waveforms; for the SYN-10/4, a channel can use 1 of 4 waveforms. To indicate which waveform a channel should use, the waveform number is loaded at the waveform address for that channel. For example, assume that channel 1 is to use waveform number 2: This requires that a 2 be loaded at F882.

Frequency modulation (FM) is accomplished by loading FF hex into the appropriate location. For example, channel 1 will modulate channel 3 if FF is loaded at F881. The arrangement of which channel can modulate which channel is fixed. One channel can modulate a channel that is two over (i.e., channel 1 can modulate channel 3, channel 2 can modulate channel 4, 3 can modulate 5, and so forth). Even-numbered channels can modulate only even channels, and odd-numbered channels can modulate only odd channels. To turn off the modulation, a zero is loaded into the appropriate location.

Notes can be generated only after the synthesizer is loaded with timbre waveforms. Two memory locations are used to accomplish this task: F8C0 and F8C2. A waveform number is assigned to a timbre waveform. The number is first loaded at F8C0, and then the waveform is sequentially loaded into F8C2. To load the 1024, 12-bit-word waveform 2048 bytes are sequentially loaded into F8C2. The first byte to be loaded at F8C2 is the least significant byte of the 2-byte word. Only the 12 most significant bits (MSBs) of each 2-byte word are used by the synthesizer. It is possible to partially load the front part of a waveform because each time a waveform number is loaded at F8C0, the internal counter in the synthesizer is reset to zero.

Finally, the output of the synthesizer can be scaled. For maximum output, a 0F hex should be loaded at F8C3; for minimum output, a zero should be loaded at F8C3. Only the 4 least significant bits are used for the scale. The

TABLE 2 FCW in hex and decimal for seven octaves of the equally tempered musical scale

Note	Frequency	FCW dec	Hex	FCW frequency	Note	Frequency	FCW dec	Hex	FCW frequency
C0	32.703	120	78	32.697	Fc#	369.99	1358	54E	370.03
C0#	34.648	127	7F	34.605	G3	391.99	1439	59F	392.10
D0	36.708	135	87	36.784	G3#	415.29	1524	5F4	415.26
D0#	38.891	143	8F	38.964	A3	440	1615	64F	440.05
E0	41.203	151	97	41.144	A3#	466.16	1711	6AF	466.21
F0	43.654	160	A0	43.596	B3	493.88	1813	715	494.00
F0#	46.249	170	AA	46.321	C4	523.25	1920	780	523.16
G0	48.999	180	B4	49.046	C4#	554.37	2035	7F3	554.49
G0#	51.911	191	BF	52.043	D4	587.33	2156	86C	587.46
A0	55	202	CA	55.041	D4#	622.26	2284	8EC	622.34
A0#	58.27	214	D6	58.310	E4	659.25	2419	973	659.13
B0	61.735	227	E3	61.853	F4	698.46	2563	A03	698.36
C1	65.406	240	F0	65.395	F4#	739.98	2716	A9C	740.05
C1#	69.296	254	FE	69.209	G6	783.98	2877	B3D	783.92
D1	73.416	269	10D	73.297	G4#	830.58	3048	BE8	830.51
D1#	77.782	285	11D	77.656	A4	880	3230	C9E	880.11
E1	82.406	302	12E	82.288	A4#	932.32	3422	D5E	932.42
F1	87.308	320	140	87.193	B4	987.76	3625	E29	987.73
F1#	92.498	339	153	92.370	C5	1046.5	3841	F01	1046.6
G1	97.998	360	168	98.092	C5#	1108.7	4069	FE5	1108.7
G1#	103.82	381	17D	103.81	D5	1174.7	4311	10D7	1174.7
A1	110	404	194	110.08	D5#	1244.5	4567	11D7	1244.4
A1#	116.54	428	1AC	116.62	E5	1318.5	4839	12E7	1318.5
B1	123.47	453	1C5	123.43	F5	1396.9	5127	1407	1397
C2	130.81	480	1E0	130.79	F5#	1480.0	5432	1538	1480.1
C2#	138.59	509	1FD	138.69	G5	1568.0	5754	167A	1567.8
D2	146.83	539	21B	146.87	G5#	1661.2	6096	17D0	1661.0
D2#	155.56	571	23B	155.58	A5	1760	6459	193B	1759.9
E2	164.81	605	25D	164.85	A5#	1864.6	6843	1ABB	1864.6
F2	174.62	641	281	174.66	B5	1975.5	7250	1C52	1975.5
F2#	185.00	679	2A7	185.01	C6	2093.0	7681	1E01	2092.9
G2	196.00	719	2CF	195.96	C6#	2217.5	8138	1FCA	2217.4
G2#	207.65	762	2FA	207.63	D6	2349.3	8622	21AE	2349.3
A2	220	807	327	219.89	D6#	2489.0	9135	23AF	2489.1
A2#	233.08	855	357	232.97	E6	2637.0	9678	25CD	2637.0
B2	246.94	906	38A	246.87	F6	2793.8	10253	280D	2793.7
C3	261.62	960	3c0	261.58	F6#	2959.9	10863	2A6F	2959.9
C3#	277.18	1017	3F9	277.11	G6	3135.9	11509	2CF5	3135.9
D3	293.66	1078	436	293.73	G6#	3322.3	12193	2FA1	3322.2
D#3	311.13	1142	476	311.17	A6	3520	12918	3276	3519.9
E3	329.62	1210	4BA	329.70	A6#	3729.3	13687	3577	3729.4
F3	349.23	1282	502	349.32	B6	3951.0	14500	38A4	3950.9

SCALE increases the output when a few channels are being used and decreases the output to prevent overflow distortion when many channels are being used. When 2 or 3 channels are being used, a 4 or 5 should be loaded at F9C3; When 30 or so channels are being used, a zero should be loaded at F8C3.

Attack- and Decay-Envelope Program Tables 3 and 4 list two BASIC programs used to generate attack- and decay-envelope files. The first program, CLAR/ADE.BAS, generates the attack and decay envelopes for a clarinet.

TABLE 3   *A basic program to generate attack- and decay-envelope files for a clarinet. The program title is CLAR/ADE.BAS.*

```
1Ø REM CLARINET ATTACK AND DECAY
11Ø F$ = "CLAR.ADE"
12Ø OPEN "O",1,F$
13Ø FOR I=Ø TO 127
14Ø READ D
15Ø PRINT #1,HEX$(D);" ";
16Ø NEXT I
17Ø CLOSE 1
18Ø PRINT: PRINT F$,"SAVED"
19Ø END
199 REM ATTACK
2ØØ DATA Ø,4,14,3Ø,53,95,143,19Ø
21Ø DATA 235,25Ø,255,254,253,25Ø,24Ø,23Ø
22Ø DATA 222,212,2Ø7,2Ø2,2ØØ,2ØØ,2ØØ,2ØØ
23Ø DATA 2ØØ,2ØØ,2ØØ,2ØØ,2ØØ,2ØØ,2ØØ,2ØØ
24Ø DATA 2ØØ,2ØØ,2ØØ,2ØØ,2ØØ,2ØØ,2ØØ,2ØØ
25Ø DATA 2ØØ,2ØØ,2ØØ,2ØØ,2ØØ,2ØØ,2ØØ,2ØØ
26Ø DATA 2ØØ,2ØØ,2ØØ,2ØØ,2ØØ,2ØØ,2ØØ,2ØØ
27Ø DATA 2ØØ,2ØØ,2ØØ,2ØØ,2ØØ,2ØØ,2ØØ,2ØØ
299 REM DECAY
3ØØ DATA 2ØØ,198,196,194,191,188,185,179
31Ø DATA 172,164,154,142,132,12Ø,11Ø,11
32Ø DATA 92,85,78,72,66,62,58,54
33Ø DATA 49,46,43,4Ø,37,35,33,31
34Ø DATA 28,26,24,22,2Ø,19,18,16
35Ø DATA 15,14,12,11,1Ø,9,8,7
36Ø DATA 6,5,5,4,4,3,3,2
37Ø DATA 2,1,1,1,1,Ø,Ø,Ø
```

The attack and decay envelopes are defined by 64 bytes. The BASIC program generates the file CLAR.ADE from the data statements of the program. The data is stored in the ASCII hex format, with the space character (20 hex) separating each data point. The first 64 bytes form the attack; the second 64 bytes form the decay. At present the PLAY program does not support a steady-state envelope.

The second program, TRUM/ADE.BAS (Table 4), generates the attack and decay envelopes for the trumpet. This program generates the file TRUMPET.ADE.

The PLAY program requires that the attack/decay and the timbre waveform data be one file. The following section discusses the generation of the timbre file. The PIP program concatenates the two files as follows:

PIP CLAR.ADT = CLAR.ADE, CLAR.TIM

The attack/decay file CLAR.ADE is placed in front of the timbre waveform file CLAR.TIM

TABLE 4   *A basic program to generate attack- and decay-envelope files for a trumpet sound. The program title is* TRUM/ADE.BAS.

```
10 REM TRUMPET ATTACK AND DECAY ENVELOPES
110 F$ = "TRUMPET.ADE
120 OPEN "O",1,F$
130 FOR I = 0 to 127
140 READ D
150 PRINT #1,HEX$(D);" ";
160 NEXT I
170 CLOSE 1
180 PRINT: PRINT F$," SAVED"
190 END
199 REM ATTACK
200 DATA 0,35,50,58,65,100,132,137
210 DATA 150,210,250,255,255,255,255,255
220 DATA 255,255,255,255,255,255,255,255
230 DATA 255,255,255,255,255,255,255,255
240 DATA 255,255,255,255,255,255,255,255
250 DATA 255,255,255,255,255,255,255,255
260 DATA 255,255,255,255,255,255,255,255
270 DATA 255,255,255,255,255,255,255,255
299 REM DECAY
300 DATA 255,250,244,235,222,214,204,195
310 DATA 185,170,155,140,132,122,114,105
320 DATA 94,85,78,73,68,62,58,54
330 DATA 48,45,40,36,32,29,27,25
340 DATA 22,20,18,16,14,12,11,11
350 DATA 10,9,8,8,7,7,6,5
360 DATA 5,5,4,4,3,3,2,2
370 DATA 2,1,1,1,1,0,0,0
```

Fast Fourier Transform Program (FFT)   The FFT program supplied with the synthesizer is a frequency-to-time FFT, of two versions: FFT48.BAS and FFT40.BAS. FFT48.BAS requires 48K of memory and uses two arrays, one for the input data and the second for the results. FFT40.BAS requires 40k of memory and uses one array. The input data is loaded into the array. During execution of the program, the data is destroyed and the results end up in the array. Both programs require about 17 min to execute the FFT. If a BASIC compiler is available, the FFT program should be compiled; the compiled version will execute the FFT transform in about 5 min.

The synthesizer requires the timbre waveform to be 1024 12-bit words. The FFT program generates these waveforms, executing a 1024 point FFT and generating a file of 1024 16-bit words. The PLAY program uses only the most significant 12 bits. This requires the results to be less than 32767 and greater than -32767. If properly commanded, the FFT scales the results so they fall within the limits. The commands of the FFT are given in the following discussion.

The input data array (frequency) starts at 1 and goes to 1024. The first element in the array is the constant amplitude term, which normally is zero. The second term in the array is the amplitude of the fundamental; this element is usually set to 32767. The third term is the amplitude for the second harmonic. The fourth term is the amplitude for the third harmonic, and so forth. Although there are 1024 elements in the array, rarely would the input waveform consist of more than 20 terms. Normally the real terms are used to specify the amplitude of the harmonic, and the imaginary terms are set to zero.

The FFT40.BAS program has all the commands of the FFT48.BAS program, except that it does not have the R command because it only uses one array; and the D command is used to display the array. Some timbre waveforms are supplied with the disk. These files are identified with the extension TIM (for example, CLAR.TIM, TRUMPET.TIM, CELLO.TIM, and so on).

FFT *Commands*   The FFT program has the following commands:

DATA (D)   This command displays all 1024 points of the data array. The data array is in the frequency domain and is the input to the FFT.

FFT (F)   This command starts the FFT. The program takes 17 min to execute the transform.

RESULTS (R)   This command displays the results of the FFT. The 1024 points are in the time domain.

PLOT (P)   This command plots every sixteenth point of the results array.

CHANGE (C)   This command has the following subcommands that allow the user to change the data and results array:

RANDOM (R)   This subcommand allows random points in the data array to be changed.

FIND (F)   This subcommand finds the maximum and minimum value in the results array and the scale factor required to bring all the results within the limits of plus and minus 32767.

SCALE (S)   This subcommand allows the entire results array to be scaled so that they will fall within the boundary of plus and minus 32767.

ZERO (Z)   This subcommmand sets all data in the data array to zero.

COMMAND (C)   Return to main command mode.

SAVE (S)   This command allows data or results to be saved on a floppy disk. If the results are to be used by the PLAY program, they must be saved in hexadecimal format. The data must be saved in decimal format if the file is to be reloaded into the data array by the LOAD (L) command. This command asks which format the data is to be saved in.

LOAD (L)   This command allows loading a data file into the data or results array. The disk file must have been saved in decimal format.

The WAVEFORM *Program*   This program helps generate both the attack/decay envelopes and the timbre waveform. It is interactive and requires the CRT terminal to have graphics. The program plots the attack/decay envelope and the timbre waveform as parameters are changed, enabling the user to see the effect of the changes on the waveform. The program can also lay a scale with the waveform, to allow the user to hear the waveform.

The program is written in PASCAL. The routine called PLOT must be customized to fit the graphics of the host system; the program has been written to plot a 128-point array. Therefore the procedure PLOT must be written to accommodate the graphics of the system. The procedure as written expects to see a memory-mapped video display at F000 hex with a graphics matrix of 160 by 204 points (Solid State Music's VB3 video board).

WAVEFORM *Commands*   The WAVEFORM program has six commands, and each command has a number of subcommands. Following are descriptions of each command and its function:

ATTACK (A)   This command creates or modifies an attack envelope and has four subcommands:

POINTS (P)   The attack envelope has 128 points. When the program first comes up, all the points are zero. Points in the envelope can be inserted by the P subcommand. The P subcommand also connects each point with a straight line.

VIEW (V)   This subcommand plots the attack envelope on the CRT.

LIST (L)   This subcommand lists all points that have been inserted by the P subcommand.

NEW (N)   This subcommand sets all the envelope points to zero.

DECAY (D)   This command creates or modifies a decay envelope. It has exactly the same subcommands as the ATTACK (A) command.

WAVEFORM (W)   This command has three subcommands:

HARMONICS (H)   This subcommand modifies the harmonic content of a waveform. The subcommand requests the number of the harmonic that is to be modified. 0 is used for the fundamental, 1 for the first harmonic, 2 for the second harmonic, and so forth. The fundamental and up to 15 harmonics can be modified. The subcommand next asks for the value of the harmonic, which can range from 0 to 1000.

LIST (L)   This subcommand lists values for the fundamental and all harmonics.

VIEW (V)   This subcommand plots the timbre waveform on the CRT.

PLAY (P)   This command plays a scale of quarter-notes using the timbre waveform, attack envelope, and decay envelope that have been generated.

SAVE (S)   This command saves the attack/decay envelope and the timbre waveform on floppy disk. The command requests a file name for the data.

The SCORE *Program*   This program compiles a music file, thus generating a play file that can then be played by the PLAY program. The SCORE program is written in BASIC, and the music score is BASIC data statements merged with the SCORE program. Because the SCORE program ends at statement 999, the music statements should start at 1000. Table 5 is an example of a music file. The number 5 in statement 1000 indicates the number of channels

TABLE 5   *A basic program used by the* **SCORE** *program to generate a play file. This example is the first four measures of "Pictures at an Exhibition".*

```
1000 DATA 5
1002 DATA 0,2,1,2,2
1004 DATA 1,0,0,0,0
1005 REM CHAN 0 FM FOR CHAN 2
1006 REM CHAN 1 HARMONY CHAN 2 MELODY
1007 REM CHAN 3 HARMONY CHAN 4 HARMONY
1010 DATA "6GN1Q","6FN1Q","6B!10","6CN2E","6FN2E"
1020 DATA "6DN2Q","6CN2E","6FN2E","6DN2Q","6B!1Q"
1030 DATA "6CN2Q","6GN1Q","6FN1Q","6GN1Q","6FN1Q"
1040 DATA "6B!1Q","6CN2E","6FN2E","6DN2Q","X"
2010 DATA "0DN3W","0DN3Q","0DN3W.","7DN3Q","7CN3Q"
2020 DATA "7DN30","7AN30","7AN3Q","X"
3010 DATA "9GN3Q","9FN3Q","9B!3Q","9CN4E","9FN4E"
3020 DATA "9DN4Q","9CN4E","9FN4E","9DN40","9B!3Q"
3030 DATA "9CN4Q","0GN3Q","9FN3Q","9GN3Q","9FN3Q"
3040 DATA "9B!3Q","9CN4E","0FN4E","9DN4Q","X"
4010 DATA "0B!2W","0B!2Q","0B!2W.","7B!2Q","7AN2Q"
4020 DATA "7B!2Q","7CN3Q","7FN3Q","X"
5010 DATA "0GN1W","0GN1Q","0GN1W.","7GN1Q","7AN1Q"
5020 DATA "7GN1Q","7FN1Q","7DN1Q","E"
```

TABLE 6   *Note notation used in Table 5.*

Each note is written as "SANXOTMS"
where:
S = Slur (—)
    S is optional. If not present, note will have an attack and a decay. If present at front, note will not have an attack. If present at rear note will not have a decay. The slur is used to connect two notes.
A = Amplitude (0,1,2,3,4,5,6,7,8,9,)
N = Note (A,B,C,D,E,F,G)
X = Sharp (#),Flat(!),Normal (any other char.)
O = Octave (1,2,3,4,5,6)
T = Time (X,T,S,E,Q,H,W)   X = Sixty-fourth
    T = Thirty-second   S = Sixteenth   E = Eighth
    Q = Quarter   H = Half   W = Whole
M = Multiplier (.,')
    M is optional. If omitted T = T
    The multiplier is used to dot a note or to double the duration of a note.
      If M = . Then T = 1.5T (Dotted note)
      If M = ' Then T = 2T

that will be used. The five numbers in statement 1002 indicate which timbre waveforms should be used for each channel, respectively. The five numbers in statement 1004 indicate which channels contain FM information. In the example given, channel 0 contains FM data and is used to FM modulate channel 2. Table 6 shows the structure of the note notation.

Normally a music file is created by using the CP/M editor. To compile the music for the PLAY program, three steps are required: (1) the BASIC interpreter is loaded, (2) the SCORE program is loaded, and (3) the music file is merged with the SCORE program. Afterward the program may be executed. The merge command allows an ASCII file to be loaded at the end of a program that has already been loaded. If a BASIC program does not have a MERGE command, the music has to be typed as data statements directly into the BASIC program after the SCORE program has been loaded.

The SCORE program generates 4 bytes of data per note: amplitude (1 byte), time (1 byte), and frequency (FCW, 2 bytes). The interpretation of the amplitude is shown in Table 7. Maximum amplitude is represented by a 9; a 5 causes the amplitude to be half of maximum. The time byte indicates the musical duration of the note. Table 8 shows how time is interpreted by the SCORE program. We must also allow for two or more notes to be slurred together (i.e., one or more notes will not have an attack or a decay). The time byte MSB is set if the note is not to have an attack envelope. The bit after the MSB is set if the note is not to have a decay.

Two bytes are used to specify a frequency. The relationship between the note and the frequency is dictated by the characteristics of the synthesizer. The values used by the SCORE program are given in data statements 130 through 140; the data statements can be changed to alter the note relationships. Figure 12 shows the relationship of each note on a standard keyboard to the frequency defined by the FCW word in Table 2.

The PLAY Program   The main purpose of the PLAY program is to control the synthesizer and play the music compiled by the SCORE program. This pro-

---

TABLE 7   *Interpretation of amplitude data in Tables 5 and 6*

Music amplitude	Amplitude data generated by program SCORE	Interpreted by PLAY program as
9	1	MAXIMUM AMPLITUDE
8	2	0.875 MAX. −1.2 dB
7	3	0.750 MAX. −2.5 dB
6	4	0.625 MAX. −4.1 dB
5	5	0.500 MAX. −6.0 dB
4	6	0.375 MAX. −8.5 dB
3	7	0.250 MAX. −12.0 dB
2	8	0.125 MAX. −18.0 dB
1	9	0.062 MAX. −24.0 dB
0	0	0

TABLE 8   Interpretation of note duration data in Tables 5 and 6

Note	Data generated by SCORE
64th note	Ø
64th dotted	1
32d	2
32d dotted	3
16th	4
16th dotted	5
8th	6
8th dotted	7
Quarter-note	8
Quarter dotted	9
Half-note	1Ø
Half dotted	11
Whole note	12
Whole dotted	13
Whole + whole	14
End of data	15
No attack	128
No decay	64

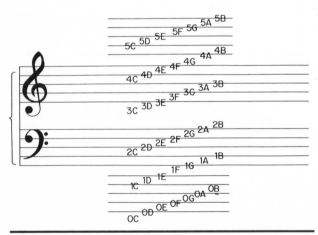

FIG. 12   Nomenclature used by the synthesizer for all notes on an equally tempered musical scale.

gram also loads the synthesizer with timbre waveforms and does miscellaneous bookkeeping.

Two PLAY programs are supplied with the synthesizer: SPLAY.ASM and RPLAY.ASM. The SPLAY program uses a software timing loop to determine the duration of a note. The RPLAY program uses a real-time clock for note-duration timing. The SPLAY program requires fewer modifications than the RPLAY program before it will run on a system because it does not require a real-time clock. However, the timing of RPLAY is more accurate than that of SPLAY. Both are 8080 assembly language programs and essentially identical.

The RPLAY program requires a timer so that a note can be played for the correct duration. The RPLAY program expects to see an Intel 8253 programmable interval timer located at address F4F8. If a different timer is used, three subroutines must be changed: TIME, SETIME, and ZEROTIME. The wait loops PWAIT and XWAIT must also be altered. The TIME subroutine changes the basic note-duration time. The timing device should be programmable so that its sample period can be varied from 1 to 30 ms. The attack and decay routines expect a sample period of about 4 ms.

The XPLAY routine (which does not implement attack and decay) expects a sample period of 16 ms. ZEROTIME sets the counters in the 8253 to zero. SETIME sets up the initial sample period of the 8253. The two wait loops, PWAIT and XWAIT, are identical and determine when a new sample period has begun. They must be changed to accommodate other timing devices.

PLAY *Commands*   The PLAY program has nine commands. Here is a description of each command and its function:

CP/M (C)   Return to CP/M (warm boot).

FM (F)   Modify FM table. This command has five subcommands:

  SET (S)   Set a channel for FM. The software requests the number of the channel to be set. If a channel is set, it FM-modulates the channel that is two removed, i.e., channel 1 modulates channel 3, channel 2 modulates channel 4, and so on.

  RESET (R)   Clear a channel of FM. Software requests the number of the channel to be cleared.

  TABLE (T)   Display FM table.

  ZERO (Z)   Zero entire FM table.

  COMMAND (C)   Return to the main command mode.

INITIALIZE (I)   Zero all synthesizer amplitudes.

GET (G)   Get music file from memory.

MONITOR (M)   Jump to ROM monitor.

PLAY (P)   Play music with attack and decay envelopes. Typing any character after the music has started will terminate the music and return the program to the main command mode.

SCALE (S)   Set DAC scale. The scale is used to increase the output as follows:

Synthesizer output = digital output $\times$ 2 exp (SCALE)

The SCALE (S) command is often used to increase the output when a few channels are being used. If the SCALE is set too high, an overflow occurs and the output is distorted. The SCALE always resets to zero whenever the main processor is reset.

TIME (T)   Set the timing. This determines the rate at which the music is played.

WAVEFORM (W)   Each channel must be assigned a timbre waveform. The waveforms must be loaded into the synthesizer and each channel assigned a waveform. The W command has seven subcommands that allow waveforms to be fetched and loaded into the synthesizer. Means are also provided to modify waveform assignments; each music file contains information on the waveform assignment for that given piece. When the music file is fetched with the GET (G) command, a waveform table is set up. This table can be modified with several W subcommands:

CLEAR (K)   Set all waveform assignments to zero.

MODIFY (M)   Change the waveform number of a channel. Software requests the channel number and the new waveform numbers.

TABLE (T)   Display waveform-assignment table. The waveform number assigned to each channel is displayed. The first number at the upper left-hand corner is the waveform number for channel 1. The next number to the right is the waveform number for channel 2. The table displays the assignment for all the channels. The table also displays the file name of the waveform that was loaded into the synthesizer.

FETCH (F)   Fetch the timbre waveform from the floppy disk. The software requests the file name of the waveform.

LOAD (L)   Load the timbre waveform into the synthesizer. The waveform must have been previously fetched. The software requests a waveform number. If the synthesizer can hold only four waveforms, the number should be between $\emptyset$ and 3. If the synthesizer can accommodate 16 waveforms, the number should be between $\emptyset$ and 15. The same waveform can be loaded into more than one synthesizer waveform location.

ZERO (Z)   Zero all waveforms in the synthesizer. This command clears all waveforms that have been loaded into the synthesizer.

COMMAND (C)   Return to the main command mode.

DDT (D)   Program jumps to DDT. If PLAY program was not loaded with DDT, the system crashes.

XPLAY (X)   Play music without attack and decay envelope. Typing any character after the music has begun causes the program to return to the main command mode.

REFERENCES

1. Tierney, J., C. M. Rader, and B. Gold: "A Digital Frequency Synthesizer," *IEEE Trans. Audio Electroacoust.*, vol. AU-19, March 1971, pp. 48–56.
2. Heaberlin, A.: Multichannel Digital Synthesizer and Modulator, U.S. Patent 4,003,003, Jan. 11, 1977.
3. Snell, J.: "Design of a Digital Oscillator Which Will Generate Up to 256 Low-Distortion Sine Waves in Real Time," *Computer Music J.*, vol. 1, no. 2, 1977, pp. 4–25.
4. Moorer, J. A.: "Signal Processing Aspects of Computer Music: A Survey," *Proc. IEEE*, vol. 65, no. 4, August 1977, vol. 65, no. 4, pp. 1108–1137.
5. Chowning, J. M.: "The Synthesis of Complex Audio Spectra by Means of Frequency Modulation," *J. Audio Engineering Society*, vol. 21, no. 7, pp. 526–534, September 1973.

CHAPTER ELEVEN

Digital Filters Utilizing Microprocessors

Robert D. Grappel

Hemenway Associates,
Boston, Massachussetts

11.1   Real-Time Analog Processing with Computers

A filter is a device or process that separates one element or class of
elements from a mixture of such elements. By this definition, many
computer programs are in fact filters. For example, a mailing-list
program that picks out desired addresses from a data base is a filter,
and a string pattern-match algorithm in a text editor is a sort of filter.
Nearly every computer program must separate special data items
from the input at some point. Hence, it is not unusual to consider
using a computer in a filter. However, the most common meaning of
filter in the electronic context is as a type of circuit that separates
signals at certain frequencies or bands of frequencies from an input
spectrum. These filters, usually constructed from resistors, amplifiers,
capacitors, and inductors, seem far removed from the realm of digital
computing.

Electronic filters work in the analog domain; computers deal in the
digital domain. A computer cannot deal with a continuous stream of
inputs, and it cannot continuously change its outputs. The digital

circuit must get an input, perform some processing, and form an output—all of which takes time. Clearly, a digital filter (a filter designed around a computer or special digital hardware) must somehow change the continuous inputs and outputs into instantaneous "snapshots."

Figure 1 illustrates the basic requirements of a computer designed for analog processing. The input analog signal is sampled by an analog-to-digital converter (ADC). This device takes a nearly instantaneous reading of the input voltage and converts it into a digital word (8 bits wide for most of the examples in this chapter). The computer (or other digital processing hardware) performs computations on this input and then converts it to a digital output word. This word is then converted back to an equivalent voltage using a digital-to-analog converter (DAC). This process is repeated rapidly, over and over again. It is similar to the process by which a series of still photographs shown fast enough becomes a movie. The number of samples per second processed by the ADC or DAC is called the *sampling rate*.

Sampling Rate Limitations The sampling rate required by a given filter depends upon the type of inputs it must handle. Clearly, if the input changes very rapidly between samples, then information about the input shape may be lost. As shown in Fig. 2, the waveform is changing dramatically between the sample times, yet the input seen by the ADC looks constant. It is almost as though the sampling process is filtering out frequencies (rates of change) that occur in less than one sample period. A measurement of a change in the input requires at least two samples of the change. Likewise, it takes a minimum of two points to detect a peak or valley. A fundamental theorem of information theory states that the highest frequency a sampled process can detect is one-half of the sampling rate, or alternatively, the sampling rate must be greater than twice the highest frequency which is to be present in the input. This minimum sampling rate is called the Nyquist rate or Nyquist frequency.[1] If frequencies higher than one-half the Nyquist frequency are present in the input to the digital filter, they will be aliased by the sampling process into signals falling within one-half the Nyquist rate. Aliasing is the folding of signals from one frequency band down into a lower band. The result is considerable noise and distortion. Such frequencies must be removed from the input spectrum before sampling; this is usually done with a normal analog low-pass filter. The Nyquist frequency is one of the important parameters of digital filter design.

Why is the Nyquist frequency so important? Digital processing takes time, and even the ADC and DAC processes take some time. The more sophisticated the digital processing going on, the longer it will take. Thus there is a definite limit to the sampling rate that a given system can attain. All too often this limit proves lower than the Nyquist frequency, and so the system must be redesigned. The Nyquist frequency has been the driving force for many generations of digital filter designs. Semiconductor manufacturers are continually developing faster devices in an attempt to get the sampling rate high enough to handle the desired input frequencies. Improvements in software are also responsible for many increases in processing speed.

But why use computers, ADCs, and DACs when filters can be built with simple, cheap components such as resistors, capacitors, and op amps? The primary reason is flexibility. It is easier to change software than to solder joints and traces on a printed circuit card once it is in production. A digital filter can be tailored for many different tasks. A second reason is the imperfection of standard filter components. Resistors have some capacitance and inductance, inductors have resistance and capacitance, op amps have phase shift and dynamic range limitations, and so on. Although digital filters also have limitations, they approach the theoretical limits more closely. Digital filters have superior time and temperature stability than do their analog counterparts. Digital filters also give better performance at very low frequencies, whereas the large resistors, capacitors, and inductors required in analog filters create size, weight, and cost problems.

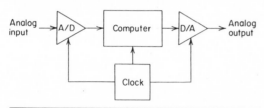

FIG. 1   *The basic elements required for a computer designed for signal processing.*

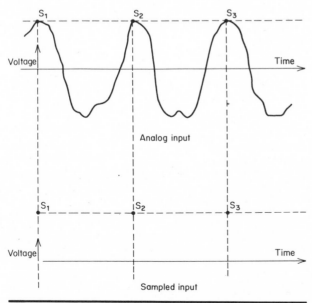

FIG. 2   *Sampled input to a computer of a waveform whose frequency equals the sampling rate.*

11.2   Simulating Analog Components Digitally

There are a number of techniques for mathematically describing and designing digital filters. This chapter presents one of the "wave filter"[2,3] approaches, which is probably the easiest method to use when first designing digital filters. With this technique we assume each electronic part has a digital equivalent. These digital equivalent parts are then connected using software or digital parts to create a digital circuit equivalent to the analog circuit desired. This section is not rigorous; its purpose is to show that analog filters may be modeled with simple digital algorithms. Later, in the discussion of digital filters, more precise approaches are used. The following analog parts descriptions refer to Fig. 3.

Amplifier   A perfect amplifier produces an output that is simply an enlarged copy of its input. The output is the product of the input and some constant (called the gain) that is a property of the amplifier. The perfect amplifier introduces no distortion or phase shift into the input waveform, nor does it produce any offsets or clipping. Typically the gain is greater than 1, but it does not have to be. In a digital filter, gain is represented by a multiplier.

Resistor   A resistor voltage divider causes an output that is simply a smaller version of its input. It can be viewed as a type of amplifier whose gain is less than 1. A resistor voltage divider simply attenuates the signal passed through it without any distortion, phase shift, offset, or clipping. These circuit elements are also simulated using a multiplier.

Capacitor   A capacitor is a more complicated device; its behavior depends upon associated resistances and inductances. When exposed to a change of input voltage, its current is a function of time, so the output voltage waveforms from a circuit containing a capacitor are therefore altered. As shown in Fig. 3, the output behaves as an exponential when an input change is made. The parameter of the exponential, called the time constant (the product RC), is a property of the capacitor and associated resistances. A capacitor is simulated in digital systems with a unit delay (i.e., a delay of 1 clock period used by the ADC) and multiplication by a constant.

Inductor   Like the capacitor, the inductor in conjunction with associated resistances behaves as an exponential with a time constant (R/L) that is a property of the inductor and its associated resistances. This device is simulated using the unit delay and multiplication by a negative constant.

Avoiding the Computation of Exponentials   What are the implications of all this for sampled filters? It seems that the filter must be able to compute exponentials, which would be a formidable and time-consuming task for a microprocessor-based filter design. Fortunately, calculation of exponentials is *not* required for a sampled filter. For both the capacitor and the inductor, the exponential consists of a constant multiplied by the time over which the change occurs. In a sampled filter, this time is fixed by the sampling rate (i.e.,

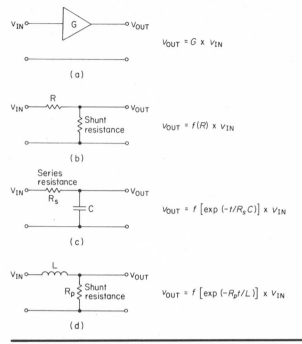

FIG. 3 *Four electronic parts which can be simulated using digital processing techniques: (a) amplifier, (b) resistor, (c) capacitor, and (d) inductor.*

the unit delay previously mentioned). Hence each exponential is really just a constant for any given capacitor or inductor. The output for any given sample is simply some constant times the value of the input one sample period earlier. The following equation is useful for either a capacitor or an inductor:

$$v_{OUT}(n + 1) = v_{IN}(n) \times \text{constant}$$

where $(n + 1)$ represents a unit delay relative to n. It becomes evident that a simulation of the behavior of filter components requires the following capabilities:

1. Multiplication by a constant
2. Delay by one sample period
3. Add values
4. Subtract values

Items 3 and 4 come into play when components are connected to form circuits.

Digital Delays Multiplications, additions, and subtractions are common computer processes, but what does a delay mean? Very simply, it means storage of data for a given period of time. To delay by one sample period means to save the value during one computation period for use during the next computation period. Thus, during each computation period the following events occur in a typical digital filter:

1. Obtain sample from input ADC
2. Process input data and data stored from previous computation periods using digital filter algorithm.
3. Store data for future computation periods.
4. Send output data to DAC
5. Go back to step 1 and repeat process.

11.3 Single-Pole Digital Low-Pass Filter

Consider the single-pole low-pass filter shown in Fig. 4a.[4] Figure 4b shows how this filter attenuates frequencies higher than its pole frequency but passes frequencies lower than the pole with a gain of 1. A differential equation with the output voltage as the unknown can be written using Kirchhoff's laws and the characteristics of resistors and capacitors:

$$v_{IN}(t) = Ri(t) + v_{OUT}(t) = RC \frac{dv_{OUT}}{dt} + v_{OUT}(t) \tag{1}$$

This is a first-order equation with constant coefficients. The output response $v_{OUT}(t)$ depends upon two things: the input voltage $v_{IN}(t)$ and the natural or transient behavior of the filter. Assume a charge has been stored on the capacitor. If the input is then set to zero, the output response from that time on will be the natural response of the circuit. For this situation the voltage across the resistor is the same as that across the capacitor. Hence the circuit equation describing the low-pass filter may be written:

$$\frac{dv_{OUT}}{dt} = \frac{-1}{RC} v_{OUT}(t)$$

where $v_{OUT}(t)$ indicates the natural response of the circuit. This equation is called the homogeneous part of the circuit equation. Its solution gives the natural response $v_{OUT}(t)$ of the circuit. One solution is an exponential, as follows:

$$v_{OUT}(t) = V_c \exp(-at)$$
where $a = 1/RC = 2\pi f_{pole}$
  V_c = initial capacitor voltage

A complete derivation of the behavior of a circuit must consider both the natural and forced responses. The forced response is that due to the input $v_{IN}(t)$. The output response resulting from both causes is

$$v_{OUT}(t) = \int_{T_0}^{T} [a \exp(-a(t-x))] v_{IN}(x) \, dx + V_c \exp(-at)$$

The second term is simply the natural or zero-input response, and the first

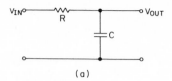

(a)

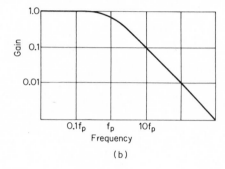

(b)

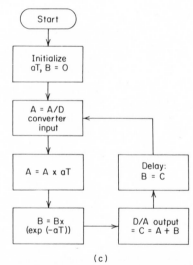

(c)

FIG. 4 *Development of a single-pole low-pass digital filter.* (a) *The analog circuit to be simulated.* (b) *Desired gain as a function of frequency.* (c) *Flowchart.*

term is the behavior caused by the forcing function. The integral is in the form:

$$\int_{T_0}^{T} f(t - x)\, g(x)\, dx$$

where $f(t - x) = a \exp(-a(t - x))$ (2)

$\qquad\quad g(x) = v_{IN}(x)$

Such an integral is called a convolution integral. It states that the response of a circuit to a pulse whose width is short compared to the time constant of the circuit may be approximated by the response of the circuit to an impulse of equal area. This approach works whether the pulse is rectangular or has some other shape. The integral sums up the contributions of all inputs the circuit has seen.

The lower limit T_0 is arbitrary. Usually it is convenient to either let T_0 equal zero or let it approach minus infinity. In general terms, this says that we have been running the circuit for a long time. If T_0 is not zero, then the constant V_c is related to the circuit output voltage at time T_0:

$$V_c = v_{OUT}(T_0) \exp (aT_0)$$

If T_0 is a very large negative number, then V_c must be vanishingly small. We assume that $v_{out}(T_0)$ is bounded, which means that the natural response term must vanish in the past and the total response of the low-pass filter becomes:

$$v_{OUT}(t) = \int_{-\infty}^{T} [a \exp (-a(t - x))] \, v_{IN}(x) \, dx \tag{3}$$

This equation is handled quite easily with a computer. Assume a sample of $v_{IN}(t)$ is available every T seconds. Each successive value of $v_{OUT}(t)$ would be:

$T = 0$: $v_{OUT}(0) = av_{IN}(0)$

$T = 1$: $v_{OUT}(1) = av_{IN}(1) + av_{IN}(0) \exp (-a)$

$T = 2$: $v_{OUT}(2) = av_{IN}(2) + av_{IN}(1) \exp (-a) + av_{IN}(0) \exp (-2a)$

$T = 3$: $v_{OUT}(3) = av_{IN}(3) + av_{IN}(2) \exp (-a) + av_{IN}(1) \exp (-2a)$

$\qquad\qquad\qquad + av_{IN}(0) \exp (-3a)$ $\hfill (4)$

$\qquad \vdots$

$T = n$: $v_{OUT}(n) = a \sum_{k=0}^{n} v_{IN}(n - k) \exp (-ak)$

Filters of this type, whose output depends only upon present and past input values, are called nonrecursive filters and are discussed further in later sections of this chapter.

In Eq. 4, the older terms become less and less important as time passes. We can take advantage of that fact to simplify our implementation of the filter. Likewise, we can simplify handling of exponentials by noting that:

$$\exp (-nat) = [\exp (-at)]^n$$

Because the exponential need be calculated only once for the sampling rate, the entire calculation becomes easy. The flowchart in Fig. 4c illustrates the processing of a digital single-pole low-pass filter. Note the delay formed by storing the output C in temporary B.

11.4   Single-Pole Digital High-Pass Filter

A single-pole high-pass filter, as shown in Fig. 5a, can also be implemented with one resistor and one capacitor. A high-pass filter is transparent for frequencies higher than its pole frequency while attenuating frequencies lower than that frequency. Figure 5b indicates the frequency response for this circuit.

The loop equation for the single-pole high-pass filter is:

$$v_{IN}(t) = v_{OUT}(t) + \frac{1}{C} \int i_c \, dt = v_{OUT}(t) + \frac{1}{RC} \int v_{OUT}(t) \, dt \qquad (5)$$

This equation is the same as that for the low-pass filter (Eq. 1), except the derivative term is changed to an integral term. Mathematical steps similar to those used in analyzing the low-pass filter may be used to analyze the high-pass filter. The net result is a sign change in the summation shown in Eq. 4. Instead of adding contributions from past samples, the high-pass filter subtracts these contributions (i.e., the more current through the resistor, the lower the output voltage). Changing one instruction in the filter from an Add to a Subtract changes the entire behavior of the filter. This illustrates the flexibility of computer-based digital filters.

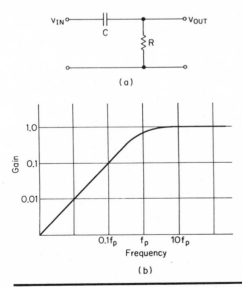

FIG. 5   (a) The high-pass circuit simulated digitally, and (b) its desired frequency response.

11.5 Nonrecursive Filters

The previous sections suggest that a general equation may be derived for digital filters which consists of a sum of terms, each term being a constant multiplied by an input sample with some degree of delay.[5,6] Such an equation describes what is called a "nonrecursive" filter. It can be written as a difference equation as follows:

$$Y(nT) = \sum_{i=0}^{n} A_i X(nT - iT) \tag{6}$$

where $X(nT)$ represents present input sample
$\quad X(iT)$ represents past input samples
$\quad Y(nT)$ represents present output sample
$\quad A_i$ represents a series of constants

This type of filter can be implemented with tapped delay lines or shift registers. Such filters are commonly called transversal filters. Of course, the concept is easily adaptable to software routines, but its upper frequency limit is determined by the speed of the microprocessor. Because no feedback is used (the summation uses only past input samples), the circuit (or algorithm) is unconditionally stable. That is, it will not oscillate under any set of conditions. An impulse input will result in a set of output values that decay toward zero. Consequently, this type of circuit is also called a "finite impulse response" (FIR) filter.

11.6 Recursive Filters

Consider the circuit in Fig. 6. The voltage at the junction of C_1 and C_2 depends upon both v_{IN} and v_{OUT}. Equation 6 is valid only for equating an output $Y(nT)$ to past and present values of $X(nT)$. Figure 6 requires $Y(nT)$ to depend upon past and present values of both $Y(nT)$ and $X(nT)$. This feedback requires an extension to the general nonrecursive filter equation (Eq. 6). For Fig. 6, the filter output becomes the sum of two summations: The first is the nonrecursive terms, and the second is an equivalent sum, one that uses output samples (with some degree of delay) instead of input samples. The equation is now called "recursive" because feedback, is involved. The recursive equation is general; it can describe all filters, including nonrecursive types. Thus, nonrecursive filters are a subset of the recursive filter class.

The equation for a recursive digital filter can be stated in difference form as:

$$Y(nT) = \sum_{i=0}^{n} A_i X(nT - iT) + \sum_{i=0}^{n} B_i Y(nT - iT) \tag{7}$$

where B_i = constant multiplier for each delay (iT)
$\quad Y(iT)$ = past output samples

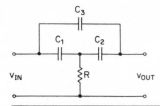

FIG. 6   *Simulation of a circuit of this type digitally would require recursive techniques.*

This equation is normally written as a z-transform:

$$Y(z) = X(z) \sum_{i=0}^{N} A_i z^{-i} + Y(z) \sum_{i=0}^{M} B_i z^{-i} \tag{8}$$

where z^{-i} represents delay operator
$\quad\quad i$ represents number of past unit delays

A unit delay equals the sample period previously mentioned. Equation 8 may be interpreted as: The present output is equal to the present and past inputs each multiplied by the respective coefficient A_i plus the past outputs each multiplied by the respective coefficient B_i. Using this equation, designing a digital filter becomes a task of picking the proper constant multipliers for each summation.

11.7   Hardware Considerations in Digital Filters

As illustrated in Fig. 1, the software-operated digital filter needs additional hardware to interface with the analog world. Because the ADCs and DACs could take up a book of their own, this discussion is very brief. There are three parameters that influence the choice (or design) of the conversion hardware: speed, accuracy, and dynamic range. The speed requirement comes from the Nyquist limit, the accuracy requirement is driven by the desire for a low-noise filter with little output distortion, and the dynamic range requirement comes from the need to be able to process the input signals without clipping or distortion. These requirements interact, however, and tradeoffs are always a necessary part of the design.

Interface Accuracy   Commercial ADCs and DACs come in 4-, 6-, 8-, 10-, 12-,14-, and 16-bit models. The 8-bit converters seem the most logical for use with 8-bit microprocessors because they are relatively cheap, easy to interface, and fast enough for many applications. There is a direct relationship between the number of bits and cost. Eight bits (signed) provide better than 0.8 percent resolution, which is sufficient for most digital filter work using microprocessors.

Interface Speed The speed requirements of interfaces are based upon the Nyquist frequency of the filter. The converters must be able to perform the conversions fast enough to keep up with the sampling rate. There is an inverse relationship between converter accuracy (number of bits) and a converter's conversion speed. For a given price range, converters with low resolution (a small number of bits) are faster than those with high resolution.

Dynamic Range The number of bits in the converters also determine the dynamic range of the filter. Dynamic range equates to the range between the highest and lowest levels that may be converted without distortion. Dynamic range is computed with the following equation:

Dynamic range in dB $= 20 \log (2^{n-1})$

where n is the number of bits in the converter. An 8-bit signed converter is thus capable of about 42-dB dynamic range, which is sufficient for many medium-quality digital filter applications.

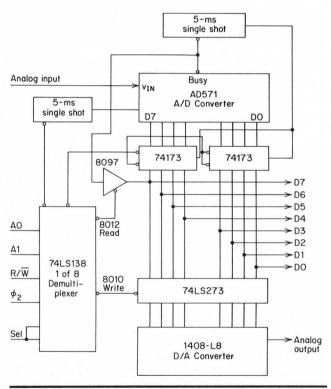

FIG. 7 *The analog-input and analog-output section of the digital filters discussed in this chapter.*

A Practical ADC *and* DAC *Design Example*　As an example of the type of practical hardware used in a digital filter, consider the schematic in Fig. 7. This ADC and DAC interface was designed by Richard Lord of Upward Concepts, Durham, N.H., for use with a Southwest Technical Products computer system. This interface plugs into an input-output (I/O) slot on the processor bus and behaves like two memory locations. A 1408 DAC is addressed by writing into the first of these memory locations (address 8010 hex). An AD571 ADC is addressed by reading from that same address. The AD571 is actually a 10-bit device, so this interface uses only the upper 8 bits. To initiate a conversion by the AD571, a write is done into memory location 8012 (hex). The AD571 feeds back a busy flag in the high-order bit of this same memory location. The software must wait for the AD571 to clear this bit before reading the value. This interface takes about 25 μs for a conversion.

11.8 Software Considerations in Digital Filters

Software Multiplication　One elemental operation required of a digital filter is multiplication. As shown in Fig. 4c, a voltage sample provided by the ADC (or a delayed voltage sample) is multiplied by a constant. The 6800 microprocessor used in this chapter does not have a multiply instruction, so this operation must be done with a software subroutine. A typical 8-bit multiplication with a 16-bit product may take several hundred clock cycles, i.e., hundreds of microseconds for each multiplication. Some 8- and 16-bit microprocessors do have multiplication instructions, yet even these take tens of microseconds. This implies that a fairly complex filter requiring several multiplications may operate only at lower frequencies if implemented with one of the slower microprocessors. The filter design may fail to meet the Nyquist limit for higher frequencies because the multiplications take too long to fit into the required sampling rate.

How can we speed up the loop between samples? In recent years software engineers have developed many tricks to optimize algorithms for digital filters.[7] One of the most obvious is to reduce the number of multiplications per loop.[7] The flowchart in Fig. 4c shows two multiplications per loop. This procedure can be reduced to one multiplication per loop using some algebraic manipulation. Starting with the iterative version of Eq. 4:

$$v_{OUT}(n) = av_{IN}(n) + av_{IN}(n-1) \exp(-a)$$

we let $a(\exp(-a)) = 1 - a$. This can be done only if this equation is simulating a simple RC low-pass filter.[11,12] The above equation becomes:

$$v_{OUT}(n) = av_{IN}(n) + (1 - a)v_{IN}(n-1)$$
$$= a[v_{IN}(n) - v_{IN}(n-1)] + v_{IN}(n-1)$$

We now have an additional subtraction in place of the removed multiplication. However, subtraction takes 1 instruction, whereas an 8 $\times$ 8 multiplication takes approximately 52 instruction periods (8 times around the multiplier loop plus initialization). This technique speeds up the flowchart of Fig. 4c by nearly a factor of 2.

Another solution to the multiplication problem is to build a special piece of hardware to perform the multiplication for the host processor. One such circuit that performs an 8 × 8 multiply was published in Ref. 8. This design uses eight inexpensive transistor-transistor logic (TTL) chips and can perform the multiplication in less than 10 μs. The microprocessor software simply sends the multiplier and multiplicand to the hardware and then reads back the product. This sort of hardware makes digital filters practical even when using relatively slow processors.

Fractional Multiplication   The multiplication subroutine is the most time-consuming part of the software. In the example being developed here, A/D samples and the constant multipliers are 8-bit quantities. The result of the multiplication is a 16-bit quantity, but only the most significant 8 bits are used; the rest are truncated. It is therefore a waste of time to compute the entire 16-bit product when only 8 bits will be used. Also, because the example program is being developed on an 8-bit machine (a Motorola 6800) that does not readily handle 16-bit values, a full 8 × 8 multiply is not especially fast. Note, however, that Motorola's 6809 processor does have an 8 × 8 multiply instruction which forms a 16-bit product in approximately 10 μs. In this 6800 example, to get maximum speed we use a special multiply subroutine called "fractional multiply," so named because the multiplier is assumed to represent a fraction rather than an integer. Here the multiplicand is an 8-bit integer and the multiplier is assumed to be $n/256$, where n is the actual value of the multiplier passed to the subroutine. The multiplication thus executes only those steps required to form the 8-bit result desired. Figure 8 shows the fractional multiply subroutine coded for the 6800. It expects the multiplicand in the A accumulator and the multiplier in the B accumulator. The product is returned in the A accumulator. Note that because of the fractional multiply scheme, there is no need to check for overflows or to use multiple precision arithmetic. Three bytes of memory could be saved and some speed gained by coding TEMP in the base-page instead of letting it be relocatable as shown.

Sources of Error   There are three sources of error in the finite-word-length implementation of a digital filter. The first source is the signal quantization in the ADC. This is usually not very serious, appearing as noise with zero mean and a uniform distribution over the range plus or minus one-half of the least significant bit. The second source of error is the quantization of the multiplier coefficients. Rounding off these coefficients can lead to serious troubles. It is possible to have a filter whose output does not decay to zero when the input is turned OFF. This means the filter is not asymptotically stable. The third source of error occurs in the arithmetic operations of the filter algorithm. When two n-bit numbers are multiplied, the product has $2n - 1$ bits. This must be rounded off to n bits for the further stages of the filter. These round-offs can lead to filter oscillations and other types of instabilities. The usual way to estimate the effects of roundoffs is to associate a noise source with each

```
        NAM FRACMUL
* CALLED WITH PARAMETERS IN A AND B ACCUMULATORS
* PRODUCT RETURNED IN A ACCUMULATOR
*
* CODED FOR 6800 MICROPROCESSOR
*
* USES ONE TEMPORARY RAM BYTE
*
FRACML STA A TEMP      SAVE CONTENTS OF A
       CLR A
*
MLOOP  LSR TEMP        ARG 1 = ARG 1/2
       ASL B           CARRY = MSB(ARG2)
       BCC NONADD      CARRY = 0?
*
       ADD A TEMP      ADD IF CARRY = 1
*
NONADD BNE MLOOP       LOOP AGAIN IF ARG2 NE O
*
       RTS             OTHERWISE DONE
*
TEMP   RMB 1
*
       END
```

FIG. 8   *Subroutine to perform fractional multiplication; 8-bit multiplier times 8-bit multiplicand returns the most significant 8 bits of product.*

multiplication. The noise source is assumed to have a uniform distribution over the interval of numbers that are rounded to the same number at the output of the multiplier. The analysis of such errors is beyond the scope of this chapter, but it results in a definite noise floor related to the number of bits used in the filter calculations. This is why devices such as Intel's 2920 signal processor have such wide multipliers: the more bits, the less noise.

Adder Overflow Limit Cycles   Multiplier roundoff is not the only mechanism that can generate oscillations in a digital filter. If two n-bit numbers, each greater than $n/2$, are added in an n-bit adder, the sum will overflow, yielding a result modulo 2 to the nth power. This nonlinear effect can be the source of severe distortion, causing and sustaining "limit cycles" or oscillations with no input signal present. These oscillations are typically quite large in amplitude. Furthermore, increasing the word length on the least significant bit side will not attenuate the oscillations, as was the case for multiplier roundoff cycles. There are two possible solutions: (1) use adders wide enough to ensure no overflows, or (2) use saturation arithmetic. This type of arithmetic simply means that the adder output is forced to the maximum positive value if positive overflow occurs, and it is forced to the maximum negative value if negative overflow occurs. Saturation adders cannot induce limit cycles, and their overflow distortion is reduced. They can introduce other forms of distortion, however, and they require additional software to check for overflows and perform corrections.

Software for the Low-Pass Filter   The low-pass filter may be described as a single real pole. The location of this real pole is given by:

$$a = 2\pi f_{pole} = \frac{1}{RC}$$

i.e., a is the reciprocal of the time constant of the filter.

The low-pass digital filter described in earlier sections is implemented by repeatedly solving Eq. 4 with the 6800 system. Equation 4 can be rewritten in more convenient notation as follows:

$$y_1 = y_0 \tag{9}$$
$$y_0 = By_1 + Gx \tag{10}$$

where $B = \exp(-aT)$
    $G = aT$
    T = sampling period
    x = input sample from ADC
    y_0 = output sample sent to DAC
    y_1 = output sample delayed one sample period

If the low-pass filter program is allowed to operate at maximum interrupt rate, the listing in Fig. 9 will accept 1700 samples per second. In this case we have $T = 1/1700 = 5.88 \times 10^{-4}$. Suppose we require the filter to have a cutoff frequency of 100 Hz. We compute the following constants:

$$a = 2\pi f_{pole} = 2\pi(100) = 628$$
$$G = aT = 628\,\frac{1}{1700} = 0.3694$$
$$B = \exp(-aT) = \exp(-0.3694) = 0.6911$$

The fractional multiplier routine assumes B and G are fractions. We therefore convert these constants to a fraction of a full 8-bit register, i.e., a fraction of 256. Thus, $B = 256(0.6911) = 177$ (rounded to nearest whole number), and $G = 256(0.3694) = 95$ (rounded).

The listing for the low-pass digital filter program is shown in Fig. 9; the measured frequency response is shown in Fig. 10. Note that the response is down 3 dB at 100 Hz, as required. As the frequency approaches one-half the Nyquist rate (850 Hz), the response begins to become irregular.

The filter software described here forms a single-pole low-pass design using the constants just derived. It is written with an initialization section (executed only once) and an interrupt handler section that is called for each sample. The program shown is coded in Motorola 6800 assembler language. It assumes A/D and D/A hardware as previously described.

The initialization section sets the interrupt vector in memory to point to the interrupt handler (filter program). The form of initialization required to do

```
        NAM FILTER
*
* LOW-PASS DIGITAL FILTER PROGRAM
*
ATOD   EQU $8010      A/D INTERFACE ADDRESS
DTOA   EQU $8010      D/A INTERFACE ADDRESS
STROBE EQU $8012      START A/D CONVERSION
TEMP   EQU $ 10       TEMPORARY STORAGE
SAMPLE EQU $ 11       SAMPLE STORAGE
*
INITR  LDX #IFILTR
       STX $A000      INITIALIZE IRQ VECTOR
       CLR STROBE     START A/D CONVERSION
       CLR SAMPLE     INITIALIZE SAMPLE
       CLI            ALLOW INTERRUPTS
*
* FILTER IS NOW RUNNING, AND WILL CONTINUE AS LONG
* AS THE PERIODIC INTERRUPTS CONTINUE
*
*
IFILTR LDA A ATOD     GET SAMPLE FROM A/D
       STA A STROBE   RE-START A/D
       LDA B #95
       BSR FRACML     FIRST MULTIPLY
       PSH A          SAVE RESULT
       LDA A SAMPLE
       LDA A #177
       BSR FRACML     SECOND MULTIPLY
       PUL B
       ABA            SUM TERMS
       STA A DTOA     D/A OUTPUT
       STA A SAMPLE
       RTI            DONE!
*
FRACML LSR TEMP       SAVE CONTENTS OF A
       CLR A
*
MLOOP  LSR TEMP       ARG 1 = ARG 1/2
       ASL B          CARRY = MSB(ARG2)
       BCC NONADD     CARRY = 0?
*
       ADD A TEMP     ADD IF CARRY = 1
*
NONADD BNE MLOOP      LOOP AGAIN IF ARG2 NE 0
*
       RTS            OTHERWISE DONE
*
TEMP   RMB 1
*
       END
```

FIG. 9 *Complete listing of the single-pole low-pass digital filter program using the 6800 microprocessor.*

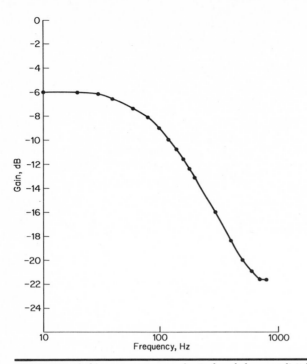

FIG. 10 *Measured frequency response of a single-pole low-pass digital filter having a pole frequency of 100 Hz.*

this depends upon the system being used. The A/D hardware is strobed to begin a conversion of the input voltage. The delayed-sample storage is cleared. Interrupts are enabled, and the filtering process begins.

The interrupt handler performs the actual filter operation. It reads the A/D value and then strobes the converter to begin another conversion. This conversion will complete long before the next sample, so the software need not check for completion. The attenuation constant is multiplied by the sample value, and this result is temporarily saved. The delayed sample is multiplied by the filter constant; this result is added to the result of the first multiply. The product becomes the D/A output and is stored as the delayed sample. This completes the filter process.

Note that this software could also perform as a high-pass filter by changing the addition of the two multiplication results to a subtraction.

11.9 Special Computing Devices for Digital Filtering

Beyond the microprocessor-with-A/D-and-D/A approach, some large-scale integration (LSI) components are especially designed for digital filter applications. Incorporating a programmable computation (add, subtract, multiply) facility with fast ADCs and DACs on a single chip, these components provide digital filters in a few simple packages. The Intel 2920 analog microprocessor is one such device; Fig. 11 shows its block structure.[9,10,11] This device uses an on-chip, erasable, programmable read-only memory (EPROM) to hold its program. It executes each and every instruction in 400 ns. A low-pass filter can be written in about 10 instructions using the 2920, which yields a possible sampling rate of about 250 kHz.

The American Microsystems S2811 signal-processing peripheral[12] incorporates the digital processing stages of a filter in a form that allows it to operate several orders of magnitude faster than the simple methods described in this chapter. Its block diagram is shown in Fig. 12. It executes instructions in 300 ns and can run simple filters at sampling rates above 1 MHz.

11.10 A Practical Digital Resonant Filter

Suppose that a filter which passes only a single frequency is desired. Such a filter is called a *resonant filter* because it resonates at a given frequency. In the analog world, such a filter can be built from a capacitor and inductor connected in parallel. One way to build a filter that passes only a single frequency is to first make a low-pass filter which removes all frequencies higher than the desired frequency. Next, make a high-pass filter that removes all frequencies lower than the desired frequency. The result of these two filters is that only the desired frequency is left, all others having been removed by one of the filters.

The Low-Pass Filter Section Recalling the discussion of the digital low-pass filter, Eqs. 9 and 10 must be used to remove high frequencies above the selected resonant frequency.

The High-Pass Filter Section A similar description holds for the high-pass filter, except that the sign of the constant B is negative. Hence, the resonant filter can be totally described by:

$$y_2 = y_1 \tag{11}$$
$$y_1 = y_0 \tag{12}$$
$$y_0 = B_1y_1 + B_2y_2 + Gx \tag{13}$$

where B_1 = low-pass filter constant
$\quad\quad B_2$ = high-pass filter constant (negative)
$\quad\quad G = aT$
$\quad\quad x$ = input sample from ADC
$\quad\quad y_0$ = output sample sent to DAC
$\quad\quad y_1$ = delayed output of low-pass filter
$\quad\quad y_2$ = delayed output of high-pass filter

This description is in the form of the general filter equations derived in previous sections. The whole task of resonant filter design becomes the choice of the constants B_1, B_2, and G.

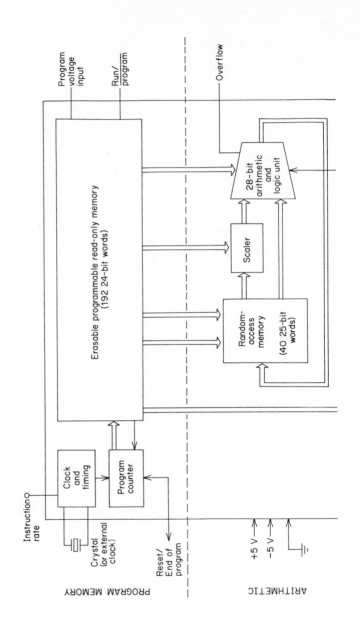

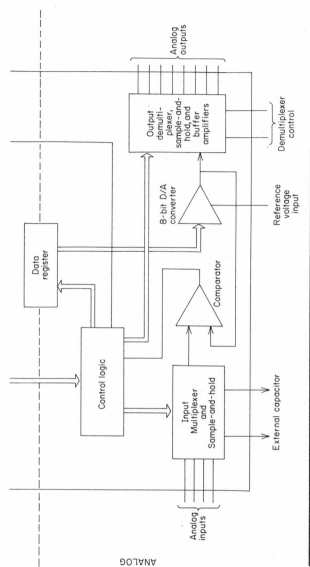

FIG. 11 Block structure of the Intel 2920 analog microprocessor.

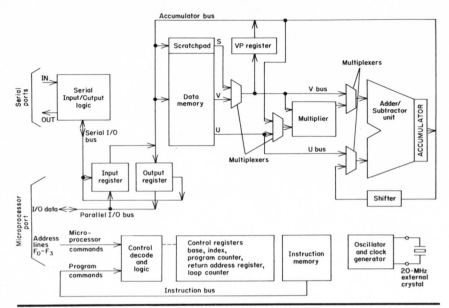

FIG. 12   Block diagram of the American Microsystems S2811 signal-processing peripheral.

Analog filters are usually designed through the location of poles and zeros of the transfer function in the S plane. Each pole or zero can be expressed in the form $(x + iy)$, $(x - iy)$, where x is the real part of the complex frequency and iy is the imaginary part. The transfer function $T(s)$ for any filter may be written as the product of poles and zeros expressed in factored form. Just as analog filters can be characterized by the locations of their poles and zeros, digital filters can be designed using these locations. The behavior of the digital version is similar to that of the analog counterpart so long as the input frequencies are reasonably below the Nyquist limit.

A resonant filter is realized by a complex-conjugate pole pair. One pole is $(x + iy)$; the second pole is $(x - iy)$. The following relationships hold for these poles:

$$f_o = \frac{y}{2\pi} = \frac{\cos^{-1}[B_1/2(-B_2)^{1/2}]}{2\pi T} = \text{resonant freq. of pole}$$

$$Q = \frac{y}{2x} = \frac{-2\pi f_o T}{\ln(-B_2)} = \text{sharpness of pole}$$

Hence, starting with the desired resonant frequency, first compute the imaginary part of the pole location using $y = 2\pi f_o$. Next, choose the Q desired for the filter and solve for the real part of the pole location using $x = y/2Q$. Given the pole locations, constants B_1 and B_2 are computed:

$$B_1 = 2[\exp(-xT)]\cos(yT)$$
$$B_2 = -\exp(-2T)$$

where T is the sampling period of the filter. Note that B_2 is negative, as mentioned. Also, observe that the constant x (the real part of the poles) is similar to the constant $a = 1/RC$ of previous sections. The gain constant G may be computed from:

$$\text{dc gain} = \frac{G}{1 - B_1 - B_2}$$

which then leaves all parameters of the filter determined.

Suppose that a filter with a resonant frequency of 50 Hz is desired and the sampling rate is to be 1 kHz. We calculate a value of 314.159 for y. The filter Q is chosen to be 50, which provides a value of 3.1459 for x. The values of 1.896 and -0.993739 are calculated for B_1 and B_2, respectively. Choosing $G = 1$ arbitrarily gives a dc gain of approximately 10 for this filter.

REFERENCES

1. Nyquist, H.: "Certain Topics in Telegraph Transmission Theory," *Trans. AIEE*, vol. 47, April 1928, pp. 617–644.
2. Antoniou, A.: *Digital Filters: Analysis and Design*, McGraw-Hill, New York, 1979, pp. 309–348.
3. Pogge, R. D.: "Simulate Analog Circuits with Digital Filtering Circuits," *EDN*, Oct. 5, 1976, p. 93.
4. Grappel, R. D.: "A Simple Digital Filter," *BYTE*, vol. 3, no. 2, February 1978, pp. 168–171.
5. Leon, B. J., and S. C. Bass: "Designers Guide to Digital Filters," *EDN*, Jan 20, 1974, pp. 30–75.
6. Mick, J. R.: "Basic Digital Filter Theory," *Schottky and Low Power Schottky Data Book*, Advanced Micro Devices, Sunnyvale, Calif., 1976, pp. 5.3–5.11.
7. Ham, P. A. L.: "Simple Digital Filters," *Wireless World*, July 1979, p. 54.
8. Hall, T.: "This Circuit Multiplies," *BYTE*, vol. 2 no. 7, July 1977, pp. 36–39.
9. Hoff, M. E., and M. Townsend: "Single-Chip N-MOS Microcomputer Processes Signals in Real Time," *Electronics*, Mar. 1, 1979, pp. 105–110.
10. Holm, R. E.: Implement Complex Analog Filters with a Real-Time Signal Processor," *EDN*, Nov. 20, 1979, pp. 171–180.
11. Karwoski, R. J.: "Implement Digital Filters Efficiently with a Specially Configured Computer," *Electronic Design*, Sept. 1, 1979, p. 110.
12. Blasco, R. W.: "V-MOS Chip Joins Microprocessor to Handle Signals in Real Time," *Electronics*, Aug. 30, 1979, pp. 131–138.

CHAPTER TWELVE

Parallel and Serial Microprocessor Data Interfaces

David F. Stout

Dataface, Inc.,
Santa Clara, California

DATA TRANSFER OVERVIEW

Microprocessors transfer data to/from other devices in the system using parallel bidirectional lines. Microcomputer chips have this same capability, but some microcomputers also transfer serial data, in which case separate pins are used for input and output. Other specialized microcomputers also have separate analog input and output lines. Analog data transfer devices are discussed in several other chapters in this handbook; this chapter concentrates on digital data interfaces.[1]

12.1 The Buffer-Gate Array

At least six types of buffer gates are used in parallel-bus interfaces. Figure 1 shows the logic symbols for six of the common buffer gates available, with four, six, or eight gates to a package. Data are transferred through the gate only when the enable line (EN, the line going

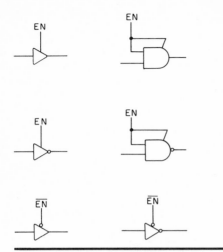

FIG. 1   *A few of the common inverting and noninverting buffer gates used in parallel microprocessor interfaces. The line on top of each gate is the tristate enable line. (From Ref. 1 with permission)*

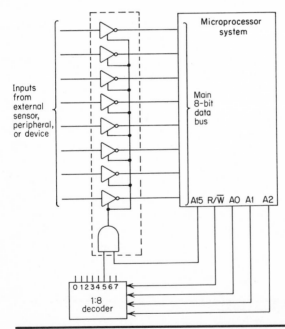

FIG. 2   *An array of eight buffer gates used to transfer an external byte of information onto the microprocessor data bus. This transfer takes place when the address bus contains 8005 (hex). (Adapted from Ref. 1 with permission)*

into the data side of the gate symbol) is enabled. If a LOW enable ($\overline{EN}$) is required, the small circle is used in the symbol.

The outputs of these gates are in the high-impedance state when the enable line is OFF. In this state each output is free to assume the logic level of other gates tied to it. Buffer gates of the types shown in Fig. 1 are typically used as inputs to the microprocessor data bus. All devices driving this data bus must have tristate capability so that only the addressed device is able to place data on the bus.

Figure 2 shows a representative application for buffer gates in a microprocessor system. A buffer-gate package typically has one or two enable inputs. If the device is designed with one enable input, it enables all gates in the package simultaneously. If two enable lines are brought out, at least three configurations are commercially available: (1) the two enable lines are ORed, (2) the two enable lines are ANDed, or (3) each enable line controls half the gates. If an OR (or NOR) or AND (or NAND) is used internally, it can be utilized to perform part of the address decoding. For example, in the circuit in Fig. 2 the AND decodes address 8005 (hex) by taking the AND of address bit 15 and the sixth output of a 1-of-8 decoder that is attached to the three lowest-order address bits. Because buffer gates are typically used as inputs to the microprocessor system, the line $R/\overline{W}$ must be HIGH if the gate array is to be enabled. This can be done in a number of ways. If the 1-of-8 decoder has an enable or strobe input, the $R/\overline{W}$ can be applied to that input.

Buffer gates can also be used as microprocessor data-bus outputs. However, the outputs will contain the correct information for only several microseconds (or less). In most applications the output information must be stored (or latched) so that the external circuitry has time to perform its function. This topic is discussed in Sec. 12.2, *Latch — D Flip-Flop.*

Buffer gates are also useful for converting from one type of logic level to another. This is often required when converting from CMOS to transistor-transistor logic (TTL) because most CMOS output circuits handle only one or two low-power TTL inputs. These same buffers are also useful for interfacing two systems that operate at different V_{CC} levels. Typical devices in this class are the 74C901 inverting TTL buffer and the 74C902 noninverting buffer.

12.2   Latch — D Flip-Flop

Latches and D flip-flops are widely used as parallel-output ports for microcomputer systems. These devices are readily available, with four, six, or eight to a package. Latches differ from D flip-flops in one minor respect. A latch has a $\overline{\text{LATCH ENABLE}}$ input. When this terminal is HIGH, the latch outputs follow the D inputs. When $\overline{\text{LATCH ENABLE}}$ goes LOW, the data on the D inputs, which satisfy setup and hold-time requirements, is retained on the outputs until $\overline{\text{LATCH ENABLE}}$ returns to the HIGH state. The D flip-flop, however, is an edge-triggered device; a clock input moves data from the D inputs to the corresponding output. D flip-flops sensitive to either positive or negative clock edges are available.

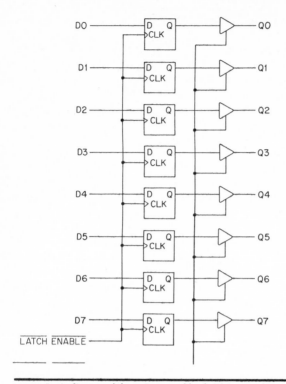

FIG. 3   *Logic diagram of the 74C373 octal latch. The output lines are active when the $\overline{OUTPUT\ ENABLE}$ line is HIGH. Data are transferred from each D input to each Q output when the $\overline{LATCH\ ENABLE}$ line goes HIGH. The outputs become latched when $\overline{LATCH\ ENABLE}$ returns to the LOW state. (Adapted from Ref. 1 with permission)*

Figure 3 is the logic diagram for the 74C373 octal latch. The logic diagram for the 74C374 octal D flip-flop is identical, except that the $\overline{LATCH\ ENABLE}$ is called the clock input. The $\overline{LATCH\ ENABLE}$ is normally maintained in the LOW state. Whenever data stored in the eight latches are to be updated, the $\overline{LATCH\ ENABLE}$ line momentarily receives a positive pulse, and the data inputs are latched over to the outputs. The $\overline{LATCH\ ENABLE}$ signal is usually derived from an address decoder that uses some of the address lines, the $R/\overline{W}$ line, and a clock signal. The address decoder sometimes requires three to five equivalent gates in series to handle all the needed inputs. The time delays of all these gates must be carefully evaluated to make sure the $\overline{LATCH\ ENABLE}$ signal arrives slightly after the D inputs have stabilized but not after the D inputs are changing to something else.

12.3   Parallel Peripheral Interface (PPI)

This class of device is also known as the peripheral interface adapter (PIA), programmable peripheral interface (PPI), or universal peripheral interface.

Every microcomputer chip set has programmable large-scale integrated (LSI) devices available for parallel interfacing to the outside world. Although each manufacturer has a slightly different way of implementing a parallel interface, one basic characteristic is common to all: Data are transported in or out of the microcomputer system on a parallel bus whenever the correct address appears on the chip. A R/$\overline{W}$ line is also required to inform the device which way data are flowing. Most of these devices can perform some of the address decoding so that external gates are kept to a minimum.

A Typical Peripheral Interface Device   The 6820 PIA is a representative parallel input-output (I/O) device made by several companies. As shown in Fig. 4, this chip has a 8-bit data-bus interface on the microcomputer side and two bidirectional 8-bit ports on the peripheral side. There are also four control-interrupt lines on the peripheral side; two lines are bidirectional, and two are inputs to the PIA.

Note from Fig. 4 that each of the two peripheral data buses has a group of supporting logic. Each side has a data-direction register that controls the direction of data flow (to or from the microprocessor). Each side has a control register that sets up the mode of operation for that bus. Each side has an interrupt input and a bidirectional control line. Finally, each side has an output register (a set of latches) that temporarily stores the bus content until changed by a new command.

Before the PIA can be used, control registers CRA and CRB must be programmed so that the correct mode of operation is set up. The data-direction registers are next programmed, to fix the direction of data flow. The PIA is then ready for use.

The two input lines CA1 and CB1 are used primarily as interrupt inputs. They affect the status of PIA interrupt flags in the two control registers and the PIA interrupts $\overline{IRQA}$ and $\overline{IRQB}$. These flags and interrupts can each be programmed to respond to CA1 and CB1 inputs in four different ways, as shown in Table 1. Each input can be made positive- or negative-edge-sensitive according to the status of 2 control bits. In two of the four modes, the $\overline{IRQ}$ output lines are not affected; in the other two modes, both interrupt flags and $\overline{IRQ}$ output lines are active.

The other two control lines, CA2 and CB2, can be made to perform exactly like CA1 and CB1 if CRA5 (or CRB5) is in the LOW state. Table 2 shows the modes of operation for these two lines if they are used as inputs.

Control lines CA2 and CB2 can also be used as outputs if CRA5 (or CRB5) is HIGH. However, in this case CA2 and CB2 operate quite differently, as shown in Tables 3 and 4.

Section A peripheral bus   Each peripheral data line can be independently programmed to act as an input or output. This programming is performed by writing a 1 into the corresponding data-direction-register bit for those lines that are to be outputs. A LOW state in a data-direction-register bit makes the corresponding A line an input. If the data-direction register contains all 0s, then during a microprocessor-read-peripheral-data instruction, the data on each A peripheral line appears directly on the corresponding microprocessor

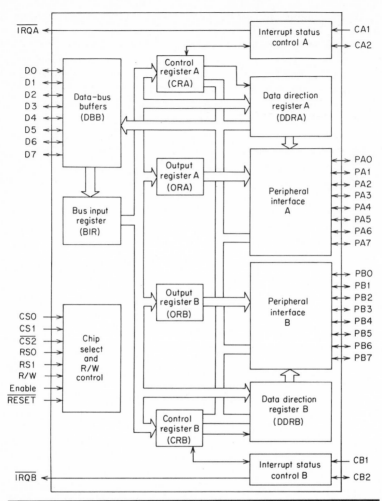

FIG. 4   *A block diagram of the 6820 peripheral interface adapter (PIA). This chip is made by several companies which manufacture the 6800 microprocessor chip set (Motorola, Inc., American Microsystems, Inc., and others). (Adapted from Ref. 1 with permission)*

data line. Likewise, in the write mode a microprocessor write into the PIA causes an immediate transfer of the data bus to the A peripheral bus.

   Section B peripheral bus   The B peripheral data lines perform similarly to those on the A side, except that as inputs, the B peripheral lines do not source current as a TTL device. However, they have a high input impedance. Also, as outputs, the B lines can source up to 1 mA for directly driving the base of a power transistor. A standard TTL output typically sources only 0.1 mA.

TABLE 1   Four Modes of Operation for Control Inputs CA1 and CB1

Control-register inputs		Input CA1 (CB1)	Interrupt flag CRA7 (CRB7)	Interrupt to microprocessor $\overline{\text{IRQA}}$ ($\overline{\text{IRQB}}$)
CRA1 (CRB1)	CRA0 (CRB0)			
0	0	↓	Set HIGH on ↓ of CA1 (CB1)	Always HIGH
0	1	↓	Set HIGH on ↓ of CA1 (CB1)	Goes LOW when CRA7 (CRB7) goes HIGH
1	0	↑	Set HIGH on ↑ of CA1 (CB1)	Always HIGH
1	1	↑	Set HIGH on ↑ of CA1 (CB1)	Goes LOW when CRA7 (CRB7) goes HIGH

TABLE 2   Four Modes of Operation for CA2 and CB2 when Used as Inputs*

Control-register inputs		Input CA2 (CB2)	Interrupt flag CRA6 (CRB6)	Interrupt to microprocessor $\overline{\text{IRQA}}$, ($\overline{\text{IRQB}}$)
CRA4 (CRB4)	CRA3 (CRB3)			
0	0	↓	Set HIGH on ↓ of CA2 (CB2)	Always HIGH
0	1	↓	Set HIGH on ↓ of CA2 (CB2)	Goes LOW when CRA6 (CRB6) goes HIGH
1	0	↑	Set HIGH on ↑ of CA2 (CB2)	Always HIGH
1	1	↑	Set HIGH on ↑ of CA2 (CB2)	Goes LOW when CRA6 (CRB6) goes HIGH

*CRA5 (or CRB5) must be LOW.

TABLE 3   Four Modes of Operation for CA2 when Used as an Output*

Control-register inputs		Conditions needed to clear CA2	Conditions needed to set CA2
CRA4	CRA3		
0	0	LOW on ↓ of enable after a microprocessor read of PIA side A data	HIGH on ↑ or ↓ transition of CA1
0	1	Low after a microprocessor read of PIA side A	HIGH on ↓ transition of enable
1	0	LOW on ↓ of CRA3 as a result of a write into control register A	LOW if CRA3 is LOW
1	1	HIGH if CRA3 is HIGH	HIGH on ↑ of CRA3 as a result of a write into control register A

*CRA5 must be HIGH.

Microprocessor Addressing of the PIA   The 6820 has eight control inputs from the microprocessor system. Three of these lines, CS0, CS1, and $\overline{CS2}$, perform part of the address decoding for the PIA. They replace two external-address decoding gates. The PIA cannot be accessed (read or write) unless CS0 = CS1 = 1 and $\overline{CS2}$ = 0 simultaneously.

The R/$\overline{W}$ line must be HIGH whenever the PIA is being read and LOW during a write operation. The $\overline{RESET}$ line must be maintained in the HIGH state for normal operation; if it is momentarily brought LOW, all internal PIA registers are cleared. The enable line is normally one of the microprocessor system clock lines. The enable line must go LOW after the address and R/$\overline{W}$ lines have stabilized. This guarantees that a correct address will be clocked into the PIA.

The control lines RS0 and RS1 access the various registers in the PIA. These lines, in conjunction with bits previously stored in the control registers, allow the microprocessor to select one of six PIA registers. Table 5 indicates the programming requirements for these registers.

Whenever RS1 = **0** and RS0 = **1**, we select control register A. The control-register bits have no effect in this selection process because it would be illogical for a bit in a register to address itself. Likewise, unconditional access to control register B is obtained by letting RS1 = RS0 = **1**.

Table 6 is the complete format for the two control registers; the details of each group of bits are in Tables 1 to 5.

PIA programming example   Assume we are using the A peripheral bus to send or receive data for a machine. The machine also requires the CA2 control signal to start some operation. The input control signal CA1 alerts the microprocessor that the operation is complete. Figure 5 is a schematic of this 10-wire PIA-machine interface.

TABLE 4 Four Modes of Operation for CB2 when Used as an Output*

Control-register inputs		Conditions needed to clear CB2	Conditions needed to set CB2
CRB4	CRB3		
0	0	LOW on ↑ of enable after a microprocessor write into PIA B data register	HIGH when interrupt flag CRB7 is set by active transition of CB1 input
0	1	LOW on ↑ of enable after a microprocessor write into PIA B data register	HIGH on ↑ of enable
1	0	Follows CRB3	Follows CRB3
1	1	Follows CRB3	Follows CRB3

*CRB5 must be HIGH.

TABLE 5 Addressing the Six PIA Registers

RS1	RS0	Control-register bit*		Internal register selected
		CRA2	CRB2	
0	0	1	X	Peripheral register A
0	0	0	X	Data direction register A
0	1	X	X	Control register A
1	0	X	1	Peripheral register B
1	0	X	0	Data direction register B
1	1	X	X	Control register B

*X = don't-care state.

TABLE 6 Control-Word Format

	Bit number					
	7	6	5 4 3	2	1	0
CRA	IRQA1	IRQA2	CA2 control	DDRA access	CA1 control	
CRB	IRQB1	IRQB2	CB2 control	DDRA access	CB1 control	

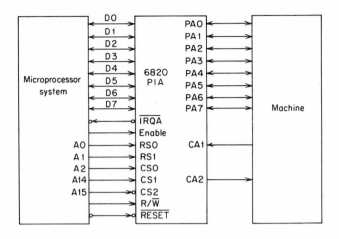

PIA Register	Address (HEX)
Data direction A and peripheral A	4004
Control A	4005
Data direction B and peripheral B	4006
Control B	4007

FIG. 5   *A method by which a 6820 PIA is used to control a machine while receiving directions from the 6800 microprocessor. (From Ref. 1 with permission)*

After a system reset has occurred, several setup instructions are required before the PIA can begin the normal data flow. The following sequence is a typical setup procedure for this type of PIA:

1. System $\overline{\text{RESET}}$ gets LOW momentarily, setting all PIA registers to zero.
2. The microprocessor writes a 00111000 into the A control register (hex address 4005). This command makes the CA2 output HIGH (its inactive state), disables the CA1 input, and sets CRA2 equal to zero so that data-direction register A can next be addressed.
3. The microprocessor writes a 11111111 into the A data-direction register (hex address 4004 with CRA2 cleared). These 1s in the data-direction register cause the contents of the peripheral register to be outputs.
4. Sending data from the microprocessor through the PIA to the machine requires that we again access the control register and change CRA2 to the HIGH state. The next data written into hex 4004 will then be directly transferred to the peripheral data bus.
5. Suppose we want to activate CA2 at this point to make the machine process the 8-bit word just sent to it. Because CA2 is HIGH in the standby state, we need a command to make it go LOW momentarily. This is performed by writing a **0** into CRA3.

6. At the same time as the above operation, we also write a **1** into CRA0. This sets up control input CA1 so that it looks for a negative transition.

7. When the machine sends over a negative transition on CA1, the flag bit in CRA7 is set to the HIGH state, and the PIA $\overline{\text{IRQA}}$ (interrupt) output goes LOW.

8. The $\overline{\text{IRQA}}$ line from the PIA is usually wire-oRed with other $\overline{\text{IRQ}}$ lines. Therefore, the microprocessor must check the status of all devices having an $\overline{\text{IRQ}}$ output. This PIA is checked by performing a read operation on control register A. The microprocessor will observe that CRA7 is HIGH. (This read operation resets CRA7 to the LOW state and sets $\overline{\text{IRQA}}$ back to the HIGH state.)

9 Because the microprocessor has found out that CA1 is LOW, it must read the peripheral data bus from the machine. First, CRA2 must be changed to a **0** so the data-direction register can be accessed. Next, write 00000000 into the data-direction register, to cause the peripheral data bus to change into inputs.

10. Next, change CRA2 to the HIGH state so that the peripheral data register can be accessed. A read operation on that register then transfers the 8-bit word from the machine to the microprocessor.

12.4   Serial Data Interfaces

Data are most economically transferred over long distances in a serial format. One would never expect to perform a parallel transfer of an 8-bit microcomputer data bus to a peripheral device 200 mi (320 km) away because doing so would require eight telephone lines or eight separate radio frequencies operating simultaneously. Even for peripheral devices only a few feet from the computer, serial communication is quite common. The most widely used microcircuit for interfacing the parallel microcomputer data bus to a serial device is called the *universal asynchronous receiver-transmitter* (UART). The transmitter section of this device performs a parallel-to-serial conversion; the receiver section does the reverse.

Several typical serial interfaces with microcomputers are video displays, tape recorders, telephone lines, and radio links. Peripheral devices requiring high data-transmission rates are usually interfaced with parallel devices.

The UART is an asynchronous device because no clock reference is separately transmitted to synchronize the transmitter to the receiver. At the receiver end, the required clock reference is extracted from the single data line. The clock at both ends typically operates at 16 times the data rate. Data rate is measured in bauds (Bd), which is the number of signal changes per second. A low-speed Teletype operates at 110 Bd; thus, the internal clock in the UART for a Teletype must operate at $16 \times 110 = 1760$ Hz.[2]

If synchronous serial communication with a computer is required, the universal synchronous receiver-transmitter (USRT) may be used.[3] This chip contains all the logic necessary to interface a word-parallel system, such as a microcomputer, with a bit-serial synchronous communication network.

Many LSI microcircuits are available that handle either synchronous or asynchronous serial communications. This class of device is called the universal synchronous-asynchronous receiver-transmitter (USART).

As shown in Fig. 6*a*, an asynchronous serial data word is organized as follows:

1. The serial line is normally HIGH between words. This is called a *mark*, and a LOW state is called a *space*.
2. A start bit is always LOW.
3. The data bits (5 to 8 in number) follow the start bit.
4. The parity bit (odd or even) is computed from the number of data bits used.
5. Either 1 or 2 stop bits (HIGH level) are utilized.

In many asynchronous applications there are long periods of time between data words. During this interval the serial line remains in the HIGH state while the receiver is watching for a transition to a LOW state. When this transition occurs, the receiver initiates a checkout procedure to see if the transition is really data or just a noise spike. If real data are detected, the receiver begins to accept the data word.

Figure 6*b* shows the format for a serial bit stream using synchronous communication. The sync characters are transmitted only between blocks of data (i.e., during idle periods). At the end of every sync word, the receiver readies itself for another block of data. Some devices allow for the use of two sync words.

If the serial communication link is purely digital, the USART merely needs buffering and/or level translation at the communication-line-computer interface. However, most serial communication is done through analog lines. This requires a system called a modulator-demodulator (modem) to convert digital levels to some type of analog levels. A frequency shift keying (FSK) circuit is most commonly used; this is an FM circuit in which one frequency represents

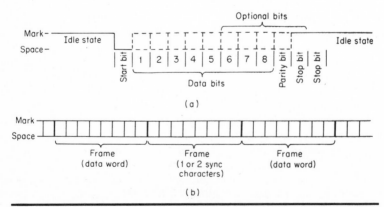

FIG. 6   (a) *Serial format of each word used in asynchronous communication devices*; (b) *format for synchronous words. (From Ref. 1 with permission)*

a logical HIGH and another discrete frequency represents a logical LOW. Phase or amplitude modulation can also be utilized for this serial analog interface. However, phase shift keying (PSK) is more complex and expensive than FSK, and amplitude modulation is too susceptible to noise degradation.

12.5 Universal Asynchronous Receiver-Transmitter

Alternate names for such a device are UART, USART, parallel-serial-parallel converter, serial communications interface, programmable communication interface, and asynchronous-communications interface adapter (ACIA).

It is helpful to visualize the UART as two separate systems on a chip: the receiver and transmitter systems. Figures 7 and 8 show these two parts of a typical UART in abbreviated block-diagram form. In a real chip the X16 clock input, the five control lines, and the 8-bit data bus are common to the receiver and transmitter. We show them separately for clarity. In most UARTs the five control lines time-share the data-bus inputs.

Referring to Fig. 7, note that the five control inputs are first stored in latches when the mode-control line is triggered. The input data are then applied to

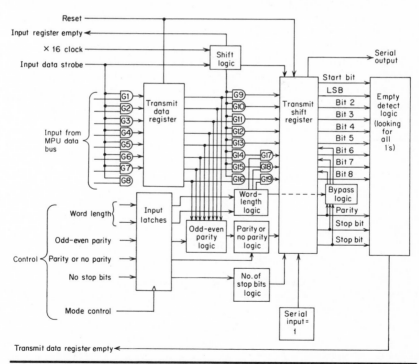

FIG. 7 *Typical logical arrangement for the transmitter section of a UART. (Adapted from Ref. 1 with permission)*

the parallel data bus. The input-data strobe rises to gate the parallel word into the transmit-data register (eight D flip-flops). A number of other things occur while the input-data strobe is HIGH:

1. The word-length logic uses its 2 input bits to decide whether the word length is 5, 6, 7, or 8 bits. The logic utilizes gates G17 to G19 to transfer variable-length words from the transmit-data register to the transmit-shift register. Bypass logic must also be programmed so that the parity and stop bits bypass data bit 8 if a 7-bit word is chosen, bypass data bits 7 and 8 if a 6-bit word is chosen, or bypass data bits 6 to 8 if a 5-bit word is chosen.
2. The parity/no-parity logic is activated. This logic also has bypass circuitry so that the stop bits will be routed around the register used for parity if no parity is chosen. The odd-even parity logic computes a value for the parity bit using the transmit data register output lines. The word-length logic must be a factor because the parity calculations depend upon the number of bits examined.
3. Injecting a HIGH state in appropriate sections of the transmit-shift register selects either 1 or 2 stop bits.

When the input-data strobe falls, the shift logic begins to serially transmit bits out of the transmit-shift register. Sixteen cycles of the X16 clock are required for each bit shifted out of the serial output terminal. At the bottom of the shift register, HIGH bits are inserted as the word is shifted out. When the empty-detect logic determines that the shift register is completely filled with **1s**, a transmit-data-register-empty signal is activated. This signal is used by the device controlling the UART to generate the next data word.

The input data bus is used for a third function in most UART devices. By appropriate addressing, the eight data lines can read the status of many internal circuits to determine if the UART is in the proper mode. For example, the 8 status bits of the 6850 UART contain the following information:

Bit 0: Receiver data register full (see Fig. 8)
Bit 1: Transmit data register empty (see Fig. 7)
Bit 2: Data carrier detect (used in conjunction with a modem)
Bit 3: Clear to send (used with a modem)
Bit 4: Framing error (stop bit missing in a received data word)
Bit 5: Receiver overrun (one or more receiver characters lost)
Bit 6: Parity error
Bit 7: Interrupt request (can be used to determine that a received character is ready to be sent to the CPU)

Figure 8 is an abbreviated block diagram of the receiver portion of a UART. This circuit is the inverse of the transmitter circuit; it receives serial data words and converts them into parallel. Its mode of operation is set up using four of five control inputs. Word length is controlled by inserting the serial input data into the shift register at selectable points using gates G1 to G4. The parity circuits check the serial data as they pass by and activate status-register bit 6 if an error is detected. No input is needed in the receiver for the 1- or 2-stop-bit mode control used in the transmitter.

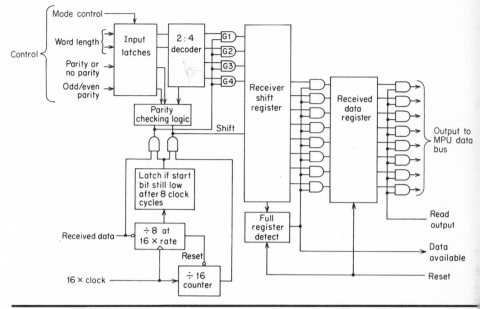

FIG. 8   A simplified block diagram of the receiver portion of a UART. (Adapted from Ref. 1 with permission)

Received data first pass through circuitry that is looking for the negative edge of the start bit. This negative edge gates the X16 clock in a ÷8 counter. If the start bit is still LOW after a count of 8, it has been determined that a valid start bit is present. Because the X16 clock runs at 16 times the bit rate, eight counts is the middle of the start bit. A latch is then set that resets a ÷16 counter. Each time this counter times out (16 cycles of the X16 clock), we will be centered on a new data bit. At each of the bit center locations, a shift pulse is generated that clocks the present value of the received data into the shift register. This process therefore samples the received serial data at the middle of each bit period where the bit has stabilized.

When the start bit arrives at the full-register detector, the full-register flip-flop is set. This activates the data-available status line, which can be polled by the CPU. In some chips an interrupt is generated so that the CPU will know the UART needs attention.

12.6 UART *Application: A Cassette Modem*

The low-priced audio cassette recorder is one of the most popular storage mediums for small microprocessor systems. However, before this storage medium could become widely accepted, a standard recording method had to be formulated. This was done in November 1975 at a symposium in Kansas City, Missouri. As one might expect, the standard has been nicknamed the Kansas City standard (KCS or KCS format).[4]

A KCS circuit can be designed to interface with any of the available single-chip UARTs. The UART is a digital device; i.e., both the parallel and serial interfaces handle digital data. The KCS specifies how the UART serial input-output must be converted from or to an analog format, i.e., sine waves of several frequencies. Low-cost cassette recorders do a poor job of recording and reproducing digital data. The KCS works on a principle of frequency modulation, with only two frequencies used: 1200 and 2400 Hz. This modulation method, called *frequency shift keying* (FSK), allows serial data to be transmitted at speeds to 300 Bd. Tape-speed variations up to ± 25 percent are possible with some of the better KCS implementations. Here is the basic KCS:

1. A mark (logic HIGH) bit consists of 8 cycles at a 2400-Hz frequency.
2. A space (logic LOW) bit consists of 4 cycles at a 1200-Hz frequency.
3. Each recorded character consists of a start bit (logic LOW), 8 data bits, and 2 or more stop bits (logic HIGH).
4. The interval between characters is unspecified.
5. The 8 data bits are organized as least significant bit first, most significant bit last, and a parity bit (optional). The total number of data bits, including parity, cannot exceed 8.
6. If fewer than 8 data bits are used, the unused bit locations are left in the HIGH state (2400 Hz).
7. Data are organized in blocks of arbitrary length, preceded by at least 5 s of marks (2400 Hz).
8. To minimize errors from splices and wrinkles at the start of the tape, the beginning of the first block of data occurs at least 30 s after the beginning of a clear leader.
9. The KCS is designed around the use of a X16 clock for both transmit and receive. The X16 clock is reconstructed from the received data using frequency-multiplication techniques (16 × 1200 Hz = 19,200 Hz is the standard X16 clock used).
10. Transitions from mark to space and vice versa occur at the zero crossover point in the serial waveform. This eliminates excessive harmonic generation, which could be a source of noise.

There is a valid reason for recording 8 cycles of 2400 Hz for a mark and 4 cycles of 1200 Hz for a space: This technique allows the receiver at playback to determine how fast the tape is going. If the tape is played back 10 percent slow, the 1200 Hz becomes 1080 Hz and the 2400 Hz becomes 2160 Hz. However, the receiver multiplies 1080 by 16, to obtain 17,280 Hz, which is used as the receiver X16 clock and is sent to the UART. The receiver system therefore slows down all processes by 10 percent and synchronizes to the slower tape speed.

The Receiver Circuit Figure 9 is a typical receiver for a cassette interface modem. Figure 10 shows waveforms at various points in the circuit. The input to the circuit is taken from the "ear" output of the recorder. The signal is first filtered to remove noise outside the 1200- to 2400-Hz frequency range. Next, a level detector, or slicer, changes the sine-wave inputs into a rectangular

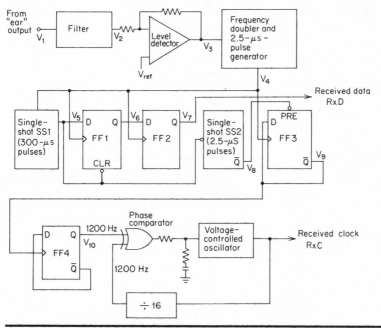

FIG. 9   The receiver portion of a modem designed to interface a low-cost audio cassette recorder to a UART and a microprocessor. (From Ref. 1 with permission)

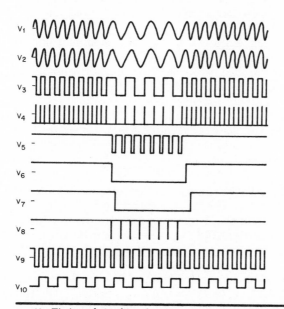

FIG. 10   Timing relationships of various waveforms in Fig. 9. (From Ref. 1 with permission)

waveform v_3 so that it can be digitally processed. This circuit uses positive feedback to produce steep edges on the rectangular waveform. The next block produces a short positive pulse v_4 for each transition (positive or negative) of the rectangular signal. These pulses are spaced at 208 μs when the mark (2400-Hz) bit is received and at 416 μs when a space (1200-Hz) bit is received. There will be 16 pulses during the mark and 8 pulses during a space. These short pulses trigger single-shot SS1, which generates relatively long pulse widths v_5 of approximately 300 μs. SS1 is a retriggerable single-shot; i.e., if it is retriggered while an output pulse is present, the new pulse is tacked onto the first pulse, with no gap between. Therefore, if mark pulses occur at 208-μs intervals and the single-shot pulse width is 300 μs, the output continuously remains HIGH. If a space occurs (416 μs), the single-shot times out, causing the waveform to go LOW for 116 μs. Whenever the output of SS1 goes LOW, it clears FF1, causing its output v_6 to also go LOW. If a mark is present, the output of FF1 remains in the HIGH state. We therefore have recovered digital data at the output of FF1. However, this data has short spaces and long marks. FF2 places symmetry back into the recovered data v_7 by using trigger pulses from the frequency doubler.

Single-shot SS2 generates a short negative pulse $\overline{v_8}$ each time v_5 has a negative transition. Each pulse presets FF3 so that its $\overline{Q}$ output v_9 goes LOW. The next pulse from the frequency doubler v_4 toggles FF3. A study of v_4 and v_8 in Fig. 10 shows that v_9 is at 2400 Hz when v_4 is 4800 Hz. However, when v_4 is at 2400 Hz, the output v_9 is still at 2400 Hz because v_8 keeps presetting FF3 between the slower-rate pulses. The output v_9 is therefore always 2400 Hz, although the symmetry is poor in the space period. FF4 is a simple toggle flip-flop that places symmetry in the waveform and changes the frequency to 1200 Hz.

The last few blocks in Fig. 9 are a X16 frequency multiplier utilizing a phase-locked loop (PLL) chip and a $\div$16 counter. Essentially, this frequency multiplier has a voltage-controlled oscillator (VCO) tuned to approximately 19,200 Hz. This output goes to the clock input of the UART. The same output is also divided down by a four-stage counter so it becomes 1200 Hz. A phase comparator compares this frequency with the 1200 Hz from FF4. If there is any difference in frequency or phase between these inputs, a correction voltage is sent over to the VCO. This voltage levels out at a voltage that provides a precise phase lock of the two inputs.

The Transmitter Circuit   The transmitter portion of a cassette interface modem is very simple compared with the receiver. A typical circuit is shown in Fig. 11a. All this circuit must do is generate 2400 Hz when a HIGH (or mark) state is received from the UART and generate 1200 Hz when a LOW (or space) is received. The various waveforms for the circuit are shown in Fig. 11b.

A 4800-Hz clock is coupled to the clock input of the two flip-flops in the circuit. When the UART data output TxD is LOW, v_2 is HIGH. A HIGH level on the JK inputs of FF1 causes it to divide by 2. Likewise, FF2 divides again

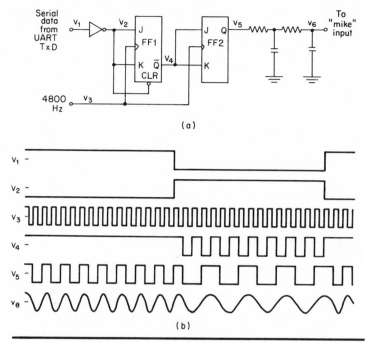

FIG. 11 *A typical modem transmitter for a cassette interface:* (a) *the circuit low-pass filters the digital output from a flip-flop, and* (b) *waveforms at various points in the circuit.* (*From Ref. 1 with permission*)

by 2, and the output v_5 is at 1200 Hz. A low-pass filter clips off the square corners and makes a quasi sine wave at v_6.

When v_1 is HIGH, v_2 is LOW, causing FF1 to remain in the reset state. This keeps the JK inputs of FF2 HIGH, so that it divides the 4800-Hz clock by 2. The resulting 2400-Hz square wave is filtered and passed onto the cassette recorder mike input. Because changes from one output frequency to the other occur during zero crossover, high-order harmonics should not be prevalent.

12.7 Universal Synchronous Receiver-Transmitter

Such a device is also known as a USRT, USART,[5] programmable communication interface (PCI), and synchronous serial data adapter (SSDA).

Such devices provide a bidirectional serial interface for synchronous transfer of data. Bidirectional does not mean that the serial communication takes place on one wire; rather, one chip handles both serial directions on separate pins simultaneously. This is called the full-duplex mode. Figure 12 is a block diagram of a Motorola 6852 SSDA, which is a second-generation USRT. The 6852 is designed to operate with an 8-bit microprocessor data bus. It can be

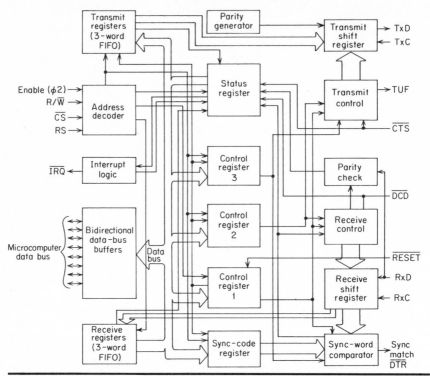

FIG. 12   *Block diagram of the Motorola synchronous serial data adapter (SSDA). This is a second-generation USRT chip (Motorola, Inc.). (From Ref. 1 with permission)*

programmed to handle numerous data formats by storing command information in three internal control registers. The sync code is also stored during the preliminary programming of the 6852. Up to three words of transmitted data can be stored in a first-in first-out (FIFO) set of registers. Received data can likewise be collected in three FIFO registers. The state of eight internal registers is always available by reading the status register. Thus we have eight write-only registers and four read-only registers in the synchronous serial interface chip.

Referring to Fig. 12, observe that the $\overline{\text{RESET}}$ line interfaces only with control register 1. When this line goes LOW, both the transmitter and receiver sections are latched into a reset condition. Also, peripheral control bits PC1 and PC2 are cleared, the error-interrupt enable (EIE) is cleared, and the transmit-data-register available (TDRA) is cleared. All these control bits can later be set by software control using the three control registers.

Initialization   The SSDA requires several programming steps before it can be used for transmitting or receiving. The first step is to load control word **1** (C1) into the SSDA. Table 7 shows that we only require RS = **0** and R/$\overline{\text{W}}$ =

0 to perform this command. The programming of the bits in C1 depends upon the application. For example, if we are initially programming the SSDA (after a $\overline{\text{RESET}}$) for full-duplex operation, C1 would probably be 00000000. This is done with a CLEAR command for the address of C1. Referring to Table 7, observe that this command does the following:

Bit 0:   Maintains receiver at inhibited state until later in initialization sequence.

Bit 1:   Maintains transmitter at inhibited state.

Bit 2:   Sync stripping not active (this will be done later).

Bit 3:   Enables synchronization when bit 2 is later enabled.

Bit 4:   Transmitter-interrupt-status bit and $\overline{\text{IRQ}}$ placed in standby state.

Bit 5:   Receiver-interrupt-status bit and $\overline{\text{IRQ}}$ placed in standby state.

Bits 6 and 7: Code of 00 allows the addressing of control register 2 (C2) on the next SSDA command.

The second step in the initialization of the SSDA is a write operation into C2. To address this register, we need RS = **1** and R/$\overline{\text{W}}$ = **0** plus the AC1, AC2 bits previously left in C1. Again assuming full-duplex operation, we write 10111101 into C2. This instruction sets up the SSDA as follows:

Bit 0:   Selects the sync match mode.

Bit 1:   Causes a 1-bit-wide pulse to appear at the SM/$\overline{\text{DTR}}$ terminal each time a sync match occurs.

Bit 2:   A HIGH level on this bit chooses the single-word transmitter-receiver FIFO mode. If this bit was LOW, 2 words could be moved into or from the two FIFOs.

Bits 3 to 5: These 3 bits choose the transmit or receive word length as shown in Table 8. Note that we selected 8 bits plus odd parity in this example.

Bit 6:   A LOW level causes the transmitter to send mark characters (HIGH logic level) automatically whenever data is not available for transmission from the transmit FIFO.

Bit 7:   If this bit is HIGH, the error-interrupt circuitry is enabled, allowing the $\overline{\text{IRQ}}$ status bit to go HIGH and the $\overline{\text{IRQ}}$ output to go LOW when any of the following occur:
1. Receiver overrun (more than 3 words trying to load receiver FIFO).
2. $\overline{\text{DCD}}$ goes HIGH.
3. Received-data parity error.
4. $\overline{\text{CTS}}$ goes HIGH.
5. Transmitter underflow (transmitter FIFO empty).

The third initialization step is to load control register 3 (C3). First write in another C1 command of 01000000. Bits 7 and 6 (AC2 and AC1) of C1 now allow us to address C3 (see Table 7). If we also make RS = **1** and R/$\overline{\text{W}}$ = **0**, the addressing is complete.

TABLE 7 SSDA Programming Model*

Register name and address				Register content							
RS	R/W̄	AC2	AC1	Bit 7	Bit 6	Bit 5	Bit 4	Bit 3	Bit 2	Bit 1	Bit 0
Control 1 (C1)				(AC2)	(AC1)	Receiver interrupt enable (RIE)	Transmit interrupt enable (TIE)	Clear receiver sync	Strip sync char.	Transmit reset (TxRs)	Receiver reset (RxRs)
0	0	X	X								
Control 2 (C2)				Error interrupt enable (EIE)	Transmit sync code if underflow (Tx sync)	Word-length select 3 (WS3)	Word-length select 2 (WS2)	Word-length select 1 (WS1)	1-byte-2-byte transfer (1B/2B)	Periph. cont. 2 (PC2)	Periph. cont. 1 (PC1)
0	0	0	0								
Control 3 (C3)								Clear transmit, underflow status (CTUF)	Clear C̄T̄S̄ status (CLR C̄T̄S̄)	1 or 2 sync char. control (1S/2S)	External-internal sync mode control (E/I sync)
1	0	0	1								
Status (S)				Interrupt request (IRQ)	Receiver parity error (PE)	Receiver overrun (Rx OV)	Transmit, underflow (TUF)	Clear to send (C̄T̄S̄)	Data-carrier detect (D̄C̄D̄)	Transmit-data register available (TDRA)	Receiver data available (RDA)
0	1	X	X								
Sync code				D7	D6	D5	D4	D3	D2	D1	D0
1	0	1	0								
Receive data FIFO				D7	D6	D5	D4	D3	D2	D1	D0
1	1	X	X								
Transmit data FIFO				D7	D6	D5	D4	D3	D2	D1	D0
1											

*X is a don't-care logic level.

TABLE 8   *Word-Length Selection in Control Word 2*

Bit 5 WS3	Bit 4 WS2	Bit 3 WS1	Word length
0	0	0	6 bits + even parity
0	0	1	6 bits + odd parity
0	1	0	7 bits
0	1	1	8 bits
1	0	0	7 bits + even parity
1	0	1	7 bits + odd parity
1	1	0	8 bits + even parity
1	1	1	8 bits + odd parity

The data-bus content written into C3 for our example is 00001110. This word does the following:

Bit 0:   A LOW selects the internal synchronization mode, whereby the sync character(s) begin a new block of data.

Bit 1:   A HIGH indicates that a single sync character is required to flag the start of a block of data.

Bit 2:   Writing a HIGH into this location clears the clear-to-send ($\overline{CTS}$) status bit and its associated interrupt. The USRT is then available for external transmitter control through the $\overline{CTS}$ input, if required.

Bit 3:   A HIGH written into bit 3 clears the transmit-underflow-status bit (TUF) and its associated interrupt. This readies the device for transmission applications that use the TUF bit.

Bits 4 to 7: Not used by the SSDA.

After all three control registers are programmed, the sync-code register can be loaded. First write 10000000 into control register 1 so that AC2 and AC1 will address the sync-code register. Now select RS = **1** and R/$\overline{W}$ = **0** to complete the addressing. Simultaneously with RS = **1** and R/$\overline{W}$ = **0**, the sync-code word is placed on the data bus to be written into the SSDA.

The last initialization step is to release the transmitter- and receiver-reset control bits so that both sections of the SSDA will be ready for operation. We now sequence through typical transmit and receive procedures.

Transmitter Operation   The next control register 1 command should include AC2 = AC1 = 1 to activate the transmit data FIFO. The word on the data bus will then be parallel-loaded into the 3-byte transmit FIFO. Enable ($\phi2$) pulses clock data into and through all three stages of the FIFO. The byte then transfers over to the transmit-shift register, where it is serially transmitted at the rate of the transmit clock. Data move from the last register of the FIFO to the transmit-shift register during the last half of the last bit of the previous character. This transfer is initiated by the transmitter clock, whereas movement of bytes in the FIFO is clocked by the enable ($\phi2$) pulses.

Data is transmitted least significant bit first. The parity bit is optionally attached after the most significant bit. If the shift register becomes empty and a new byte is not available in the FIFO, a transmit underflow occurs. This sets bit 4 (TUF) in the status register and lowers the $\overline{\text{IRQ}}$ output. This interrupt is seen by the microprocessor, which in turn reads the status register to determine the needs of the SSDA. If the microprocessor notes that the TUF bit is set, another byte is sent over to the SSDA on the 8-bit data bus. However, if the microprocessor chooses not to send over another byte, the transmitter begins shifting out marks (HIGH logic level) or sync characters, depending upon the state of C2 bit 6. The underflow condition is also indicated by a positive pulse approximately one Tx Clk wide on the TUF terminal, which coincides with the transfer of the last half of the last bit preceding each underflow character.

When transmitter underflow occurs and data are to be sent again, the TUF status bit should first be cleared; this is done with bit 3 of C3. Because we need AC2 = 0 and AC1 = 1 to program C3, C1 will probably need to be accessed first. The clear underflow command will also reset the $\overline{\text{IRQ}}$ output. AC2 must then be returned to the HIGH state so that the data bus will again have access to the transmit FIFO.

If the SSDA is to be automatically controlled externally by some device such as a modem, the $\overline{\text{CTS}}$ input can be used. The $\overline{\text{CTS}}$ output from the modem is connected directly to the SSDA $\overline{\text{CTS}}$ input. When this line is HIGH, the transmitter-shift register is inhibited and reset. The TDRA status bit is also inhibited if $\overline{\text{CTS}}$ is HIGH and the internal sync mode is selected. If external sync is being used, TDRA is unaffected by $\overline{\text{CTS}}$, to provide transmit FIFO status for preloading and operating the transmitter under control of the $\overline{\text{CTS}}$ input.

The transmit FIFO can be cleared by setting the transmitter-reset bit (TxRs); this also clears the TDRA status bit. After one $\phi2$ pulse has occurred, the transmit FIFO becomes available for new data.

Receiver Operation   Data and a synchronous clock are applied to the SSDA at the Rx Data and Rx Clk inputs. The data is a continuous stream of bits, with no means of identifying character boundaries within the data stream. Synchronization must therefore be achieved at the beginning of a block of characters; once it has been achieved, we assume it to be retained for all successive characters within the block. The one or two sync characters received before synchronization is complete are not transferred to the receiver FIFO.

Once synchronization has been achieved, subsequent characters are automatically transferred from the receiver-shift register into the receiver FIFO. The characters are clocked through the FIFO to the last empty location by $\phi2$ pulses. The receiver-data-available-status bit (RDA) indicates when data are available to be read from the last FIFO location (location 3) when operation is in the 1-byte transfer mode. If the 2-byte transfer mode is utilized, the RDA status bit indicates that data are available when the last two FIFO register locations are full. This data-available status also causes an interrupt request ($\overline{\text{IRQ}}$ goes low) if the receiver-interrupt-enable (RIE) bit is set. The microcomputer then reads the SSDA status register, which indicates that data are available to read in the last stage of the receiver FIFO. The IRQ and RDA status bits are reset by the FIFO read command. If two or more characters are resident in the receiver FIFO, a second $\phi 2$ pulse causes the FIFO to update, and the RDA and IRQ status bits again are set. A third $\phi 2$ pulse is required to clock the second word out of the FIFO.

Parity is automatically checked as data is received, and the parity-status condition is maintained with each character until the data is read from the receiver FIFO. Parity errors cause an $\overline{IRQ}$ output if the EIE has been set. Because the parity bit is not transferred to the data bus, it must be checked in the status register. Thus, in the 2-byte transfer mode the parity error must be checked before reading the second word. This parity error is stored in the FIFO along with the second word, and it activates the status register as it reaches the third position.

If the receiver FIFO is completely full with 3 words and the shift register transfers in another word, the overrun-status bit will be set. This also causes an interrupt output if the EIE has been set. The transfer of the overrunning character into the FIFO causes the previous character stored in position 1 to be lost. The overrun-status bit is cleared by reading the status register, followed by a read command of the receiver FIFO. Overrun cannot be cleared without providing an opportunity for detection of its occurrence in the status register.

A positive transition on the $\overline{DCD}$ input causes an interrupt output ($\overline{IRQ}$ goes LOW) if the EIE is set. This interrupt is cleared by reading the status register while $\overline{DCD}$ is HIGH, followed by a receiver FIFO Read command. The $\overline{DCD}$ status bit subsequently follows the state of the $\overline{DCD}$ input when it goes LOW.

REFERENCES

1. Stout, D. F., and M. Kaufman: *Handbook of Microcircuit Design and Application,* McGraw-Hill, New York, 1980, Chaps. 10 and 11.
2. Smith, R. L.: "Understanding the UART," *Popular Electronics,* June 1975, p. 43.
3. Etcheverry, F. W.: "Binary Serial Interfaces: Making the Digital Connection," *EDN,* Apr. 20, 1976, p. 40.
4. Peschke, M., and V. Peschke: "BYTE's Audio Cassette Standards Symposium," *BYTE,* No. 6, February 1976, p. 72.
5. Smith, L.: "USART: A Universal Microprocessor Interface for Serial Data Communications," *EDN,* Sept. 5, 1976, p. 81.

CHAPTER THIRTEEN

Keyboard Data Input Techniques

David F. Stout

Dataface, Inc.,
Santa Clara, California

OVERVIEW OF SCANNING TECHNIQUES

Many circuit techniques have been developed for scanning (sampling) switch arrays. The most familiar switch array is the standard typewriter alphanumeric keyboard. This type of array typically has 60 or more keys that must be rapidly scanned so the user is not aware of any time delay between a key depression and an appropriate response from the system. All switches must be periodically examined by the scanning circuit, either singly or in groups. The most common technique is to examine eight or ten of the switches simultaneously. To perform this group-examination scheme, the switches are arranged in an X-Y array if both terminals of each switch are available. If one terminal of each switch must be at ground or some given voltage, more hardware is required to perform the scan.[1]

In the following pages we look at three scanning techniques. Each method is unique, because of the constraints of the switch array used. The first method, using an X-Y switch array, is by far the most widely used. Many microcircuits have been designed using implementations of this basic technique.

13.1 X-Y *Matrix Switch Array*

The X-Y array scanning technique is a common method used by most alphanumeric keyboards.[2,3] As shown in Fig. 1, two buses are required. An output bus goes in the X direction; an input bus goes in the Y direction. The inset shows that a switch is placed at each intersection of an X line and a Y line. A number of microcircuits are available that implement this technique. However, we present the concept using a microprocessor because with a microprocessor the technique has much more flexibility, although it ties up most of its time for this one task.

Operation of this circuit is as follows. The microprocessor starts a scanning sequence by first raising line D0 to the HIGH state. Lines D1 to D7 remain LOW while D0 is HIGH. These states are stored in the 8-bit latch. The microprocessor next reads the state of the input-data bus by activating the eight input buffers. These lines are vertical in Fig. 1. For example, if switch 02 is depressed, the microprocessor reads 00000100, where D0 is the least significant bit. This word is decoded by microprocessor software into whatever format is needed by the system.

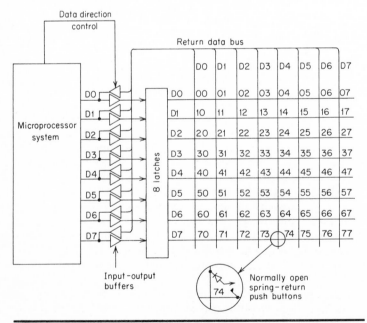

FIG. 1   A common switch-scanning technique which uses two buses intersecting in an X-Y array. (From Ref. 1 with permission)

After the read and decode cycle, the microprocessor advances the HIGH output line to D1. This new word 00000010 is again stored in the eight latches, the bus is read again, and the cycle repeats itself. The 64-switch keyboard is completely scanned after eight output and eight input instructions have been performed. This complete scan can be performed in less than 100 μs if efficient software is used. After each complete scan, the complete state of the switch array is stored in 8 data words of 8 bits each. This data can be processed by the system using software independent of the scanning circuit or its software.

This scanning technique has a potential problem when two or more keys are simultaneously depressed. Suppose switches 12 and 22 are closed: this causes a short circuit between the D1 and D2 output lines. If these two output lines are in opposite states, we may destroy some devices in the latch circuits. Placing a diode in series with each switch eliminates this problem.

Some commercial microcircuits that utilize the X-Y scanning technique have a feature called n-key rollover. If a key is depressed before a previously depressed key is returned to the OFF position, the second key still generates a code. Likewise, a third key generates a code if the first two keys are still down. With true n-key rollover we could have any number of keys down, and any new key depression would still generate a code. However, some manufacturers of these devices caution the user that if any combination of depressed keys forms a right triangle in the X-Y array, the last key down in this set of three will not be encoded. A microprocessor-controlled encoder as shown in Fig. 1 does not have this problem. For example, suppose all the switches 02, 12, 22, . . . , 72 and 03, 13, 23, . . . , 73 are simultaneously depressed. On the first output code 0000001, the corresponding input will be 00001100. The software will be able to determine that switches 02 and 03 are depressed. On the next output cycle 00000010, the input will again be 00001100. The software now finds that the 12 and 13 switches are depressed. The same mutually exclusive tests are made all the way down to the 72 and 73 switches. No interaction between switches occurs. Because the X-Y switch array is scanned at a high rate, each new key closure merely changes the input code back to the microprocessor. The microprocessor program is written to detect each change in the input code by looking at individual bits in each input word as it arrives.

13.2 A Musical Keyboard Scanner Using a PIA

The circuit described in this section could alternatively be called an n-key rollover keyboard encoder, software-controlled music keyboard scanner, or a multiple-closure switch-array encoder. n-Key rollover or multiple closure means that there is no limit to the number of simultaneous key depressions the circuit can handle.

The circuit in Figs. 2 and 3 is capable of generating switch-closure codes compatible with a music synthesizer designed by the author. It is organized in octaves; i.e., circuit sections can be added or subtracted in whole octaves. The software also counts to the base 12 and stores information in a format directly usable by a music system.

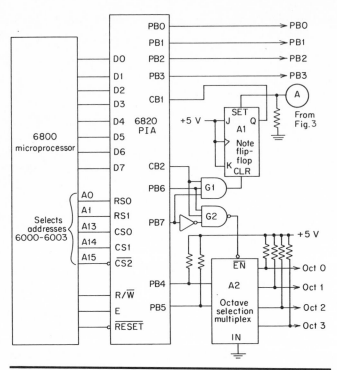

FIG. 2   *Control circuit for a four-octave musical-keyboard scanner using the 6820 PIA device. (Adapted from Ref. 1 with permission)*

Hardware Description   This circuit is designed to interface with a multiple-channel music synthesizer. Data and control lines coming from the microprocessor are organized to handle both the synthesizer and this keyboard simultaneously. Address decoding gates (that is, G1 and G4) must therefore be three-input devices.

The synthesizer circuit has two modes: select channel 1 or channel 2 (see Table 1). The scanning circuit also has two modes. The first mode clears the note flip-flop (A1): the second mode samples keys on the keyboard by activating multiplexer A2. These modes are set up by the states of the 2 most significant bits in the PIA data word (PB6 and PB7). After the correct mode is placed on these lines, a control line (CB2) is momentarily raised to the HIGH state, to cause a mode transfer to the appropriate circuit. This two-step mode control utilizing three lines is required because the data-bus bits PB6 and PB7 are controlled with different instructions occurring at an earlier time than the control line CB2. The scan-keyboard mode causes the microprocessor to examine each note on the keyboard for a switch closure. If a key is depressed, a signal is generated that sets the note flip-flop. The microprocessor looks at the note flip-flop after each note is addressed to see if a note has been depressed. After the note has been examined, the note flip-flop is cleared to make ready for the next note scan.

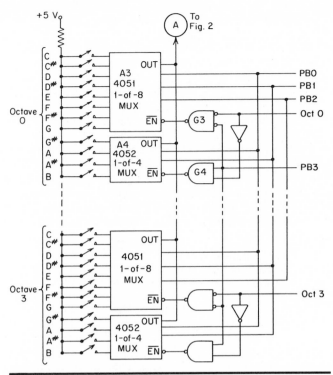

FIG. 3   *Two octaves of a four-octave musical-keyboard scanner circuit. (Adapted from Ref. 1 with permission)*

TABLE 1   **Four modes of keyboard scanner and synthesizer circuits**

PB6	PB7	CB2	Action Taken
0	0		Output T1 to synthesizer 1
0	1		Output T2 to synthesizer 2
1	0		Scan keyboard
1	1		Clear note flip-flop

At this point it is useful to describe the interface between the microprocessor and the keyboard. The circuit described in this section is designed to be controlled by a 6800 microprocessor and its family of peripheral chips. The 6820 peripheral interface adapter (PIA) is used as the parallel interface between the microprocessor and the scanner. This is a dual device, and we will assume the B side is used for the musical keyboard and the A side for various control inputs.

The B side of the PIA has an 8-bit data word latch that can be used for microprocessor input-output from or to an external device. This application uses these 8 lines as microprocessor outputs for both the synthesizer and the scanner.

The 6820 has an input control signal called CB1 that may be used to sense the status of some external device. In this case it senses the output of the note flip-flop A1. A PIA output signal called CB2 is often used to control an external device. Here we use CB2 to clear the note flip-flop and enable A2.

Scanner Circuit Operation   The note flip-flop A1 is first cleared when the microprocessor sends a PB6 = PB7 = CB2 = 1 command through the PIA. This command is decoded with G1. The microprocessor then moves into the scan mode, with PB6 = CB2 = 1 and PB7 in the LOW state. This is decoded by G2, after which a data word already present at PIA output bus B selects one of four octaves using A2. Bits PB4 and PB5 are used for octave selection; the note selection within an octave is performed with bits PB0 through PB3. We can therefore scan four octaves having 12 notes each using this decoding scheme.

Device A2 is a 1-of-8 multiplexer. We use only four of its outputs in this circuit. Because the common input terminal of this device is tied to ground, we will get a LOW level for the selected output. The pull-up resistors on each output line make the standby state HIGH. Each output enables two other multiplexers (see Fig. 3) in the selected octave circuit. These two multiplexers service 12 keyboard notes. We also could have used a 16-channel multiplexer for note selection within each octave. However, 4- and 8-channel multiplexers are much cheaper (and more readily available) than 16-channel multiplexers.

When a note is depressed, a HIGH level is transferred to the appropriate multiplexer input pin. When the microprocessor scans that particular input, the HIGH level is transferred through one of the note-selection multiplexers, where it sets the note flip-flop. The microprocessor then samples the CB1 line to see if the note flip-flop has been set. If not, the next note is selected for examination. If the note flip-flop has been set, an 8-bit word is stored in memory, with a code corresponding to that particular note.

The multiplexer for each octave uses a 1-of-8 multiplexer (a 4051) for the lower eight notes. The upper four notes are sampled with a 1-of-4 multiplexer (half of a 4052). The $\overline{\text{ENABLE}}$ ($\overline{\text{EN}}$) input of the 4051 is LOW (selected) only when PB3 is LOW and the appropriate octave select line is LOW. PB3 is LOW only for the first eight notes of an octave. When PB3 goes HIGH, notes 9 through 12 are selected and the $\overline{\text{EN}}$ line to the 4052 goes LOW. For example, note that the output of G3 (the $\overline{\text{EN}}$ for A3) goes LOW only when both PB3 and OCT0 are LOW. Also observe that the output of G4 (the $\overline{\text{EN}}$ for A4) goes LOW only when PB3 is HIGH and OCT0 is LOW.

Software Description   Figure 4 shows the flowchart and instructions for a method of scanning the four-octave keyboard just described. This program begins by clearing all temporary registers in memory location $0100 through $0106 (the $ means hexadecimal number). Each of these temporary registers is listed in Table 2. The PIA is initialized so that the B side is an output bus. We next send out PB6 = PB7 = 1 to clear the note flip-flop. PB6 and PB7 remain latched in the output register while CB2 is momentarily pulsed to the

TABLE 2   *Function of seven temporary registers in Fig. 4*

Address of register (hex)	Name of register	Register function
0100	N	Note number on keyboard
0101	T1	Higher of two notes activated
0102	T1P	T1-present counter; three scans of activated T1 needed before synthesizer notified
0103	T1M	T1-missing counter; three scans of missing T1 needed before synthesizer turned off
0104	T2	Lower of two notes activated
0105	T2P	T2-present counter, similar to T1P
0106	T2M	T2-missing counter, similar to T1M

HIGH state, causing the output of G1 also to go momentarily HIGH, thereby clearing the note flip-flop. Immediately after the note flip-flop is cleared, the PIA is programmed to look for a CB1 input from the note flip-flop Q output. While the flip-flop is being sensed, the PIA output bus B addresses note 00. If this note is activated (depressed), A3 transfers a HIGH level over to the SET input of the note flip-flop.

Whenever any note is found in the HIGH state, the program must determine whether it has a higher or lower pitch than a stored note that was previously evaluated as the highest note activated. At any given instant the note being sampled is N, and the highest-pitch note previously stored is T1. If N > T1, the new note is higher than the old highest note. The old note is renamed T2, and the new note is named T1. If N < T1, the new note is stored as T2 and T1 remains undisturbed.

The program next moves into a debouncing routine. Each time T1 is found in the HIGH state, a counter called T1P is incremented. This counter keeps track of the number of times T1 was present. Because each key is scanned sequentially, the entire keyboard is scanned between samples of any particular note. Another counter, called T1M (T1 missing), is cleared whenever T1P is incremented. Counter T1M counts the number of times T1 is found in the LOW state. The number of scans used to detect a valid T1 present or missing is set at 3 in the program. Other numbers can be used, depending upon the switch-bouncing characteristics of the keys used. When three HIGH values of T1 are detected, the program sends the code corresponding to that particular note to the synthesizer channel 1. When T1M reaches a count of 3, synthesizer channel 1 is turned OFF. Likewise, T2P and T2M control the ON-OFF status of synthesizer channel 2. Neither synthesizer is notified of a T1 or T2 ON-OFF state until that particular note is found in three successive scans of the entire keyboard. This technique debounces all keys and prevents chattering keys from falsely operating the synthesizer.

The program advances N in a base 12 format. Each time N is incremented, its least significant digit is compared to hexadecimal C (decimal 12). If a match

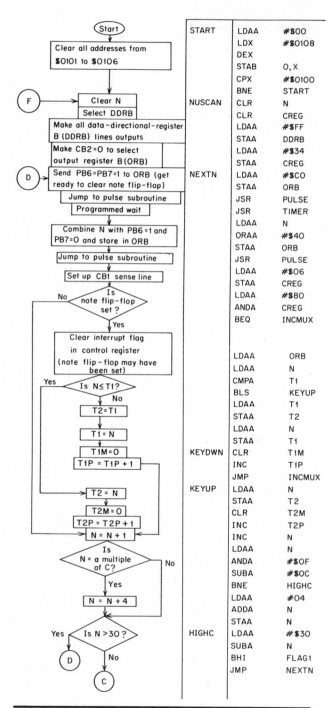

FIG. 4 *Flowchart of a four-octave musical-keyboard scanning program. (Adapted from Ref. 1 with permission)*

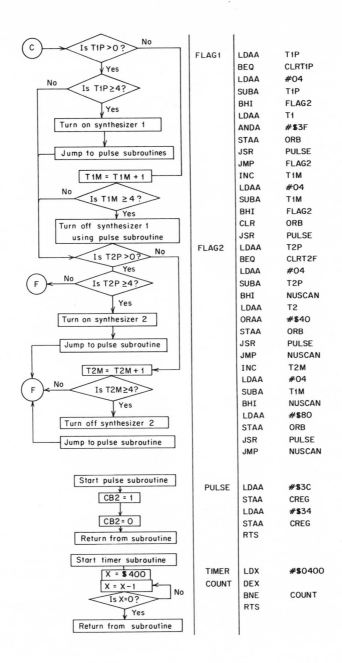

FLAG1	LDAA	T1P
	BEQ	CLRT1P
	LDAA	#04
	SUBA	T1P
	BHI	FLAG2
	LDAA	T1
	ANDA	#$3F
	STAA	ORB
	JSR	PULSE
	JMP	FLAG2
	INC	T1M
	LDAA	#04
	SUBA	T1M
	BHI	FLAG2
	CLR	ORB
	JSR	PULSE
FLAG2	LDAA	T2P
	BEQ	CLRT2F
	LDAA	#04
	SUBA	T2P
	BHI	NUSCAN
	LDAA	T2
	ORAA	#$40
	STAA	ORB
	JSR	PULSE
	JMP	NUSCAN
	INC	T2M
	LDAA	#04
	SUBA	T1M
	BHI	NUSCAN
	LDAA	#$80
	STAA	ORB
	JSR	PULSE
	JMP	NUSCAN
PULSE	LDAA	#$3C
	STAA	CREG
	LDAA	#$34
	STAA	CREG
	RTS	
TIMER	LDX	#$0400
COUNT	DEX	
	BNE	COUNT
	RTS	

is found, N is advanced by 4, so that the most significant digit is incremented by 1. Because we are starting the count at 0, a count of 12 decimal is the first note of the next octave.

If a four-octave synthesizer keyboard is used, the maximum N is 30 (hex). A test is made each time N is advanced to see if the limit 30 has been exceeded. If not, the program counter returns to the clear note flip-flop routine (NEXTN). If the end of keyboard is detected, a T1P > 0 test is performed. If the result is false, the T1M (T1 missing) counter is incremented. When this counter reaches 4, synthesizer 1 is turned OFF. If the result of the T1P > 0 test is true, another test to see if T1P ≥ 4 is performed. If this is true, synthesizer 1 is activated with a clean debounced value of T1. This note stays latched in the synthesizer tone-generation circuit until T1M advances to 4. The synthesizer is turned OFF by loading an all-zero data word. The T2P test is entered after the T1 synthesizer ON-OFF routine is complete or if 0 < T1P ≤ 3.

The program requires approximately 100 μs for each key and another 50 μs for each activated key. A complete scan of 60 notes therefore takes approximately 6 ms. If four scans are required for debouncing, a 24-ms delay occurs from the time a note is depressed until it is transferred over to the appropriate synthesizer channel. If more debouncing time is required, a timer loop can be inserted after the clear note flip-flop routine. This timer loop is shown as a subroutine called TIMER. If the index register is loaded with $0400, as shown, the delay per keyboard scan will be approximately 8 ms in addition to the 6 ms for the rest of the program.

13.3 A BCD *Thumbwheel Switch Scanner*

Instrument front panels commonly utilize binary-coded decimal (BCD) switches and displays to simplify human operation and interpretation. An array of BCD thumbwheel switches provides a compact method of entering large numbers into an instrumentation system. In many cases this BCD number of N digits must be converted into its binary equivalent. The following pages describe a technique for scanning four BCD thumbwheel switches and converting the four BCD words into a 14-bit binary word.

Figure 5 shows one simple method of interfacing the four BCD switches with the microprocessor address and data buses. Each BCD switch has four outputs with weights 1, 2, 4, and 8. For example, if the number 9 is selected, the 1 and 8 output lines are internally connected to the common terminal. Pull-up resistors are needed on each switch output terminal because the various weighted outputs are open-circuited if not internally connected to the grounded common terminal. The resulting BCD code is inverted at this point, but the 74LS240 buffers again invert the code. For the 74LS240 devices the maximum pull-up resistor sizes must be

$$R_{max} = \frac{V_{CC} - V_{IH,min}}{I_{IH,max}} = \frac{(5 - 2)V}{40 \ \mu A} = 75 \ k\Omega$$

where $V_{IH,min}$ is minimum recognizable HIGH input voltage

$I_{IH,max}$ is maximum input current with HIGH level applied

Resistors of 10 kΩ would be sufficient. With a worst-case input current of 40 µA; the HIGH-level input voltage will be $V_{IH,min} = RI_{IH,max} = 10^4 \times 40 \times 10^{-6} = 0.4$ V below V_{CC}.

A 74LS240 is selected when both its enable lines are driven LOW. When the enable lines are HIGH, the device's outputs go into the high-impedance state. The LOW enable signals are generated using a 74L154 decoder. The two lowest addresses decoded by the 74l154 are used in this application. A particular output on this device is selected when G1 and G2 are both LOW and A, B, C, and D contain a number corresponding to the desired output. G1 and G2 will be LOW for addresses F000 through F015. A0 through A3 select the exact address within that range. Whenever the computer program issues a read command for address F000, the two least significant thumbwheel digits are transferred over to the data bus. A read command at address F001 moves the two most significant digits to the data bus.

Figure 6 is a flowchart of a program to scan the four BCD thumbwheel switches and convert the data into a 14-bit binary word. An ASSEMBLY language listing of the flowchart using the 6800 language is given in Table 3. The program starts by clearing UP8 and L08, that is, the upper and lower 8-bit segments of the 16-bit output register. This register could be part of RAM or

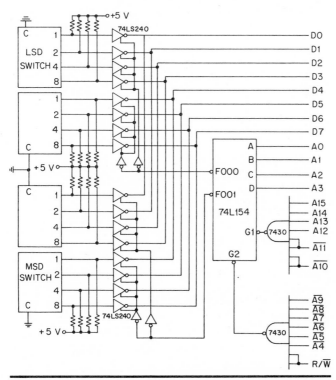

FIG. 5 A simple method for interfacing the four BCD thumbwheel switches with the data and address buses of the microprocessor. (From Ref. 1 with permission)

TABLE 3   ASSEMBLY *language program to implement the flowchart of Fig. 6 using the 6800 microprocessor language*

BCDBIN	CLR	UP8	Begin subroutine by clearing 16-bit
	CLR	L08	output word
	LDAA	THH	Read TH = D7–D4, H = D3–D0
	LSRA		
	LSRA		Move thousands to lower 4 bits and
	LSRA		zeros into upper 4 bits
	LSRA		
	STAA	TH	Store thousands in TH
	LDAA	THH	Read THH again
	ANDA	#$0F	Keep hundreds and mask out
	STAA	H	thousands; store in H
	LDAA	TU	Read tens = D7–D4, U = D3–D0
	LSRA		
	LSRA		Move tens into lower 4 bits; move zeros
	LSRA		into upper 4 bits
	STAA	T	Store tens in T
	LDAA	TU	Read tens = D7–D4, U = D3–D0
	ANDA	#$0F	Keep units and mask out tens; store in
	STAA	U	U
START	LDAA	#$03	
	STAA	C	C, D = $03E8 (1000 decimal)
	LDAA	#E8	
	STAA	D	
TEST TH	LDAA	TH	Is TH = 0 ?
	BEQ	HUNDRD	Yes, go to hundreds test
	LDAA	L08	
	ADDA	D	L08 = L08 + D
	STAA	L08	
	LDAA	UP8	
	ADCA	C	UP8 = UP8 + C + carry
	STAA	UP8	
	DEC	TH	TH = TH − 1
	BRA	TEST TH	D0 another 1000s loop
HUNDRD	CLR	C	Begin 100s loop
	LDAA	#$64	C, D = $0064 (100 decimal)
	STAA	D	
TESTH	LDAA	H	Is H = 0 ?
	BEQ	TEN	Yes, go to tens test
	LDAA	L08	
	ADDA	D	L08 = L08 + D
	STAA	L08	
	LDAA	UP8	
	ADCA	C	UP8 = UP8 + C + carry
	STAA	UP8	
	DEC	H	H = H–1
	BRA	TESTH	Do another 100s loop
TEN	LDAA	#$0A	Begin 10s loop
	STAA	D	C, D = $000A (10 decimal)

TABLE 3 ASSEMBLY *language program to implement the flowchart of Fig. 6 using the 6800 microprocessor language* Cont.

TESTT	LDAA	T	Is T = 0 ?
	BEQ	UNIT	Yes, to units routine
	LDAA	L08	
	ADDA	D	L08 = L08 + D
	STAA	L08	
	LDAA	UP8	
	ADCA	C	UP8 = UP8 + C + carry
	STAA	UP8	
	DEC	T	T = T − 1
	BRA	TESTT	Do another 10s loop
UNIT	LDAA	L08	
	ADDA	U	L08 = L08 + U
	STAA	L08	
	LDAA	UP8	
	ADCA	#0	UP8 = UP8 + carry
	STAA	UP8	
	RTS		Exit subroutine

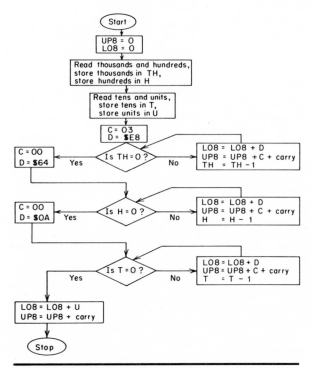

FIG. 6 *Flowchart for scanning the four BCD thumbwheel switches shown in Fig. 5 and converting the data into a 14-bit binary word. (From Ref. 1 with permission)*

some type of output register.The thousands and hundreds switches are read next. This input port, called THH (thousands and hundreds), is read twice. During the first reading the hundreds bits (D0 to D3) are deleted by shifting the thousands bits (D4 to D7) to the right four places. The LSRA instruction shifts zeros in from the left so that the upper 4 bits are cleared after this operation. This new 8-bit word is stored in register TH (part of RAM) for use later in the program. During the second reading of THH, the hundreds data are saved by masking out the upper 4 bits using the ANDA #0F instruction. These data are saved in register H. The tens and units data are similarly processed and saved in registers T and U.

The program begins the BCD-to-binary conversion routine at START. A hexadecimal number $03E8, which corresponds to decimal 1000, is loaded into registers C and D. Next, the TH register contents are compared with zero. If they are equal to zero, the program immediately jumps to the hundreds routine. If TH > 0, D is added to UP8 and C is added to L08. The L08 + D operation is performed first, and any resulting carry is added into the UP8 + C operation. TH is then decremented, and the loop repeats itself until TH becomes zero. At this point UP8 and L08 contain a hexadecimal number corresponding to the number of thousands on the BCD thumbwheel switch.

The hundreds and tens routines are identical to the thousands routine. In these cases $0064 is added to UP8, L08 for each hundred and $000A is added for each ten. The number of units is added directly with no test loop because hex and decimal whole numbers between 0 and 9 are identical.

REFERENCES

1. Stout, D. F., and M. Kaufman: *Handbook of Microcircuit Design and Application,* McGraw-Hill, New York, 1980, Chap. 16.
2. Peatman, J. B.: *Microcomputer-Based Design,* McGraw-Hill, New York, 1977, pp. 219–252.
3. *SC/MP Applications Handbook,* pub. no. 420305239-001A, National Semiconductor Corporation, October 1976, pp. 2C2-1–2C2-14.

CHAPTER FOURTEEN

Voice Recognition

Frank Koperda

IBM Corp., Information Systems Division,
Boca Raton, Florida

HISTORICAL OVERVIEW

Voice recognition, the subject of research for more than 20 years, is a potential application for microprocessors. Initial experimental systems utilized large processors because of the necessary extensive computations. Eventually "minicomputers" were developed; their computing power has increased and new mathematical and programming techniques have evolved. Because today's microprocessor is approaching the computing power of the minicomputer, it is now practical to consider a voice-recognition system based upon a microprocessor.

There is a twofold rationale for a voice-recognition system: (1) It is an easier means for noncomputer professionals to enter data into the computer. (2) In certain applications, such as in semiautomated quality-control inspection procedures, computer users need to use their hands. The cost and generally limited vocabulary of some commercial units have prevented their wide acceptance. One common limitation, for example, is that the system and speaker have to be "trained" to adapt the system to the particular characteristics of the speaker. Ideally, a truly general voice-recognition system would be capable of recognizing a large vocabulary of words, independent of the speaker.

This chapter describes an experimental system being developed by the author as a hobby. Although not yet totally implemented, major portions of the system have been completed and are operating. Based upon the results to date, the remainder of the system has been planned and is currently being constructed. The approach to the system design utilizes information about the speech waveform that has been reported in the literature as well as characteristics which can be observed on an oscilloscope or plotter.

14.1 System Goals

The audio waveform created from speech is a complex signal of considerable variation, depending upon the speaker's physical characteristics, emotional state, and learned speaking habits.[1] Fundamentally, speech is created by the vibration of the vocal cords, which gives rise to the sounds, such as the vowels. In addition, different sounds are created by air passing through constrictions formed by the tongue, nose, and lips (for example, the /s/ and /f/ sounds). These basic sounds are modified by the size and shape of cavities in the mouth, nose, and other air passages in the head. Differences in all these physical factors cause variations in the speech waveform from speaker to speaker, and even from day to day in the same person.

To be effective, therefore, a recognition system must be able to deal with these variations; that is, the system should be speaker-independent.[2] In speech waveforms, the variations are manifested as changes in frequency, relative amplitude, and time duration. The system must be designed to normalize these factors, to create parameters independent of absolute time, amplitude, and frequency. This system's approach is to use ratios of quantities that can be measured by the system.

Two additional goals are to make the system insensitive to extraneous sounds and to give it the ability to recognize continuous speech. Insensitivity to extraneous sounds is desired so the system can be used in practical applications where background noise must be tolerated. For example, in a manufacturing location, nearby machinery or other people create sounds. Requiring a noise-free environment is not feasible in such a situation. The ability to recognize continuous speech is also a practical consideration. Certain systems quite accurately recognize discrete words, spoken with distinct interword gaps. Continuous speech, consisting of more than one word spoken in a normal sequence, is much more difficult to recognize because the system must determine when one word ends and the next begins. Since many applications require recognition of sequences of words, a system that restrains the speaker to an artificial way of saying phrases is not satisfactory.

The final goal is to design a system that can be implemented using microprocessors. With this restriction, it is not practical to use some of the approaches that have been investigated in the past because many require processing power in excess of that available with a microprocessor. For example, many research approaches utilize the fast Fourier transform (FFT) to convert the time-domain signal into the frequency domain.[3] It is not practical to implement a real-time FFT on a microprocessor, so the system described here does not convert to the frequency domain. Similarly, because the microprocessor is not as powerful as larger computers, this design utilizes multiple processors to provide concurrency and hence greater apparent processing power. These are examples of the types of tradeoffs necessary when designing a microprocessor-based voice-recognition system.

14.2 System Overview

Six steps in the recognition of speech are common to most voice recognition systems: (1) converting the input analog signal into a digital form by sampling, (2) compressing or selecting the relevant data for subsequent processing, (3) determining the boundaries of the word, (4) detecting patterns within the word, (5) pattern classification, and (6) association of pattern sequences with words in the vocabulary.

With a powerful processor, it is possible to time-share the processor among these six tasks. With microprocessors, however, it is more practical to use several processors in a "pipelined" architecture. The first processor in the pipeline performs one or more of the six tasks and passes the resulting data on to a second processor. The first processor can then continue on the next speech segment while the second performs subsequent steps in the processing. The number of processors required depends upon the complexity of the steps, the speed of the processor, cost considerations, and the desired accuracy.

Figure 1 is a block diagram of the pipelined system described in this chapter. It incorporates three separate microprocessors in addition to the signal-

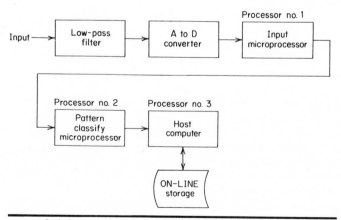

FIG. 1   *Block diagram of pipeline speech-recognition system.*

input hardware. The input stage consists of a microphone preamplifier whose characteristics attenuate frequencies above about 8 kHz. The analog-to-digital converter (ADC) changes the input to a digital representation of the analog voice signal. Processor 1, the input microprocessor, receives the data from the ADC and determines when a voice signal, as opposed to noise, is present. It also detects signal peaks (local maxima and minima) and records their amplitude and the time interval between peaks. This significantly reduces the amount of data that must be handled in subsequent processing. The selected data is passed on to Processor 2, which decides when the compressed data constitutes a pattern and then generates parameters based upon the type of pattern. Processor 3, the host computer, uses the sequences of parameters to decide which word has been spoken and to take the programmed action, such as print the word or control an external device. The pipeline configuration essentially follows the six processing steps in the recognition procedure. Sections 14.3 to 14.8 provide information about accomplishing each of the six steps and details about the specific configuration that has been implemented.

An alternate approach, one that reduces computational time at the expense of additional hardware, is to separate the speech into 8 to 15 frequency bands using filters and then sample the filter outputs. The frequency and amplitude information can then be used directly in Fourier series and other frequency-domain computations. In essence, the fine detail of the speech waveform has been transformed from the time domain to the frequency domain. However, the filters are relatively expensive and implementing them digitally requires significant computing power, which is not consistent with the desire to use current microprocessors.

14.3   Input-Signal Processing

The speech waveform for the word "ship" shown in Fig. 2 illustrates the type of signal that must be processed by the system. The first processing step is to sample the analog waveform and to convert the amplitude of the signal at the sampling instants into a digital word that can be manipulated by the computer. Important considerations in this conversion are the sampling rate and filtering requirements.

Analog-to-Digital Converters (ADCs)   The basic equipment used to convert an analog signal into its digital equivalent is the ADC, which is essentially a digital voltmeter that can be controlled by the processor. Many different techniques are available to perform the conversion, including successive approximation, voltage-to-frequency conversion, and dual-slope integration.[4] The successive-approximation (S/A) method is fast enough for sampling speech, and low-cost integrated circuit (IC) versions are readily available.

The S/A technique compares the input voltage and a known voltage to generate the successive bits in the binary representation. First the unknown input voltage is compared to a reference voltage equal to half the full-scale range

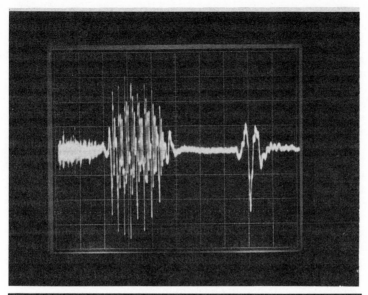

FIG. 2 *Pattern of the word "ship."*

of the ADC. A decision is made as to whether the input voltage is greater than the reference voltage. If it is, the most significant bit is set to binary **1**. The next comparison occurs between one-half the reference voltage added to one-fourth the reference voltage. The second bit is set to **1** if the signal voltage is greater than this comparison voltage. By proceeding in this fashion, the total binary representation of the input signal value is generated. This comparison process is inherent in the IC, so the processor merely needs to initiate the conversion and read the data at its completion.

IC ADCs are available with up to 12 bits resolution (1 part in 4096), with 8 bits being quite common and inexpensive. Based upon experimental results obtained with the system, it appears that an 8-bit ADC is adequate for the approach described in this chapter.

The speed requirement for the ADC is determined by the sampling rate and the desired time resolution. As discussed in the next section, a minimum sampling rate of 6 kHz is required. However, to provide time resolution, the conversion time should be only a small fraction of the 160-μs period associated with the 6-kHz sample rate. In the implemented system, an ADC having a conversion time of 20 μs is used; this is equivalent to a sampling rate of 50,000 samples per second.

Another way to encode data is pulse-code modulation (PCM). There are several forms of PCM, including delta modulation (DM) and differential pulse-code modulation. These alternative analog conversion techniques are discussed in later sections.

Sampling Rate Requirement The frequencies in a speech signal range from somewhat less than 100 Hz to in excess of 8 kHz. The Nyquist criterion for sampling states that a periodic signal can be described completely by $2f$ periodic samples, where f is the highest frequency component of the signal. Thus, accurate representation requires a sampling rate of at least 16,000 samples per second or a sampling interval of about 60 μs. This requires, however, that there be no frequencies greater than 8 kHz; in reality, there are higher frequencies present due to harmonics. To prevent errors caused by inadequate sampling speed ("aliasing errors"), the input signal should be band-limited by using a low-pass filter with a cutoff frequency of about 8 kHz. In the implemented system, the sampling rate of 50,000 samples per second allows a signal bandwidth of 25 kHz which, when coupled with the characteristics of the microphone equalization preamplifier, ensures that the sampled data accurately represents the speech signal.

Noise Suppression The physical environment in which a person speaks is seldom free of background noise. To help suppress these extraneous signals, a unidirectional microphone with a windscreen is recommended. This type of microphone helps ensure that the speech signal will have a significantly higher amplitude than that of the background noise.

Low-frequency (high-pass) filters also can help reduce noise generated by low-frequency mechanical equipment such as electric motors. These filters can be implemented by using analog techniques. However, the microprocessor can provide their digital equivalent. Random sounds with a duration of up to several milliseconds can be efficiently detected and eliminated with a microprocessor. The approach used here is further discussed in Sec. 14.5, *Discrete Word-Boundary Determination*.

14.4 Data Compression

The amount of data generated by sampling the voice signal at 16,000 samples per second would require a large amount of storage if each sample amplitude were stored. In addition, this quantity of data would overburden the microprocessor in the subsequent processing steps. As a result, it is desirable to find some technique either of reducing the amount of data stored or of storing it more efficiently, without losing the information needed for subsequent recognition.

One technique for reducing the amount of data is to use a different encoding scheme. For a continuous waveform, such as a speech signal, DM can be used. This approach encodes the differential change (the delta) in the signal magnitude between sampling instants. If the differential is less than a preset value, no data is recorded, thus significantly reducing the amount of data for slowly varying signals. In practice, a delta modulator can be implemented with an integrator having a constant input with reversible polarity.

Starting at time $t = 0$, the output of the integrator is a ramp (the integral of a constant), as shown in the first segment of Fig. 3. This output is compared to the input signal at each clock time. When the integrator output exceeds the input signal, the polarity of the integrator input is reversed. The integrator output now decreases, as in the second segment of Fig. 3. When the integrator output becomes less than the input signal, the integrator input polarity is again reversed. In this way the integrator's output "tracks" the signal input using a triangular wave that lags slightly behind the differential changes in the input. By recording the times at which the integrator polarity is reversed, a digital representation of the signal is obtained. Either the number of clock pulses in each interval or a **1** or a **0** at each clock pulse can be recorded.

The precision with which the integrator output tracks the actual signal depends upon the clock rate and the magnitude of the integrated voltage. With the proper selection of these parameters, and depending upon the desired precision (quantization resolution), the amount of data can be reduced significantly, as low as 2 kbyte/s for speech signals.

A further improvement (see Fig. 4) can be obtained by using several fixed input levels to the integrator. When the input is changing rapidly (i.e., has a high slope or large differential), a large integrator input voltage is used, thus allowing the integrator output to "catch up" to the input signal more rapidly. When the differential is small, a smaller integrator input voltage is used, thus minimizing overshoot of the integrator. To encode the signal, both time of reversal and indication of which integrator input voltage is used must be recorded.

In both approaches, determining the actual value of the input requires a numerical integration of the recorded data. The recognition algorithm used in the system described here depends on ratios of actual amplitudes of the input

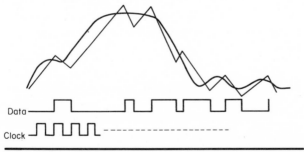

FIG. 3   *Delta modulation.*

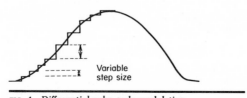

FIG. 4   *Differential pulse code modulation.*

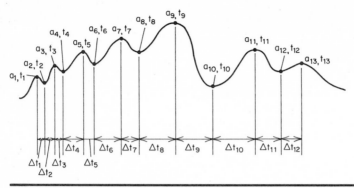

FIG. 5   *Frequency and amplitude separation.*

signal. For this reason the DM encoding technique was not used because the requirement for numerical integration would have increased computation, even though the amount of data stored might be less.

Using a similar idea, however, the system employs immediate processing of the data, to select only those data points needed in subsequent processing. As the data from the ADC is received, it is immediately compared to the previous sample to determine if a change in the sign of the slope has occurred. If it has, the amplitude value is stored. In addition, the value of the time interval since the last slope change is recorded. In a sense, the approach is a peak detector in which the input signal is approximated by a triangle wave of variable amplitude and frequency, as shown in Fig. 5.

This approach also separates the amplitude and frequency characteristics of the speech signal to the extent that the signal frequency is related to the time intervals between slope reversals. This is called the frequency and amplitude separation (FAS) method of data collection. The reciprocals of the time intervals do represent true frequencies in the sense of the mathematical description of sinusoids. However, they are indicative of the frequency components in the waveform. As an indication of the data compression provided, most small words (like "ship") require about 500 bytes of storage.

The FAS method does require that the time intervals be measured with reasonable precision. Experimentally, it appears that sampling at least every 80 μs (12,500 samples per second) is required. As noted earlier, the implemented system uses a 20-μs interval (50,000 samples per second), providing more than adequate time resolution.

14.5   Discrete Word-Boundary Determination

The next step in a voice-recognition system is word-boundary determination, the process of determining if a word is present and where it begins and ends. Although this seems to be a trivial process, difficulties arise because of such factors as background noise and electronic interference. There are at least four signal characteristics that can be used to distinguish speech from noise: amplitude, frequency, duration, and sound patterns. Individually, none of these characteristics is sufficient for all cases, but, when used in conjunction with each other, an effective means of word detection is possible.

Because of the multiple characteristics being used, word-boundary determination must be done in several stages within a system. Easily identified word boundaries are determined at the time of input, to allow isolated (discrete) words to be identified. For continuous speech, where one word rapidly follows or is slurred into another, word-boundary determination must be done at a later step of the recognition process.

Variable-Amplitude Threshold A variable-amplitude threshold input section is useful for determining the start and end of valid voice input. This technique is used to lower the threshold amplitude until a signal that exceeds the threshold voltage is received. The pattern-recognition component in the system identifies the data as background noise and increases the threshold amplitude. After a delay that is short compared to the length of a valid speech sound, the threshold amplitude is reduced slightly and the sequence repeats. By using this approach, the system continues to search for a valid speech signal without burdening the system with erroneous noise data.

An interesting phenomenon that occurs in speech can cause end-of-word-detection problems. At the end of a word, the vocal chords have lost their excitation but are still oscillating. The speech waveform begins as erratic decay that sometimes can be interpreted as multiple speech dead times. This decay can cause an ambiguity in defining the exact end of a word. To help more clearly delineate the end of a word, the variable-amplitude threshold can again be used to advantage. When the interval between slope reversals exceeds 10 ms, the threshold amplitude is increased and the sampling rate is reduced to 1,000 samples per second (1-ms intervals). After a short delay, the original threshold level is restored, but sampling still continues at 1-ms intervals. When the input amplitude again exceeds the threshold amplitude, the sampling rate increases to its maximum rate.

There is another phenomenon that can cause false word-end detection. When a word consists of multiple phonemes (the basic acoustic unit of words), there is a finite transition time between phonemes that can be greater than 10 ms. It is very useful to be able to detect these transition times for future processing. After a 10-ms period has elapsed, the pause may be caused by a true end-of-word or by an end-of-phoneme. Further sampling of the input data at the 1-ms time interval and the original amplitude threshold can determine which case exists. If a signal amplitude greater than the threshold is encountered after 10 ms, then an end-of-phoneme signal is saved. If multiple consecutive 10-ms periods exist, during which no signal is detected, then the pause is the end of a word. The 10-ms criterion used was determined experimentally and may vary in the final implementation.

Frequency The frequency of the input signal, as reflected in the time interval between slope reversals, may also be used to distinguish between noise and the presence of voiced input. Many types of background noise (such as that caused by motor-driven machinery) have a low frequency. Although an analog filter could be used to block this noise, a microprocessor can provide a similar function. The microprocessor can check the frequency of an input and determine if it is below 300 Hz. If the FAS method is used for data compression, the microprocessor can reject all input data until the interval between slope changes exceeds about 1.5 ms, or half the period of a 300-Hz sinusoid. Similarly, the endpoint of a word can be determined by the lack of a minimum 300-Hz input. Thus, the microprocessor acts as a fast-attack and fast-decay comparator and low-frequency filter. Even if the background noise is loud, false detection is minimized.

Pattern   Another way to distinguish between noise and voice is to examine input patterns. Most noise above 300 Hz is random and of short duration. By examining the pattern and the length of the noise, it is possible to ignore large-amplitude noise. On the basis of experimental results, if an isolated sound lasts less than 100 ms, a word is not in progress and the preceding data can be ignored.

Continuous Speech   These techniques have proved effective for rejecting noise and identifying word boundaries in discrete speech or in continuous speech in which words are distinctly separated. Sometimes, however, these techniques may not be effective when speech habits result in connected speech. For example, the southern "you all" is often spoken as the single word "y'all," and therefore must be considered as a distinct word for recognition purposes. Because the specific system being described has not been implemented completely, its ability to recognize continuous speech has not been evaluated. Most likely, additional techniques will be required for word-boundary detection, or certain combinations of words will have to be considered as single words for recognition purposes.

Detection Algorithms   The preceding requirements for noise suppression, data compression, and word boundary detection using the FAS approach enable the construction of an algorithm for the initial processing of the speech signal. Figure 6 is a flowchart of an algorithm that has been experimentally successful for accurately tracking voice input. On a standard 8-bit microprocessor, the algorithm takes about 100 lines of assembler code.

The top third of Fig. 6 samples for a slope reversal and should be less than 80 μs (preferably faster), so that peak times can be accurately determined. The section on the right side of Fig. 6 shows that changing the sampling rate has no effect on the amount of data needed to represent the waveform. Only when the slope of the waveform changes sign are any data saved. Thus, increasing the sampling rates simply provides more precision in determining the time between peaks. When a slope reversal occurs, the maximum or minimum amplitude can be either saved or forwarded to the next microprocessor. The time between slope reversals also is saved, and the scanning continues looking for the next slope change.

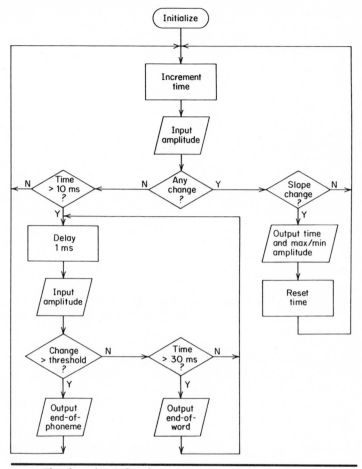

FIG. 6   *Flowchart of FAS algorithm.*

The lower-left section of Fig. 6 suppresses data output during speech dead times, such as between words or during some consonants. A slow sampling rate and variable-amplitude threshold help eliminate background noise and false end-of-word detection. Because data is not saved until a word actually exists, a considerable amount of data need not be analyzed subsequently. For simple words (e.g., the word "one"), the FAS method reduces the input waveform to only 256 to 512 bytes of data.

As a side benefit, data resulting from the FAS method allows very simple speech-output hardware. A digital-to-analog converter (DAC) may be used in conjunction with the transition time. This data is sent to the DAC to generate triangular wave shapes that approximate the speech waveform. For higher-quality output, the microprocessor can construct a sine-wave segment between two points.

14.6   Definitions of Linguistic Terms

The subsequent sections use certain linguistic terms that may be unfamiliar to most people. Although the definitions are not considered technically rigorous by pure linguists—indeed, there is much disagreement among linguists as to what is the technically correct definition of many of these terms—their purpose here is to provide a common basis for understanding the terms used in the remainder of the chapter. Definitions of the linguistic components of speech are best clarified by numerous examples. This section also illustrates that voice recognition must concern itself mainly with sounds, not the traditional spellings of words.[5]

Morpheme   A morpheme is the smallest unit of meaning in language. In English, all words are made up of at least one morpheme. Many morphemes are words in their own right, for example, "pin" and "fish." Some morphemes must be combined with others to make what we refer to as words. For example, the morphemes "un," "pin," and "ing" have their own meanings, with "un" being a negative and "ing" indicating an action, but neither can be used independently.

Phoneme   A phoneme is the basic unit of distinctive sound. For example, the word "cat" has three phonemes, with each letter representing a phoneme. This is not always the case because some phonemes require more than one letter, such as the sound represented by "ou" in "house." On the other hand, some letters represent a number of phonemes. For example: "a" can represent the three different phonemes heard in "cat," "father," and "make." Occasionally, a letter does not represent a phoneme at all, as, for example, the silent "e" in "tame." These inconsistencies between spellings and sounds (grapheme-phoneme inconsistencies) are very common in the English language and have led linguists to invent phonetic alphabets, where one symbol represents only one phoneme.

Consonants   Consonants are all the letters of the alphabet except the vowels "a," "e," "i," "o," and "u." Taken singly, most consonants represent a single phoneme. There are exceptions, as, for example, the letter "c," which has no sound exclusive of its own; it sometimes borrows the sound of "k" (cat) and sometimes the sound of "s" (cent). Consonants taken in combination produce even more phonemes, as is discussed in the *Digraph* section.

Vowels   Vowels are the five letters "a," "e," "i," "o," and "u" ("y" also may be used as a vowel). Every English morpheme contains at least one vowel. Vowels present an extreme number of grapheme-phoneme inconsistencies. Even taken singly, vowels represent more than one phoneme, depending on the spelling of the word (graphemic environment). The sounds of "a" in "pan" and "pane" are affected by the silent "e." Vowels are often "overruled" by consonants; for example, the /o/ sound, as in "boat," is significantly affected by the "overruling r" in "more."

Digraph   A digraph is a combination of two vowels or two consonants that results in only one phoneme. Examples are the "ch" in "chair" and the "ai" in "sail."

Diphthong   A diphthong is a combination of two adjacent vowels in a morpheme, where each vowel is sounded and each produces sounds it does not produce in other graphemic environments. The "oi" in "oil" and "ow" in "out" are diphthongs.

14.7   Pattern Detection Within a Word

The next processing step in the voice-recognition system begins the analysis phase. There is some uncertainty as to what constitutes the intelligence of speech and what characteristics of a speech waveform allow the brain to recognize words. However, it appears that the intelligence recognized by the brain is related to patterns of frequency and amplitude. Taking this view, speech consists of patterns of several types and transitions between patterns.

It is difficult to describe precisely what constitutes a pattern because of the many waveforms that can occur in speech. A rough definition of a pattern might be multiple occurrences of a particular distinctive waveform.

Observing the waveforms of phonetic sounds on a scope or plotter resulted in identifying three general pattern characteristics. Most unaspirated sounds, such as /s/, appear random in nature, but even randomness can be defined as a distinct characteristic. The vowel sounds are complex periodic oscillations caused by vocal-chord vibrations. Stop consonants are characterized by a short pause followed by a high-amplitude burst of sound. Variations of basic sounds are caused by the mouth, temporary positions of the tongue and lips, and the permanent characteristics of other facial features. Thus, each pattern variation is unique to an individual, and so the patterns must be defined broadly to be useful.

The patterns do not remain constant, even within a phoneme. As one phoneme ends and another begins, there is a transition between patterns that may range from silence to a complex blending of the initial and final pattern. The first processing task, therefore, is to recognize the existence of a relatively stable pattern that, in subsequent analysis, can be classified for use in identifying the spoken word.

The saved input data are the time intervals and amplitudes of maxima and minima. The time intervals are very useful for determining random variation; the amplitude values are used for identifying oscillations. However, neither can be used independently to determine the parameters of a pattern.

Pattern Characteristics   The random waveform sounds change slope polarity frequently, and the time between slope reversals is usually less than 160 μs. Potential stop consonants (/b/, /d/, /g/, /p/, /t/, /k/; see Table 2, p. 14–23) are detected in the data-input section or during the pattern-detection phase of analysis and are identified by a pause followed by a high-amplitude signal.

If a 10-ms interval between large amplitude changes occurs, the following pattern is probably a stop consonant.

Amplitude variations associated with periodic oscillations are more difficult to detect. Most types of oscillations observed are damped; that is, the peak amplitudes within a pattern decrease progressively in size, as shown in Fig. 7a. The damped type of oscillation can be detected by subtracting successive peak amplitudes, determining the absolute values of the change, and noting that three or more points form a negative slope. The data resulting from performing this algorithm are shown in Fig. 7b.

Pattern-Detection Procedure   Determining the precise beginning and ending of a pattern is difficult. Simple words such as "one" contain three to four distinct types of patterns, and each type has 10 to 12 repetitions. Detection of these groups of the same pattern type is a complicated problem because of variations in the same pattern and the leading and trailing transitions between patterns.

In the system being described, the detection of the beginning and ending of a pattern depends upon recognition of the random and decaying oscillation signals previously described. As soon as one or the other is detected, the data is tagged as the beginning of a pattern. When the data no longer satisfies the characteristics of the identified pattern, the data is tagged as the end of the pattern and a search for the next pattern begins.

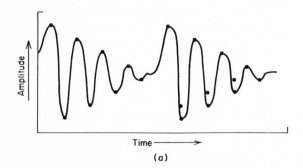

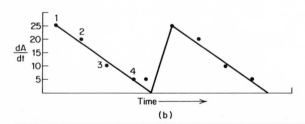

FIG. 7   (a) *Damped oscillation;* (b) *absolute value of change in damped oscillation.*

In more detail, the procedure is as follows. At the identified beginning of a word, the program concurrently examines the data for both randomness, as indicated by slope reversals in less than 160 μs, and decaying oscillations, as indicated by periodic monotonic decreases in the absolute values of the peak amplitudes. If the randomness criterion is satisfied for about 30 slope reversals, the search for damped oscillations is terminated. The random-pattern analysis continues until seven time intervals fail to satisfy the criterion, at which time the end-of-pattern is declared. Similarly, when damped oscillations are found, the end-of-pattern is declared after the appearance of seven slope reversals which do not satisfy the criterion.

After an end-of-pattern is declared, the preceding data are examined to determine the number of slope reversals in the pattern. If there are fewer than about 40, it is assumed that the data represent a transition period and they are ignored in subsequent analysis.

This procedure was derived from experimental results and observations of speech waveforms. Tests to date indicate that it is effective in segmenting the word for subsequent analysis. Due to variations in speakers and utterances of a single speaker, the same word may result in differing members of identified patterns. These multiple patterns must be resolved in the subsequent pattern-classification and word-recognition portions of the system.

14.8 Pattern Parameters and Analysis

After segmenting the word into patterns using the procedures described in Sec. 4.7, the next step is to derive a set of measurement parameters that can be used for the further classification and trends of the patterns. If patterns are described too precisely, the chances of finding them again in the same word are small. If patterns are examined too coarsely, the distinction between vowels, for example, is very difficult. To produce speaker-independent recognition, some degree of variation must be accommodated.

A number of parameters can be used to describe a speech waveform. Some parameters require large amounts of mathematical manipulation, implying significant processing time or additional hardware. Cost, performance, and accuracy must be balanced to create a reasonable system configuration.

Types of Patterns   In the system being described, two independent searches of a pattern are made to extract the necessary parameters. One search does a detailed analysis of types of oscillations; another search develops the trends of the pattern. In each search, both time and amplitude data are examined. The analysis is based upon changes in time and amplitude between peaks, and the parameters are expressed as ratios, so as to make the resultant parameters independent of the absolute time and amplitude.

Eighteen parameters currently are calculated in this system; sixteen are grouped into four categories. The remaining two parameters are single values: one is a number and the other is an average taken over the total pattern. The eighteen parameters can be summarized thus:

1. Damped oscillations—amplitude analysis (four ratios)
2. Damped oscillations—time-interval analysis (four ratios)
3. Peaks—amplitude analysis (four ratios)
4. Peaks—time-interval analysis (four ratios)
5. Number of repetitions
6. Average time interval

Damped Oscillations—Amplitude Analysis   As described earlier, a damped-oscillation pattern is identified by comparing the absolute value of the amplitudes of successive peaks and noting that three or more of them are monotonically decreasing. Within a pattern of this type, there typically are a number of repetitions of the damped behavior. Within each repetition, the number of oscillations (peaks) appears related to the particular vowel. The existence of the repetitions and of the varying number of peaks in a repetition is illustrated in Fig. 8 for two vowel sounds.

The pattern data based upon these observations is examined to identify the repetitions. The total number of repetitions is determined and saved. Similarly, the number of positive peaks in each repetition is saved. The time intervals between the first five positive peaks also are saved for use in the later time-interval analysis. The saved data are indicated graphically for two repetitions in Fig. 9. For convenience, only the positive peaks are used in this analysis. The concept could be used with both positive peaks (maxima) and negative peaks (minima), but this has been found unnecessary in this experimental system.

If we let R be the total number of repetitions (reps) in the pattern, four ratios arbitrarily named r_1 through r_4 are calculated:

$$r_1 = \frac{R}{\text{no. of } P_2\text{'s in } R \text{ reps}}$$

$$r_2 = \frac{R}{\text{no. of } P_3\text{'s in } R \text{ reps}}$$

$$r_3 = \frac{R}{\text{no. of } P_4\text{'s in } R \text{ reps}}$$

$$r_4 = \frac{\text{total no. of peaks } (P) \text{ in } R \text{ reps}}{R}$$

Because it is conceivable that the denominator of some of these ratios might be zero, the program must test its value to avoid an attempt to divide by zero.

All calculations are done by using integer arithmetic, which is usually faster than floating-point arithmetic. This is why the ratios are designed to provide numbers greater than 1. The ratio r_4 provides the average number of peaks in a damped oscillation; this number is a clue as to the type of vowel or pattern. If there are more than 16 damped-oscillation segments ($R > 16$), the pattern is a candidate for classification as a vowel.

Damped Oscillations—Time-Interval Analysis   Referring again to Fig. 9, a similar set of ratios, arbitrarily designated r_5 through r_8, are calculated. They

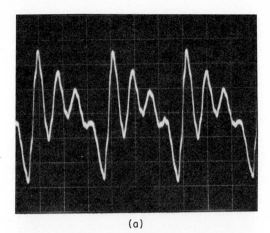

(a)

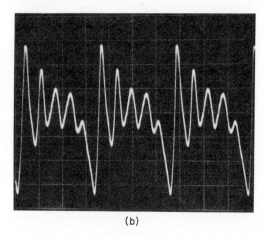

(b)

FIG. 8   *Patterns of (a) the vowel /a/, and (b) the vowel /o/.*

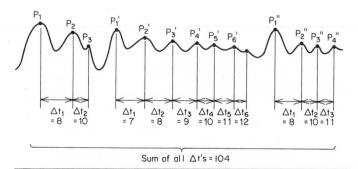

FIG. 9   *Example of damped oscillation analysis.*

represent the average time intervals associated with each of the first four peaks and with the entire pattern.

The ratios are calculated as:

$$r_5 = \frac{\text{sum of } \Delta t_1\text{'s in } R \text{ reps}}{\text{no. of } P_2\text{'s in } R \text{ reps}}$$

$$r_6 = \frac{\text{sum of } \Delta t_2\text{'s in } R \text{ reps}}{\text{no. of } P_3\text{'s in } R \text{ reps}}$$

$$r_7 = \frac{\text{sum of } \Delta t_3\text{'s in } R \text{ reps}}{\text{no. of } P_4\text{'s in } R \text{ reps}}$$

$$r_8 = \frac{\text{sum of all } \Delta t\text{'s in } R \text{ reps}}{R}$$

Again, the program should test the denominator for zero before attempting division. Also note that r_8 is the average time duration of the damped oscillations.

As a specific example of the calculation of r_1 through r_8, consider the waveform in Fig. 9, which shows three repetitions of a damped-oscillation pattern so that $R = 3$. The number of P_1's, P_2's, P_3's, and P_4's, are 3, 3, 3, and 2, respectively. The time intervals are as shown in the figure. Using this data, the ratios are:

3/3, 3/3, 3/1, 13/3, 23/3, 28/2, 20/2, 104/3

Peaks—Amplitude Analysis   This analysis provides four additional ratios that describe characteristics relating to the peaks in the waveform. Both positive and negative peaks (maxima and minima) are used, and the ratios represent relative occurrences of certain characteristics compared to the total number of peaks P in all repetitions R. The ratios arbitrarily are designated as r_9 through r_{12}. In the calculation of r_9, "equality" means that the peak amplitudes are equal to within 6 of the 8 data bits; that is, the subsequent peaks vary less than 4 parts out of 2^8, or 256.

The ratios are defined as:

$$r_9 = \frac{P}{\text{no. of sequential peaks almost zero in total pattern}}$$

$$r_{10} = \frac{P}{\text{no. of sequential peaks equal in total pattern and} > \text{zero}}$$

$$r_{11} = \frac{P}{\text{no. of sequential peak amplitudes monotonic (positive or negative) in total pattern}}$$

$$r_{12} = \frac{P}{\text{no. of sequential peaks in total pattern for which differentials alternate}}$$

The last parameter requires further explanation. The denominator is determined by considering three peaks at a time. If $P_1 > P_2 < P_3$, then one differential $(P_1 - P_2)$ is positive, and differential $(P_2 - P_3)$ is negative. This is what is meant by alternating differentials. It is extended to P_4, P_5, ... , until the condition is no longer true.

Peaks — Time-Interval Analysis This analysis is analogous to that used for the amplitude data. Because the numbers of peaks and time intervals in the pattern differ by only 1, P is used in calculating the ratios. With the same interpretations of equality and alternating differentials, the ratios r_{13} through r_{16} are defined as:

$$r_{13} = \frac{P}{\text{no. of sequential } \Delta t\text{'s} < 280 \ \mu\text{s in total pattern}}$$

$$r_{14} = \frac{P}{\text{no. of sequential } \Delta t\text{'s} = \text{or} > 280 \ \mu\text{s in total pattern}}$$

$$r_{15} = \frac{P}{\text{no. } \Delta t\text{'s monotonic (positive or negative) in total pattern}}$$

$$r_{16} = \frac{P}{\text{no. of sequential } \Delta t\text{'s in total pattern for which differentials alternate}}$$

Parameter-Calculation Procedure The remaining two parameters are the number of repetitions in the pattern (earlier defined as R) and the average time interval in the entire pattern. This is defined as:

$$r_{17} = \frac{\text{sum of all } \Delta t\text{'s in total pattern}}{P}$$

The total procedure is summarized in Fig. 10. The word-boundary and data-compression (selection) procedures were described earlier and are shown in more detail in Fig. 6. This procedure executes very quickly on a microprocessor. It is implemented in about 300 lines of assembler code and requires about 600 bytes of storage.

Pattern Analysis Specific computer routines that examine the parameters described have not yet been completed. As a result, experimental evidence that the 18 parameters are sufficient for voice recognition has not yet been obtained. Development of the pattern-analysis and word-recognition algorithms may result in modifications, additions, or deletions to the set of parameters. However, the work to date suggests that this set may be sufficient. On the basis of manual computation and visual observation of the ratio parameters for many different words, several observations can be made that will be the basis for developing the analysis routines.

There are multiple parameters generated for a pattern, and a decision as to the nature of a particular pattern cannot be made until all patterns are considered. The pattern must be examined as a total entity because of the number of identifying characteristics within that pattern.

The hard consonant (such as /t/ in "two") has as its main characteristic r_{13}, r_{14} (small ratio). Words like "one" (Fig. 11, p. 14–25) and "four" have similar parameters (r_9 through r_{16}) across a pattern and similar oscillation types in the amplitude domain (r_1 through r_4) but vary in the time domain of the oscillations (r_5 through r_8). Unaspirated sounds have a large number of random changes and small average time within a pattern (r_{13}, r_{17}).

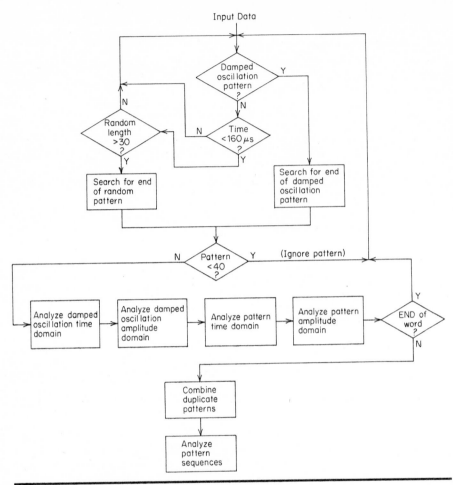

FIG. 10 *Block diagram of pattern classification.*

These observations can be illustrated by using the actual ratios generated by the system for the word "ship." A facsimile of the output is shown in Table 1. Pattern 1 shows a large number of peaks which change slope (r_{12}). The time associated with this change is short (r_{17}), and the short time interval is the predominant occurrence (r_{13}). The large number of damped oscillations (R and r_{15}) is consistent with the idea of randomness because all pattern types can exist in a random pattern. Pattern 1, then, is at the least an unaspirated sound (that is, /s/, /t/, /f/); to help distinguish these ratios (r_5 through r_8) indicate a probable /s/ sound. Patterns 2 to 3 represent the middle of the word. Pattern 3 is terminated by a stop-consonant flag derived by the input processor. Pattern 4 then identifies the /p/ as the stop consonant.

TABLE 1 Parameters for "ship"

| | Damped oscillations | | | | | | | | | Peaks | | | | | | | | |
| | Amplitude | | | | | Time interval | | | | Amplitude | | | | Time interval | | | | |
	r_1	r_2	r_3	r_4	R	r_5	r_6	r_7	r_8	r_9	r_{10}	r_{11}	r_{12}	r_{13}	r_{14}	r_{15}	r_{16}	r_{17}
Pattern 1	1	1	1	3	109	4	5	6	38	15	2	8	2	2	8	3	16	23
2	1	1	2	3	5	21	32	44	80	42	42	2	2	13	40	2	2	37
3	1	1	1	2	12	8	27	34	128	0	0	1	2	50	50	2	2	39
4	1*	1	1	4	3	7	32	16	64	0	12	2	3	...	10	2	2	48

*Represents an inter-phoneme-gap flag.

It appears that the unique identification of vowels will be very important in the success of this, or any, speech-recognition system. There are many similar words that differ in only the vowel sound, as, for example, "hit," "hat," and "hot." As shown in Table 2, half the phonemes are vowel-like sounds (i.e., vowels, semivowels, and diphthongs). Although characterized by the multiple repetitions of decaying oscillations, unique identification appears to depend upon the ability to identify the frequency content of the sound.

Some techniques for voice recognition depend heavily upon a frequency-domain analysis of the sound. Directly (by use of a filter bank) or indirectly (by the FFT, for example), the relative energy in certain frequency bands has been measured. Vowel-like sounds typically show three or more distinct frequency ranges, called "formants," in which significant energy is concentrated. Table 3 shows the frequencies on which these bands of energy are centered for the vowel sounds.[6] The values are averages taken over different speakers uttering a variety of words.

In this system, the burden of converting to the frequency domain was not considered reasonable, so all analyses are being done in the time domain. However, some frequency information is inherent in the time-interval data that has been saved by the system. The exact relationships have not been derived, but it is expected that the average values of the various time intervals can be related consistently to the formant frequencies. For example, the average length of the repetitions in the first cycle of a damped-oscillation waveform appears to be related to the third formant frequency, and r_8 is related to the first formant frequency.

Phoneme Sequences   The concepts discussed serve to associate the individual patterns with phonemes. The procedures do not result in a unique relationship between any given pattern and a single phoneme. The patterns resulting from transitions between phonemes and limitations in the analysis techniques limit the ability to totally and accurately identify phonemes.

However, it is expected that the procedures will narrow the possible phonemes for a given pattern to a manageable number. To a greater or lesser degree, the procedures will permit the construction of possible phoneme sequences that approximate the actual phoneme sequence in the word. Using the phoneme sequences in conjunction with the calculated ratios, a search technique of the dictionary of words, their phoneme sequences, and probable variations of these sequences can be constructed to lead to the actual word recognition.

As a more specific example, the word "six" (phonetically, /siks/) is rather easily separated into a sequence of four types of phonemes: a random sound, a vowel sound, a stop consonant indicated by a pause, and a final random sound. The identification procedures discussed for the vowel sounds can provide more detail about the vowel sound. Similarly, random sounds will be analyzed to separate some of the fricatives, such as distinguishing /s/ from /z/.

An intelligent pattern-analysis algorithm is very necessary for identifying phoneme sequences. Some patterns are meaningless because they merely

TABLE 2 *Orthographic representations of phonemes in American English and representative words*

Vowels		Semivowels		Diphthongs	
IY	beet	W	wag	eI	bay
I	bit	L	lamb	oU	boat
E	bet	R	rod	aI	buy
AD	bat	Y	yes	aU	how
UH	but			oI	boy
A	hot			jU	few
OW	bough	(These sounds are particularly			
U	foot	dependent upon their location			
OO	boot	in the word and			
ER	bird	surrounding vowels.)			

Nasals		Consonants Stops		Whisper	
M	miss	B	big	H	hand
N	knot	D	dig		
NG	sing	G	give		
		P	pin		
		T	tin		
		K	cat		

Fricatives		Affricates	
V	van	DZH	gem
TH	then	TSH	chin
Z	zip		
ZH	rouge		
F	fan		
THE	thin		
S	sod		
SH	shove		

TABLE 3 *Table of formant frequencies for vowels*[6]

Typewritten symbol for vowel	Typical word	F1	F2	F3
IY	beet	270	2290	3010
I	bit	390	1990	2550
E	bet	530	1840	2480
AE	bat	660	1720	2410
UH	but	520	1190	2390
A	hot	730	1090	2440
OW	bought	570	840	2410
U	foot	440	1020	2240
OO	boot	300	860	2240
ER	bird	490	1350	1690

indicate a transition, and some patterns are only repeats of previous patterns. An exact match of the parameters for each phoneme is not possible because of the variations of each voice. What *is* possible is a trend analysis of the patterns. The key parameters of each pattern parameter are used, and a best-fit approach is used for comparison.

14.9 Word-Identification Techniques

The final step in the word-recognition sequence is the association of phoneme sequences to words. This will be done by establishing a dictionary that relates actual words to phoneme sequences and other identifying parameters. Finding the exact word involves searching the dictionary for a reasonable match.

The more powerful 16- and 32-bit microprocessors perform this task more efficiently than do the 8-bit microprocessors. Their powerful instruction sets, larger addressing space, additional addressing modes, and word size can be used to reduce computation time and main storage requirements.

The search technique, the amount of storage, and the desired sophistication of "understanding" will influence the amount of storage required for the dictionary. Simple digit-recognition systems might require as little as several hundred bytes of storage. Very complex phrase- or sentence-understanding systems require multimegabyte dictionaries with syntactical parsing that breaks down a sentence into nouns, verbs, and other components of a sentence.

A number of well-known searching techniques are available. In some cases, combinations of the techniques are used in a sequential procedure. The following sections introduce three of the search techniques likely to be useful in this system: binary, indexed, and hashing.

Binary Search   The binary search technique can be very efficient for a reasonable number of entries, such as might be encountered in digit recognition. The lookup table can reside in memory; a search divides the table in half and decides which half the observed phoneme sequence is in. That half is cut in half, and a similar decision is again made. This process continues until the word is found. A table of 1024 entries can be searched with only 10 decisions by using this method.

Indexed Search   An indexed search is used for larger vocabularies. A table of parameters is maintained that gives an address of a group of words with similar properties. For example, an index table composed of phonemes can be used for start-of-word sounds. If the first pattern of a word contains an /s/ sound, the /s/ entry has associated with it a starting address for a table in memory. The table contains all words with a starting /s/ sound, their likely phoneme sequences, and other key parameters. This table of phoneme-constructed words can have the English spelling as part of its entry. This spelling entry could be used to directly print the word or to initiate some other computer response.

Hashing Parameters Hashing algorithms take all the key parameters from the phoneme sequence and generate an address based upon some algorithm. Some key parameters that can be used are the number of unique patterns, the placement of vowels within a word, and beginning sounds. Hashing algorithms are very efficient for converting the large number of parameters (40 to 50 bytes) in a word to a 16- to 24-bit address.

14.10 Hardware Implementation

There are many possible hardware configurations for performing voice recognition. The configuration that was implemented is shown in Fig. 1. Now that some of the problems and possible techniques associated with recognition have been mentioned, a more descriptive functional hardware implementation is possible. Using this system, the parameters associated with a word can be determined in about 1.5 s, and several words may be in the process of being analyzed because of the pipeline architecture.

The first processor is the input and includes an ADC that has 128 bytes of random access memory (RAM) and 512 bytes of read-only memory (ROM). The sampling rate of the ADC is 50,000 samples per second. Implemented in the code are the variable-amplitude threshold, word-boundary determination, and the data-compression algorithms. About 500 to 1000 parameters per second are transferred to the next processor for subsequent processing.

Processor 2 has 8 kbyte of RAM and 8 kbyte of ROM. It performs the pattern-detection algorithm and calculates the 18 ratios. The data from Processor

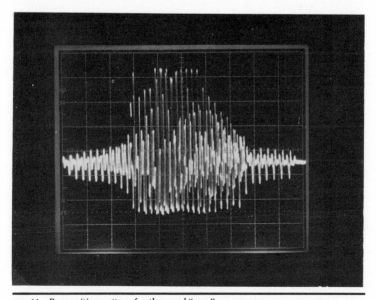

FIG. 11 *Recognition pattern for the word "one."*

1 is received and buffered while the previous word is being analyzed. This processor sends 100 to 200 parameters per second to the subsequent processor.

Processor 3, the system processor, has a standard complement of input-output (I/O), devices, such as keyboard/CRT and disk (diskette). This processor has 64 kbyte of RAM and will perform the dictionary lookup using a combination of indexed and hashing search techniques. It will also perform the response to the verbal request.

14.11   Status

As indicated earlier, not all of this system has been constructed. Processors 1 and 2 have been implemented, and the software up through the calculation of the ratio parameters is operational. The basic operating system kernel is currently being written.

Because the system implementation is incomplete, it is not now possible to verify the accuracy of its voice-recognition capabilities. It is certainly likely that, when completed, the system will not be completely successful initially. Further experimentation, which could involve modifications to the procedures described in this chapter, may be necessary. It is even conceivable that the system cannot reach its initial goals because of limitations in currently available microcomputer processing power or fundamental errors in the experiments, research, or heuristic reasoning upon which the system is based.

Nevertheless, this experimental system represents an investigation that is possible only because of the emergence of the microprocessor. The problem of voice recognition has been a topic of research for more than 20 years and a low-cost, speaker-independent, large-vocabulary system has yet to become commercially practical. Someday professionals will find a microprocessor-based system which meets the elusive goals and which could be of significant value in hundreds of practical applications. In the meantime, voice recognition continues as a fascinating and challenging problem for researchers in this field.

ACKNOWLEDGMENTS

I would like to express appreciation to my wife Bonita for her linguistics support and to Dr. Thomas J. Harrison for his efforts in the preparation of this chapter.

REFERENCES

1. Dinneen, Francis P..: *An Introduction to General Linguistics*, Holt, New York, 1967.
2. Dixon, N. Rex, and Thomas B. Martin: *Automatic Speech and Speaker Recognition*, IEEE Press, New York, 1979.
3. Rabiner, L. R., and R. W. Schafer: *Digital Processing of Speech Signals*, Prentice-Hall, Englewood Cliffs, N.J., 1978.

4. Harrison, Thomas J.: *Handbook of Industrial Control Computers*, Wiley-Interscience, New York, 1972.
5. Heilman, Arthur W.: *Principles and Practices of Teaching Reading*, Merrill, Columbus, Ohio, 1972.
6. Peterson, G. E., and H. L. Barney: "Control Methods Used in a Study of the Vowels," *J. Acoust. Soc. Am.*, Vol. 24, No. 2, March 1952, pp. 175–184.

CHAPTER FIFTEEN

A Slow-Scan Television System Using a Microprocessor

Clayton W. Abrams

International Business Machines Corp.,
General Products Division,
San Jose, California

INTRODUCTION

Slow-scan television (SSTV) is a low-resolution scheme that reduces the bandwidth of conventional television. SSTV is used as a communications medium where bandwidth is an important factor. This chapter begins with a discussion of analog TV systems at various scanning rates. The major portion of the chapter is devoted to a microprocessor-based SSTV system that can be used in many applications; typical applications include picture telephones, high-frequency communications, and weather-satellite reception.

SSTV was conceived in the 1920s, and its popularity as a communications medium is increasing. In the 1970s, SSTV gained worldwide attention with NASA's Apollo moon pictures, with the Mariner and Viking Mars pictures, and, more recently, with the Voyager Jupiter and Saturn pictures. In all cases the SSTV principles are similar—only the system specifications and technology employed differ.

15.1   SSTV *Specifications*

In most cases SSTV specifications are derived from fast-scan conventional television. The fast-scan specifications, which have been standardized for the past 30 years, are basically

525 lines per frame
 60 fields per second
 30 frames per second

These specifications were not derived arbitrarily; they resulted from numerous investigations[1] and were basically designed to provide a resolution approximately equal to 16-mm motion pictures.

Resolution is the number of alternating black and white lines that can be resolved in the horizontal or vertical directions. The vertical resolution of a television image is the maximum number of discernable horizontal lines that can be resolved in the height of the picture. The horizontal resolution of a television picture is a measurement of the maximum number of alternating black and white vertical lines that can be viewed. In digital electronics this parameter is usually referred to as "pixels per horizontal scan line." Pixel is derived from "picture element," which is defined as the smallest spot resolvable on the face of the picture tube.

If an SSTV specification is to be derived, a few compromises must be made in resolution. Unfortunately, no straightforward method exists to relax the fast-scan specification. In most cases the resolution is a *de facto* result of the bandwidth of the system. Bandwidth is a restriction placed upon the system as a result of the communications medium selected for the SSTV system. Table 1 is a bandwidth criterion for the communications medium in which an SSTV system could be used.

TABLE 1   *Communications channel bandwidths*

Medium	Bandwidth
Telephone*	4 kHz
AM broadcast	10 kHz
Narrow-band FM	±5 kHz
Wideband FM	±15 kHz
HF broadcast	3 kHz

*CCITT recommendation for multiplex voice-grade lines

The bandwidth of an SSTV system has a direct relationship to the required horizontal resolution. The calculation of bandwidth can be approximated in the following manner.[1] The first point to consider in the bandwidth approximation is the sampling frequency of the pixels:

Sampling frequency
= pixels per line × lines per field × no. of fields per second

The Nyquist theory dictates that the minimum sampling frequency be twice the maximum frequency of the video. This is an approximation because in reality the sampling rate is considerably greater than twice the spatial resolution. For example, if the samples are taken at a rate twice the highest frequency component at the zero crossing points of the frequency, the sampled output is zero. Therefore, the video bandwidth of an SSTV system can be approximated by the following:

Video bandwidth = sampling frequency ÷ 2

This calculation includes a further assumption that the aspect ratio of the SSTV system is 1:1.

The aspect ratio of the picture is the relationship of frame width to height. In conventional television the relationship is 4:3, which closely approximates 16- and 35-mm film. Once a bandwidth is selected, the next process is to determine the number of lines per field and the number of fields per second. Most of the parameters are determined by experimental results. Following is some background on this subject. Experiments have been conducted on SSTV to address the following[2]:

1. Interlaced versus noninterlaced SSTV
2. Number of lines per field

These experiments concluded that 90 percent of the observers preferred noninterlaced pictures with a greater number of lines. The same experiment varied the number of lines from 225 to 135. Subjectively, the pictures were significantly better at the high lines per field; however, they were satisfactory for many applications at the rate of 135 lines per field.

Additional experiments conducted by the author have shown that with 128 lines per field systems, a significant improvement in quality can be achieved by increasing the number of pixels per line. A minimum-quality picture is possible at 128 pixels per line; the quality improves with 256 pixels per line. Figure 1 shows the effect of bandwidth versus fields per second for 128-line SSTV pictures.

Another parameter to consider when specifying an SSTV system is image continuity, which is the rate at which fields are repeated. The rate of field repetition must be chosen to satisfy two requirements:

1. Portrayal of motion in a continuous fashion
2. Avoidance of flickering

The motion of the subject material can be restricted by application. For example, if the application is to be used for picture telephones, most material to be

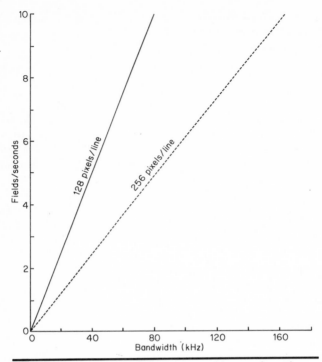

FIG. 1   *SSTV Bandwidth versus fields per second for a 128-line video picture.*

transmitted will be the head and shoulder views of a person. In experiments, the following observations were made[3]:

Rate	Subjective comments
30 frames per second	Normal TV
20 frames per second	Slight jerkiness in motion
15 frames per second	Noticeable jerkiness in motion
6 frames per second	Quite jerky—no coordination between lips and sound

The quality of the motion can be improved if digital electronic techniques are employed. If only portions of pictures are transmitted in which motion is detectable, the bandwidth of the system can be further reduced. Experiments have shown that low bandwidths are possible using this scheme.[4]

The flickering of a television display system is quite different from jerky motion. In conventional television systems, this problem was caused by two factors:

1. Brightness of the displayed image
2. Viewing conditions

Tests have shown[5] that with a display brightness of 3 ft-L, a field rate of 40 fields per second is the limit of flickering which can be noticed. The use of digital technology in SSTV system displays allows the field rate to be much lower than that in the older analog systems. This is accomplished by receiving the picture at a slow rate, storing the picture digitally, and then displaying the picture at a fast rate.

A High-Frequency Communications SSTV Specification The following sections of this chapter are devoted to the description of an SSTV system designed for a high-frequency (HF) communications application. The system has proved adequate for amateur radio communications in which motion was not allowed. The bandwidth of the system was the most important factor.

The bandwidth of this system is 1.25 to 2.5 kHz, which is compatible with all the communications media in Table 1. The specifications of this system are:

Vertical resolution = 128 to 256 pixels per line
Frame rate = one frame per 8.3 seconds
Noninterlaced video
Vertical resolution = 128 lines per frame
Horizontal sync pulse width = 5 milliseconds
Vertical pulse width = 30 milliseconds
Horizontal line period = 66.66 milliseconds
Horizontal retrace time = 5.0 milliseconds

Despite these relaxed specifications, satisfactory pictures have been transmitted via communications media where conventional television was not possible.

15.2 Analog SSTV Systems

The first SSTV systems[6] designed were entirely analog. These systems suffered from many shortcomings; however, many of the principles employed are used in the more recent digital designs. One common technique is SSTV modulation.

SSTV modulation is generated by frequency-modulating (FM) video and sync information onto a subcarrier. The carrier is typically in the audio range and varies in frequency proportionally to the video amplitude. A lower audio frequency from video is used to designate sync. The HF SSTV scheme, which is discussed in this chapter, uses a sync frequency of 1200 Hz, and the video information varies between 1500 and 2300 Hz.

SSTV Analog Display Systems A block diagram of a typical analog SSTV display system is shown in Fig. 2. The SSTV signal is applied to a limiter stage that performs limiting, automatic gain control (AGC), and audio filtering of the signal. The discriminator changes the FM-modulated SSTV signal to an AM signal. To recover the sync signal, a tuned circuit discriminator is used to recover the horizontal and vertical sync information.

A second detector recovers the video information, usually by full-wave rectification and filtering. This signal drives the cathode of a cathode ray tube (CRT). The vertical and sync pulses are used to drive the deflection circuitry

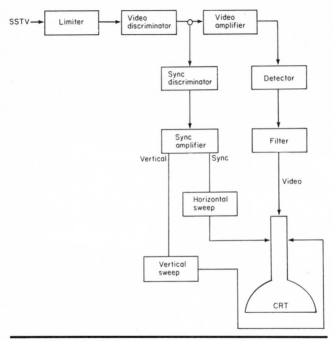

FIG. 2   *SSTV analog display system.*

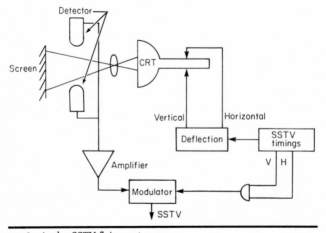

FIG. 3   *Analog SSTV flying spot scanner.*

of the CRT, which produces a raster on the CRT screen. A video signal on the CRT's cathode varies the intensity of the CRT raster, which creates a picture on the screen. The screen of the CRT tube must have a phosphor that will retain the SSTV image for an entire slow-scan frame. This is the greatest drawback of all SSTV analog display systems.

SSTV *Analog Image Generation*   Analog SSTV images can be produced by two methods: TV cameras and flying-spot scanners. Figure 3 is a block diagram of an analog flying-spot scanner. This device is useful for generating stationary images, such as test patterns. A spot is formed on the CRT face and imaged on a pickup screen. The spot's motion is controlled by the deflection circuitry, which is timed to the SSTV rate.

A more popular means of analog SSTV generation is the use of a sampling TV camera. Figure 4 is the block diagram of a sampling TV camera. The sampling TV camera functions like an oscilloscope. In this application, the TV camera yoke is rotated by 90°. The SSTV pixels are sampled on successive fast-scan vertical lines, and at the completion of an SSTV line, the sampling is moved to the right 1 pixel (Fig. 5). The process is repeated until an SSTV frame is generated. One restriction to using this sampling technique is that the subject must be stationary in front of the camera for the SSTV frame rate. This concept of scanning alternate horizontal lines with a constant vertical

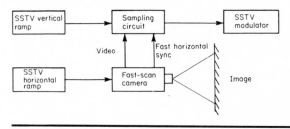

FIG. 4   *Analog SSTV sampling camera.*

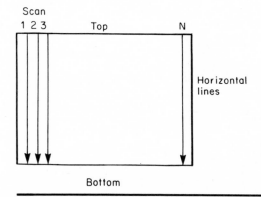

FIG. 5   *Sampling technique used for the fast-scan camera.*

displacement is further discussed in Sec. 15.6, *Microprocessor Software Design,* under *Fast-Scan Television Camera Interface Software* (p. 15–26).

15.3   Digital SSTV Systems

The analog SSTV systems previously discussed present a basis for all digital systems. The digital concepts are primarily used for the temporary storage of digital TV images. Prior to discussing a digital system, three concepts should be presented:

1. Pixels in horizontal lines are represented by bytes or nibbles (half-bytes) in the digital electronics scheme.
2. The analog video signal is represented digitally by discrete steps called gray levels. The gray-level steps must be as linear as possible. The number of gray levels that can be displayed and stored is a very important parameter in a digital SSTV system.
3. Digital systems replace critical components from the older analog designs. The resultant advantages outweigh the increased cost of the digital system.

Digital Display Systems   Figure 6 is the block diagram of a typical SSTV digital display system. The SSTV signal is demodulated in a manner similar to that used in the analog system. The major difference between the two systems is the display. The analog system utilized a CRT, which stored the picture temporarily on the phosphor on the screen. The digital system replaces the long-persistence CRT with a memory bank and logic.

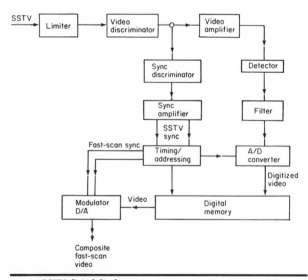

FIG. 6   *SSTV digital display system.*

Once the SSTV video signal is received by the demodulator, it is passed to an analog-to-digital converter (ADC), which converts the analog signal to a digital gray level. The digitalization of the signal is a function of the hardware components selected and the specifications of the system. Once in digital form, timing signals gate the gray-level value into memory at the appropriate time. All these operations occur at the SSTV rate.

Because the picture is now placed into a digital memory bank, it is relatively easy to address the memory at a fast rate and generate video. The video rates are converted as follows:

1. Reception of an SSTV signal at a slow rate
2. Display of a picture in memory at a fast-scan rate

The SSTV timing is derived from the incoming signal. The vertical sync pulse starts the reception of a frame, and the horizontal sync gates a pixel counter. The pixel counters are used to clock the ADC and memory address counters.

When a picture is displayed in memory, the timing is derived from an oscillator and counters operating at a fast-scan rate, which is a function of the number of pixels per line and the number of pixels per memory location. Another limiting factor is the size of the memory. If the system requirements dictate high resolution, the the memory size will increase proportionally.

Digital SSTV *Image Generation* Digital image generation is similar to the analog techniques in that a TV camera is the input transducer. The main differences are how the images are stored. As previously discussed, digital television is accomplished by placing a picture into random access memory (RAM). In most cases the RAM is some sort of electronic memory unit.

SSTV digital images can be generated either a line or a frame at a time. Both schemes have advantages based upon the application. The SSTV is generated by feeding the composite video from a closed-circuit TV into a circuit that limits and clips the video to a level compatible with a sync separator. The sync information is next stripped from the video. The recovered sync pulses are used to generate addresses and timing for the digital memory.

The video information is fed directly to an ADC and in turn to the memory unit. Because the A/D sampling must be accomplished at a fast rate, the requirements for this device are very stringent. The memory unit is used to store a frame or line; in both cases the digitized data is clocked out of RAM at an SSTV rate. The data output from RAM is fed directly to a digital-to-analog converter (DAC) and in turn to an SSTV modulator.

15.4 *Microprocessor* SSTV *Systems*

The preceding section described the methods previously employed in SSTV system design. These older systems were very inflexible because of hardware constraints. If the hardware had been made more flexible and the logic functions were more easily changed, the entire systems approach would have been more useful and expandable. The use of a microprocessor solves this flexibility problem. If most of the logic functions are replaced with microprocessor software, the system can be customized for the specific application.

The following sections present design considerations of a system using a microprocessor for random logic replacement. Because little difference exists between hardware and software in their basic form, some guidelines are provided to allow tradeoffs.

Another important decision when designing a microprocessor-based SSTV system is to use the system bus concept: Unique cards are designed for specific functions that are plugged into a bus. This configuration enables the system to be configured very quickly. Standard cards can be used to serve various common functions, i.e., memory, CPU, and input-output (I/O). Special cards can be designed for SSTV and plugged into the bus, with their logical interconnections accomplished by software, which is effectively the glue that bonds the system.

Hardware Design Considerations   We now examine a microprocessor-based SSTV system based upon the specifications in Sec. 15.1. Figure 7 is a block diagram of a system showing each critical element. The microprocessor system can be any general-purpose system that contains a standard bus structure.

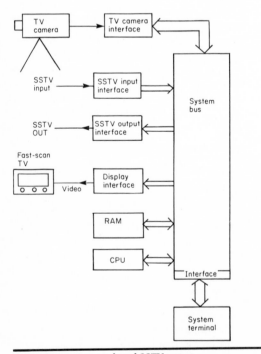

FIG. 7   *Microprocessor-based SSTV system.*

The blocks designated as memory, CPU, and system terminal are standard, commercially available components. The four unique functional components that must be constructed for this application are:

1. SSTV input
2. SSTV output
3. Fast-scan display
4. TV camera interface

Following is a brief description of these blocks. A more complete description is in Sec. 15.5, *Microprocessor Hardware Design.*

SSTV *input interface* The SSTV input blocks[7] capture an SSTV picture into microprocessor memory. The SSTV signal is detected by circuitry identical with the analog system described in Sec. 15.2. A medium-speed ADC converts the various information to a digital microprocessor input. Because the data rates of SSTV are slow compared to those of the microprocessor, all control and timing are generated by software in the microprocessor system.

SSTV *output interface* The SSTV output blocks[7] generate SSTV signals. The SSTV modulator is a sinusoidal voltage-controlled oscillator (VCO) running at the SSTV subcarrier frequency (1500 Hz). The input to the SSTV monitor is from a DAC that changes the VCO frequency proportional to the video.

A single bit from the output port is connected to the SSTV modulator, which causes the VCO to output a sync frequency (1200 Hz). This configuration is similar to the SSTV input in that all control signals and timings are derived from the software.

Fast-scan display interface The fast-scan display interface[8] displays an SSTV picture contained in the microprocessor memory of a conventional television set. Because the data rate is considerably faster than that of the processor, some external means other than the microprocessor addressing of the pixels in memory must be utilized. This is accomplished by halting the processor and letting other hardware gain control of the bus and address memory at the fast-scan rate. The picture data from memory is transferred to a DAC, mixed with sync pulses, and displayed on fast-scan TV.

This interface scheme requires little software because all timings and signals are derived from the interface card. This technique of addressing memory is called direct memory access (DMA).

TV camera interface The TV camera interface is used to interconnect a standard closed-circuit TV camera with the microprocessor system. The sampling scheme of this interface[9] employs a technique similar to that described for the analog sampling camera in Sec. 15.2.

Pixels are sampled at a slow rate from successive lines by the interface's hardware, which is controlled by the microprocessor software. The sampling scheme is shown in Fig. 5. This interface is software-dependent and requires critical software timings to transfer an entire picture from the TV camera to microprocessor memory in the minimum amount of time.

Software Design Considerations   As discussed, the software for the microprocessor system in this application is the logic element that binds all the interface cards together. One criterion for the software in a real-time SSTV application is speed; thus the software must be as efficient as possible. Therefore, ASSEMBLY language programming is a requirement for all interface devices.

The biggest advantage of using a microprocessor for a controller is that it expands the function of the older hardware designs. For example, enhancements such as image processing and graphics can be utilized (this subject is discussed further in Sec. 15.6).

The programming of a microprocessor in this logic-replacement application is first accomplished by defining all ports by function, address, and bit assignment. The next step is to define how memory will be formatted to contain SSTV picture. This is a function of the number of pixels, lines, and gray levels to be displayed. Consider the system defined in Sec. 15.1. If 16 gray levels are to be displayed or received, this format is equal to 4 bits or 1 nibble per pixel. If 2 pixels are packed into one 8-bit byte in the system, the picture requirements are:

$$\text{Memory bytes} = \text{lines per frame} \times \text{pixels per line} \times 0.5 \text{ byte per pixel}$$
$$= 128 \times 256 \times 0.5$$
$$= 16{,}384 \text{ bytes per frame}$$

The next step is to define where the program and picture will reside in memory. In this application, the picture area is limited by the hardware and will reside in the lower 16K of RAM followed by the control program.

Probably the most important concept in the creation of software is modularity: The program should be structured so each function is broken down into small independent parts. The human interface to the system should be considered as much as possible. This is usually accomplished by displaying a program menu on the systems terminal; program options can be selected from the menu.

SSTV *Program Structure*   Figure 8 is the block diagram of the program structure for the SSTV system.[8] The software structure is organized in a manner similar to that used in the hardware structure. Three functions that can be selected are:

1. SSTV transmit or receive
2. Fast-scan display
3. TV camera

Once selected, each function executes program modules. A program module is a portion of a program that accomplishes a specific task. Each task can be broken down into submodules (subroutines). This technique, called program structure, should resemble a tree if flowcharted. The submodules should be small; one guideline is to have no more than 50 lines of code per module.

Program module designs can be rated for strength or weakness.[10] One factor with a direct relationship to module strength is *coupling*; which is the degree

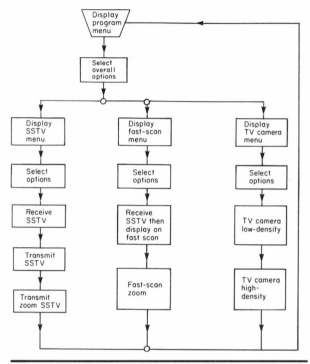

FIG. *8* *SSTV program structure.*

to which one module makes use of another. Experience has shown that programs which have low coupling tend to be more reliable and easier to maintain. The design of each program module is discussed in more detail in Sec. 15.6.

15.5 *Microprocessor Hardware Design*

This section details the SSTV interface components discussed in Sec. 15.4.

SSTV *Input Interface* The SSTV input interface is shown in the block diagram in Fig. 10 (page 15-15). The interface consists of three parts:

1. SSTV detection/amplification
2. ADC
3. I/O port

SSTV *Detection* The SSTV detection is made possible by using a number of circuits.[6] These circuits range from FM discriminators to phase-locked loops (PLLs); their main purpose is to recover SSTV video and sync pulses. One of the more popular circuits is a linear discriminator.

The linear discriminator should exhibit a response curve similar to the one in Fig. 9. This response curve can be achieved by tuned circuits or active filters.

The sync pulses from the detector are shaped and placed on bits of the input port to be sampled by the microprocessor software. The SSTV-detected video is amplified to a level compatible with the ADC. The amplifier produces 0 V for 1500 Hz and +5 V for 2300 Hz.

ADC   The ADC is composed of three parts: sample-and-hold (S/H), A/D, and I/O ports (Fig. 10). The S/H is used in conjunction with the ADC to shorten the aperture time for the converter by rapidly sampling the SSTV signal and then holding its value until the A/D conversion is completed. The aperture time is the amount of time between the hold command signal and the point when the S/H stores analog voltage.

There are four types of ADCs:

1. Counter or servo
2. Dual-slope integrating
3. Successive approximation
4. Parallel

Each type of converter operates by slightly different principles; this subject is not discussed in this chapter. A successive-approximation (SA) type ADC was selected for this application. To select the ADC speed requirements, the SSTV sampling rate must be first calculated, as follows:

$$\text{Sampling rate} = \frac{\text{horiz. line period} - \text{retrace time}}{\text{pixels per line}}$$

$$= \frac{(66.66 - 5.0)\text{ ms}}{256}$$

$$= 240.8\ \mu\text{s per pixel}$$

You can see from this calculation of the conversion time that a medium-speed ADC is required; an ADC with a conversion speed of 50 μs was selected. The S/H selected has an aperture delay of 50 ns. With this configuration, the software must not take longer than 190.8 μs to digitize the SSTV signal and place the results in RAM.

I/O *Ports*   The I/O ports are the interface between the microprocessor bus and the outside world. Two integrated circuits (ICs) are commonly used in this circuit: the 8255 programmable peripheral interface (PPI) for 8080-based systems and the 6821 peripheral interface adapter (PIA) for 6800-based systems. These ICs are general-purpose programmable I/O ports. They contain two 8-bit bidirectional ports and from 2 to 4 control lines per port.

Within the IC are two control registers that allow each register and control line to be configured as inputs or outputs. The ports are attached to the microprocessor bus and addressed as either memory-mapped I/O or I/O ports, depending upon the architecture of the system.

SSTV *Output Interface* A block diagram of the SSTV output interface is shown in Fig. 11. The interface consists of four parts: a modulator, an amplifier, a DAC, and an output port.

The modulator is a free-running oscillator with a sinusoidal output. The oscillator must be controlled by changes in frequency with an analog voltage. This type of oscillator is called a VCO. An IC ideal for this application is the XR-2206, which is comprised of five blocks: a VCO, an analog multiplier, a sine shaper, a unity gain amplifier, and a set of current switches. The internal current switches transfer the oscillator current to any one of the two external timing resistors, to produce two discrete frequencies externally selectable.

A control line from the output port is fed to the modulator for the sync input. When OFF, an analog signal is applied to the VCO. The amplifier in Fig. 11 is used to scale the analog voltage for the proper swing from 1500- to 2300-Hz in modulator frequency.

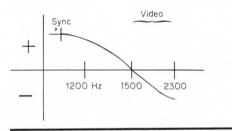

FIG. 9 *SSTV double-sided discriminator.*

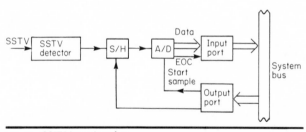

FIG. 10 *SSTV input interface.*

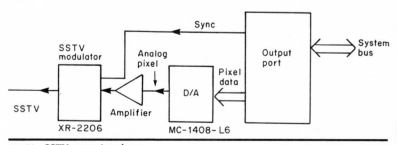

FIG. 11 *SSTV output interface.*

The DAC selected is a monolithic converter that consists of six switching current sources: a diffused resistor ladder, a bias circuit, and a reference control amplifier. The converter functions in an R-2R ladder configuration and has excellent linearity and fast settling times. The device selected is an MC-1408-L6. Connected to the DAC is an output port that transfers pixels from microprocessor RAM to the modulator under program control.

Fast-Scan Display Interface   A block diagram of the fast-scan interface design is shown in Fig. 12. The interface can be broken down into four major parts: CRT controller, memory access, video modulator, and counters/timers.[8]

The interface functions by displaying pixels at a rate far in excess of the microprocessor's ability to address memory. Therefore, DMA is utilized. Three schemes of DMA are possible with microprocessors:

1. Halting the processor
2. Cycle stealing
3. Multiplexing the CPU with the DMA device

Each technique has advantages; however, the cycle-stealing method will not be fast enough for this application. Multiplexing is advantageous because

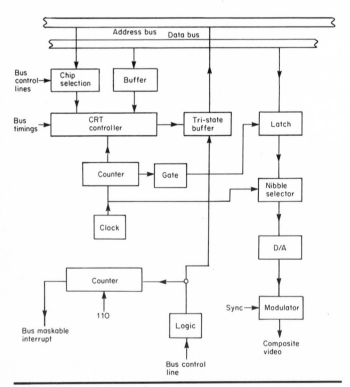

FIG. 12   *Fast-scan display interface.*

the microprocessor and memory share the RAM at the same time. In this application, the processor gains control of memory accessing during 1 cycle and controls the DMA device hardware during the alternate clock cycle of the microprocessor.

An alternate result is accomplished by halting the processor by hardware grounding of a pin on the CPU or by issuing a wait command by software. The halting method is the easiest one to implement and is used in this SSTV design approach.

The CRT controller block (Fig. 13) is the heart of the video interface. This block consists of a single IC that controls all display timings. The CRT con-

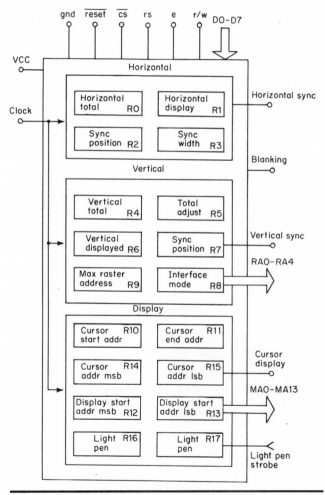

FIG. 13 *Internal functions of the MC-6845 CRT controller IC.*

troller IC is typical of a number of high-density special-function ICs that replace numerous low-density standard devices.

The CRT controller IC is designed to interface with microprocessors and provide all timings necessary to refresh RAM at video rates. To accomplish this, 18 registers are preloaded from the microprocessor. (The descriptions are in Fig. 13.) This application requires two hardware constraints:

1. The memory accessing rate must not exceed the RAM specified rate.
2. The memory picture buffer will not exceed 16,384 bytes.

The memory accessing rate is calculated by:

$$\text{Byte rate} = \frac{\text{horizontal line duration} - \text{retrace time}}{\text{bytes per line}}$$

Because 2 pixels are equal to 1 byte, the data rate of memory accessing is one-half the fast-scan pixel rate. Figure 14 is a photograph of a display using this accessing technique. The density of this picture is 128 pixels per line, 128 lines per frame, and 16 gray levels. The memory accessing rate is 651 ns.

The remaining blocks in Fig. 12 function as follows: a clock-derived signal latches the data present on the data bus at the correct time. Once latched, a multiplexer gates the data a nibble at a time to a DAC, which is a ladder network constructed with discrete resistors. Sync signals are outputted from the CRT controller chip. The sync pulse widths and their relationship to memory addressing are preprogrammed by software prior to displaying a picture. The sync pulses and video are mixed in a single transistor modulator stage to generate composite video.

Fast-Scan Television Camera Interface   A block diagram of the fast-scan camera interface is shown in Fig. 15. The interface[9] is designed to accept any standard video source. In this application, the source is a television camera.

FIG. 14   *Photograph of a fast-scan display using data stored in RAM from an SSTV system.*

The interface consists of a video amplifier, sync separator, ADC, position counters, and I/O ports. The video is initially amplified to a 2-V swing. A dc restoration circuit clamps the sync signal's maximum excursions to ground. The horizontal and vertical sync signals are then separated from the composite video signal.

The amplified video signal is then passed to an S/H circuit that is strobed from an output port of the microprocessor. The S/H is connected to an ADC that is a medium-speed SA converter.

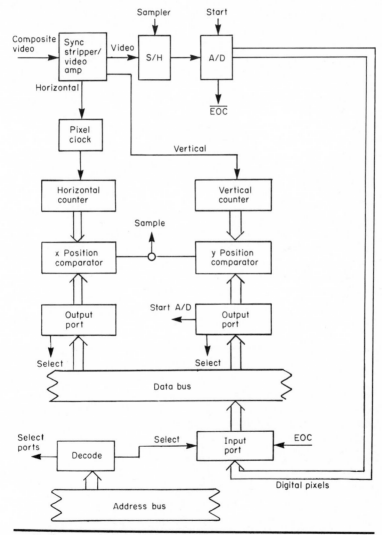

FIG. 15   Fast-scan television camera interface.

Because the sampling rate is a direct function of the microprocessor software, low-cost components may be used. The ADC consists of an MC-1408-L8 DAC and an MC-14559 SA register.

The horizontal and vertical sync pulses previously derived are connected to two counters. One counter contains an x location, the other a y location in the picture. The x location equates with the pixel location on the y line of a picture frame. The horizontal sync pulse is connected first to a pixel counter, which drives the x location counter at the pixel rate.

Both the x and y counters are connected to comparators that are in turn connected to output ports from the microprocessor. When the comparator equals the output-port count, a sample pulse is provided to the S/H. The analog video signal will be retained in the S/H, awaiting an ADC start pulse issued from an output port. The digitized point in the picture is now placed on the input port of the microprocessor after the appropriate conversion time. The input port can now be read by the microprocessor software and placed in computer memory.

15.6   Microprocessor Software Design

As discussed in Sec. 15.4, the software is the glue that bonds the hardware. When designing a system, tradeoffs must be made as to the number of functions that can be placed in the software. Hardware functions tend to be inflexible, making expansion difficult, whereas software functions are usually limited by speed, size of memory, and programming difficulty.

In the SSTV hardware previously described, the designs were based upon a maximum amount of flexibility at low hardware costs. The fast-scan display board is the only board with a fixed format of gray levels and pixels. This design was inflexible because of the hardware speeds and low-cost components utilized. Because the hardware designs allow a large amount of flexibility in software, functions can be added very easily.

Figure 8 presented a block diagram of a typical SSTV software package containing all the basic functions of a typical system. This structure contains numerous routines that can be called as macros to perform high-level functions. Several of these functions are discussed at the end of this section.

Program Organization   First, prior to program coding and flowcharting, the memory was mapped. Because the SSTV system outlined in Sec. 15.1 was to be implemented, the memory requirements necessary to contain an entire SSTV picture were:

$$\text{Memory requirements} = \text{lines per frame} \times \text{pixels per line} \times 0.5 \text{ byte per pixel}$$
$$= 128 \times 256 \times 0.5$$
$$= 16,384 \text{ bytes per frame}$$

The 16K memory size was predicted upon a pixel density of 256 pixels per line. Because the display hardware was restricted to 128 pixels per line, the

16K high-resolution region was broken down into two low-resolution regions of 8192 bytes each. Since all picture formatting is accomplished by software, each programming routine can format the gray-level picture depending upon its own requirements.

Receive and Transmit* SSTV *Software The receive and transmit software represents examples of real-time software. The software was written with a technique in which all timings were developed using tight delay loops in the software. This technique does not require special hardware for timings, but it must rely upon the CPU cycle time having a fixed value. Because most microprocessor CPU cards are controlled by crystal oscillators, accurate timings can be derived by counting CPU cycles with the software.

Figure 16 is the flowchart for a software routine that transfers an SSTV picture from an SSTV demodulator and places it in memory. This routine is typical of most real-time software; its basic structure consists of the following four general operations:

1. I/O ports are first initialized.
2. All program counters are initialized.
3. The real-time function is executed.
4. A software counter is decremented until zero, and the software executes a return from subroutine.

Receive* SSTV *Software Let us examine how the receive software functions (Fig. 16). After initialization, the software waits for a vertical sync pulse. After that pulse falls, a short delay is executed before placing a pixel in memory. After the delay, a subroutine is executed that:

1. Samples a pixel with the S/H and ADC
2. Formats pixels for storage in memory with 2 pixels per byte
3. Stores the formatted pixels in memory

The sampling of pixels is accomplished by issuing an S/H pulse from an output port, then starting the A/D conversion. When the A/D conversion is completed, the value presented to an input port is loaded into the microprocessor. A program delay is then executed prior to the sampling of the second pixel.

Transmit* SSTV *Software The transmit SSTV software (Fig. 17) is similar to the receive software, with one exception: the data flow is from microprocessor memory to an output port. The routine first initializes counters and ports and then loads a byte from memory into the microprocessor. After loading, the byte is formatted for pixels and temporarily saved in registers. The pixels are then transferred to an output port, which is connected to a DAC and an SSTV modulator.

The number of pixels transmitted are counted until a complete pixel line is counted. At this time a horizontal sync pulse is transmitted by outputting to a port a bit that switches the SSTV modulator to produce a 1200-Hz signal. A program delay establishes the pulse duration. The output port bit is then switched OFF. The entire process is continued until the last line is transmit-

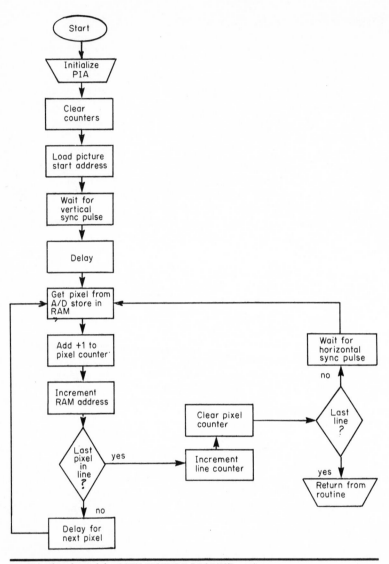

FIG. 16   *Flowchart of the SSTV PICTURE RECEIVE routine.*

ted. At this time a vertical pulse is transmitted using a process similar to that of the horizontal pulse, except that the duration is longer.

***Transmit Zoomed* SSTV**   This is an enhancement method that can be easily accomplished with software; its implementation is simplified with digitized video.

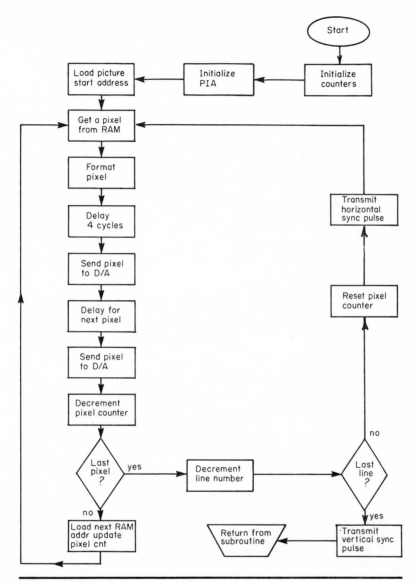

FIG. 17 *Flowchart for transmitting an SSTV picture.*

Figure 18 is a flowchart of a software routine that allows a picture to be displayed on SSTV with a 2× magnification. Any power of this magnification could be transmitted using an extension of the techniques shown in Fig. 18.

In this example, a byte is fetched from memory and separated into pixels. Each pixel is outputted to the SSTV modulator port twice, with pixel delays

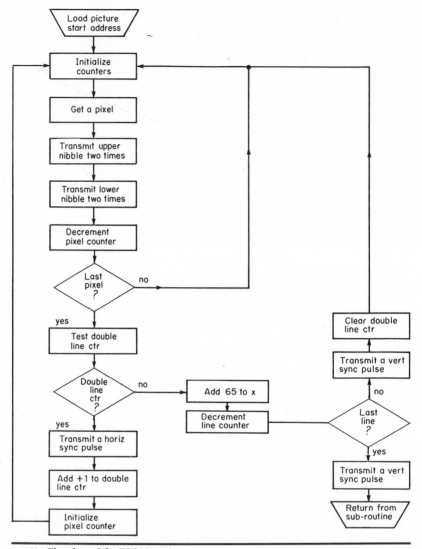

FIG. 18   *Flowchart of the ZOOM routine.*

between each transmission. This process continues for a pixel line. Upon completion of the line, the initial pixel is accessed again. The line transmission is again repeated. The net result is a transmission of one-quarter of the picture with $2\times$ magnification.

The zooming technique is quite effective and limited only by the resolution of the picture. As the zoom magnification increases, contouring occurs. Contouring is the displaying of gray-level steps, like blocks on an analog display.

Fast-Scan Television Software The fast-scan software is primarily used to control the hardware display interface card. The display interface card contains a processor with some degree of intelligence. The intelligence consists of programmable registers within the CRT controller IC, which customizes the video for the specific application.

Figure 13 is a block diagram of the internal structure of the MC-6845 CRT controller IC. The CRT controller is configured as a memory-mapped port to the microprocessor. Before the display interface can be used, the internal registers must be preloaded with data from calculations made from manufacturer specifications. The preloading is accomplished as follows:

1. The CRT controller register number is stored in the appropriate port.
2. The value for the register is stored in another port.
3. The preceding steps are repeated until all registers in the controller are initialized.

Once initialized, the fast-scan display can be selected by executing a wait command with the microprocessor software.

Each microprocessor type responds differently to a wait command. With the 6800 microprocessor, the wait command causes the bus available (BA) line from the CPU IC to go to the HIGH state. This condition causes all cards on the bus to switch into a tristate condition (floating state). The display interface then gains control of the bus, and memory is accessed by the CRT controller and displayed on the TV screen.

The display interface card contains a timer clocked with a 300-bd pulse train. The countdown provides an interrupt to the processor every 1.1 s. At this time the CPU gains control of the bus. The software then determines if the display duration is sufficient by counting down a software counter. The process is repeated until the counter is decremented to zero.

Prior to displaying the picture, processing may be required. The following discussion considers two of the many possible processing techniques: fast-scan formatting and fast-scan picture zooming.

Fast-scan formatting If the picture to be displayed is in a high-resolution format of 256 pixels per line, the picture must be formatted or compressed to be displayed at a low resolution of 128 pixels per line. One method of formatting is shown in Fig. 19. In this routine, pixels are averaged together and replaced in memory as follows:

1. Two pixels are separated and added.
2. The sum of the addition is logically shifted right in the accumulator.

This shifting technique is a simple method of dividing by 2. The pixel is then replaced in memory.

Fast-scan picture zooming Figure 20 is a method of zooming during display formatting of the picture. In this example, the picture is in a low-resolution format of 128 pixels per line. The picture is moved to an alternate 8K region by doubling pixels and lines. The technique is similar to SSTV zooming. Because the resolution is low, contouring is very pronounced.

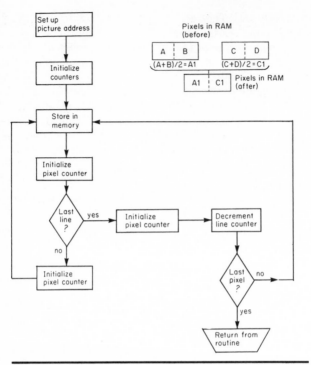

FIG. 19   *Flowchart of the SSTV FORMAT routine.*

Fast-Scan Television Camera Interface Software   The software for the fast-scan camera represents another example of real-time software. To understand the fast-scan television camera software, the raster scan picture sampling method discussed in Sec. 15.2 must first be understood. Figure 5 demonstrates how this scanning is accomplished; a software flowchart for this technique is shown in Fig. 21. This software takes a 6-bit pixel (64 gray levels) from the interface and places it in memory. The software stores the x and y coordinate locations of a pixel into their respective output ports. The software then polls a bit of an input port assigned to the A/D end-of-conversion signal. When conversion is completed, the value is saved in memory. The whole process must be completed within 2 TV scan lines or 128 μs because the picture is digitized at a density of every other fast-scan horizontal line.

The code must be written as efficiently as possible because it must both save the pixel value and perform software housekeeping. The housekeeping in this example increments memory pointers and location counters. Code was written for a 6800 microprocessor to accomplish this within 89 machine cycles. If the CPU was operated at a 1-MHz rate, the software overhead would be 89 μs. To this time the A/D conversion must be added, which is 12 μs maximum and results in a total line-scan time of 101 μs, which provides a 27-μs safety margin.

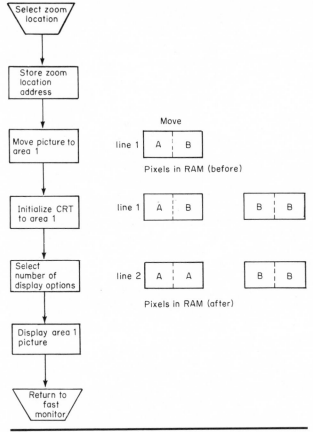

FIG. 20   *Flowchart for displaying a zoomed fast-scan picture.*

The entire process is repeated for the next y location, with the x location kept constant. The y location is incremented by 2 because every other line of a fast-scan frame is digitized. At the completion of 128 y locations (vertical scan lines), the x location is incremented to set up for reception of the next pixel location.

To display the picture on the fast-scan interface, the pixels must be reduced to 16 gray levels and reformatted by the software because of hardware restrictions in the display interface. The picture is then rotated 90° in memory and then formatted to be displayed on fast scan.

Image Processing   With a system as previously described, an unlimited number of image-processing techniques are possible, including image enhancement, distortion correction, pattern recognition, and object measurements. Because this topic is the subject of numerous textbooks and papers, only two

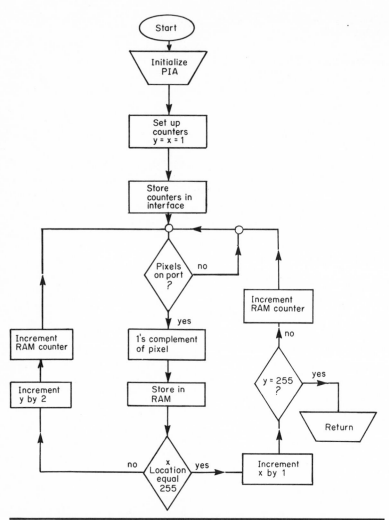

FIG. 21   Flowchart of the fast-scan television camera INTERFACE routine.

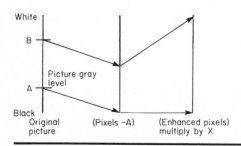

FIG. 22   Contrast enhancement technique.

applicable techniques are presented here: contrast enhancement and noise reduction.

Contrast Enhancement Contrast is the quality of a photograph determined by the magnitude of brightness differences between adjacent parts of the photograph. The human eye is sensitive to contrast and actually sees objects more accurately in high-contrast pictures than in low-contrast ones. The microprocessor contrast-enhancement technique takes washed-out low-contrast pictures and brings out details that would otherwise go unnoticed by the human eye.

The algorithm for accomplishing contrast enhancement is shown in Fig. 22. Assume that the original picture is washed out and contains a gray-level range from A to B. The enhancement is accomplished by first subtracting a gray level from all pixels. The results are then multiplied by a factor (x) and replaced in the original picture. The multiplication factor is a factor of the contrast range desired. With 16 gray levels, the optimum factor was found to be 1.5.

Noise Reduction Noise appears in television pictures as random fluctuations in gray scale. The sources of picture noise depend upon where and how the original picture was developed. With SSTV systems, most noise results from signal fading caused by atmospheric conditions.

One method of noise reduction is the accumulation of several digitizations of a noisy picture. Because the noise is always fluctuating, the exact value of any given pixel is different with each digitization. Noise adds to the nominal pixel value in some instances but subtracts from it in others. The average effect over several digitizations thus sums to zero. In theory, noise reduces by the square root of the number of pixels digitized. The software averaging is accomplished by digitizing the current pixel, loading the corresponding pixel from memory. The two values are added and then divided by 2 using a logical shift right. The resultant gray level is then replaced in memory.

REFERENCES

1. Miller, Donald C.: "Techniques for Bandwidth Reduction of TV Images," *Amateur Television Magazine*, November 1978, p. 9.
2. "Line-Interlaced and Noninterlaced TV Pictures," *Bell Syst. Tech. J.*, January 1967, p. 199.
3. "Frame Repetition and Picture Replenishment," *Bell Syst. Tech. J.*, January 1967, p. 261.
4. "Combining Intraframe and Frame-to-Frame Coding for Television," *Bell Syst. Tech. J.*, July/August 1974, p. 1137.
5. Fink, Donald G.: *Television Engineering*, McGraw-Hill, New York, 1952, chap. 13.
6. Miller, Donald C., and Ralph Taggert: *Slow-Scan Television Handbook*, 1st ed., 73 Publications, December 1972.
7. Abrams, Clayton W.: "SSTV Meets the SWTPC 6800," *73 Magazine*, November/December 1978.
8. Abrams, Clayton W.: "Display SSTV Pictures on Fast-Scan TV," *Ham Radio Magazine*, July 1979, copyrighted 1979 by Communications Technology, Inc.
9. *Digisector Operations Manual*, The Microworks, Del Mar, Calif.
10. Myers, Glenford J.: *Reliable Software through Composite Design*, Petrocelli/Charter, New York, 1975.

CHAPTER SIXTEEN

Hardware-Oriented State-Description Techniques

Jack V. Landau

Teradyne, Inc.,
Woodland Hills, California

AN OVERVIEW OF THE TECHNIQUE

There are many ways in which people approach the task of developing microprocessor software. The most common approach is to simply write the software in assembly language based upon whatever methodology the programmer is most familiar with. Structured programming based upon the use of an appropriate high-level language, such as PASCAL, is helpful. Nevertheless, some ad hoc assembly language technique is usually chosen because:

1. The programmer may have a hardware background or little software training, and structured techniques seem too esoteric.
2. A high-level language compiler may not be available or may be deemed to produce code too wasteful of memory.
3. The language itself may appear inappropriate since it does not relate to the hardware elements of the machine the microprocessor is to control.

The software methodology described here,* which utilizes state descriptions, is often a good compromise. State diagrams are a natural way to describe machines or processes that operate sequentially and are part of the background of every engineer trained in digital logic design. This approach allows efficient software to be developed directly from such diagrams using the type of assembler available with most microprocessor development systems. Benefits much like those attributed to structured programming are attained, yet the resulting code is more memory-efficient than simple assembly language.

State diagrams have been widely used for synthesizing and analyzing digital circuits. This chapter shows how to apply these techniques to certain types of software and then introduces a *state language* that:

1. Conveniently describes software state diagrams in both human and machine-readable forms
2. Is easily translated into tabular binary data (called a *state table*) by conventional macroassemblers

A small and efficient assembly language program (the *state processor*) that interprets the state table is then described. The state processor evaluates the conditions required for state transitions and causes the actions described in the original state diagram to take place when the state transitions occur.

16.1   State-Description Techniques

The concept of *state*, as used in digital circuitry, refers to the collective values of all of a circuit's memory elements. Hence, a circuit with n flip-flops has, in theory, 2^n possible states. Embodied in the circuit's state is all the information about previous states and inputs that the circuit needs to remember so as to respond correctly to future inputs.

A circuit is designed in such a way that for a given state, say sA, a specific input $i1$ causes an output of $o1$ and a transition to a new state sB. This situation is shown in Fig. 1a for a simple circuit having two flip-flops, A and B. State sA is represented by A's being set and B's being reset; state sB is represented by the opposite case.

Figure 1b shows a common way of representing the same circuit in a state diagram. Each state is denoted by a circle enclosing the state name, with directed lines between the circles indicating the possible state transitions. Each line is labeled with the input that causes the transition, a slash (/), and the output required when the transition occurs.

Figure 2a shows the flowchart of a comparable software situation. Here we assume that the computer is controlling a machine that must wait in some state sA until either of two conditions is satisfied. Depending upon which condition occurs, the machine performs certain actions and enters one of two new states. The conditions $c1$ and $c2$ might refer to properties of the machine's

---

*Based upon Jack V. Landau, "State Description Techniques Applied to Industrial Machine Control," *Computer*, February 1979. © 1979 IEEE.

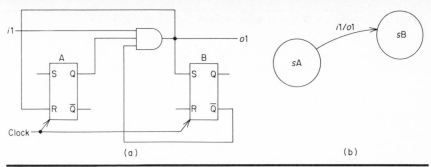

FIG. 1   A sequential digital circuit shown in the form of (a) a circuit diagram, and (b) a state diagram. Only two states are shown, although the two flip-flops theoretically allow for encoding four states.

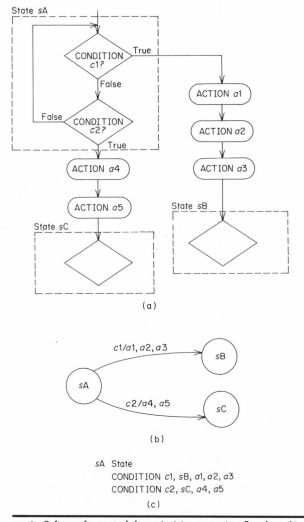

FIG. 2   Software for control shown in: (a) a convenient flowchart, (b) the corresponding state diagram, and (c) the state language description.

performance that the software detects through sensors (such as a liquid reaching a certain speed), to operator inputs (such as a certain switch depression), or to a certain amount of elapsed time.

Unlike a digital circuit, where all outputs could change almost simultaneously, a computer performs tasks sequentially; thus the software events that make up a state transition must be shown as a series of separate actions to be performed in a specified order. The action list a1, a2, a3 in Fig. 2b illustrates how this is shown on a software state diagram.

Appropriate Applications   Although a state diagram could be used to describe any sequential digital circuit, it is typically used only when it clarifies a circuit's operation for the designer. The same reasoning applies to software. The state-diagramming technique, along with the state language and state processor, are useful only for programs that can be conveniently visualized as sequences of states. Furthermore, most of the useful tasks that a program performs should be clearly associated with individual states or their transitions if the state-diagramming technique is to be useful.

Software that performs a user-machine interface function often meets these criteria. When a machine is perceived as doing a sequence of things one at a time as commanded by its user, it is convenient to think of the machine's state as being defined by its current activity. Software for appliance controllers and for many industrial machines has been suitable for state description.

On the other hand, the software for controlling a heating and air conditioning system would probably not lend itself well to state description when the actions to be performed consist mainly in actuating compressors, valves, fans, and heating elements, based upon the current values of various temperatures in the system and the desired temperature entered at the thermostat. The concept of machine state has little meaning here—little information about past events influences current or future actions of the controller. From the point of view of logic circuits, one would say that this controller consists primarily of combinational rather than sequential logic. Likewise, software for scientific problem solving or business data processing is frequently poorly suited to state diagramming.

Techniques Related to State Description   Decision tables and their associated programming languages have been used for at least 20 years to organize certain types of complex procedures.[1] Here the emphasis is on tabular enumeration of all possible combinations of conditions and the actions to be performed when the conditions are met. The state concept can be incorporated into decision tables, as it can into any programming language, but decision tables do not provide the graphic clarity and easy readability of statements that Fig. 2b,c shows for state-oriented machines.

References 2 and 3 deal directly with some of the approaches set forth in this chapter. They explain various manual techniques for designing software in terms of states and explain the benefits of this approach from the authors' viewpoints.

16.2 The State Language

The essential elements of the state language are the STATE and CONDITION statements. For translation reasons (discussed later), each statement occupies a new line and comprises a name field, a command field, and an argument field. Figure 2c shows a state language example corresponding to the state diagram in Fig. 2b.

STATE *Statement* The STATE statement identifies the beginning of a new state description and assigns a name to that state through its name field, sname:

   sname   STATE   optional parameters

Optional parameters in the argument fields of STATE statements may be used to identify events that occur in a large percentage of the states, conditions that are active in a large percentage of the states, or messages or data to appear in operator displays. For example, suppose the machine being described has a user-operated reset switch that may be activated in 75 of the machine's 100 states to cause the machine to assume an initialization state. It would be tedious and wasteful of memory to include an individual CONDITION statement for this switch in each of the 75 states. Instead, the parameter RESET would be used in the argument field of each state for which this switch is active, and the state processor would be designed to perform the required state transfer for this condition. For example, the state named GRIND3 in a hypothetical kitchen blending machine might be described as:

   GRIND3   STATE   RESET,TCYCLE

Here the RESET parameter indicates that the user reset switch is active in this state, and the TCYCLE parameter indicates that the time remaining in this blend cycle is to be displayed to the user during this state.

CONDITION *Statement* One or more CONDITION statements must follow each STATE statement to describe the means for transferring to other states. The name field is not used:

   type   id, nsname, action-list

The condition is identified by the command field *type* in conjunction with the first argument *id*. For very simple machines, having only a few conditions, type could be the command CONDITION in all cases, and the different conditions would be identified simply by the id argument, as in Fig. 2c. However, when there are many conditions, they should be grouped according to function, and a type command should be assigned for each function to improve readability. For example, user-operated switches might have the type SWITCH, and machine sensors might have the type SENSOR; the id argument would identify the specific switch or sensor.

Use of the state language occasionally requires invoking a condition that is always true. For clarity in this special case, the type NEXT is used and the id argument is omitted:

NEXT   nsname, action-list

The nsname argument tells what the name of the next state must be when the condition described by type and id is true. If the condition is not true, the next CONDITION statement is evaluated. If none of the conditions is true, the machine remains in the same state and the first CONDITION statement is evaluated again.

The *action-list* gives the names of assembly language subroutines that the state processor will call in sequence when the condition described by type and id is true. These are the actions to be performed before a transfer to the new state. The action-list may be of arbitrary length and empty.

The choice of meaningful mnemonics is especially important in a state-description language because there are so few different types of statements. A CONDITION statement to test for depression of the START switch, transfer to the RUN state, activate the motor solenoid, and initiate a 15-s timer might look like:

SWITCH   START, RUN, MOTORSOL, TIMER15

Logical Functions   As noted, each condition in a state is evaluated in sequence by the state processor. This leads to a situation quite different from that of digital circuit states, where the conditions in each state are inherently evaluated simultaneously. Figure 3 shows how the logical NOT function is achieved by relying upon the fact that the first CONDITION statement is always evaluated before the second. While condition $c3$ is true, the machine remains in the same state sJ. The second CONDITION statement (NEXT) is evaluated only when $c3$ is not true, and it unconditionally transfers the machine to state sK after executing actions $a1$ and $a2$.

The state language example in Fig. 4 extends this same concept to achieve the logical AND function. No CONDITION statement following the first one will be evaluated until condition $c4$ is false. Transfer from state sP to state sQ then requires condition $c5$ to be true as well, at which time action $a3$ is performed.

Whenever two CONDITION statements in one state have the same nsname argument, the state transfer will occur when the logical OR of the two conditions is true. Figure 5 illustrates this situation, since state sY appears in both CONDITION statements. No actions are performed in this example when the state transfer occurs.

In practice, the need for such logical functions has been relatively slight, partly because of appropriate choice of condition type and id values. Hence, simple techniques such as these, which utilize the inherent properties of the state processor, have been preferable to extensions of the state language, which would increase the memory requirements and execution time of the state processor.

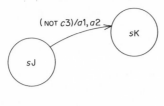

sJ State
    CONDITION   *c*3, sJ
    NEXT   sK, *a*1, *a*2

FIG. 3 *The logical* NOT *function as a consequence of sequential evaluation of the CONDITION statements.*

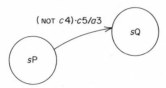

sP State
    CONDITION   *c*4, sP
    CONDITION   *c*5, sQ, *a*3

FIG. 4 *State language describing the transfer between states as the logical* AND *of two conditions.*

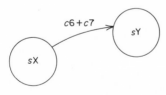

sX State
    CONDITION   *c*6, sY
    CONDITION   *c*7, sY

FIG. 5 *A state transfer based on the logical* OR *of two conditions.*

16.3 *State Language Translation*

It is highly desirable that the translation from state language to encoded state-table data be performed automatically, not only to eliminate the possibility of human error but to save considerable time when several hundred states are involved. It is also important to be able to use existing standard software to perform the translation—preferably the same assembler that is being used for the assembly language software. Otherwise, the use of state language techniques is limited to the few organizations that are large enough to develop customized assemblers to support their work.

These goals dictated the selection of the name-command argument field format used in the state language. This format meets the requirements of common assemblers having a macrodefinition capability, so that the state language can be translated simply by writing macros for the STATE statement and for each CONDITION statement type used. Assemblers actually used include the IBM System/370 assembly language, the assembly language for the Singer System Ten (a business data processing computer), and a general-purpose language development program named DUAL.[4]

STATE *Macro* Figure 6 shows the state language translation requirements. The STATE macro serves primarily to establish an address for the name field sname in the assembler's symbol table. If optional parameters are used in the argument field, they can typically be encoded into the first byte of the state-table entry for that state.

CONDITION *Macros* The macro for each condition type generates 1 byte to identify the type and id for the condition; if there are many conditions, 1 byte

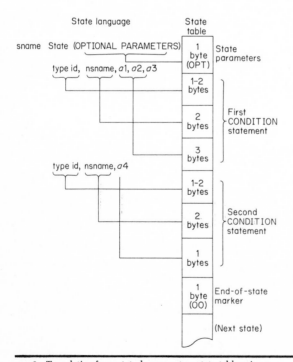

FIG. 6   *Translation from state language to a state table using a conventional macro assembler. The state in this example contains two CONDITION statements.*

can be used for the type and a second byte for the id. The mnemonics to be used in the various arguments (such as id) must have been equated previously to the desired code values in the state table. The absolute address in the state table of the state corresponding to nsname is then entered in the next 2 bytes. Finally, each entry in the action-list (a1, a2, a3 in the first example) is encoded in a subsequent byte of the state table using only the least significant 7 bits of each byte. The most significant bit of the last byte (a3 in this case) is set to 1 to indicate the end of the list; this allows any number of entries in the action-list. If the action-list is empty, a 1-byte default entry of 80 (hex) is made in the state table.

To allow for an arbitrary number of CONDITION statements in each state, the state-table code 00 (hex) is not used for any type-id; it instead serves as a 1-byte end-of-state marker. This byte should be generated by the STATE macro for the subsequent state.

If the assembler has no macro capabilities, the software state diagram should be transcribed directly to data-declaration statements compatible with the assembler being used. Using mnemonics throughout for clarity, a separate declaration statement can be used for the type-id, the next state address, and each action-list entry. It is especially important that the next state (nsname) be identified symbolically so that the assembler establishes the correct address in each assembly; then, if states are subsequently added to or removed from the system, there will be little chance of errors in the linkages between the original states.

16.4   *Application to an Industrial Sewing Machine*

One extensive application of these state-description techniques has been in the control of the Singer Company's Centurion programmable industrial sewing machine. A brief description of this application serves as an example.

In the garment-fabrication industry, a sewing-machine operator typically performs the same operation for days or weeks at a time. For example, the operator might attach a pocket or a shirt front in an assembly-line operation. After many months, an operator becomes very skillful at handling certain operations, but the benefits the factory owner derives from these skills are offset by the enormously high rate of employment turnover in this industry.

The Centurion "learns" a sewing operation by monitoring once a trained operator performing the operation manually. The sewing speed and length of each seam in the operation are memorized and saved in a sewing-program library in battery-protected CMOS random access memory (RAM). Thereafter, a less-experienced operator can quickly achieve high-quality work by simply guiding the fabric under the needle while the machine automatically controls the sewing speed and seam length it learned originally. As the trainee becomes more proficient at guiding the fabric, the sewing speed can be increased.

Dozens of different sewing-machine operations may be stored in the sewing-program library simultaneously with industry-compatible identification numbers used for library storage and retrieval. A lighted, touch-sensitive console is used for all operator interactions, such as entering the identification number for a newly learned sewing program or changing the sewing speed of an existing program.

Control is based upon a state processor driven by a 6800 microprocessor. Figure 7 shows the relationship between the various elements of the state language and the hardware elements of the machine. Action subroutines (referenced in the action-list argument of CONDITION statements) initiate all the electromechanical machine operations, such as establishing motor speed and direction and actuating solenoids to raise the presser or trim the thread. Action subroutines also carry out all the modifications to the sewing-program library.

The operator console for this machine contains a large number of lights and other displays that must be coordinated with the current state of the machine. One byte at the beginning of the state-table entry for each state provides the state processor with a code indicating which lights are to be on and what alphanumeric data are to be displayed (if any). Operator commands entered through the console are recognized through CONDITION statements.

Table 1 summarizes the various types of CONDITION statements needed for the state language description of the machine and the types of actions performed by the various action-list entries. The state language refers, altogether, to 46 different conditions and 76 different action subroutines. Table 2 quan-

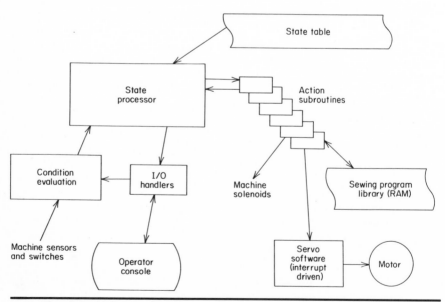

FIG. 7   The relationship between the software and hardware components in the programmable industrial sewing machine.

TABLE 1   *Conditions and actions used in the industrial sewing machine.*

CONDITION STATEMENTS

Type command	Number of different conditions (*id* codes)	Meaning
SENSOR, SENNOT	7	Test of battery voltage, treadle position, and other mechanical switches on machine. (SENNOT is logical complement of SENSOR.)
KEY, KEYNOT	18	Test of touch-sensitive user controls. (KEYNOT is logical complement of KEY).
COND	20	Tests of software conditions including timers, status of the sewing-program library, and various flags and registers.
NEXT	NONE	Unconditionally true.

ACTION SUBROUTINES

Number of different sub-routines (*action-list* codes)	Actions performed
15	Operate solenoids and motor (e.g., sew until needle up, sew until needle down, raise presser foot).
10	Add, delete, and modify entries in sewing-program library.
12	Search library for various data.
30	Set software flags and registers.
9	Machine diagnostic routines.

TABLE 2   *Characteristics of the state language for the industrial sewing machine.*

Number of states:	235
Number of CONDITION statements:	570
Number of *action-list* entries:	858
Number of state-table bytes per state:	16 (average)
Number of state-table bytes per CONDITION statement:	5.75 (average)

tifies the size of the state language description and the amount of memory required in the corresponding state table.

The definition of the various machine states and the sequencing between them evolved naturally in the course of specifying how the machine was to operate. Most of the states correspond to situations in which the machine is waiting for some operator action, such as activating or releasing the speed control treadle or touching a switch on the console. In some other states, the machine is waiting for a mechanical event, such as the motor's reaching a certain speed or completing a certain number of stitches.

It would be a mistake to apply the state concept in the purest sense of using the current state to embody every bit of information about previous states and inputs that must be remembered. Doing so would lead to unnecessarily complicated state diagrams because at points in the machine's cycle the operator frequently makes a yes/no decision which does not affect the machine's operation until much later. Instead of remembering the outcome of such decisions by a separate series of states, the machine uses action subroutines to set appropriate flags or values in RAM that can be tested later by CONDITION statements.

A Sewing Example   Figure 8a shows a small portion of the software state diagram that illustrates how the state-processor technique was applied to this machine. Assume that in the SEW state the machine is being operated manually, with the position of the treadle controlling the sewing speed. Each time the action routine TRDLSEW is called, it causes the motor speed to be adjusted to correspond to the current treadle position. This routine must be called continuously during the SEW state if the motor speed is to vary continuously with treadle position. Figure 8b shows the state language for Fig. 8a.

The machine is transferred to the WAIT state when the treadle is brought to the NEUTRAL position. In this process, the machine is stopped by electrically braking the motor until 400 r/min is reached (DYNBRAKE), sewing at this speed until the needle is all the way down in the fabric (NEEDLEDN), and then applying the mechanical brake (MECHBRAKE). It is essential, for sewing reasons, to always stop with the needle down, and the mechanical brake will not stop the machine with sufficient accuracy at speeds above 400 r/min.

When the machine is stopped in the WAIT state, a foot-operated jog switch can be used to advance the machine exactly one stitch as follows (see also Fig. 8):

NEEDLEDN—Start by positioning the needle in the down position if necessary (the WAIT state may have been entered from some other state that, unlike the SEW state, would not have left the needle down).

NEEDLEUP,NEEDLEDN—Take one stitch by sewing until the needle is up and then until it is down again.

MECHBRAKE—Stop by applying the mechanical brake.

This sequence leaves the machine in the JOGHOLD state, waiting for the operator's foot to be removed from the jog switch. The SENNOT CONDI-

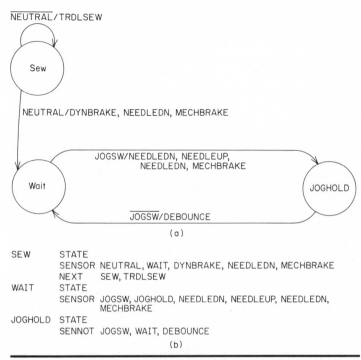

NEUTRAL/TRDLSEW

Sew

NEUTRAL/DYNBRAKE, NEEDLEDN, MECHBRAKE

JOGSW/NEEDLEDN, NEEDLEUP,
NEEDLEDN, MECHBRAKE

Wait

JOGHOLD

JOGSW/DEBOUNCE

(a)

```
SEW        STATE
           SENSOR  NEUTRAL, WAIT, DYNBRAKE, NEEDLEDN, MECHBRAKE
           NEXT    SEW, TRDLSEW
WAIT       STATE
           SENSOR  JOGSW, JOGHOLD, NEEDLEDN, NEEDLEUP, NEEDLEDN,
                   MECHBRAKE
JOGHOLD    STATE
           SENNOT  JOGSW, WAIT, DEBOUNCE
```
(b)

FIG. 8   *An example of (a) a state diagram, and (b) the corresponding state language for the industrial sewing machine. Sewing stops with the needle down when the treadle is in the neutral position; the jog switch then causes a single stitch to be made.*

TION statement is true when the jog switch is *not* activated, and the machine returns to the WAIT state after calling a 50-ms time-delay routine (DEBOUNCE) to ensure that switch bounce will not be mistaken for a subsequent jog switch command. Debounce was unnecessary on the way from WAIT to JOGHOLD because of the relatively large amount of time required to take one stitch. State transfers (omitted from Fig. 8 for simplicity) would take the machine from the WAIT state back to the SEW state after the treadle is pressed again.

16.5   Implementation of a State Processor

Figure 9 shows the flowchart of actions the state processor performs in executing the functions called for by a state table such as that shown in Fig. 6. At the beginning of each state, the state processor must take the actions called for by any parameters included in the STATE statement argument field. In the case of the industrial sewing machine, this involves activating certain displays on the operator console. Each condition in the state is then evaluated in sequence. When a condition is evaluated as false, the subsequent bytes in the state table (which identify the next state and action subroutines) are skipped, so that the next condition can be evaluated. If the state processor reaches the end-of-state marker without finding any true conditions, it is repositioned to the first condition in the state. If a true condition is found, the corresponding action subroutines (if any) are called in sequence, and the state processor is positioned to the new state address in the state table.

The inherent loop structure of the state processor (Fig. 9) makes it convenient to perform periodic tests of inputs that require constant monitoring. Although not shown in Fig. 9, such tests could be inserted at the beginning of each new state or prior to the evaluation of each condition, depending upon the frequency of polling required. This technique was used in the sewing machine to monitor input signals indicating loss of an ac phase and excessive motor temperature. Interrupts were used only for events requiring immediate response, such as determination of motor speed from periodic measurements of rapidly occurring tachometer pulses.

Preventing Random Results   The sequential way in which the state processor evaluates the conditions in each state could lead to a situation in which the state transfer that occurs is not predictable solely upon the basis of the condition values but is influenced by when a condition becomes true relative to the current activity of the state processor. This is not necessarily a problem— in fact, it did not impact the industrial sewing machine application at all—but the situation should be understood by the user.

Using Fig. 2c as an example, suppose it is known from the nature of the machine that if condition c1 ever occurs, it will always occur *before* condition c2, and in this case a transfer to state sB is required. Condition c2 could, however, occur by itself, in which case a transfer to state sC is required. Although the order of the CONDITION statements in Fig. 2c would ostensibly provide for the correct priorities, in some instances both conditions could become true in sequence after the state processor had evaluated c1 but before it had evaluated c2. The result would be an undesired transfer to state sC.

When it is necessary to guarantee which state transfer will take place when each of several conditions in the same state becomes true, the state processor can sample and save the values of all the conditions before the conditions for possible state transfers are evaluated. The CONDITION statements will then all be based upon the same sampled value of the conditions rather than upon the instantaneous values of the conditions.

Overhead Costs   When considering the application of state-description techniques, memory and execution-time overhead must be taken into account. If the cost of memory is important, the memory required for the state processor itself (typically 100 to 200 bytes) should be compared to the size of the state table (typically 6 bytes per CONDITION statement). Figure 10 illustrates how memory is utilized in the industrial sewing machine and shows that the size of the state processor is clearly insignificant in relation to the sizes of the other software components.

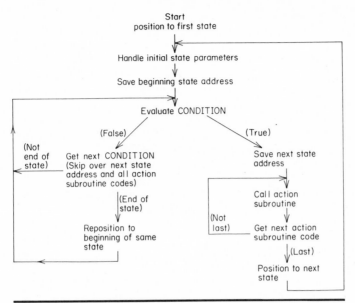

FIG. 9   *Flowchart of the state processor.*

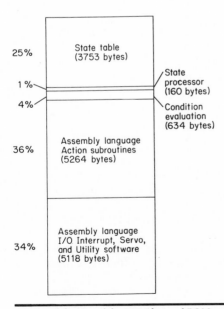

FIG. 10   *Utilization of the 14,929 bytes of ROM control software in the industrial sewing machine.*

The execution-time overhead due to the state processor may also be important in some applications. Using the 6800-based state processor in the sewing machine as an example, the minimum overhead per state is 180 μs, assuming the state processor enters a new state, finds the first condition true immediately, calls the designated action subroutines, and transfers to the next state. This time is based upon the assumption that the 6800 microprocessor operates with its standard 1-μs cycle. Regardless of how the control program is structured, the condition must be evaluated and all the action subroutines must be performed, so the time required for these activities must be added to the 180-μs overhead to obtain the total execution time per state.

State-processor timing was of little concern for the sewing control application. The Centurion machine is fast by sewing machine standards—100 stitches per second—but a software overhead of several hundred microseconds was tolerable compared to the 10-ms stitch rate.

16.6 Benefits of State-Description Techniques

The original impetus for using software state-diagramming techniques was the apparent lack of any other suitable graphical method for describing the behavior of complex industrial machines. The compactness and clarity exhibited in Fig. 2b made conventional flowcharting methods such as in Fig. 2a unthinkable when 25 or more states had to be shown on a single page. Once such diagrams have been generated, a major programming chore is avoided by simply transcribing the diagrams into the state language.

Language Benefits   In microprocessor applications in which the product volume has been fairly large, high-level languages such as Fortran and Basic have never been acceptable; they were either not available to the programmer, or the resulting object code occupied too much memory relative to the same application coded in assembly language.

The state language approach is superior to any of these techniques because:

1. Users have reported that it feels natural for describing the class of machines for which it is appropriate. The language seems to be as understandable to nonprogramming personnel as are the software state diagrams.
2. It imposes a useful structure on the resulting software, achieving many of the benefits sought by other structured programming techniques. It has been easier to coordinate the work of multiple programmers on the same project, and fewer mistakes have been made. There are fewer opportunities for a programmer's coding style to influence the programs.
3. It yields some of the benefits associated with high-level languages in that one statement replaces several assembly language statements.

Figure 11 illustrates the type of statement efficiency obtained with the state language. Figure 11a shows a typical CONDITION statement testing condition $c1$ and, if true, performing actions $a1$ and $a2$ before branching to

```
CONDITION c1, STATEH, a1, a2

            (a)


CALL    CONDC1      evaluate condition c1
BE      NEXTCOND    condition false: try next
CALL    A1          condition true: perform a1, a2
CALL    A2
B       STATEH      transfer to new state
NEXTCOND.......................evaluate next condition

            (b)
```

FIG. 11   (a) *A CONDITION statement, and* (b) *the assembly language it replaces.*

STATEH. At least five separate statements, such as those in Fig. 11*b*, would be required to realize the same function in a typical assembly language. Extensive studies have shown that the number of statements a programmer writes per day depends little upon the language used, suggesting that the state language can improve productivity significantly.

Implementation Benefits   In addition to the benefits state diagramming offers as a programming language source, other benefits have been realized in the course of actual implementations:

1. The state language is easily transportable between different microprocessors because it does not contain any information related to the processor's instruction set. The prototype for the industrial sewing machine described earlier was developed upon an entirely different microprocessor from that used in the production model. Nevertheless, the state language description did not have to be changed at all in the transition.
2. As with most table-driven techniques, state description requires less memory than assembly language does. In practice, the CONDITION statement in Fig. 11*a* would occupy 5 to 6 bytes, and the corresponding assembly language in Fig. 11*b* would occupy at least 10 bytes (optimistically assuming 2-byte instructions). Based upon the industrial sewing machine statistics in Fig. 10, this means a savings of some 3500 bytes of read-only memory (ROM) over a pure assembly language approach.
3. Software checkout proceeds in an orderly way because of the system's organization. The operation of the state processor is simple and can be verified quickly. The subroutines that evaluate conditions and perform actions are individually checked, and the state language and the machine's functional performance can be checked more easily because the state processor and its associated subroutines are known to work correctly.

The maximum benefit is achieved when all the techniques described here—software state diagrams, state language, state table, and state processor—are used together. These techniques require no complex software or hardware tools for implementation, and the small amounts of overhead involved have clearly been justified by the benefits achieved through the structuring of the software and the overall savings in memory utilization.

REFERENCES

1. Metzner, J. R., and B. H. Barnes: *Decision Table Languages and Systems*, Academic Press, New York, 1977.
2. McPhillips, A. S.: "Designing Logic With Software," *Proc. Delaware Bay Microcomputer Conf.* March 1978. (IEEE Catalog no. 78CH1330-OC.)
3. "Programming with Finite-State Machines," in *Computer Program Management*, I. L. Auerbach (ed.), Petrocelli/Charter, New York, 1975, sec. 14-02-03.
4. *Dynamic Universal Assembly Language (DUAL)*, Proprietary Software Systems, Inc., Beverly Hills, Calif., 1977.

CHAPTER SEVENTEEN

Multiple Microcomputers in Small Systems

C. W. Carter

Corning Glass Works, R&D Division, Corning, New York

Single-Chip Microcomputers and Small Measurement Systems

The single-chip microcomputer (μC) can enhance the functionality of many low-cost instruments.* It can add intelligence and labor-saving conveniences, providing the computing power to eliminate or reduce manual calibrations, calculations, and sequencing.

The single-chip microcomputer has an advantage in small measurement systems. Despite falling prices, classical multichip designs using a microprocessor (μP) with a bus architecture can be prohibitively expensive. The total recurring cost (including inventory, assembly, and testing) is generally proportional to the number of component parts. Additionally, the μC reduces circuit real estate and power requirements—important considerations in many small instruments.

A good selection of μCs is now available, ranging from simple control processors to versions of more powerful multichip families.

*Much of the material in this chapter is adapted from Ref. 2, C. N. Carter and J. J. Kalinowski, "Dual-μC Design Adds Memory, Processing, and Software Control Without Adding Chips," *Electronic Design*, vol. 28, no. 2, Jan. 18, 1980, p. 82.

Single-chip parts are available with various combinations of random access memory (RAM), read-only memory (ROM), input-output (I/O), and bus expansion capability.

In applications requiring more RAM, ROM, I/O, or computing speed than available in a μC, the designer may tend to select a multichip μP-based design, with significant cost impact. At this point, a multiple μC design should be considered.

The techniques described in this chapter will aid the system designer in developing multiple μC designs; however, the techniques are general in nature and can be applied to multichip μP designs.

17.1   Small Measurement Systems Defined

In this context, measurement systems are instruments that display a quantity which is a function of one or more input variables. The inputs usually consist of analog voltages from sensors. Data taking and display are done in real time. Display update rates of 1 to 2 Hz are common, but the actual data rate may be much faster. The primary output device is usually a digital display, but printed and linearized analog outputs may be desirable options. Operator input of supplemental process data or values for calibration standards may be required.

A small measurement system might be described as low-cost. It is probably a high-volume instrument that can be placed in a significant number of installations requiring the measurement. Examples are pH meters, temperature sensors, and electronic test equipment.

The Corning pH/Ion Meter 135 is a design example. When used with appropriate electrodes, this instrument can measure the temperature and pH of a solution or precisely determine ion concentrations. Three commonly used laboratory techniques for determining concentration are automated. The equation relating electrode voltage to concentration is solved, and the concentration is read out directly in units of the user's choice. A semiautomatic calibration procedure, compensating for electrode variances, eliminates the conventional interactive potentiometer adjustments. Temperature compensation for electrode response is provided.

Enhancing Small Measurement Systems   Consider, for example, the governing equation for an ion-selective electrode[1] that relates ion concentration in solution to electrode voltage (Fig. 1):

$$E = E_o + \frac{S(T + 273.16)}{298.16} \log \frac{C + C_b}{C_i + C_b} \tag{1}$$

where E = electrode voltage (mV)
$\quad E_o$ = electrode offset potential (mV)
$\quad S$ = electrode slope in mV per decade concentration at 25°C
$\quad T$ = solution temperature in °C

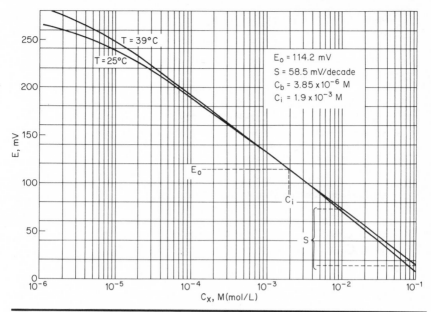

FIG. 1 *Typical ion-selective electrode response curve.*

C = solution concentration
C_b = blank correction term for low concentrations
C_i = isopotential concentration at which E is independent of T

This equation is solved for the calibration constants E_o, S, C_i, and C_b, given measurements of E and T on solutions of known concentration C. For measurement readout, Eq. 1 is solved for C.

Equation 1 can be simplified to

$$E = E_o + S \log C \tag{2}$$

By omitting T and C_i, temperature compensation of electrode slope is eliminated, requiring calibration and measurement to be done at the same temperature. Omitting C_b reduces accuracy at low concentrations. However, Eq. 2 is easily plotted on semilog graph paper for calibration purposes, or C can be read directly from a meter movement with an appropriate scale.

Equation 1 and others of similar complexity are easily processed by a μC, thus allowing rather sophisticated processing that enhances instrument capabilities. Arithmetic operations are performed using a floating-point arithmetic package. Functions such as log and antilog are easily implemented with series-expansion algorithms. Floating-point and function subroutine packages are often available from the μC vendor or a user's library.

User-entry of values for calibration standards allows the calibration constants to be calculated from sensor voltage readings on the standards. The actual calibration procedure involves measurements of several standards and the simultaneous solution, by the μC, of the resulting equations.

Linearized analog output is sometimes required for devices such as strip-chart recorders. The readout value is output via a digital-to-analog converter (DAC) to obtain this feature.

Noise-prone sensor systems (e.g., high-impedance ion-selective electrodes) often render digital displays unacceptable. Even minor fluctuations in a digital display at a 0.1- to 10-Hz rate are annoying because the user cannot easily determine a visual average, as is often done when reading an analog meter. A digital filter implemented in a microcomputer reduces the problem.

17.2 Classical Multichip μP Architecture

The classical μP system design of Fig. 2 is ideal for many measurement systems because it is very flexible and easily modified, especially in larger instruments with greater memory and I/O requirements.

Figure 2 satisfies the functional requirements of an ion analyzer. An integrating analog-to-digital converter (ADC) provides the required 1 part in 40,-000 precision over a range of -2 to $+2$ V. A conversion rate of 3 Hz is acceptable. The user interface consists of a scanned-matrix keypad and refreshed seven-segment displays connected to a peripheral interface chip. The memory requirements are satisfied by 6K $\times$ 8 ROM and 384 $\times$ 8 RAM. Additional circuits, such as display drivers and electrode amplifiers, are not shown in Fig. 2 for simplicity.

Advantages of this design are expandability and flexibility. Additional memory and I/O are easily connected to the address and data buses; however, bus buffering and additional address decoding may be required. By adding and/or changing ROMs and I/O interfaces, optional features may be offered to users. A circuit board based upon the Fig. 2 design may even be used in several different instruments.

In some systems where size, cost, and power consumption are critical factors, the 14 integrated circuits (ICs) of Fig. 2 may be excessive. Systems requiring faster data rates may have software timing conflicts between the display refresh and the ADC, necessitating additional display hardware.

17.3 A Dual μC Design

The μC system shown in Fig. 3, also for a Corning 135, implements the identical functions of Fig. 2. The chip count is reduced from 14 to 7. The design is based upon two μCs with a total of 6080 $\times$ 8 ROM, 192 $\times$ 8 RAM, and 8 $\times$ 8 I/O ports. One I/O port on each μC is used for interprocessor communications, leaving six ports for interfacing. In the design example, two ports on the slave μC are used to interface an additional 256 $\times$ 8 RAM.

The increased computing power allows more real-time tasks to be pulled into the μCs, reducing hardware. Specifically, the slave is assigned only one

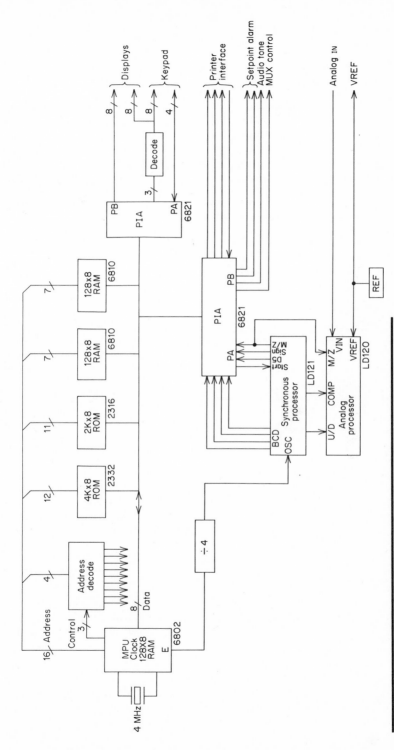

FIG. 2 Single μP design for pH/ion meter. Reprinted with permission from Electronic Design, vol. 28, no. 2; copyright Hayden Publishing Co., Inc., 1980.

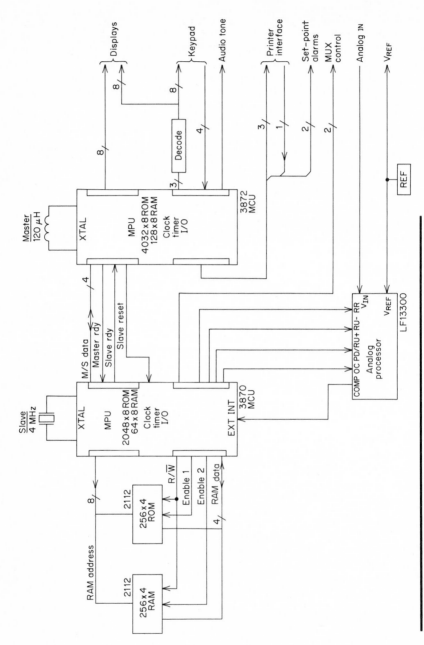

FIG. 3   *Dual µC design for pH/ion meter. Reprinted with permission from Electronic Design, Vol. 28, No. 2; copyright Hayden Publishing Co., Inc., 1980.*

real-time task: the digital functions of the integrating ADC. The master is assigned all other real-time tasks, such as display refresh and keypad scanning and debouncing. This eliminates the synchronous processor and divide-by-4 of Fig. 2.

For software design simplicity, the two μCs are programmed in a master-slave relationship. The master uses the slave as a smart peripheral, sending it commands and transferring data. Each master-slave exchange begins with a command from the master, followed by a data transfer if required by the command. After each exchange, the slave returns to a dormant state to await the next command. In this way the master controls the direction and use of the interface.

For simplicity, commands to the slave are defined as action or data-transfer commands. Action commands direct the slave to perform specific tasks, such as A/D conversions or calculations based upon voltage readings and parameters stored in the slave's RAM. Data-transfer sequences begin with the transfer of a command to the slave, which identifies a data block, a block length, and the transfer direction.

Master-Slave Communications   The master and slave communicate commands and data over a 4-bit bidirectional data bus. All transfers on this bus are synchronized under software control by MASTER RDY and SLAVE RDY (Figs. 4 to 9). This interface is convenient for transferring 8-bit bytes in 2 bus cycles, and its implementation requires only one I/O port on each μC. For convenience, the master can reset the slave at any time by asserting SLAVE RESET.

In a master-to-slave exchange (Figs. 4 to 6), the slave waits for the master to assert MASTER RDY before responding with SLAVE RDY. The master then places data on the bus and drops MASTER RDY. After the slave reads the data, it drops SLAVE RDY, confirming receipt. The master is then free to reassert MASTER RDY for the next 4-bit transfer.

A slave-to-master exchange (Figs. 7 to 9) occurs only when requested by the master. The slave waits for the master to assert MASTER RDY before placing data on the bus and asserting SLAVE RDY. After the master reads the data, it drops MASTER RDY, confirming receipt. The slave acknowledges by low-

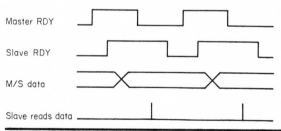

FIG. 4   *Master-to-slave transfer timing diagram. Reprinted with permission from Electronic Design, Vol. 28, No. 2; copyright Hayden Publishing Co., Inc., 1980.*

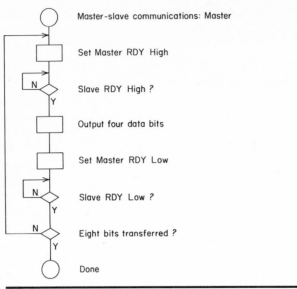

FIG. 5   *Master-to-slave transfer: flowchart for the master.*

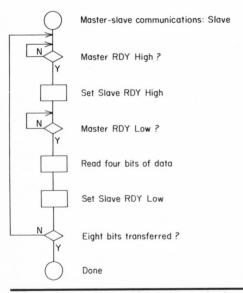

FIG. 6   *Master-to-slave transfer: flowchart for the slave.*

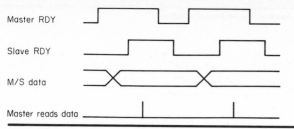

Master RDY

Slave RDY

M/S data

Master reads data

FIG. 7   *Slave-to-master transfer timing diagram. Reprinted with permission from Electronic Design, Vol. 28, No. 2; copyright Hayden Publishing Co., Inc., 1980.*

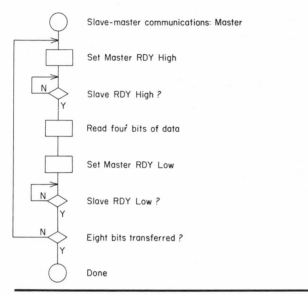

Slave-master communications: Master

Set Master RDY High

N Slave RDY High ?
Y

Read four bits of data

Set Master RDY Low

N Slave RDY Low ?
Y

N Eight bits transferred ?
Y

Done

FIG. 8   *Slave-to-master transfer: flowchart for the master.*

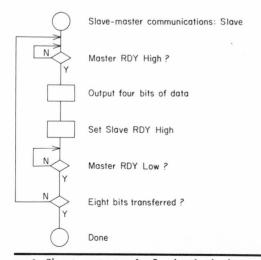

Slave-master communications: Slave

N Master RDY High ?
Y

Output four bits of data

Set Slave RDY High

N Master RDY Low ?
Y

N Eight bits transferred ?
Y

Done

FIG. 9   *Slave-to-master transfer: flowchart for the slave.*

ering SLAVE RDY. The master is then free to reassert MASTER RDY for the next 4-bit transfer. After transferring the specified number of bytes, the slave again looks for commands from the master.

17.4 Extension to Multiple Slaves

The dual μC scheme is extended to multiple slaves in Fig. 10. The master communicates with the selected slave as shown in Figs. 4 to 9. To facilitate communications with multiple slaves, the signals SELECT and SLAVE RDY B are added to the communications interface. The master uses these additional signals to simultaneously communicate an 8-bit slave selection code to all slaves (Figs. 11 to 13). Each slave controls SLAVE RDY and SLAVE RDY B with open collector drivers. By checking SLAVE RDY or SLAVE RDY B for a High state, the master determines if all slaves have responded with an open switch to a step in the sequence. Open collector drivers are often available as I/O port options on μCs, eliminating additional hardware. Figure 11 shows the timing sequence for communicating an 8-bit select code to all slaves. Figures 12 and 13 diagram the program steps required to implement Fig. 11 in the master and slaves. At the end of the sequence, only the selected slave responds to SELECT Low and MASTER RDY High by closing its switch on SLAVE RDY. The master can use the absence of SLAVE RDY Low as a select-error indication.

After a slave is selected, it remains selected until the next select sequence. While selected, it communicates with the master as described in Figs. 4 to 9.

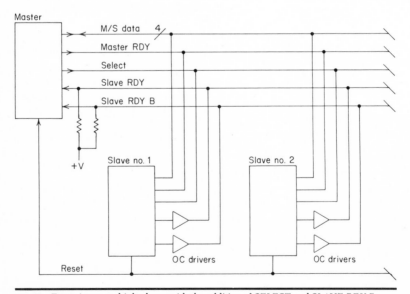

FIG. 10   Extension to multiple slaves with the addition of SELECT and SLAVE RDY B.

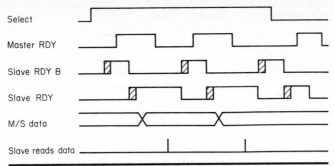

FIG. 11 *Slave SELECT sequence timing diagram.*

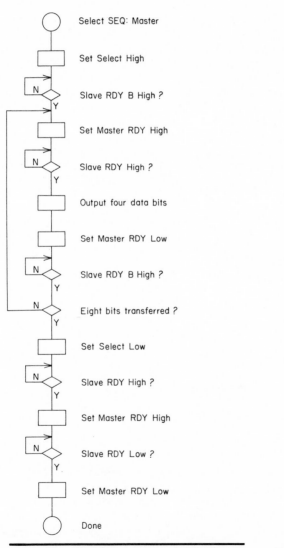

FIG. 12 *Slave SELECT sequence: flowchart for the master.*

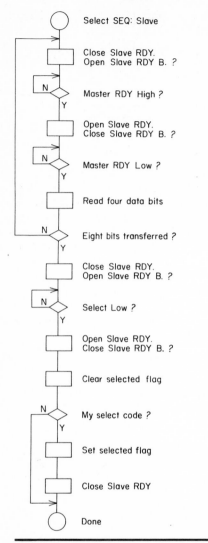

FIG. 13 *Slave SELECT sequence: flowchart for each slave.*

Nonselected slaves ignore transactions on the data bus until SELECT is asserted.

It is often desirable to allow asynchronous processing in the slaves. By interfacing the rising edge of SELECT to each slave's interrupt system, the slaves can respond to select sequences while processing previous requests from the master. Each slave can respond quickly to the select sequence and not slow bus transactions even if it is processing a long task previously requested by the master.

17.5 Partitioning Tasks Between μCs

Partitioning tasks between μCs is an additional complexity encountered in the multiple-μC approach. The following four guidelines are useful:

1. Minimize master-slave transfers.
2. Use a logical division, keeping like routines in the same μC to share common code.
3. Put a routine in the processor having the necessary I/O.
4. Avoid overburdening a processor with real-time tasks.

These guidelines are used to partition tasks in the design example. All equations that relate sensor outputs to displayed quantities are evaluated in the slave. This partitioning is convenient with the ADC interfaced to the slave. Because these equations require a floating-point arithmetic package, all other floating-point calculations are performed in the slave. Because the calculations require additional memory, the extra RAM is interfaced to the slave. To avoid timing conflicts with the software-controlled ADC, the A/D routine is the only real-time task in the slave.

The master contains all tasks required to parse operator inputs, execute commands, format display data, and control instrument sequences. It is also convenient for the master to control the printer interface, set-point alarms, and audio tone because they are related to displayed data. A set of refreshed seven-segment displays, a scanned-matrix keypad, an audio-tone generator, a serial-to-parallel printer interface, and a high-low set-point alarm system are interfaced to the master. The primary real-time tasks of the master are display refresh, keypad scanning, key debouncing, and sampling-rate control. These real-time tasks are collected in the master because they are interrelated and do not have precise timing requirements, making it easy for the master to handle them all.

An additional hardware savings is realized as a result of this partitioning. Because the stability requirements for real-time measurements in the master are not as critical as the A/D control in the slave, an inductor is used as the frequency-determining element of the master.

17.6 A Task-Scheduling Executive

An executive program that allocates processor resources can simplify real-time software design. A simple executive that executes tasks from a queue on a first-in first-out (FIFO) priority is depicted in Fig. 14. A task's activation may be blocked by external event flags and/or a real-time counter associated with the task. Tasks can be scheduled from any background or interrupt level. Tasks are executed at the background level.

This executive allows interrupts to queue time-consuming processing for background execution, making the system more responsive to other interrupts in the foreground. Tasks that must check non-interrupt-driven I/O flags can reschedule themselves for periodic execution.

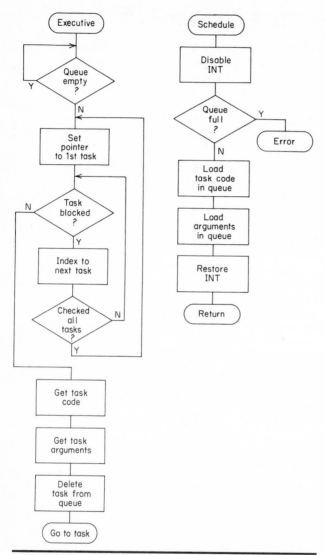

FIG. 14   *Flowchart for a simple real-time executive. Reprinted with permission from Electronic Design, Vol. 28, No. 2; copyright Hayden Publishing Co., Inc., 1980.*

The executive is entered after a power-on sequence that initializes the executive and queues the first task. Once entered, the executive controls system resources. When a task is activated, the executive passes the arguments from the task that scheduled it. When a task terminates, it exits to the executive, which activates the next unblocked task in the queue or waits for one to be scheduled by an interrupt.

An example queue entry for a task is shown in Fig. 15. The forward chain link points to the queue entry for the task queued after this one, and the reverse points to the one queued before it. The forward link of the most recently queued task is zero, as is the reverse link of the oldest task in the queue. This linked-list structure is shown in Fig. 16. In addition to the active queue, there is a linked list of free queue elements. By adjusting pointers to maintain the linked-list structure of Fig. 16, tasks can be added to the end of the list or deleted from anywhere within the list. It is necessary to have this capability because a more recently queued task will execute before the oldest task if the oldest task is blocked.

The real-time clock consists of a periodic interrupt. The INTERRUPT SERVICE routine runs through the active queue and decrements any real-time counter that is not zero. When a real-time counter decrements to zero, the task will be unblocked the next time the executive looks for a task to execute.

External event flags function similarly to the real-time counters. When the event occurs, its INTERRUPT SERVICE routine clears the associated event-flag bit in each active queue entry, unblocking tasks. A task may be blocked by several event flags and the real-time counter. All blocks must be cleared for the task to execute.

An executive with this simple FIFO priority algorithm is easily designed and coded. Its use simplifies the real-time software designer's job by providing a common routine that decides which task to activate next. However, the designer must keep task-execution times short, subdividing long tasks if necessary. Task-execution time requirements are dictated by response times needed for external events.

External events that require fast response can do time-critical processing within the interrupt subroutine and queue less-critical processing for execution in the background. The design example refreshes its displays at a 1000-Hz rate. A different digit is refreshed each millisecond within an interrupt subroutine, eliminating display flicker. The display refresh subroutine queues the keypad processing which is less critical.

The FIFO algorithm can be modified to assign priorities to tasks by modifying the executive of Fig. 14 to search for the unblocked task with highest

| FORWARD CHAIN LINK |
| REVERSE CHAIN LINK |
| TASK ADDRESS |
| EVENT FLAG BITS |
| REAL-TIME COUNTER |
| ARGUMENT 1 |
| ARGUMENT 2 |
| ARGUMENT n |

FIG. 15   *Format for a task-queue element.*

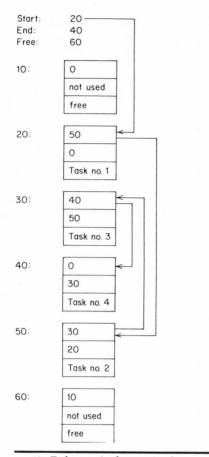

Start: 20
End: 40
Free: 60

10:
| O |
| not used |
| free |

20:
| 50 |
| O |
| Task no. 1 |

30:
| 40 |
| 50 |
| Task no. 3 |

40:
| O |
| 30 |
| Task no. 4 |

50:
| 30 |
| 20 |
| Task no. 2 |

60:
| 10 |
| not used |
| free |

FIG. 16 *Task-queue implementation depicting the linked-list structure.*

priority. This modification does not allow a higher priority task to interrupt a lower one. The highest priority task is given access to the CPU when the running task exits. The housekeeping required to implement switching between tasks is beyond the scope of this chapter and probably exceeds the requirements of small measurement systems.

17.7 Interfacing Techniques

The interfacing techniques presented in this chapter have as a primary goal the reduction of hardware at the expense of software. This usually results in a net cost reduction.

Small measurement systems often have slow data rates and limited real-time computation requirements. These factors usually result in excess processor time, which may be used to generate the timing and control signals required by external devices, replacing the hardware controllers often used in larger systems.

A Scanned-Matrix Keypad and Display   A technique for interfacing a keypad and digital display is given in Figs. 17 and 18. This type of refreshed display and scanned keypad is used in many calculators to share hardware and reduce power requirements while providing a bright display.

Once each millisecond the routine in Fig. 18 is entered via a real-time clock interrupt. The interrupt is usually available as a function of a timer included in the μC. The interrupt routine first blanks the current digit to prevent carry-over into the next. A counter is then updated to select the next digit to refresh. The counter is output on the digit-select lines, and the already decoded data is fetched from a buffer and output on the segment-select lines. A complete display of up to 10 digits may be refreshed in 10 ms or less—presenting a bright, flicker-free display to the human eye. For displays containing more

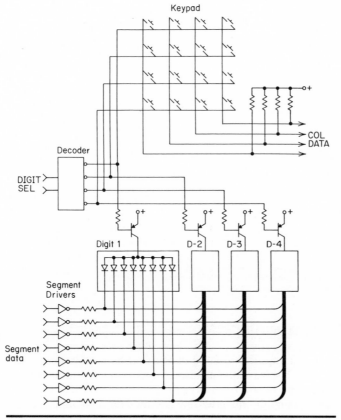

FIG. 17   *Interface for refreshed displays and scanned matrix keypad.*

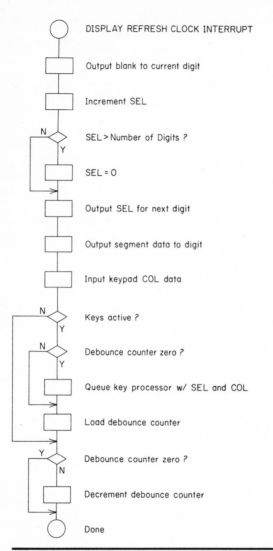

FIG. 18   INTERRUPT-*driven software driver for display refresh and keypad scanning.*

than 10 digits, faster interrupt rates are required to reduce flicker. In general, a slower interrupt rate allows more time for other processing.

Keypad scanning uses the existing digit-select lines to force the selected keypad row LOW. If a key in the selected row is active, the corresponding column input will be LOW. The software (Fig. 18) tests the row inputs each refresh cycle. Knowing the selected row and the active column, the software determines which key(s) are active. The software debounces the keys and detects new keystrokes by requiring all keys to be inactive for 50 ms before recognizing a new keystroke.

An important feature of this design is the use of the executive previously described. When a new keystroke is detected, a routine is queued to process the key. The row and column are passed as arguments to the key processor. Key processing is thus accomplished in the background, improving the response to other interrupts. By queueing and removing tasks, the key processor alters the machine sequence in response to operator actions. If multiple keystrokes are made before the first is processed, the FIFO priority of the executive ensures correct processing.

Adding Memory Via an I/O **Port** For some applications, μCs provide insufficient on-chip RAM for data storage. This is a problem if the data and address buses are not provided for memory expansion. However, it may be desirable to select a μC that does not provide an expansion facility to obtain some other feature, such as the 3872's large ROM. A similar problem is encountered if additional hardware is required to interface the desired memory device to an expansion bus.

A solution is shown in the dual μC design of Fig. 3. Two RAMs, each 256 $\times$ 4, are interfaced via two I/O ports of the 3870. The memories are accessed by cycling the address, data, and control lines in the manner specified by the memory manufacturer. Using a 4-bit data structure makes it possible to interface the equivalent of 256 bytes of RAM to two I/O ports without additional hardware.

In the design example, READ and WRITE subroutines are used to access the outboard RAMs. These subroutines transfer one 8-bit byte between the μC's internal RAM and the outboard RAMs. The low-order 4 bits are stored in one memory and the high-order in the other. Using this scheme, a complete byte is accessed with only one access to the address port. To maintain system performance, a variable is transferred to a temporary location in internal RAM for the duration of the operation.

Software Control of an Integrating ADC Most μCs provide programmable timers that can be used to measure time intervals and pulse widths. These capabilities make it relatively easy to control the analog processor of an integrating ADC.[3]

The design example (Fig. 3) shows the connection of an LF13300 to a 3870. The general techniques, however, are applicable to any integrating ADC or μC. Timing may even be obtained from software loops if the μC does not have counter/timer hardware.

In Fig. 3, 4 bits of an I/O port generate the control signals: offset correct (OC), polarity detect/ramp positive unknown (PD/RU+), ramp negative unknown (RU−), and ramp reference (RR). The comparator (COMP) output drives the 3870's external interrupt input. Timing for the LF13300 is shown in Fig. 19.

The rest state of the converter is offset correction. To start a conversion, the main-line code sets the phase of the interrupt code to 1 and sets the interval

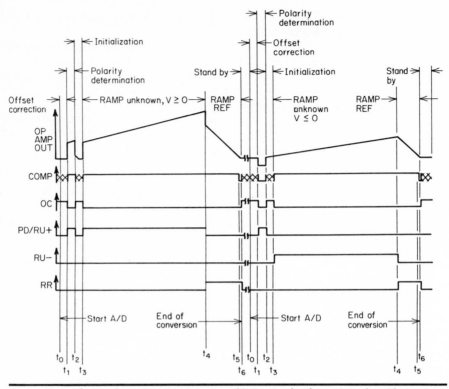

FIG. 19   Timing diagram for an LF13300 integrating A/D. Reprinted with permission from Electronic Design, Vol. 28, No. 2; copyright Hayden Publishing Co., Inc., 1980.

timer for 26 ms, the duration of the first offset-correction phase. During the conversion process, the main-line code continues background processing. At the end of the first time interval, control briefly passes to the timer INTERRUPT SERVICE routine (Fig. 20) and phase 2, polarity detection, is initiated for 250 μs. When phase 2 ends, the INTERRUPT SERVICE routine reads the comparator output and remembers the polarity of the unknown voltage. Phase 3, another offset correction, lasts for 26 ms to reset the integrator.

During phase 4, the unknown voltage is integrated for approximately 100 ms. The selection of the integration control, PD/RU+ or RU−, is based upon the polarity of the unknown. The time interval for phase 4 is resolved to 1 part in 40,000+ by counting overflow interrupts from the 8-bit timer register. Phase 4 is terminated after 156 overflows. Remaining counts in the timer register are combined with the overflow counter to form a 16-bit number. A correction factor, for the elapsed software time between reading the counter and reversing the integration, is added to determine the exact integration time for the unknown.

During phase 5, a reference voltage of opposite sign is applied to the integrator, and the time required for the integrator to return to baseline is mea-

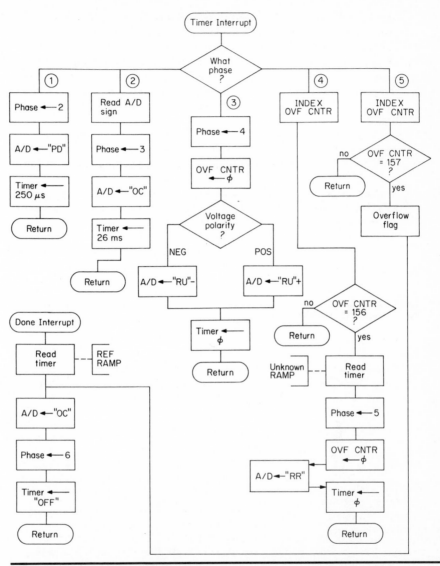

FIG. 20 INTERRUPT-driven software implementing the timing for the LF13300. Reprinted with
permission from Electronic Design, Vol. 28, No. 2; copyright Hayden Publishing Co., Inc., 1980.

sured. This time is measured by using a mode that allows the timer to run only
if the 3870's external interrupt input is HIGH. The time is resolved to 1 part
in 40,000+ by counting overflow interrupts, as in phase 4.

On the falling edge of COMP, the timer is halted and a completion interrupt
routine executed. The timer register is again combined with the overflow
counter to form a 16-bit number, and another correction factor is added for

elapsed software time between starting the reference integration and starting the timer. The unknown voltage is determined by multiplying the reference voltage by the ratio of the reference's integration time to the unknown integration time. If 157 overflows are counted during phase 5, an A/D overflow is assumed and the conversion stopped. In any case, the completion routine sets the phase to 6 to indicate completion to the main-line program. If the executive is used, the completion routine queues a routine to process the A/D reading.

The most difficult software design problem is accounting for all machine cycles in phases 4 and 5 not measured by the timer. This is critical because each count of the timer is equivalent to 1.25 machine cycles in the design example.

The only subtle design problem was a tendency of the COMP output of the LF13300 to glitch on the ramp unknown to ramp-reference transition. The glitch resulted in a premature DONE interrupt.

Using this scheme, the instrument in the design example was able to obtain a precision of 1 part in 40,000 over a range of -2000 to $+2000$ mV with an absolute accuracy of ± 0.2 mV.

17.8 Development Hints

When developing software for dual μC systems, it is usually easier to first code and debug the slave software. The slave software can be debugged in a RAM-based emulator using minimal hardware to simulate the master-slave interface. Once debugged, the slave software can be committed to an EPROM-based emulator. The master can be debugged in the RAM-based emulator using the EPROM-based slave. This approach fits the recommended top-down design, bottom-up coding approach to software. When the master and slave μCs are complete, EPROM-based emulators should be used for both in preproduction prototypes for extensive testing prior to committing to vendor-masked parts.

A logic analyzer is useful for debugging master-slave communications and other interfaces. The logic analyzer can monitor the address bus, available on the emulators, to trace program paths. It can also monitor interface lines for correct sequences.

REFERENCES

1. Kalinowski, J. J.: "Ion Measurements Come of Age with an Assist from Microcomputer Technology in Electrochemical Assay," *Ind. Res./Dev.*, February 1979.
2. Carter, C. N., and J. J. Kalinowski: "Dual-Microcomputer Design Adds Memory, Processing, and Software Control Without Adding Chips," *Electron. Des.*, vol. 28, no. 2, Jan. 18, 1980, p. 82.
3. Aldridge, D.: "Analog-to-Digital Conversion Techniques with the M6800 Microprocessor System," Motorola App. Note AN-757, 1975.

Index

ABOUT THE EDITOR-IN-CHIEF

David F. Stout is presently Vice President of Engineering at Dataface, Inc., a company using microprocessors to interface computers and communication systems with printers. He was a research associate at the University of Utah, an engineer with the Jet Propulsion Laboratory, a member of the technical staff at Martin Marietta Corp., and a senior engineering specialist at Ford Aerospace and Communication Corp. He holds BSEE and MSEE degrees from the University of Utah.

Mr. Stout has been involved with microprocessors and microcomputers since the introduction of these devices in the early 1970s. His design experience in recent years includes applications of microprocessors in display, control, and communications systems.

In addition to writing numerous articles and reports on the electronic design of atmospheric probes, auroral experiments, magnetometers, space cameras, and interplanetary biology experiments, Mr. Stout is the author of the *Handbook of Operational Amplifier Circuit Design* (McGraw-Hill) and the *Handbook of Microcircuit Design and Application* (McGraw-Hill).